Software Testing Strategies

A testing guide for the 2020s

Matthew Heusser

Michael Larsen

BIRMINGHAM—MUMBAI

Software Testing Strategies

Group Product Manager: Gebin George

Publishing Product Manager: Kunal Sawant

Senior Editor: Rounak Kulkarni

Technical Editor: Rajdeep Chakraborty

Copy Editor: Safis Editing

Associate Project Manager: Deeksha Thakkar

Project Coordinator: Manisha Singh

Indexer: Pratik Shirodkar

Production Designer: Joshua Misquitta

DevRel Marketing Coordinator: Shrinidhi Manoharan and Sonia Chauhan

Business Development Executive: Samriddhi Murarka

First published: December 2023
Production reference: 2131223

Published by Packt Publishing Ltd.
Grosvenor House
11 St Paul's Square
Birmingham
B3 1RB, UK

ISBN 978-1-83763-802-4

www.packtpub.com

For Kathleen, Rachel, and Juliana Heusser. I'll always be your dad, for anything. Also, I asked Michael, "How can I write chapter 14 and not mention Jesus, my Lord?" He said, "Put it in the dedication, where it belongs." And so, it is. Finally, to every worker at Excelon Development, past, present, and future. Your work gave me a little free time for this research and to write this book without sacrificing time with Julie, who is still in school. I am incapable of expressing all that that means to me.

– Matthew Heusser

To Christina, Nicholas, Karina, and Amber Larsen, you are all the reason I do what I do. It's an honor and a privilege to be your husband and father. Thank you for putting up with me. Additionally, thank you to the many people who have worked with me over the years and given me a chance to help make the software we use and the interactions we have with it a little better, more usable, more inclusive, and available to as many people as possible.

– Michael Larsen

Contributors

About the authors

Matthew Heusser is the 2014 Winner of the **Most Influential Agile Professional Person Award** (**MAITPP**) at Agile Testing days in Potsdam, Germany. In 2015 he received the most popular online contributor to Agile award at the Agile Awards, Marble Arch in London. In 2023, his company, Excelon Development, was listed as an INC 5000 award recipient; one of the fastest-growing privately held companies in the United States. In the same year, they were also listed as a top ten software test provider in CIO Applications magazine. He won awards through 30 years of dedicated service to the field of software delivery, including serving as lead organizer for the initial Great Lakes Software Excellence Conference, member of the board of directors of the association for software testing, senior editor of *"How to Reduce the Cost of Software Testing"*, and organizer of a half-dozen peer workshops on software delivery – all while making active contributions on software projects.

I've tried to credit people in the book for their testing ideas, but special thanks go to Homer Austin, Kathleen Shannon, and Dean Defino for teaching me a love of logic and proof. My father, Roger Heusser, taught me perseverance and commitment to a profession. It was my friends, Mike Pettee, Joe Cerven, Mary Colborn, Nikki Johnson, and others who helped me pick up after a life setback and re-orient myself with new goals. Asimov, Heinlein, Clarke, and Gygax taught me to love reading and want to write, but it was Eric Matthews and Steve Hoek who encouraged me to think deeply about software delivery, and Esther Schindler who encouraged me to write about it.

Michael Larsen has been working in software testing, one way or another, since 1991. He has been involved with a variety of companies and products over the years. He lives in the San Francisco Bay Area and has been an advocate for quality since launching his TESTHEAD blog in 2010 (`https://mkltesthead.com/`). He has served as a member of the Board of Directors and President of the **Association for Software Testing** (**AST**), and the Marketing Chair for the **Pacific Northwest Software Quality Conference** (**PNSQC**).

I owe a huge debt of gratitude to Shannah Miller and Marcia Bednarcyk, who took a chance on a young musician looking for work 30+ years ago and said, "Hey, why not?"

About the reviewers:

Cansu Akcay is a Software Test Engineer based in London with 10 years of industry experience. She is the founder of CA Software Testing LTD (`http://casoftwaretesting.co.uk/`). Cansu has worked as a Senior Software Test / QA Engineer, collaborating with various QA teams in manual and automation testing on multiple types of applications. She has also worked with large, medium, and small (start-up) local and global companies. Cansu manages an Instagram account (*@ca.softwaretesting*) where she shares tips and the latest updates on testing.

Stephen Spady is a Principal Software Engineer in Test with over 30 years of experience in software testing and development. Throughout his extensive career, he has held various roles, including software test engineer, software development engineer, lead, manager, software architect, test architect, and systems engineer. Notably, he dedicated 13 years to Microsoft, where he played a pivotal role in developing test automation and **continuous integration/continuous delivery (CI/CD)** systems for Microsoft Word, Office, RichEdit, Netdocs, and CRM.

Over the course of his career, Stephen has actively contributed to the advancement of AI technologies, conducting research and development for their application in software design, development, and testing. Stephen holds a Bachelor of Science in Computer Engineering from the University of Nebraska–Lincoln.

Table of Contents

6

Testing Related Skills   133

7

Test Data Management   153

Part 2: Testing and Software Delivery

8

Delivery Models and Testing   169

9

The Puzzle Pieces of Good Testing   193

13

Testing Activities or a Testing Role?   279

14

Philosophy and Ethics in Software Testing   293

15

Words and Language About Work   309

16

Testing Strategy Applied   323

Index   339

Other Books You May Enjoy   350

Preface

We live in an age where software is everywhere. It is inescapable at this point. Some of it is trivial, meant for entertainment or passing time, while some software is the most mission-critical possible, maintaining the delicate balance between life and death for a person. Most software that we will interact with will fall somewhere within that continuum. It may be on the web, on our phone, on our watch, or measuring the weight of our workout water bottle, reminding us to hydrate ourselves at important times. Even if we don't interact with it directly, software runs in many areas of our lives that we don't even consider, including our financial institutions, our power plants, medical imaging systems, or in running continuous trials to find the best way to synthesize chemical reactions or fight deadly viruses.

What do all of these areas of software interaction have in common? Someone has to create them and deploy them but perhaps most importantly, someone has to test them. Over the past couple of decades, there has been a move away from that "someone" and more towards "something", meaning automated tests in some capacity doing all of the testing work. Surely, software can do the work of a thousand testers, right? Yet it has come back in the news media and in high profile cases that maybe, just maybe, having people who truly understand testing is important, necessary, and should be prepared to do that work. That person does not need to have the title of "tester" to do testing. They can be a software developer, a lone hobbyist working on a passion project, or someone working with a server farm running systems, making sure they are operable, and people are able to access them. Testing happens at many levels and over the entire software development life cycle.

At its most basic level, testing is the actual experimentation that takes place in the scientific method. It's the asking of "What if?" questions. It's the joy of being sneaky and difficult with software, to try to find areas where the software is vulnerable and open to attack, where the person doing the testing can either support or refute the ideas at hand. Is the software fit for use, or is there a problem here?

Our goal with this book, *Software Testing Techniques*, is to help you, our esteemed reader, take hold of the fun and adventure that is software testing (and yes, it most certainly can be fun, and it is often quite literally an adventure). We want to give you skills, processes, techniques, and perhaps some novel ways of looking at the puzzle pieces of software testing. If that sounds like fun to you, buckle in and join us.

Our scope - beyond button-pushing

Patrick Bailey, a professor at Calvin College, once did a research report where he asked people their role and, if they could only do one form of testing, what would it be? Bailey found, strikingly, that people tend to associate the most valuable kind of testing with their role. Programmers found unit testing valuable, internal customers found User Acceptance Testing, Business Analysts found system testing, and so on more valuable.

Project Managers, for example, tend to see work as an assembly line. Anyone with a mantra like "plan the work, work the plan" and a documentation bias is going to like the idea of writing the tests down and then executing them. When we have seen that tried, the results, are, frankly, lower value. So, the company criticizes the button-pushers, maybe laughing at them. Thomas Moore wrote about this in 1551 in his book *Utopia*. To borrow from that author: First, we create bad testers and then we punish them.

That may be the first mistake, which used to be the most common. Today, we see people who saw that first mistake, know it is foolish, and view all human testing as that sort of low-value, scripted exercise. This group sees testing as something else – automation of the GUI, lower-level unit checks, and perhaps API tests. All those have their part and place in this book, but they also fail to capture the improvisational element of good testing. We'll cover that improvisational effort in *Chapter 1*, at the GUI level, where it is most obvious, and then try to maintain that spirit throughout additional chapters.

In other words, this book is not limited to "just" button-pushing testing, but there is something that happens in the hands of someone skilled that needs to be studied and applied at all levels, throughout the process.

The scope of our book is about all the ways to find out the status of the software, quickly, by exercising the code. We'll be the first to admit that is not a complete picture of software quality. It does not include how to create good requirements, or how to perform code inspections or pair programs. We see testing as a feedback mechanism, it is not the only one, and there is more to quality than that feedback.

"Just testing", we thought, was more than enough for one book. That feedback is important. It is often neglected; it is often done poorly. The second part of the book covers test integration into a delivery process. The third part covers "Practicing Politics", on how to give feedback that can be effectively used by the organization.

If you've ever heard "Why didn't we test that", "Why didn't we find that bug", or, perhaps worst of all, "Okay, you found that bug and prioritized it as must fix and we insisted it could be delayed, but why didn't you advocate more effectively?", then this book is for you. This book is also for you if:

- *If you keep seeing bugs in software that seem obvious that you wish other people caught.*
- *If you want to get better at finding information quickly and expressing it well to change the outcome of the process.*
- *If you want to come up with ways to use the information you find to reduce the bug injection rate.*
- *If you want to be able to diagnose and explain how you made key risk/reward tradeoffs.*

Hopefully, by now you realize that testing is serious, grown-up, risk-management work. Any beginner can follow the process, and any mid-level tester can tie up most software teams in delays waiting to fix things. The real value in testing is beyond that, in making smart risk/reward decisions, to invest limited resources in risk management.

You can think of this as three levels of testing. On level one, you go through the basic motions of using the application in the most simplistic way. This is the "happy path." The second level of tester is on a bug hunt. The person viewing testing views their job as to find bugs, or, as one person once put it, to "cackle with glee" as they "make developers cry." Where the first level is probably overly agreeable, the second level can be actually adversarial to development. It is on the third level that we look at how much time will be invested in what risks in order to "not be fooled" about quality while making minimal disruptions to delivery speed. In some cases, finding problems with the product early can increase delivery speed.

What is Testing?

Not too long ago or far away, one of the authors, Matthew, was the testing steward at a Health Insurance Company in West Michigan. The insurance company had contracted with a local but nationally known consultancy to come in and work on some software maintenance. One of the consultants, a brilliant coder, shoved the keyboard away in frustration, shouting, *"This is totally untestable!"*

Matt picked up the keyboard and mouse and started to exercise the software, saying, *"Sure it is, watch!"* This was followed by, *"Oh, you don't mean the code is untestable, you mean you have no way to have a computer run it through pre-defined exercises and check the results. You mean it isn't ... test-automate-able, maybe?"*

This is another example of what Pat Bailey was talking about in his research at Calvin. To the programmer, "tests" were automated pieces of code that checked the functionality. To Matt, the employee of the insurance company, testing was the process of figuring out information about the software.

At almost the exact same time as this story, one of our mentors, Dr Cem Kaner, was giving a talk on *"Testing as A Social Science"*, (`https://kaner.com/pdfs/KanerSocialScienceTASSQ.pdf`). In that presentation, Dr Kaner defined software testing this way.

Software Testing is:

- A technical investigation

- Conducted to provide quality-related information

- About a software product

- To a stakeholder

This book tends to use that as an operating definition. Testing is where you try to find out if the thing you built will actually do the things you are asking it to do. While you can fool yourself with a schedule, a bad design, and code that doesn't work, Testing is the first process designed to make sure that we are not fooled. Kaner went on to make this argument, "Much of the most significant testing work looks more like applied psychology, economics, business management (etc.) than like programming".

This will probably upset a lot of programmers, and maybe some DevOps people too. After all, the holy grail of testing in the 2020s is to automate all the checking of things. In general, that means running all the checks, quickly, and reporting results automatically with No Humans Involved, or NHI.

People seem to stop and forget that the holy grail seems to be fiction, with a great deal of energy wasted searching for a legend. The yellow brick road led to the Emerald City headed by a wizard that was a lie. People forget that Zeitgeist, the spirit of the age, implies not truth but a sense of fashion that will go out of style.

It's not that we are against automation or tooling. Our problem is the dearth of information on how to do testing well.

Given a test framework (or exercise) …

What test should we run (or write) first?

What does that test result tell us?

When should we stop?

When we stop, what do we know?

This sounds like an interactive exercise, where the results of the first test inform the second. It is possible to select some subset of that exercise, turn it into an algorithm, write it up in code, and run it routinely to see if what worked today runs differently tomorrow. Some people call this regression testing. It is even possible to create automated checks before the code, sometimes called **Test Driven Development (TDD)**. Even if the tests are automated, the process of figuring out what to run and what that tells us is the process we are more interested in.

Some people make a distinction between the institutionalized, run-it-every-time bits of code and the feedback-driven process of exploration. In particular, Michael Bolton uses the term "Checks" to be the algorithmic unthinking comparison, and 'Testing" to be the more expansive activity that often includes checking. We find this helpful in that "automated testing" loses some of the flavor of Dr Kaner's definition that we saw earlier. To that, we would add Heusser's First Observation: After the first time you run an automated test to see if it passes, it really ceases to be a true test. Instead, it becomes automated change detection – and what programmers do is create change!

Our goal for the reader is to be able to do more than memorize the material and more than perform an analysis of software according to a set of rules to come up with test ideas. We believe in this book we have synthesized a large amount of material that superficially disagrees with itself and is inconsistent. We've interpreted that through our own ideas, laying out some test approaches that have the most value, and then giving advice on how to balance them. When you're done with this book, you should be able to look at a user interface or API, identify many different ways to test it and have the tools to slice up your limited time to determine how much time to spend on what test approaches, describing them to someone else.

Whew. It's finally here. The book is final. It is ready to be out.

This book is about our (Matthew Heusser and Michael Larsen) stories. We are proud of it. It includes how we test, why we test, what influenced our thinking about testing, and a few exercises for you. To do that we had to do a few unconventional things, like change our "person" between I, you, we,

Matt, and Michael. We had to write about opinions, which you can disagree with, and experiences, which might not be relevant for you. One of our biggest challenges was what to cut, to understand what would be the most valuable to you, the reader. After doing hundreds of interviews on podcasts, consulting broadly, and attending a hundred or so conferences, we think we have some idea of what that might be. Yet a book takes our potential audience for feedback even wider. We look forward to hearing from you, the reader, about what we could have phrased more carefully, and what we should add, subtract or change. For today though…

On with the show.

Who this book is for

This book is for anyone who wants to understand the process and mindset of software testing, to put into practice the ideas and methods that will help them better test and understand the systems they work with, and to advocate for those who can't speak for themselves in the software development process. Note, that does not presuppose that the person reading this book is a dedicated software tester. We encourage everyone who has any involvement in software development, including programmers, product and project managers, business analysts, systems administrators, and anyone who has a vested interest in the software their organization creates to be as capable and robust as possible.

What this book covers

Chapter 1, Testing and Designing Tests, this chapter introduces testing as a risk management activity, focusing on powerful test ideas for important software parts. It discusses the theory of error, unscripted testing, and various methods including model-driven and soak testing.

Chapter 2, Fundamental Issues in Tooling and Automation, addresses common pitfalls in test automation and shares lessons from years of experience. It covers concepts like the minefield regression problem and the battleship problem, concluding with solutions to these automation challenges.

Chapter 3, Programmer-Facing Testing, focuses on developer testing and covers unit testing, test-driven development, and testing web APIs, among other topics. It concludes with a practical exercise in creating unit tests, using Ruby as an example.

Chapter 4, Customer-Facing Tests, explores the nuances of customer-facing test automation, discussing GUI automation patterns, specification by example, and low-code/no-code tools, aiming to enable readers to analyze and optimize user interface testing.

Chapter 5, Specialized Testing, delves into specialty areas of testing and covers performance and load testing, security, accessibility, internationalization, and regulated testing, each with its unique challenges and methodologies.

Chapter 6, Testing Related Skills, expands beyond test design and execution and focuses on skills like recognizing bugs, communicating problems, planning and documenting work, and metrics, and influencing change in testing processes.

Chapter 7, Test Data Management, addresses the test data management problem and provides techniques for creating, storing, editing, deleting, and restoring data states to drive efficient application testing and reliable test tools.

Chapter 8, Delivery Models and Testing, broadens the scope of how testing interacts with software delivery models like Waterfall, Scrum, and DevOps. Through this, this chapter helps readers understand and optimize the interaction between testing and these models.

Chapter 9, The Puzzle Pieces of Good Testing, breaks down the components of testing, like recipes, coverage, and defects, and encourages readers to reassemble these elements into a cohesive test strategy tailored to their needs.

Chapter 10, Putting Your Test Strategy Together, builds on the previous chapter, to guide readers through analyzing current testing states, prioritizing risks, and communicating and implementing a comprehensive test strategy.

Chapter 11, Lean Software Testing, introduces Lean Software Testing and combines test and operations management techniques. It covers topics like the Seven Wastes, flow, constraints, and a lean approach to metrics and measurement.

Chapter 12, Case Studies and Experience Reports, uses case studies and experience reports, and offers real-life lessons and strategies from the field, providing practical insights into testing challenges and solutions.

Chapter 13, Testing Activities or a Testing Role?, explores the nuances of who should perform testing activities, discussing cultural conflicts, risk mitigation teams, and various testing models like shift-left and continuous testing.

Chapter 14, Philosophy and Ethics in Software Testing, ventures into the philosophical and ethical dimensions of testing. This chapter examines the limitations of testing, the value of ethical reasoning, and the importance of clear communication in testing processes.

Chapter 15, Words and Language About Work, focuses on communication and emphasizes the importance of precise language and context in testing, exploring different testing schools of thought and the distinction between process and skill.

Chapter 16, Testing Strategy Applied, applies the book's concepts to practical scenarios, including a reference implementation for a mobile test strategy and a critical examination of AI in software testing, offering a comprehensive view of testing strategy application.

To get the most out of this book

Most of the approaches and techniques described in this book are less tool-specific and more person-specific. There are, however, a few examples in the book that will benefit from downloading software or hardware and installing them. Most of the tools and techniques are platform agnostic or have distributions that work with all platforms. Some of the examples in this book are based on Ruby, so having a working version of Ruby on your system would be beneficial. In the Specialized Testing section there is an example based around JMeter, so installing JMeter and its components would likewise be worthwhile.

Software/hardware covered in the book	Operating system requirements
Ruby	Windows, macOS, or Linux
JMeter	Windows, macOS, or Linux

If you are using the digital version of this book, we advise you to type the code yourself or access the code from the book's GitHub repository (a link is available in the next section). Doing so will help you avoid any potential errors related to the copying and pasting of code.

Download the example code files

You can download the example code files for this book from GitHub at `https://github.com/PacktPublishing/Software-Testing-Strategies`. If there's an update to the code, it will be updated in the GitHub repository.

We also have other code bundles from our rich catalog of books and videos available at `https://github.com/PacktPublishing/`. Check them out!

Download the color images

We also provide a PDF file that has color images of the screenshots and diagrams used in this book. You can download it here: `http://www.packtpub.com/sites/default/files/downloads/Software-Testing-Strategies_ColorImages.pdf`.

> **Disclaimer**
>
> With the intention of the Publisher and Author, certain graphics included in this title are displaying large screen examples where the textual content is not relevant to the graphic example. We encourage our readers to download the digital copy included in their purchase for magnified and accessible content requirements.

Conventions used

There are a number of text conventions used throughout this book.

`Code in text`: Indicates code words in text, database table names, folder names, filenames, file extensions, pathnames, dummy URLs, user input, and Twitter handles. Here is an example: "It will create a `Fizzbuz_02` object in memory, call the method, and expect the output."

A block of code is set as follows:

```
if !defined?(count_to) or count_to<1
  puts "Use: FizzBuzz01.rb (count)\n"
```

```
    puts "Where count is a round number of value one or higher"
    abort("");
end
```

Any command-line input or output is written as follows:

```
Finished in 0.001213s, 2473.2069 runs/s, 2473.2069 assertions/s.
3 runs, 3 assertions, 0 failures, 0 errors, 0 skips
```

Bold: Indicates a new term, an important word, or words that you see onscreen. For instance, words in menus or dialog boxes appear in **bold**. Here is an example: " All the *test* does is go to Excelon Development's main page, then click on **Consulting**, then **Contact Us**, and fill in the **Contact Us** form"

> **Tips or important notes**
> Appear like this.

Get in touch

Feedback from our readers is always welcome.

General feedback: If you have questions about any aspect of this book, email us at customercare@ packtpub.com and mention the book title in the subject of your message.

Errata: Although we have taken every care to ensure the accuracy of our content, mistakes do happen. If you have found a mistake in this book, we would be grateful if you would report this to us. Please visit www.packtpub.com/support/errata and fill in the form.

Piracy: If you come across any illegal copies of our works in any form on the internet, we would be grateful if you would provide us with the location address or website name. Please contact us at copyright@packt.com with a link to the material.

If you are interested in becoming an author: If there is a topic that you have expertise in and you are interested in either writing or contributing to a book, please visit authors.packtpub.com.

Share your thoughts

Once you've read *Software Testing Strategies*, we'd love to hear your thoughts! Scan the QR code below to go straight to the Amazon review page for this book and share your feedback.

https://packt.link/r/1837638020

Your review is important to us and the tech community and will help us make sure we're delivering excellent quality content.

Download a free PDF copy of this book

Thanks for purchasing this book!

Do you like to read on the go but are unable to carry your print books everywhere?

Is your eBook purchase not compatible with the device of your choice?

Don't worry, now with every Packt book you get a DRM-free PDF version of that book at no cost.

Read anywhere, any place, on any device. Search, copy, and paste code from your favorite technical books directly into your application.

The perks don't stop there, you can get exclusive access to discounts, newsletters, and great free content in your inbox daily

Follow these simple steps to get the benefits:

1.   Scan the QR code or visit the link below

https://packt.link/free-ebook/9781837638024

2.   Submit your proof of purchase

3.   That's it! We'll send your free PDF and other benefits to your email directly

Part 1: The Practice of Software Testing

This part is about how we test. It starts with a real working example of jumping into a project to test without any background. Our goal with this part is to give the reader both an overview of all the areas of risk that people can reduce by inspection, and also to give practical, hands-on advice on how to test software with little to no introduction, little to no documentation, under conditions of time pressure and uncertainty, while doing work that stands up to scrutiny. This includes all kinds of testing, including developer testing and test tooling. We've tried to present a balanced approach to test tooling to optimize your chances of success while being realistic.

This section has the following chapters:

- Chapter 1, Testing and Designing Tests
- Chapter 2, Fundamental Issues in Tooling and Automation
- Chapter 3, Programmer-Facing Testing
- Chapter 4, Customer-Facing Tests
- Chapter 5, Specialized Testing
- Chapter 6, Testing Related Skills
- Chapter 7, Test Data Management

1

Testing and Designing Tests

In the *Preface* section, we mentioned three levels of testing – checking the obvious, testing intensely (which might never end), and, finally, looking at testing as a risk management activity. We'll start with the obvious, demonstrate the forever, and then talk about the ways to look at testing as risk management – that is, how can we spend a little time now to save time and money and avoid frustrated users and damaged reputations later? To do that, we must select a few of the most powerful test ideas, with a bias toward the most important parts of the software, and then determine something of meaning from them. Risk management also includes a variety of techniques with some overlap, so that if one approach fails to find a problem, others might succeed. We'll cover that in *Part 2* of this book.

These ideas apply to both unit and customer-facing tests; they also apply to the specialized testing that we'll discuss in *Chapter 5*. To start, the examples will be customer-facing, only because we find that the most approachable to the widest audience.

This chapter will focus on the following areas:

- Understanding and explaining the impossibility of complete testing

- Learning and developing the theory of error to find defects

- Understand how a real-time unscripted test session might run

- How to perform unscripted testing

- Creating test ideas, including boundaries, equivalence classes, and the pairwise approach to testing

- Understanding other methods, such as model-driven, soak, and soap opera, as well as other alternative test approaches

Jumping into testing

Let's start with the *happy path*. This refers to the primary path and/or workflow that the software developers intend for the application to follow to do its work or provide its results. To do that, we'll look at a web application that will take some text as input and tell the user if the text is a palindrome or not. Feel free to play along at `https://www.xndev.com/palindrome`. (This exercise is free and open to the public. It was proposed at *WhatDat*, the Workshop on *Teaching Test Design*, an *Excelon* Event, in *2016*, with initial code by *Justin Rohrman* and *Paul Harju*).

For our purposes, a palindrome is a word that is the same both forward and backward. Thus, *bob* is a palindrome, while *robert* is not, because *robert* spelled backward is *trebor*. To determine if the text is a palindrome or not, we can create a very simple application with one input, one button, and one output. This user interface can be seen in *Figure 1.1*. Here, the user has typed in bob, clicked **SUBMIT**, and the answer came back as **Yes! bob reversed is bob**:

Figure 1.1 – The palindrome problem

The *happy path test* here is the process where we type in bob and we see that it is a palindrome. We then check the same for **robert**, see that it is not, and then declare the testing done. After dozens of times running this exercise for job interviews, we have seen veteran testers stop at the happy path and declare victory perhaps 10% of the time. These are people with years of experience on their resumes.

Most people can come up with the happy path; it may be where we get the idea that *testing is easy*. The focus of this book is doing better. To do that, we need to open our eyes to all the possible risks, and then figure out how to reduce them.

The impossibility of complete testing

Let's say for a moment you are hired by a company that is implementing palindrome software. The **Executive Vice President** (**EVP**) for new business explains that the software represents a huge contract with the Teachers Union of Canada, the first of many. As such, there must be no risk within the product. None. To make sure there is no risk, the software must be tested completely.

What is the EVP asking for?

Let's see just how many risks a palindrome has, starting with the first test that is not completely obvious: uppercase letters. We'll start by typing a capital B for `Bob` in the text box and clicking **SUBMIT** (`https://www.xndev.com/palindrome`).

This run of the code tells us that *Bob* is not a palindrome, because *Bob* is not the same as *boB*. To someone with a writing background, this might be a bug, because it bugs them. However, to the programmer who wrote the software, the feature is working as designed. All the software does is reverse the thing and compare it, and it shows that *Bob* and *boB* are different. This is an especially interesting bug because the programmer and some customers disagree on what the software should do. This type of problem can be addressed earlier through communication and conversation – finding a bug like this so far along means fixing the code and retesting. Possibly, it also means a long series of discussions, arguments, and conflict, ending in no change. Once the end customer sees the software, the team might face another set of arguments. Getting involved earlier and working together to create a shared understanding of what the software should do are helpful things. We'll touch on them in *Part 3*, *Practicing Politics*. For now, our focus is testing, and the product owner was convinced that the simple reversal comparison was good enough.

Speaking of testing, if you run the software on a mobile device such as a phone or tablet, the first letter of the word is capitalized. To make most palindromes *work*, the user has to downshift the first letter every time. This might be a bug. And certainly, mobile devices should be tested. This means duplicating every test in four platforms, including Chrome, Firefox, Safari (Mac), or Edge (Windows) for each of the five devices, including laptop, tablet, and perhaps three or four different phones, which makes it five combinations in each of the Linux, Mac, and PC ecosystems (three combinations). This means you don't run one test – you run 60 (4*5*3). An argument can be made that the underlying technology of these is norming, so there is much less risk. Yet once you see the combinatorics problem in one place, you'll see it everywhere – for example, with versions of the Android operating system and mobile devices.

Meanwhile, we've barely scratched the surface of palindromes. An experienced tester will, at the very least, test spaces (if you do, you'll find multiple spaces at the front or back are truncated) and special characters such as ! @ # $ % ^ & * ( ) < > , / ? [] { } \ | ; they are likely to test embedding special characters that might have meaning under the hood, such as database code (**SQL**), **JavaScript**, and raw **HTML**. An open question is how the browser handles long strings. One way to test this is to go to **Project Gutenberg** (`https://www.gutenberg.org/`, an online library of free electronic books, or eBooks, most of which are in the public domain), find a large bit of text, then search for a string reversal tool online. Next, you can add the first string to the reversed second one and run it. A good open question is, *How large a string should the code accept?*

Strings are collections of text. At the time of writing, when you google *classic palindrome sentence*, the first search results include the following:

- Mr. Owl ate my metal worm

- Do geese see God?

- Was it a car or a cat I saw?

All of these will fail in the palindrome converter because they are not the same forward and backward. A literature review will find that a palindrome sentence is allowed to have capitalization, punctuation, and spaces that are ignored on reversal.

Did anyone else notice the **Anagram** section at the bottom of the page shown in *Figure 1.1*? All that functionality is part of the next release. Anyone testing it is told to "not test it" and "not worry about it" because it is part of the next release. Yet unless the tester explicitly reminds the team, that untested code will go out in the next build!

We could also check all these browsers and devices to see if they resize appropriately. We haven't considered the new challenges of mobile devices, such as heat, power, loss of network while working, or running while low on memory. If you are not exhausted yet, consider one more: just because a test passes once does not mean it will pass the next time. This could be because of a memory leak or a programmer optimization. As a young programmer, Matt once wrote a joke into a tool called the *document repository*, where there was a 1% chance it would rename itself on load, picking a random thesaurus entry for *document* and one for *repository*. A graphic designer, offended by the term *Archive Swag Bag*, insisted Matt change it. He replied, "*Just click refresh.*" While the story was based on a joke from the game Wizardry V, it did happen. This kind of problem does happen in software – for example, in projects that store frequently used data and have a longer lookup for rare data. Errors can happen when the data is read from longer-term storage and when it is written out, and when those happen can be unpredictable.

Now, consider that this is the code for the palindrome that is doing all the heavy lifting:

```
original = document.getElementById("originalWord").value;
var palindrome = original.split("").reverse().join("");
if ( original === palindrome) {
```

```
    document.getElementById("palindromeResult").innerHTML = "Yes! " +
original + " reversed is " + palindrome;
} else {
    document.getElementById("palindromeResult").innerHTML = "No! " +
original + " reserved is " + palindrome;
}
```

All these tests are for one textbox, one button, six lines of code, and one output. Most software projects are considerably more complex than this, and that additional complexity adds more combinations. In many cases, if we double the size of the code, we don't double the number of possible tests; we square the number of possible tests.

Given an essentially unlimited input space and an unlimited number of ways to walk through a dynamic application, and that the same test repeated a second time could always yield different results, we run into a problem: *complete testing is impossible.*

> **Note**
>
> One of our earlier reviewers, Dr Lee Hawkins, argues that we haven't quite made our point that complete testing is impossible. So, here's mathematical proof:
>
> 1. We must consider that the coverage of our input space is a function, such as $f(x)$
>
> 2. A demonstration of $f(n)$ does not demonstrate that $f(n+1)$ is correct
>
> 3. A complex test would test from $f(orig)$ to $f(\infty)$
>
> 4. If $f(n)$ does not imply $f(n+1)$, proof by induction is impossible
>
> 5. If the input space goes to $f(\infty)$, or infinity, dynamic testing is impossible
>
> Thus, complete testing is impossible.

As complete testing is impossible, we are still tasked with finding out the status of the software anyway. Some experts, people we respect as peers, say this cannot be done. All testing can do is find errors. The best a tester can say is, "*The software appeared to perform under some very specific conditions at some specific point in time.*"

Like happy path testing, anyone can do and say that. It might technically be true, but it is unlikely to be seen as much more than a low-value dodge.

When Matt was a Cadet in the Civil Air Patrolin Frederick Composite Squadron, there was a scroll that hung on a nail in the cadet office. This is what it said:

"We, the willing, led by the unknowing, have been doing the impossible,
for the ungrateful.

We have been doing so much for long for so little

That we are now qualified to do anything for nothing."

– Konstantin Josef Jireček

That is what we are tasked to do: the impossible for the (often) ungrateful. By this, we mean that we must find the most powerful tests that reveal the most information about the software under test and then figure out what information the tests reveal.

Part of doing that is figuring out for ourselves, in our project, where the bugs come from so that we can find them in their lair with minimal effort.

If you aren't convinced yet, well, we ran out of room – but consider the number of combinations of possible tests in a calculator. Now, consider if the calculator might have a small memory leak, and try to detect that leak with tests. Complete testing is impossible. Say it again: *complete testing is impossible.*

Before we move on to a theory of error, we hope you've explored the software yourself and have a list of bugs to write up. Save them and use *Chapter 5* to practice writing them up. Our favorite defect is likely HTML injection; you can use an IMG tag or HR tag to embed HTML in the page.

Toward a theory of error

When people talk about bugs in software, they tend to have one root cause in mind – *the programmer screwed up*. The palindrome problem demonstrates a few types of a much wider theory of error. A few of these are as follows:

- **Missed requirement**: It would be really easy to do an operation I logically want to do… but there is no button for it.

- **Unintended consequences of interactions between two or more requirements**: On the Mars rover project, one input took meters and the other yards. Those measurements are close, but they don't work for astrophysics.

- **Common failure modes of the platform**: On a mobile app, losing internet signal or a draining battery is suddenly a much bigger deal.

- **Vague or unclear requirements**: "The input device" could be a keyboard, a mouse, or a Nintendo Wii controller.

- **Clear but incorrect requirements**: "Yes, we said it should do that. Now that we've seen it, we don't like it."

- **Missed implicit requirements**: Everyone *just knows* that the (**F)ile** menu should be the first in an editing program, with (**N)ew** immediately below that and (**C)lose** at the bottom.

- **Programmer error**: This is the one we understand and tend to assume.

- **The software doesn't match customer expectations**: Imagine building and testing the **Anagram** function as if it were written for elementary English teachers to use with students, when in fact it was for extremely picky Scrabble players – or the other way around. This might *bug* someone, or a group large enough to matter. Thus *requirements* and *specifications* are less *what the software will do*, and more *a generally shared agreement as to what the software should do, made at some point in time*.

Even this quick, sloppy list is much wider and deeper than the idea of the simple happy path of testing the obvious. The list is sloppy by design. Instead of presenting it as final, we suggest that, over time, *testers build their own lists*. More important than the list are the things in the list, and the weights attached to them – that is, the percentage of effort that corresponds to each category of error. Once you have a list and have gone past the happy path and requirements-driven approaches, you can create scenarios that drive the software to where these failures might be. Those are tests.

The list of categories, what is in them, and their weights will change over time as you find more bugs, and as the technical staff, product, and platform change. Our goal with this book is to accelerate that learning process for you and provide ideas that help you develop those powerful test ideas.

Testing software – an example

There are plenty of books that say the person doing the testing should be involved up-front. Our example will go the other way. In this example, the software engineering group does not create the "consistent, correct, complete, clear" requirements that are idealized. Their requirements did not decompose nicely into stories that have clear acceptance criteria that can be objectively evaluated. The stories did not have a "kick-off" meeting where the developers, the person doing testing, and the product owner got together to build a shared mental model.

Instead, someone plunked us down at a keyboard and said, "*Test this.*" As an example, we can use the old Grand Rapids Airport Parking Calculator, which, at the time of writing, Markus Gärtner has copied and placed on his website at `https://www.shino.de/parkcalc/`. Looking at the following figure; it is a piece of software that allows you to predict the cost of your airport parking:

PARKING COST CALCULATOR

Choose a Parking Lot	Valet Parking ∨		
Please input entry date and time	MM/DD/YYYY 🗓	12:00	⦿ AM ○ PM
Please input leaving date and time	MM/DD/YYYY 🗓	12:00	⦿ AM ○ PM
ESTIMATED PARKING COSTS	**$ 0**		

Calculate

PARKING RATES

Valet Parking
$18 per day
$12 for five hours or less

Short-Term (hourly) Parking
$2.00 first hour; $1.00 each additional 1/2 hour
$24.00 daily maximum

Long-Term Garage Parking
$2.00 per hour
$12.00 daily maximum
$72.00 per week (7th day free)

Long-Term Surface Parking *(North Lot)*
$2.00 per hour
$10.00 daily maximum
$60.00 per week (7th day free)

Economy Lot Parking
$2.00 per hour
$9.00 daily maximum
$54.00 per week (7th day free)

A Lost Ticket Fee of $10.00 will be assessed when the original parking stub cannot be produced when exiting the parking facilities (does not apply to Valet Parking).

Figure 1.2 – ParcCalc from Markus's website

The techniques we are about to list have been quickly determined and are rapid-fire, with questions to learn how they behave under different conditions. This thinking applies to unit tests, specialized tests, **application programming interface** (**API**) tests, and other risk management approaches. As Matt tested **ParkCalc** seriously for the first time in years, he wrote down what he was thinking and doing; you could look at it almost like a chess game that was documented for your benefit.

During testing, he was asking questions about the software, as an attorney might ask a suspect under examination in court. The answers led him to the next question. Instead of trying to build the software up, as a programmer does, he was trying to figure out what makes it work, a different style of thought. This thinking can apply to requirements, the API's performance, or accessibility.

Start of test notes

This is a little more complex than a palindrome – more inputs, more outputs, and many more *equivalence classes*, which are categories to break things into that "should" be treated the same. We might hypothesize, for example, that the difference between 10/1/2024 at 1:05 P.M. and 10/1/2024 at 1:07 P.M. is not worth testing. This shrinks the number of potential tests a bit as we can test one thing for the "bucket" of, say, 1 minute to 59 minutes. *Boundary values* point out that the errors tend to be around the transitions – at 59 minutes, 60, or 61. This happens when a programmer types, for example, less than (<); in this case, they should type less than or equal to (<=). These are sometimes called off-by-one errors. Unit tests, which we'll explore later, can radically decrease how often these sorts of errors occur. For now, though, we don't know if the programmers wrote unit tests.

When we run these sorts of simulations, it's common for the person performing the test to want to get the customer involved, to get some sort of customer feedback, or to try some sort of mind-meld with the product owner. These approaches can be incredibly powerful, and we'll discuss them in this book, particularly in the *Agile testing* section. For now, however, we'll strip everything down to the raw bug hunt. This is unfair for many reasons. After all, how can you assess if the software is "good enough" if no one tells you what "good enough" means?

And yet we press on...

In this example, we have a single screen and a single interaction. Later in this book, in *Chapter 9*, we'll talk about how to measure how well the software is tested when it is more complex. For now, the thing to do is "dive in." The place to dive in with no other information is likely the user interface. When Markus created the page, he did us the great favor of adding requirements in the text below the buttons. Note those requirements hinge on "choose a parking lot," which is the first drop-down element:

A software tester walks into a bar:	The tester orders:	The tester declares that testing is complete	A real customer walks into the bar and asks where the bathroom is
They run into it	A beer		
They crawl into it.	2 beers		
They dance into it	0 beers		
They fly into it	999,999,999 beers		The bar goes up in flames
They jump into it	A goldfish in a beer glass (test: water or beer?)		
	-1 beer		
	A "qwerty" beers		

Table 1.1 – A tester's view of the world

Faced with an interface like this, I tend to interleave two ideas: using the software while overwhelming the input fields with invalid, blank, out-of-range, or nonsensical data. This provides a quick and shallow assessment. The tradeoff here is coverage (checking all the combinations) with speed (getting fast results).

So, when I tested it at the time of writing, these tests looked like this:

Test Number	Type	Date Start	Date End	Time Start	Time End	Expected
1	Valet	7/29/22	7/29/22	2:00 P.M.	3:00 P.M.	$12.00
2	Valet	7/22/22	7/22/22	2:00 P.M.	7:00 P.M.	$12.00
3	Valet	7/22/22	7/22/22	2:00 P.M.	7:01 P.M.	$18.00

Table 1.2 – Valet parking test examples

You can build a similar table like this for your tests:

Test Number	Type	Date Start	Date End	Time Start	Time End	Expected
4	Valet	7/29/22	7/29/22	2:00 P.M.	2:59 P.M.	$12.00

Table 1.3 – Sample table for your own tests

Now, we find a second issue. After we return to the main page, the drop box defaults back to **Valet**. This means the correct dollar amount shows, but it looks to the reader like it was selected for valet parking.

At this point, I started clicking the calendar to find the datetime picker:

Figure 1.3 – Datetime picker

Notice that the picker says **about:blank**, which likely means an optional parameter for **about** is not populated. Beyond that, if you click away from the picker and back to the page, it gives the page focus. In older browser versions, the popup would not stay at the front focus but would stay behind the page with focus. This is fixed in current browsers. This led to testing maximizing the page and filling the entire screen.

Another bug is that, if the screen is maximized and you click the popup, it appears as a strange maximized new tab:

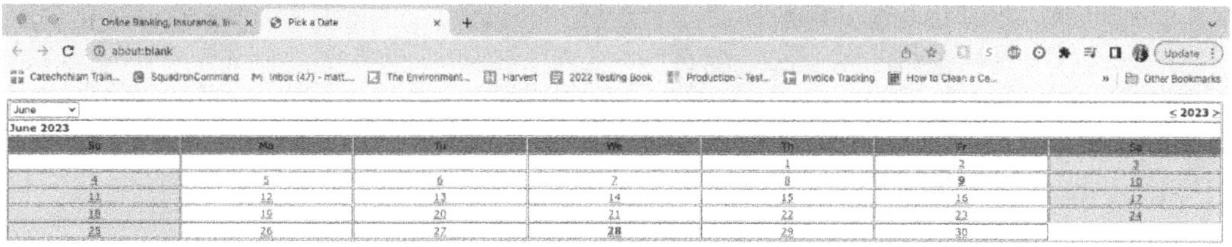

Figure 1.4 – Maximized new tab.
The intent of this screenshot is to show the maximized layout; text readability is not required.

If you start to look at the requirements, you'll see a lot of valid combinations for each type. We could decompose all the possibilities. When you look at that appendix, you will realize that the list is just too long. Exploring short-term just a little more yields these combinations:

```
30 minutes, 60 minutes, 90 minutes, 120 minutes, 121 minutes, 119
minutes
23 hours and 59 minutes, 24 hours, 24 hours and 1 minute
```

Leap years. Three interesting ideas to test are to see if the datetime picker realizes that 2024 contains February 29 but 2023 and 2022 do not, to see if the tool correctly realizes that February 28 to March 1 2023 is 1 day in 2023 and 2 days in 2024, and to hard-code, say, 2/29/2023 to 3/1/2023 as a date and see if the software realizes the date is in error.

While the first two scenarios work, the period from 2/29/2023 at 14:00 to 3/1/2023 at 13:59 seems to be -1 days, 23 hours, and 59 minutes. This is the same calculation as 3/1/2023 to 3/1/2023 14:00 to 13:59. The software seems to be calculating the date as days_since_something; numbers beyond the end of the month just get added on. Also, if you think about it, "-1 days PLUS 23 hours PLUS 59 minutes" is the same as 0 days, 0 hours, and -1 minutes:

Figure 1.5 – Highlighted date picker

While this is probably a bug, exactly how the software should work is a little less clear. It might be better to print an error message, such as Departure date from parking cannot be before arrival.

My next move is to switch over to Firefox and mess with the popup. On two monitors, I see the popup appear in the center of my first monitor, apparently with fonts selected for the second. I also see the same maximize causes popup to open in a new tab problem.

Note that today's date appears in the date picker with a yellow background. If the month has 31 days in it, then the last day is also yellow. Why we would want that, I'm not sure. I moused over the button to find the name of the JavaScript function, which is NewCal(). Then, I right-clicked and chose **View source** to find the web page code. Not finding a definition for NewCal in the source, I found the following include, which pointed to the JavaScript file name that might include NewCal:

```
<script language="JavaScript" type="text/JavaScript"
src="datetimepicker.js"></script>
```

Looking at that code (https://www.shino.de/parkcalc/datetimepicker.js) it appears to be someone else's custom date time picker, not anything from the operating system. Here's the beginning of the source code:

```
//Javascript name: My Date Time Picker
//Date created: 16-Nov-2003 23:19
```

```
//Scripter: TengYong Ng
//Website: http://www.rainforestnet.com
//Copyright (c) 2003 TengYong Ng
//FileName: DateTimePicker.js
//Version: 0.8
//Contact: contact@rainforestnet.com
```

This code appears to be from 2003 and likely hasn't kept up as people started to use more monitors, smartphones, and so on. I tried the app on my iPhone and the interface was hard to read, and the date picker was even more awkward. I could have spent a great deal of time looking at this JavaScript code if I wanted to.

With no specific goals on risks or effort, the JavaScript code for DatePicker is just one of many directions I could speed off in, with no plans or governance of where to invest my time. While the things I have found so far bug *me*, I don't know that the product owner would care. So, again, I'd try to find a person with the authority to make final decisions to talk about the expectations for the software and test process. This will guide my testing. If I know the decision maker just does not care about entire categories of defects, I won't waste time testing them. Let's say the person in charge of the product made a common reasonable decision: "*Spend about an hour on a bug hunt, don't get too focused on any one thing, and then we'll decide what to do next.*"

This statement isn't that far-fetched. A few years ago, Matt worked with a team that had made a corporate decision not to support tablets for their web application. Of course, the customer used them anyway, to the tune of several million dollars a month and growing exponentially. Instead of saying "*We don't support tablets,*" which was no longer a choice, a proposal was made to go into an empty office for a day and figure out what the largest blocking issues were. It might have been that we just needed a half-dozen bug fixes; it might have been so bad that a total rewrite was needed. Without actually using the software on a tablet, no one knew.

Timing work to an hour, it was determined that each action from the dropdown would take about 3 minutes minus 15 minutes total. That would be 15 more minutes for each platform (different browsers, different screen resolutions, different devices), then 15 minutes exploring incorrect data, and 15 minutes to double-check and document findings.

Speaking of overwhelming, the next test is to examine data that looks correct but is not. An example is short-term parking *from 10/32/2022 to 11/3/2022*, or valet from 12:00 P.M. to 70:00 P.M. Both of those return results that fit the mental model of how the software is performing – that is, the expectation is to convert complex dates into a simpler format and subtract them. 1:00 P.M. becomes 13:00 A.M., so the software can subtract and get elapsed time. Thus, *10/32* is the same as *11/1* and 70:00 P.M. is 10:00 P.M. plus 2 days (48 hours).

It's time for a new test: I tried short-term, 12:00 A.M. to 13:00 A.M. The time should be 1 hour, and the rate should be $2.00. Instead, the software says $24.00, which is the day-rate maximum. Looking at the time, I can see that this is treated as 12:00 A.M. (midnight) to 1:00 P.M., or 13 hours, at $2.00

per hour, with a daily max of $24.00 – that is, 12:00 A.M. is *midnight*, to be followed by 12:01 A.M., with 1:00 A.M. 1 hour after *midnight*.

End of test notes

After a few pages of reading how I test, you've probably realized a few things. A lot of details have been included but nowhere near as much as was performed (this example was shortened for printing purposes and yet was still full of information). In the next section, we will break down the steps we performed and analyze how and why we performed the tests listed. Let's examine what we accomplished here and see how we can use these techniques in our testing process.

Testing software – an analysis

First of all, note how messy the process is. Instead of planning my time, I jumped in. Planning happened about 15 minutes in, where I planned only the first hour. My style was to jump in and out, back and forth, quickly. Fundamentally, I skipped between three modes:

- Testing the user journey

- Testing for common platform errors

- Testing for invalid formats

If all of the notes had been included, you would have seen more elaboration on each dropdown, plus invalid format attacks on every field. The invalid format attacks are either data that looks correct but is out of bounds (The 50th of October), data that looks entirely wrong (a date of "HELLOMA"), or data that is blank. Another way to do this is to do things out of order: click buttons that would not be in the normal order, perhaps delete a comment on one device, and attempt to reply on another after it has been deleted.

It's easy to dismiss these kinds of *invalid data* approaches as "garbage in, garbage out," but they provide valuable information quickly. If the programmer makes small attention-to-detail errors on input, they probably make larger attention-to-detail errors in the logic of the program. As we'll learn later, accepting invalid inputs can create security vulnerabilities.

Thus, if I find a large number of "quick attack" errors, it tells me to look more closely at the valid exception conditions in the software. Having conversations about what is valid and not with the technical staff is one way I *force* conversations about the requirements. For example, I can ask what the software should do under certain conditions. When the answer is, "*That's interesting. Huh. I hadn't thought about that,*" we enter the realm of defects from unintended consequences or missed expectations.

Let's put this together to figure out how to be an airdropped tester, then step back to a few formal techniques.

Quick attacks – the airdropped tester

If you read the example that we discussed earlier, and you don't have a background in formal documented test techniques, then it looks like I'm just goofing around, just taking a *tour*. Michael Kelly introduced the *tour metaphor* and James Whittaker wrote a book on it. If you have seen documented test cases with each step laid out, it might look more like foolishness – where is the structure, where is the planning?

With this style of testing, the results of the previous test inform the next. The first question is "What should I test first?", after that "What did that test result tell me?", and after that "What should I test next?" It may seem impossible, but this is exactly how strategy games such as chess are played. As the situation unfolds, the experienced player adjusts their strategy to fit what they have found. I outlined the general style previously – *explore the user journey while pushing the platform to failure, and particularly pushing the inputs to failure.* And, as I mentioned previously, more information about the team, platform, and history of the software will inform better tests.

On the outside, a game of chess looks like chaos. Where is the strategy? Where is the structure, the planning? Isn't it irresponsible to not write things down?

A different aspect of the code changes each time we test it. That is different from an assembly line, where each item should be the same with the same dimensions – a quality control specialist can check every part the same way, or develop a tool to do it, perhaps by the case. With software, the risks of each build are very different. Given the limited time to test and an infinite number of possibilities, it makes sense for us to customize every test session to squeeze the most value. Later in this book, in *Chapter 9*, we'll discuss how to create just enough documentation to guide and document decisions, especially for larger software. This lesson is on the airdropped tester – the person who drops in with little knowledge of the system.

Most people working in software realize they cannot do an airdropped tester role. We know because we have challenged people at conferences and run simulations. Instead, people "wiggle on the hook," asking for documents, asking to speak to the product owner, to talk to customers. Those are all good things. The airdropped tester does it anyway, without any of that help.

After reading this entire chapter, you should be able to do *something*. For this section, we'll tell you a few secrets.

First, the ignorance of being an outsider is your friend. Employees of the company, filling out the same form year after year, might know that phone numbers are to be input in a particular format, such as (888) 868 7194, but you don't. So, you'll try without the parentheses and get an error. We call this the consultant's gambit: there are probably obvious problems you can't see because of your company culture.

Here's an example of time-and-date attacks:

Timeouts

Time Difference between Machines

Crossing Time Zones

Leap Days

Always Invalid Days (Feb 30, Sept 31)

Feb 29 in Non-Leap Years

Different Formats (June 5, 2001; 06/05/2001; 06/05/01; 06-05-01; 6/5/2001 12:34) Internationalization dd.mm.yyyy, mm/dd/yyyy

A.M/P.M. 24 Hours

Daylight Savings Changeover Reset Clock Backward or Forward

For any given input field, throw in some of these invalid dates. We'd add dates that are too early or too late, such as in ParkCalc when we tried to park a car in the past, or far in the future. Most variables are stored in an internal representation, a data type (such as an integer or a float), and these usually have a size limit. In ParkCalc, one good attack is to try the type of parking that will grow the fastest (valet) with the largest possible period to see if you can get the result to be too large. It could be too large to fit the screen, too large for the formatting tool, or too large for the internet item. Because of how they are structured, floating-point numbers are especially bad when adding numbers that contain both large and small elements. A float in C++, for example, has only 6 to 9 digits of precision. This means that storing 0.0025 is easy, as is storing 25,000, but storing 25,000.0025 will be a problem. Most programming languages these days can store at least twice as many numbers, but at the same time, a great deal of software is still built on top of older, legacy systems.

Going back to the consultant's gambit, we typically try to change the operational use. If the programmers all use phones to edit and test their mobile applications, we'll use a tablet – and turn it sideways. If all the work is done on at-home strong networks, we'll take a walk in the woods on a weak cell connection. If the answer comes back that this kind of testing isn't useful, that's good; we've gone from airdropped to actually learning about the software and the customers.

After doing this professionally for over a decade, Matt has always been able to find a serious defect that would stop release within 1 day. While the team works on fixing that bug, Matt can dive into all the other important things we've implied, such as requirements, talking to customers, talking to the team, gathering old test documents, and so on.

Generally, business software takes input through a transformation, creating output. In our ParkCalc example, there are all sorts of hidden rules such as *the seventh day free*. Without those requirements on the initial splash screen, it will be very difficult to know what the correct answer should be. Moreover, there are hidden things to test (such as a 6-day stay, 7-day stay, and 8-day stay) that you don't know to test without those requirements.

Once you've found the first few important bugs and the programmers are busy fixing them and have found enough documents to understand how the software should work, it's time to analyze and create deeper test ideas.

Next, we'll talk about designing tests to cover combinations of inputs.

Test design – input space coverage

In early elementary school, Matt wrote a little program that would take your name and echo back hello. It was in the back of computer programming magazines. Sometimes, we would do something a little cheeky; if you entered a special code, you'd get a special answer. We'll cheat a bit and show you the relevant bits of code:

```
print "Enter your name "
propername = gets.chomp();

if (propername == "victor")
  puts "Congratulations on your win!";
else
  puts "hello, " + propername + "\n\n";
end
```

Given this sort of requirement, there are two obvious tests – the top and bottom of the input statement. Type in victor, type in Matthew, see both sides execute, and we are done testing. We tend to think of this as *myopic testing*, or testing with blinders on – reducing the testing to the most trivial examples possible. What about Victor or VICTOR? Let's modify the assignment, like this:

```
propername = gets.chomp().downcase()
```

That gives us at least three test ideas – Victor, victor, and Matthew. As a tester, a blank string, a really long string, and special characters – foreign languages and such – would be good parameters to test with.

You could think of this as trying to come up with test ideas, and that's certainly true. On the other hand, what we are doing here is reducing the number of possible tests from an infinite set to a manageable set. One core idea is the *equivalence class* – if we've tested for Matt, we likely don't need to test for Matthew, Robert, or anything else that is not "victor"-ish. Looking at the code, we likely have three equivalence classes: "victor"-ish, Matt, and "special cases", such as really long strings, really short strings, foreign languages, emojis, and special ASCII codes. We're a fan of char(7) – the ASCII "bell" sound.

In the old days, we would have programs that rejected non-standard character codes; we'd have to worry if the text we entered exceeded the memory allowed for that bit of text. Ruby takes care of a great deal of that for us. Many modern applications are still built on top of those old systems, where data structure size matters or appears on a phone screen with a limited amount of room. By knowing the code and programming language, we can reduce (or increase) the amount of testing we do. Another way to do that is by understanding the *operational use* – business customers are much less likely to paste in the newest form of emotional representative object, and, when they do, are unlikely to view their pasting of an animated picture as a *fail*.

Still, these three test ideas miss the point.

Notice \n\n at the end of the `else` statement. That is a carriage return. The output of `victor` looks like this:

```
mheusser@Matthews-MBP-2 Chapter01 % ruby TestDesign01.rb
Enter your name victor
Congratulations on your win!
mheusser@Matthews-MBP-2 Chapter01 %
```

On the other hand, the output of `Matt` looks like this:

```
mheusser@Matthews-MBP-2 Chapter01 % ruby TestDesign01.rb
Enter your name Matt
hello, matt
mheusser@Matthews-MBP-2 Chapter01 %
```

Those \n characters are the carriage returns. That is what a typewriter does when the author wants to finish a line and go to the next. The extra \n\n creates the extra whitespace between `matt` and the next line. *This is an inconsistency.*

You could argue that this sort of inconsistency doesn't matter; this is a silly children's game. Yet if you train yourself to spot the inconsistencies, you'll notice when they *do* matter.

Here's another: By down-casing the `propername` method, it is also printed out in lowercase. "Matt" becomes "Hello, matt." `downcase()` should probably only go inside the comparison, which is the criterion that's used for the `if` statement. That way, the variable printed out exactly matches what was typed in.

Thus, we have Heusser's Maxim of documented testing:

> *"At the end of every human-run, pre-designed, documented test is a hidden*
> *expected result: … And nothing else odd happened."*

In *Chapter 2*, we'll discuss why we are not excited about *test cases*, and other ways to plan, visualize, and think about testing. It would be fair to write down a list of inputs and expected results, especially in later examples when the software becomes more complex. The problem comes when we fixate on one thing (the `if` statement's correctness) instead of the entire application. This becomes especially true after the programmers give fixes; it is too easy to re-test just the fix, instead of elements around the fix. Get four, five, six, or seven builds that aren't quite good enough and you can get tester fatigue. Each build can lead to less and less testing. When this happens, the "little errors", such as the capitalization mentioned previously, can get missed. We'll also discuss a formula for reducing these problems through programmer tests, acceptance tests (that can be automated), and human exploration.

Looking at the code, we can see another way to test – *statement coverage*. Statement coverage has us measure, as a percentage, the number of lines of code that are executed by the tests. We can achieve 100% statement coverage by testing `matt` and `victor`, neither of which would trip the capitalization bug. Being able to see the code and consider it is something called *white box* or *clear box* testing, while only viewing the program as it is running is sometimes called *black box* testing. Focusing on the code can also be myopic; it doesn't consider resizing the window of a windowed application or if hitting the *Enter* key on a web form will click the submit button. Looking at coverage from a clear box can be helpful, and we'll cover it when we consider programmer-facing testing in *Chapter 3*.

Often, we want to come up with test ideas before the code is created, or as it is created. In those cases, the clear/black-box distinction doesn't matter. Let's look at a second example that is a little more complex.

To do that, we'll build up an application, micro-feature by micro-feature, in ways that allow us to demonstrate some classic test techniques.

Equivalence classes and boundaries

In this section, we will look at a sample auto insurance premium calculation app.

Story 1 – minimal insurance application

The software is designed to calculate or quote the cost of auto insurance for potential customers in the United States. The first story drops just one input (**Age**), and one button (**Calculate**, or **Submit**). Here's the breakdown of insurance costs and the screen mock-up:

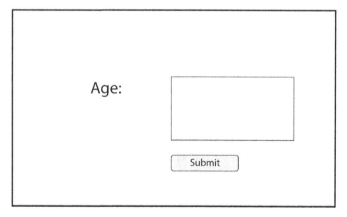

Figure 1.6 – Insurance application screen

From here, we can select the age brackets and the appropriate level of coverage:

Age	Cost
0 to 15	No insurance
16 to 20	$800 per month
21 to 30	$600 per month
30 to 40	$500 per month
41 to 50	$400 per month
51 to 70	$500 per month
71 to 99	$700 per month

Table 1.4 – Insurance rates based on age

Given what we've written so far, get a piece of paper and write down your test ideas. Recognize that every test has a cost and time is limited, so you want to run the most powerful tests as quickly as possible.

We aren't going to propose a single "right" answer. How much time you invest in testing, and how deep you go, will depend on how much time you have, what you would rather be doing, and how comfortable you are introducing errors into the wild. What we are doing in this chapter is providing you with some techniques to come up with test ideas. *Chapters 9* and *10* include ideas to help you balance risk and effort. So keep your list, finish the chapter, then review if you missed anything. For that matter, read *Chapters 9* and *10*, then consider your own organizational context, try this exercise again, and compare your lists. Another option is to work with a peer to come up with two different lists and compare them.

Now let's talk about test ideas. First of all, there is a problem with the requirements. How much do we charge a 30-year-old, again? This is a requirements error; the transition is 21-30 and 31-40. Once you get past that, you would likely ask how much to charge a 100-year-old. Assuming the company has worked out the legal problems and the answer is "error," we can look at categories of input that should be treated the same. So, for example, if 45 "passes," yielding a correct answer of $40, then we would not need to test 44, 46, or 47. Here's what that looks like on a number line, where it yields eight test ideas. The numbers on top are the specific bracket numbers, while the arrows represent the test values that we can use:

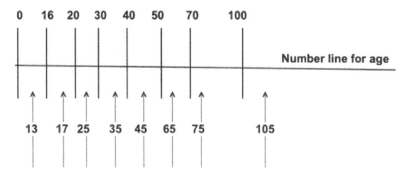

Top Data: Age equivalencies

Arrows: Ages to test
(12 and 13 "should" be equivalant)

Figure 1.7 – Age brackets and example numbers to test

As it turns out, this is terrible testing. The most common error when creating programs like this one is called the off-by-one error, and it looks like this:

```
if (age<16)
      puts "Unable to purchase insurance";
elsif (age>16 && age<20)
      puts "$600/month";
elsif (age>=20 && age<30)
      puts "$500/month";
```

The preceding code block has two errors. First, 16 is never processed because the first if is less than 16 and the second is greater than 16. 20 is processed along with the people leading up to 20, instead of with 16 to 20, where it should be. Including (or failing to include) the equals sign when using greater/less than can lead to errors around the boundaries. Errors in boundaries can also creep in when boundaries are calculated. For example, if we input Fahrenheit and then convert it into Celsius, a round-off error could miscalculate freezing or boiling by just enough that 100 degrees Celsius calculates to 99.999 Celsius. This is "not boiling." In the same case, a print statement might truncate 99.999 and print "99" when it should round to 100. We also see these kinds of errors in loops, when a loop is executed one time too many or one time too few.

The test examples listed are all smack dab in the middle, unlikely to trip any boundary condition. So, let's try again:

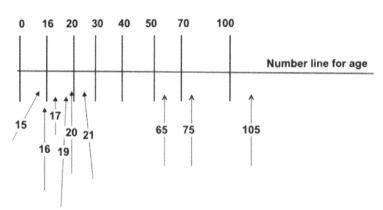

Figure 1.8 - Highlighting the possible edge conditions

The preceding example has 22 conditions out of a possible 85. It combines at least four approaches:

- **Equivalence classes**: Right in the middle of each category. 25, 35, and 45.

- **Boundaries**: Around the transitions between values. 20 and 21, 40 and 41.

- **Robust boundaries**: One above and below a boundary condition. 19, 22, 39, 42, and so on.

- **Magic numbers**: Once we've tested 100, there is nothing particularly new or special about 101. Likewise, nothing special is supposed to happen between 29 and 21. Yet we added a test at 101 and another at 29. These are robust boundaries, but they are also the boundaries of big, logical numbers – remember our code example where 16 itself was missed.

In addition to these, we might wonder what would happen if the field is left blank or text is typed in, such as special characters, (how do we process 30.5?), very large numbers, and all the other unique characters we've talked about before, or the security things we'll talk about later. It's worth noting that the best fix for this is likely to put a mask on the input, so you simply cannot type in anything except whole numbers from 16 to 99.

Even with an input mask, the only way to "know" that every line is correct is to test all the values from 16 to 99. Even that does not guarantee some sort of memory leak or programmer easter egg if a certain combination is entered. Video game fans may think of test flags, such as the "Up Up Down Down Left Right Left Right B A Start" in some console games. Simple requirements techniques will fail to find these edge cases.

This example is just too simple. It is the first feature, cranked out in a week to satisfy an executive. Let's add some spice.

Decision tables

In this section, we'll look at our next story.

Story 2 – adding a type of insurance dropdown

It should have the following coverage:

- Comprehensive /w No Deductible 3x Cost
- Comprehensive /w Deductible 2x Cost
- Minimal Coverage 1x Cost

Here's the user interface:

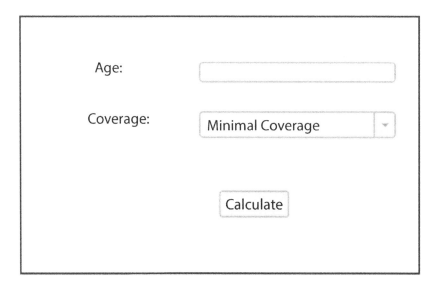

Figure 1.9 – Expanded insurance quote screen example

Notice that the UI has changed a bit; the button has now changed from **Submit** to **Calculate**, and the button does not appear to be centered. Likewise, **Age** and **Coverage** look "off." We don't even know if this is a Windows or Mac application, runs in a browser, or on a native mobile app. If it is for Windows, the UI does not tell us if the screen should have a minimize or medium-sized button or be resizable. None of these ideas come up when we look at the pure algorithm, yet we have both worked on projects where exact pixel position and font size mattered, so part of the testing was making sure the screen matched the exact appearance in a mockup. Matt once worked on an eCommerce web project where a mini-shopping cart, on the right-hand side, was too high. When it was moved down, the buttons were cut off!

Still, focusing on the algorithm, we have a problem. Our little number line now has two dimensions. To solve this, we can make a table and arrange the values using equivalence classes:

	Coverage Type		
Age	Minimal	Comprehensive, deductible	Comprehensive, not deductible
0-15	N/A	N/A	N/A
16-20	800	1,600	2,400
21-30	600	1,200	1,800
31-40	500	1,000	1,500
41-50	400	800	1,200
51-70	500	1,000	1,500
71-99	700	1,400	2,100
100	NA	N/A	N/A

Table 1.5 – Insurance quotes presented in equivalence classes

This is sometimes called a *decision table*. If every combination is one thing we "should" test, our number of combinations shoots up from 8 to 24. That gives us 100% requirements coverage and generates our test ideas to run for us. If you want to get fancy, you could put this in a web-based spreadsheet and color the cells green or red when they pass or fail – an instant dashboard!

Sadly, based on our application of boundaries, robust boundaries, and magic numbers, it's more like 22 times 3 or 66. It still could be modeled in a table – it would just be long, ugly, and hard to test.

Don't worry. That's nothing – it's about to get a lot harder.

Decision trees

In this section, we'll consider adding a vehicle's value.

Story 3 – adding a vehicle's value

Users will use an offline tool (for now) to calculate the vehicle's value, then apply the following guidelines to change the insurance quote:

Table 1-2

Price	Impact
Less than $2,000	+10%
$2,001 to $10,000	-10%
$10,001 to $50,000	No change
$50,001 to $70,000	+10%
$70,001 to $90,000	No change
$90,000 to $200,000	+20%
$200,000.00	+100%

Figure 1.10 – Quote percentage changes based on the cost of the vehicle

The 10% increase for a low-priced vehicle is correct as the data shows that "cheap" vehicles are more likely to be involved in accidents. At this point, our two-dimensional table fails us, and we have to move to a decision tree. Here's one way to model that decision tree; note that it is painful and brings us to 198 possible tests if we use robust testing, or a mere 76 with "just" equivalence class testing:

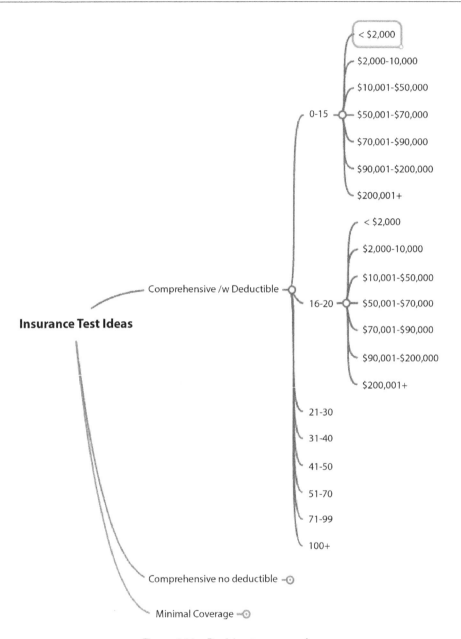

Figure 1.11 – Decision tree example

But there is a bigger issue – shouldn't the price also be tested with robust boundary conditions? Instead of seven possibilities, that's more like 20 or a total of (22 * 3* 20) 1,320 things to test in three stories that, realistically, might take a total of 30 minutes to code.

This is a problem.

In a real organization, Matt would suggest that instead of typing in the vehicle price, we select from a dropdown. If these are true equivalence classes, we could make the code handle them equally. That'll help… a little. Yet when Matt does training on this, he makes it harder, adding a "driving record" dropdown for speeding tickets (four choices) and a "years with no accident" dropdown (five more choices). That is 1,520 equivalence class tests; 26,400 with robust boundaries.

We call this the "combinatorics problem," and once you look for it, it is everywhere. When Android devices were young, it was common for manufacturers to "fork" the operating system, leaving native applications to be tested hundreds of ways on top of any existing testing. The same problem came when tablets appeared, and the possible number of screen resolutions exploded. Plus, of course, there is the logic in our own code.

The earlier example is contrived. The programmers likely used a pattern where each additional requirement functioned independently of the other. A little knowledge of what goes on under the hood might allow the testers to test each requirement once, leading to a combination like this:

- All the ages tested robustly one time (22 tests)

- All the coverage types tested once (3 tests)

- All the price of the vehicle ranges tests tested once (7 tests)

- All the driving record options tested once (4 tests)

- All the years with no accident choices tested once (5 tests)

This is 41 tests. If you think about it, though, each of the ages could also be used to test one of the coverage types, one of the vehicle ranges, one of the record options, and one of the accident choices. In seven tests, we could have tested everything except for 15 of the ages. Some companies put the test combinations on the first column of a spreadsheet, the equivalence classes on the other columns, and the tests in rows, and put an *X* every time a combination is hit. This is called a *traceability matrix*. These kinds of tests are more useful when dealing with complex equipment that might take a significant time to set up, where the interaction of the components could cause unexpected errors. It could also happen if the preceding program were coded in a naive way by someone using a great deal of `if` statements and a cut-and-paste coding style. As a tester, identifying where the real risk is, and what we can afford to skip, is a significant part of the job.

So, what do you do when there are just too many combinations? We can use a technique that allows us to make a more manageable set of parameters by making sets of combinations, combining two variables at a time. This is referred to as *all-pairs* or *pairwise testing*.

All-pairs and pairwise testing

The *giant decision tree* we mentioned earlier implies that we need to test everything. After all, a specific combination of insurance, coverage, vehicle sale price, and driving record might have an error the others do not, so we need to test all 9,240 combinations (that is, the number of possible test cases if every option is tested with every other option for an exhaustive listing).

Except, of course, no one is testing that by hand. Even if we did and found, say, three bugs that only occurred in their specific circumstances, those defects would impact about 0.03% of all cases. By covering every scenario once, we run just 22 test cases; after the seventh, we can *weigh* the scenarios, testing the ones we think are most likely. This should provide us with pretty good coverage, right? The question is how much.

As it turns out, the USA-based **National Institute of Standards and Technology** (**NIST**) ran a study on the combinatorics problem (web.archive.org/web/20201001171643/https:/csrc. nist.gov/publications/detail/journal-article/2001/failure-modes-in-medical-device-software-an-analysis-of-15-year), first published in 2001, that discovered something interesting. According to the study, 66% percent of defects in a medical device could be found through testing all the possible pairs, or two-way combinations between components, 99% could be found through all three-way interactions, and 100% through all four-way interactions. Here's the relevant table from that study, from their 2004 publication in IEEE Transactions:

TABLE 1
Cumulative Percent of Faults Triggered by n–way Conditions

FTFI No.	RAX conver-gence	RAX conver-gence	RAX interf	RAX engine	POSIX modules	Medical Devices	Browser	Server	NASA GSFC
1	61	72	48	39	88	66	29	42	68
2	97	82	54	47	*	97	76	70	93
3	*	*	*	*	*	99	95	89	98
4	*	*	*	*	*	100	97	96	100
5	*	*	*	*	*		99	96	
6	*	*	*	*	*		100	100	

Table 1.6 – Percent of faults triggered by n-way conditions

Source: *IEEE TRANSACTIONS ON SOFTWARE ENGINEERING*, VOL. 30, NO. 6, JUNE 2004. Fair Use applies.

It's an overstatement to say this set the testing world on fire, but it is fair to say this was kind of a big deal. The challenge of the day was creating test labs that had combinations of operating systems, browsers, browser versions, JavaScript enabled (or not), and so on. Mobile phones and tablets made this problem much worse. By testing pairwise, or all-pairs, it was possible to radically reduce the number of combinations. Mathematicians had done their part, developing tables to identify the pairs in a given set of interactions, called *Orthogonal arrays*. These were based on algorithms that could be put into code. In 2006, James Bach released a free and open all-pairs generator under the Gnu public license.

In 2009, a friend of ours, Justin Hunter, founded a company to make all-pairs generation available to everyone, easily, online, through a web browser. More than just all-pairs, Justin was interested in going the other way, to create additional coverage beyond all-pairs, to all-triples, all-quadruples, and up to six-way combinations. He called his company **Hexawise (The company is now a division of Idera).** It took less than 10 minutes for us to model the insurance problem in Hexawise; here is a partial screen capture of the table it generates:

Age (in Years((8)	0-15	16-20	21-30	31-40	41-50	51-70
Deductible type (3)	Comprehensive /w No Deductible	Comprehensive /w Deductible	Minimal Coverage			
Vehicle Value (7)	Less than $2,000	$2,000 to $10,000	$10,001 to $50,000	$50,000 to $70,000	$70,001 to $90,000	$90,001 to $200,000
Accident Record (5)	None in 2 years	1 in 2 years	2 in 2 years	3 in 2 years	4 or more in 2 years	
Traffic Ticket Compos...	0	1 to 3	4 to 7	8 or higher		

Figure 1.12 – Hexawise example of testing variations

Here's a sample of the output:

Search...	**57 scenarios and 283**	2-way interactions	⌄ ⓘ	

#	Age (in Years)	Deductible type	Vehicle Value	Accident Record	Traffic Ticket C...7 years)
1	15	Comprehensive /w No Deductible	Less than $2,000	None in 2 years	0
2	20	Comprehensive /w Deductible	Less than $2,000	1 in 2 years	1 to 3
3	30	Minimal Coverage	Less than $2,000	2 in 2 years	4 to 7
4	36	Comprehensive /w No Deductible	Less than $2,000	3 in 2 years	8 or higher
5	1	Comprehensive /w No Deductible	$2,000 to $10,000	1 in 2 years	4 to 7
6	0	Comprehensive /w No Deductible	$10,001 to $50,000	2 in 2 years	1 to 3
7	15	Minimal Coverage	$50,000 to $70,000	3 in 2 years	0
8	1	Minimal Coverage	$70,001 to $90,000	4 or more in 2 years	8 or higher
9	50	Comprehensive /w Deductible	Less than $2,000	4 or more in 2 years	0
10	19	Comprehensive /w Deductible	$10,001 to $50,000	3 in 2 years	4 to 7
11	16	Comprehensive /w No Deductible	$50,000 to $70,000	2 in 2 years	8 or higher
12	21	Comprehensive /w Deductible	$2,000 to $10,000	3 in 2 years	1 to 3
13	51-70	Minimal Coverage	Less than $2,000	None in 2 years	1 to 3
14	70-99	Comprehensive /w Deductible	Less than $2,000	None in 2 years	4 to 7

Figure 1.13 – Sample output from the Hexawise configuration

The thing that was most interesting to us was the slider, which allows you to select less than 57 all-pairs and visualize the amount of coverage. With this option, you can see the red elements and decide if they matter or whether you should change the ratings:

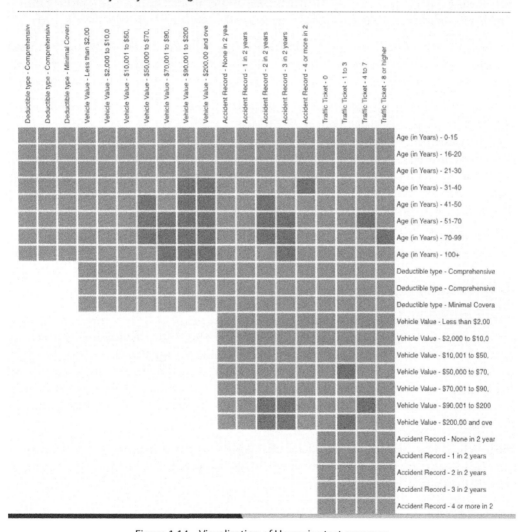

88.69% after first 40 test cases   251 of the 283 possible 2-way interactions ⊙

- Use your mouse / touchpad scrolling to zoom, click and drag to pan when zoomed
- Use the left & right arrow keys to step through coverage
- Press the 'c' key to cycle through available color schemes

Figure 1.14 – Visualization of Hexawise test coverage

Like any of the test ideas in this book, when you see a new technique, it's easy to get enamored with it and overly focus on it. This is something we call *test myopia*. While we have both run into testing projects where all-pairs was incredibly valuable, such as financial services and social media, after 15 years of having the tools at our disposal, we find *Pairwise* testing only useful some of the time. That is sort of the lesson of this book – we are climbing up *Bloom's Taxonomy* – that is, this book creates knowledge (what the techniques are), comprehension (restate them in other words), and application (actually use them) before moving to analyze, synthesize, and finally evaluate – picking the best combination of test ideas to use in limited time and under conditions of uncertainty.

Pairwise testing has a place, but it isn't a universal one and doesn't tell us when to automate versus human test, where to stop on the "slider", how to integrate the work with the developers, how to handle re-testing when a new feature might change existing functionality… there is a lot more to examine.

In the fourth edition of *Software Testing: A Craftsman's Approach*, Matt's old professor Dr. Paul C. Jorgensen discusses static applications (where you enter a value, a transaction runs, and an answer pops out) versus dynamic applications. In a dynamic application, such as a website, you might make a post, scroll down, make a comment, upload an image, and so on. Dr. Jorgesen concludes that all-pairs is more helpful for the former scenario. As the behavior of browsers and operating systems have standardized, cross-compiling tools have evolved, and responsive design frameworks have emerged. We also see less use of all-pairs on the test environment side.

Let's talk about another approach to solving the combinatorics problem – that is, using high volume – along with some less popular test techniques.

High volume automated approaches

One company had a legacy system with all kinds of tweaks and problems. Users were handled differently according to rules long forgotten. Data setup could either be by creating flat text files and importing them into a database, or *tweaking* the database so known users looked like valid test scenarios. The system did work in batch; it would run and "pick up" new users and put them into a second data set. This kind of work is called **extract, transform, load** (**ETL**). Testing took weeks, which encouraged the organization to make many changes and test rarely. As a result, releases were infrequent, slow, and buggy.

The tech lead, Ross Beehler, had a brilliant idea. What if we had two databases where, using the previous version of the software and the current change, we ran huge files in them and compared the output? Here's how it worked:

1. Create Empty Identical Databases

2. Populate DB's with static test data

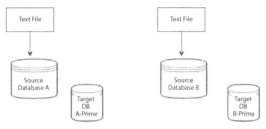

3. Run ETL process, populate downstream DB

4. Out text files to SQL Dump Utility

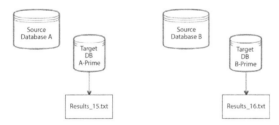

5. Compare and look up differences

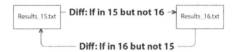

Figure 1.15 – A/B flow example from two databases

Let's elaborate a bit:

1. First, we set up two identical source databases that are empty (**A** and **B**), along with two downstream databases that are empty (**a** and **b**).

2.   Next, we get a huge text file that can be used to populate the database. Our database system had export/import capabilities, so we could export from production, clean it up, and import the data in a few lines of code. That text file could contain live customer data for unregulated environments, or anonymized data if regulated. It is possible to use truly random data, but that will not have the same impact as live data. In our case, we would test a month of realistic customer data, or tens of thousands of tests, in about 3 hours.

3.   Run the ETL. This will iterate over the data in the database (**A** and **B**) and send the results to databases **a** and **b**. Note that **B** will use the second "new, changed" version of the ETL. At the end of this process, we'll have a version of database **a** as it would exist from today's program running live, and a version of database **b** as we are expecting to test it.

We would use the database utility to export databases **a** and **b** as text files and use a simple `diff` function to compare text files.

The differences between the two were interesting. We would expect to see the planned differences and no unplanned differences.

For example, early on in the process, we had a change where diagnostic code should change; we were now supporting French users, so instead of going from French to Category 999 (unsupportable), it would go to *French, 6*. Running for tens of thousands of users, there were now a handful of 6s. Tying those back to `UserID` and searching the database, all of the 6s had a country language of FR, and none of them had a country code other than FR, and that was the only change.

Of course, some very odd combination of data could trip some other change. By using a great deal of realistic customer-like data, we were able to say with some confidence that if such an error existed, we could not have tripped it in the past month of data over so many thousands of users. If management wanted more data, we could go further back, pulling older records and simulating them. This made the tradeoff of risk and effort explicit, providing management with a dial to adjust.

We find having live data in test for this type of work to be compelling. With very little work, a company can scramble birthdates, names, and important identifying codes. Due to regulations, some companies protect the data, and de-identifying data can be expensive – we'll talk about regulated testing in *Chapter 5*. For now, if using live data is impossible, it's usually possible to simulate with randomization. When the system is an event-based, dynamic system, and we generate random steps, we sometimes call this *model-based testing*.

Other approaches

A variety of testing methodologies can be used to help get a handle on the testing problem and approach it from a variety of angles:

- **Model-driven testing**: Assuming you have a dynamic system, such as the editable web pages in a wiki, with some options (new, edit, save, comment, tag a page), you could draw circles and arrows between states, then use a tool to automate the program running, recording every step. Let it run overnight, then export the result and compare it to what you expect to see.

- **Soak testing**: Let a system sit in a corner and run for an extended period. A tool might drive the user interface to do the same thing, over and over, to see if the 10,000th time is different than the first. You can also do this with multiple users or randomization. Once a problem does occur, though, it can be difficult to figure out the root cause.

- **Data flow diagrams and control flow**: This is similar to model-driven testing without randomization. The idea is to make sure we cover all the possible transitions. One easy example of this is applications where we enter information and then come back and have to re-enter it; the programmer likely did not consider that state transition.

- **Soap opera testing**: These are a few incredibly powerful and rare scenarios. When Matt was at the insurance company, for example, he would test a claim turned in 21 days after the event happened, where the event happened the day before the end of the plan year, the family became ineligible for service, the child turned 27 and ineligible for insurance the next day, and the bill pushed the family two dollars over their deductible for the year. He also tested "just barely rejected" scenarios and looked for the reason why. Hans Buwalda calls this *soap opera testing*.

- **Use/abuse case testing**: Use cases are a way of writing down requirements; they are how the customers will use the software. Abuse cases go the other way; they assume the customer will misuse the software and plan on what the software will do in that situation.

- **Exploratory approaches**: If you've noticed, this chapter has "bounced around" quite a bit. We introduced ideas, explored them, offered to come back to them, and provided you with more information in the notes. You might be frustrated by this approach. Still, we find the best results are exploratory. A few years ago, we would do training on this, splitting the class into three groups. The first group was given a requirements document and told to design tests. The second group was given the requirements document and a tour of the user interface, while the third group was freed from the need for a requirements document or a previous tour and could design their approach as they went. Invariably, the third group, which combined test design, execution, reporting, and learning, who had new test ideas developed out of their work, both found more bugs that were more important, but also reported higher satisfaction in the work. Even with documents telling you what to test, humans that find something odd go "off script," and, once the bug is found, return to a different place. Thus, we'd argue that all good testing has an exploratory component, and the techniques listed here can inform and improve test approaches.

We'll discuss other kinds of testing not directly related to functionality, such as security and load/performance, in *Chapter 5*.

Data and predictability – the oracle problem

Once you've randomly created a wiki page with a bunch of comments and tags, how do you know what the correct page *should* look like? In practice, you dump the text to something called **wikimarkup** and, as the test runs, generate what the wikimarkup *should* be. Another term for that is an oracle, which Dr. Cem Kaner describes (`https://kaner.com/?p=190`) as a tool that helps you decide whether the program passed your test:

Calculator

Monthly payment   Purchase budget

Include taxes & fees   Monthly payment

Loan amount $ 1,717

$ 240,000

Loan term   Interest

30-yr fixed   7.736 %

Disclaimer · Feedback

Figure 1.16 – Example insurance app

Google's mortgage calculator, for example, takes four inputs: **Loan amount**, **Loan term**, **Interest**, and **Include taxes & fees**, and spits out the monthly payment. It might be possible to loop through thousands of inputs and get the answers. To know they are correct, you might have someone else code up a second version of the system. Comparing the answers doesn't prove correctness (nothing can), but it might at least demonstrate that if a mistake were made, it was reasonable to make such a mistake.

When we've made such automated oracles, we generally try to have them separated as much as possible. Have a second person write the oracle, someone with a different background, using a different programming language. This prevents the "made the same round-off error" sorts of mistakes. In our experience, when oracles make the same mistake as the software, there are often interpretation errors in the requirements, or elements left blank by the requirements. Truly random data will tend to help find the hidden equivalence classes in the data.

Oracles can come from anywhere. Your knowledge, dictionary spellings, the knowledge that the (**E)dit** menu should be to the right of **(F)ile**, prior experience, the specification… all of these can be oracles. Oracles can also be incorrect. Candidates who run the palindrome problem and are well-educated often cite palindrome sentences, such as, "*Was it a car or a cat I saw?*" and expect the spaces and punctuation to be ignored. Their oracle spots a problem, but the customer wants to just reverse the text and compare, so the sentence "should" fail.

These ideas of a fallible method to solve a problem are sometimes called **heuristic**. Heuristics, or, as we joke, "Heusseristics" are integral to testing because we combine a large variety of techniques and timing aspects to figure out if the software is correct.

The final problem this chapter will introduce is test data. The act of running the test generally pollutes the database the test runs over. In many cases, running the test a second time will create a new and different result. Clearing out the database *before* each run is tempting; it is the approach we usually take for programmer's units or micro-tests. Yet there are often problems that only occur as data builds over time. To save time, some companies like to run more than one test at the same time, or more than one tester, and these tests can *step* on each other. That means separating the data used in testing, tracking it, and coming up with a strategy to optimize between simple/repeating and powerful/longer-running can make or break a test effort. We'll come back to test data in *Chapter 7*.

Summary

In this chapter, we explained how complete testing is impossible, then showed a handful of ways to come up with a few powerful tests. We discussed a few ways of looking at testing but haven't looked at user interfaces in depth. Once you find your domain, you'll want to dive deep into it. There is a great deal more to testing than we could cover in this chapter, which just gives a feel for the depth of the work, plus some approaches worth considering.

While we touched on the idea of user interfaces, it is Michael Hunter and his 32-page treatise testing Windows applications, *You Are Not Done Yet*, that hits on how to test Windows applications. As he was at Microsoft working on systems that would be used by hundreds of millions of people with a higher cost to ship updates, we found reproducing his work here beyond our scope.

In the next chapter, we will discuss how to use tools to help us.

Further reading

To learn more about the topics that were covered in this chapter, take a look at the following resources:

1. *Pairwise Testing: A Best Practice That Isn't*, by James Bach.
2. *Software Testing: A Craftsman's Approach*. 4th Edition, CRC Publications: `https://www.oreilly.com/library/view/software-testing-4th/9781466560680/`.
3. *Use Soap Opera Testing to Twist Real-Life Stories into Test Ideas*, by Hans Buwalda: `https://www.agileconnection.com/sites/default/files/presentation/file/2018/W11_14.pdf`.
4. *The Oracle Problem and the Teaching of Software Testing*, Cem Kaner: `https://kaner.com/?p=190`.
5. A PDF version of *You Are Not Done Yet* is available at `https://www.thebraidytester.com/downloads/YouAreNotDoneYet.pdf`).

6. You can download the *Allpairs generator* from `https://www.satisfice.com/download/allpairs`. There is a command line (MS-DOS-like) version that is a `.exe` file and also a script written in Perl that runs on most Unix machines, including Mac.

7. James also teamed up with Danny Faught on PerlClip, which generates structured test data: `https://www.agileconnection.com/sites/default/files/magazine/file/2012/XDD9687filelistfilename1_0.pdf`.

2
Fundamental Issues in Tooling and Automation

One common theme in our consulting is the team that has never done *test automation* before yet is certain they have it figured out. We've also hosted hundreds of podcast interviews, and during that time have come to believe that test automation is often a faith-based concept. In 1 year, or 2 or 5, the consultant comes back and the group we advised has learned some of the same lessons recommended on that first on-site visit but could not do. Or, in some cases, they've failed.

As it turns out, there are foundational ideas in test tooling that usually can only be learned by experience. Without some resources to accelerate the learning process, your organization is likely to make the same mistakes, possibly over and over again. In the worst case, you could be like that customer, building something on a rickety foundation, only to have it fall back into the sand.

So, we suggest you don't do that. Instead, learn from our experience!

This chapter is structured as a series of lessons we have learned over years of experience. We will be discussing the following topics:

- The idea of no silver bullets – that no single idea will radically compress the test/fix cycle.

- The minefield regression problem, which recognizes that traditional test execution automation only has value on the second and subsequent runs, and that value is remarkably limited

- The battleship problem, which points out the limits of automation that cannot change strategy when defects are found

- The cost of test maintenance and the problem straddling the line between only looking for select changes (and missing others) versus signaling errors on every change

Finally, we'll introduce some solutions to these challenges.

Technical requirements

This chapter mostly contains concepts; that are designed in a way that anyone with a high school education, knowledge of the internet, and the ability to think abstractly can understand them. This chapter will proceed through metaphor, drawing inspiration from grid coordinates and games. The ability to print out worksheets, and work them with a friend with pencil and paper, may be helpful. We'll use the game *Battleships* as an example. You can find a Battleships PDF at `http://www.mathematicshed.com/uploads/1/2/5/7/12572836/battleships.pdf`, do a Google search for *Battleship game filetype pdf*, or photocopy the one in this book at the end of this section.

No silver bullets – you can't radically fix the test cycle

The earliest mass-market book about software engineering to still be in print is probably *The Mythical Man-Month*, by Fred Brooks. Published in 1975, although the book's language and tone may seem a little archaic, it contains three ideas that are still relevant today. The first is the idea that adding staff to a late project will make it later. As projects grow, the number of potential communication paths between people grows exponentially, shifting the cost from effort to communication and coordination. We'll cover how to keep those costs light and cheap in the next section. Secondly, Brooks suggested the idea of the *second system effect*, which is the idea that we don't know what will be good for the customer until we've made a first, unsuccessful attempt at it. **Rapid prototyping** and other measures fell out of this. As Brooks put it, "Plan to throw one away – you will anyway." The meat for this chapter, though, comes from an essay he snuck in the second edition of the book (1995) called *No Silver Bullets*.

In his essay, Dr. Brooks suggested that software development consists of distinct phases, such as planning, requirements, design, coding, testing, and operations. Each of these might be a sixth of the software effort. Thus, if you could make programming free and easy, eliminating it with some sort of magical artificial intelligence, the best you could ever do is reduce cost and time to market by a sixth or about 16%. Given that we were not going to make anything free, and the best we could do with some magic wiz-bang tech might be a 75% reduction in one of the activities, then the net overall impact is even smaller. Instead of a single silver bullet to slay the werewolf of runaway software development, Brooks suggested a handful of bronze bullets – many attempts to reduce the effort that might have an accretionary effect. This book represents our attempt to craft one of those bullets.

Let's talk about test automation, the idea that we have often seen described is a big button that you can press to get results very quickly.

Imagine for a minute that you had such a button. You finish your blob of code, test it, and boom – you get results.

The way most teams do automation, those results need to be investigated. Some of them will be false failures. Matt and Michael both believe in a traditional religion with a heavenly Father. We do keep our faith where it belongs – in the church house. Everyone else needs to bring data, or, failing that, logic. Linear, straightforward, *do things and inspect* automation is, after all, more change detection than testing – and it is the job of the programmers to create change! So, the test run will have *failures* or *errors* that turn out to mean the software is now doing what the programmer expected it to do.

The test run will also have some actual failures that need to be investigated. The tool-assisted case might be more complex than the simple case, which might appear to *work* on inspection. Finally, someone finds a reproducible case. Now that it is documented, the team might need to have a meeting to discuss if the bug should be fixed. Then, we wait. Then, a programmer fixes the code. Then, we get a new build and run the automation again. Hopefully, it passes this time.

All this assumes that automation is free (it isn't) and runs in no time at all (it doesn't).

In most of the organizations we have worked with, most of the time, a completely free and infinitely fastest tool process would reduce test effort by less than 50%. Not only that, but the automation effort is not free or instantaneous. More than once on a tens-of-millions-of-dollars-a-year test effort, developing a human testing program was able to get meaningful feedback to developers, so they could start working on fixes, faster than the tooling effort – that is, humans, exploring the software in the places it had most recently changed were able to file actionable bugs, while someone else was waiting for a test tooling effort to finish.

Bear in mind that Matt's first big break was speaking at Google's Test Automation Conference and Michael's title has been *automation specialist* for longer than it was tester, quality analyst, quality engineer, or anything else. This isn't an anti-automation book. The continuous delivery sections simply could not happen without significant tool-assisted tests, and Matt has been championing modern unit tests for 20 of the 27 years they have existed. What we are saying here is that the solution needs to include the whole process. For now, let's say that we don't know a generalized key to success – but an approach that often leads to failure is a sort of naive, *automate all the things* religious approach.

If you follow that religious approach, if you type in *software test automation, how do I do it* into a search engine, you are bound to go down a certain road, and, if you are paying attention, can learn some things. Like the rest of this book, our goal is to accelerate your learning and help you learn the lessons we have learned without spending many years fighting shadows in the dark that we have. The rest of this chapter is designed to disabuse you of the religious approach notion and provide some healthier alternatives.

Let's talk about how to model test effort based on a minefield metaphor.

The minefield regression problem

Again, we are talking about a certain type of test automation, something we call *click-click-click, inspect* testing. In this vision, we take the user journey and have a computer go through it, looking for problems along the way. Unit and programmer tests can do this too. The important thing is that the test doesn't have much randomization in it. Model-driven tests and other approaches have these problems to a much smaller extent, but there is a reason those approaches don't ever seem to take off or survive.

For now, someone is writing what they call a test. The implementation doesn't matter. Let's say it is an eCommerce application, so we have a half dozen "tests" that exercise the application, creating a profile, searching, finding a product, adding it to the cart, and going through the motions of checkout.

Note something about that search test – it doesn't add any value as it is created. Most of the time, for most of our customers, something will cause the search to get stuck and have some back and forth with the programmers. Perhaps there will be a bug where the location of the submit button is not predictable or there's an actual bug in the search engine. Perhaps the search results are not predictable, or the data itself is changing. Once all those elements are changed, after all the back and forth to get it working has happened, the test *works* – that is, it offers no investigatory value. The only value of the tooling is after a programmer has made a change, during something we call *regression testing*. The purpose of regression testing is to see if a feature fell back or regressed. A great example of regression testing is "click element A on-screen number 1 to get to screen number 2; screen number 2 contains element B, which you click to reach screen number 3." At some point, while screen 3 was under development, element A just disappeared. It became impossible to get to screen 2 or 3. Where screen 2 was fit for purpose before, it was now impossible to reach.

In code bases that grow organically, as a sort of *ball of mud* (check the note), these sorts of "programmers step on each other and break things they did not expect" problems are incredibly common. In code bases where multiple programmers are in the same area of the code, this is almost guaranteed.

> **Ball of mud**
>
> Brian Foote and Joseph Yoder wrote the *Big Ball of Mud* paper in the late 1990s. It's amazing, still on the web, and free. Go read it: `http://www.laputan.org/mud/`.

Modern engineering practices, which we will touch on in *Chapter 3*, will reduce the frequency of these regressions. In the meantime, let's explore the value of test automation for just regression.

Coverage model

Bear in mind that complete testing is impossible, so it is not possible to create a comprehensive *map* of the input space and combinations of transformations. As the saying goes, the map is not the territory. That is what a *model* is – an attempt to approximate or reflect what is going on in a useful way. *Models make a trade, losing comprehensiveness for comprehensibility.* As George Box put it, all models are wrong; some are useful.

In our example, we'll model the possible input space as a two-dimensional grid. You could think of it as a minefield – that is, the things you can do in the software; the mines are bugs. Another way to look at it is as a large park, filled with doggie-do. Over time, as more owners walk dogs, invariably, some forget bags and the do-do starts to build up.

In this analogy, software testing is the process of exploring the problematic software and finding and removing the poop.

Exploring the minefield as a dog park

Again, the dog park is dirty and needs to be cleaned up. To do that, we take a walk through the park with a scooper. If the dog park were software to be tested, the *dog doo-doo* would be bugs, and the area you are walking through would be the possible inputs of the software. And, of course, you would be blindfolded, only able to see what your tools can show you immediately in front of you. Here's how Doug Hoffman, of Software Quality Methods, visualized it when he presented the idea:

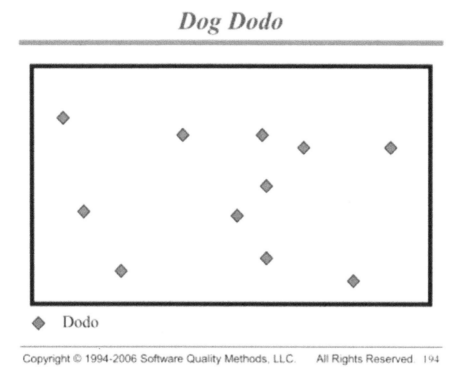

Figure 2.1 – Locations of "dog dodo" (credit: D. Hoffman)

Bear in mind that software testing in the 1980s and 1990s was heavily influenced by manufacturing, to be stable, predictable, and repeatable. People talked about creating *test cases*, held together in a *test case library*. When it came to automation, people took that library and turned it into a *test suite* that could run again and again.

In our analogy, the test suite is essentially taking a pre-planned walk through the park. By definition, because of the impossibility problem, it only covers a relatively small section of ground. The first run might look something like this:

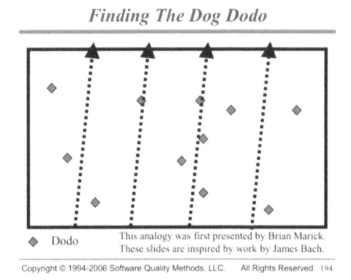

Figure 2.2 – Walking through the dog park and examining/covering the ground

Notice that we picked up a few pieces; that's good. The most common kind of test automation, as argued over and over again, will do the same thing, over and over. It is repeatable. This is touted as a good thing. However, remember that, unlike human exploration, the test script can't run on its own until the bugs have been removed. In the case of record/playback style testing, we often can't even create the test until the code works correctly. If **Add to cart** generates an error, then testing has to stop until the bug is cleared – the only value in that style of test automation is in regression.

After the test code runs, we make some changes and re-run the tooling:

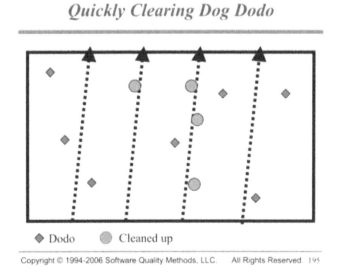

Figure 2.3 – Areas of the dog park that have been cleaned up

But we've already cleared up the four bugs on these tracks! There are no new bugs there. The only value regression testing has is when new bugs appear on the tracks that we previously covered. If you've got the data, go into your bug tracker and see how many of your bugs are regression bugs. If you don't, just track it for a couple of weeks. Numbers vary by organization, but, as it turns out, this number is certainly a fraction of the overall picture.

This leads to *Heusser's Maxim* of (traditional, pre-defined) test automation: the majority of defects found by *100% test automation* organizations are not found by tooling running regression, but instead by humans performing other activities.

Those other activities include things such as "trying to create test tooling but being blocked by bugs."

Put differently, if your team is pursuing 100% test automation, then you can either find the majority of the bugs poorly, manually, or accidentally, or you can stop being silly and study testing.

Lisa Crispin once pointed out the most charitable interpretation of the phrase "100% test automation." She defines that as pursuing a strategy where if you have steps to be followed automatically, the same every time, then at least get the computer to do that, leaving humans to explore and research things that might only need to run once, or at least slightly differently every time. *Exploratory testing* is one term for this work. And, to be fair, we have used similar language – that is, to consider what small subset of the tests to institutionalize and run on every build and then automate that.

At this point, we hope you have a healthy skepticism toward repeating the same tests over and over. Let's continue this conversation about what to automate every time we use another model of the input space. This time, we'll use the children's game of Battleships.

The Battleships problem – testing versus checking

Battleships is a grid-coordinate game, so, just like Dog Park, we will *pretend* we can flatten the input space into two dimensions – Y (up/down) and X (left/right). If it helps, you could think of the X-axis as activities, such as search, product information display, shopping cart, create/edit account, and the Y-axis as the input space within that account. If it doesn't, well, it's a model – it isn't perfect. In the childhood game, the X-axis is represented by numbers (1 to 10) and the Y-axis is represented by letters (A to J). Thus, if you "bomb" the upper left-hand corner, you would select (1,A):

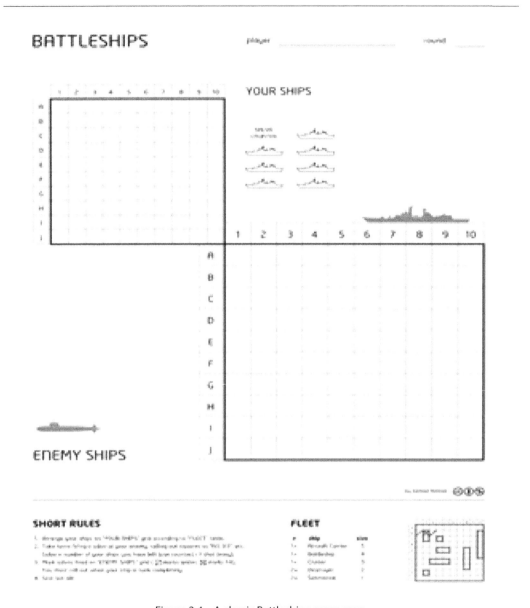

Figure 2.4 – A classic Battleships game map.

This image is only for representation purposes. You can find the actual PDF at the link provided below.

This image was taken from *Wikipedia* under the Creative Commons license. At the time of writing, you can find a Battleships PDF at http://www.mathematicshed.com/uploads/1/2/5/7/12572836/battleships.pdf or do a Google search for *Battleship game filetype pdf.*

The game itself is close to 100 years old and predates copyright law. In this section, we'll describe an exercise and our experience with it, and even include a sample sheet you can copy and reuse yourself. In this game, both players start by "seeding" the board with the following parts:

- One aircraft carrier (5 squares)
- One battleship (4 squares)
- One cruiser (3 squares)
- Two destroyers (2 squares)
- Two submarines (2 squares)

Players can place these ships vertically or horizontally but not diagonally.

Comparing Battleships to bugs

Back in the real world, the ships are bugs and represent the idea that bugs tend to *clump together* in modules. While we do not have data, this does match our lived experience.

So far, the game is played identically; players fill out the smaller sheet with where their bugs are hidden. In the children's game, the players go one after another, taking turns, declaring "miss" or "hit" back and forth. When using this to teach software testing, I add one more additional step: half the players need to plan their moves.

This is, after all, what traditional test automation does. The team defines a set of steps for the software to run through, either before the code is created as some kind of executable specification, or after the code is created as part of a test process. Human *scripted* testing, with test cases, steps, and expected results, does the same thing.

So, one team has to behave similarly to test automation, writing down their steps, while the other side has no plan.

This is when things get interesting. Highly agreeable groups will at least try the game to see what will happen. Those who like planning, especially those with experience with follow-the-steps testing, will gladly play along, coming up with strategies that create a big X, a star pattern, or a diagonal step. However, those with a disagreeable temperament and higher intelligence, especially those less familiar with "planned" testing often convey modest disgust. Being locked into a strategy means they cannot adjust in the case of a hit, pivoting around to figure out where the ship is and sink it.

Put more clearly, teams that are not constrained by a defined plan of action will inevitably beat the teams that are. After running this simulation with hundreds of two-person teams, I can only think of a few times when the scripted team won the game, sinking the other ships first. In at least half of these cases, the *exploratory* person was from a different culture, was not familiar with the basic game, and did not "wake up" to the idea that they needed to change plans when they got a hit.

The comparisons to testing jump off the page. First, we have cultural differences. Like the palindrome problem, those who are not awake and "on" could have testing in their job description, but miss a great deal of what good testing is. Second, we have the idea of coverage, which we will come back to in *Chapter 9*. Most importantly, the lesson for today is that computers cannot adjust their testing; instead, they tend to only check for the things we ask them to check for. We'll push back against that in the *The maintenance problem* section.

Automation rarely beats human intuition

We also get pushback in the simulation. People want to add **artificial intelligence** (**AI**) to their code; they want to make it smart enough that it adjusts when it finds a defect. And, if they do that on their teams, or even know of a team that has test software advanced enough to do that, then I allow them to build that into their tools. That is not quite model-driven testing, which would more likely check all the boxes. In the time this exercise has been run, no one has told a credible story where their test tooling actually can adjust and react as a human does when they find a bug or "hit" a ship in the game.

To recap, human exploration is fundamentally different from computer *test automation* because humans can plan the next test based on the results of the previous test. In 2009 at the Agile Conference, Michael Bolton gave a lightning talk where he tried to make a distinction between "what a human can do" (investigating a product with the intent to discover) and "what a computer can do" (checking pre-defined scenarios). He picked two English words to make his distinction, calling them "testing versus checking."

According to Michael Bolton, "*Testing is the process of evaluating a product by learning about it through experiencing, exploring, and experimenting, which includes to some degree: questioning, study, modeling, observation, inference, and so on.*" (Michael Bolton, *Testing and Checking Refined*, `https://www.satisfice.com/blog/archives/856`.)

His definition of testing is compatible with Dr Kaner's, which we will use in this book. Bolton defines checking as "*...the process of making an evaluation by applying algorithmic decision rules to specific observations of the product.*" (Michael Bolton, *Testing and Checking Refined*, `https://www.satisfice.com/blog/archives/856`.)

Using that language, checking is a part of testing – it is a thing that happens as we test, and it offers some value in reducing risks. It is possible to have a computer perform unassisted checking in a corner by itself – but that will have limited utility in managing risks. The focus of this book is helping people conceptualize their risks and how testing can reduce them; checking can be part of a complete breakfast. A naive misunderstanding of the dynamics – of how humans uncover problems versus what computers can do – is the source of many issues in software delivery.

So, grab a friend, make a copy, or download one (as per the instructions in the *Technical requirements* section), and go play Battleships. Consider if the tooling you are writing, or want to write, can adapt to find corner-case defects. Then, read on.

The maintenance problem

So far, we've pointed out that repeatable/repeating *tests* create less coverage than changing the approach for each build. We did this through a metaphor and didn't spend a great deal of time on how to adjust the testing to increase coverage over time. Computer-driven tests are the ultimate example of this. Humans following documented steps run this risk of missing ideas to explore, of asking *what if…?*. With computers, it's guaranteed because of the fulfillable promise of repeating tests.

So, we created a simulation that repeated tests and, surprise surprise, it's worse at finding bugs.

There are a couple of additional challenges that do not appear in the simulations.

First, there is what the test is trying to do. Consider a test like this, which Matt created in **Selenium IDE**, an open source tool that records and plays back tests. All the *test* does is go to Excelon Development's main page, then click on **Consulting**, then **Contact Us**, and fill in the **Contact Us** form:

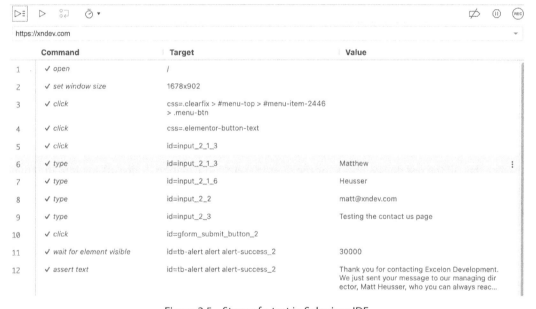

Figure 2.5 – Steps of a test in Selenium IDE

Here's the final page it is checking:

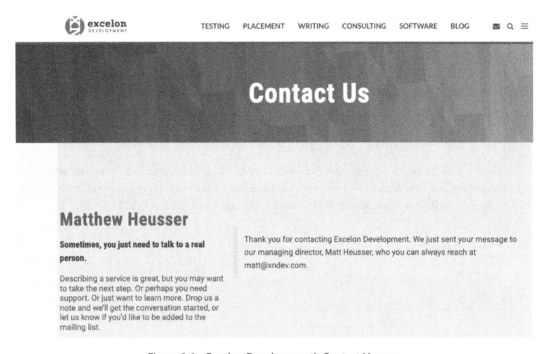

Figure 2.6 – Excelon Development's Contact Us page

Notice that all the test does is check for the message sent confirmation. It doesn't log into the email service and see if the message ever got there (one kind of common test tooling error). More importantly, it doesn't check for anything else. It doesn't check font size, that the submit button is triggered by the *enter* key, the message on the left, font type, or anything else.

As we've said before, at the end of every test case is the hidden assertion *"…and nothing else went wrong"."* The test we modeled earlier is not capable of checking that assertion. In Michael Bolton's language, the check might be helpful, but it isn't really testing, but just "applying algorithmic decision rules to a specific observation of the product."

In our words, there are all kinds of bugs that this kind of tooling will miss.

There are ways around this. One approach is to take screenshots of everything and compare them. The problem with this is that when anything changes, the test will *fail*, and the user will need to see the failing test and take a new screenshot. In extreme cases, everything will fail and need to be re-recorded. Here are two screenshots from Yahoo! Finance for the stock symbol **Apple** (**APPL**) that were taken on November 2 and November 14, 2022 – less than 2 weeks apart. In Scrum terms, this change happens within one sprint:

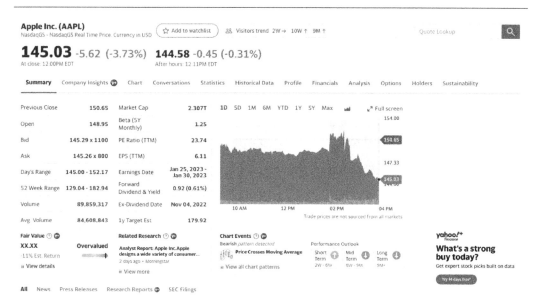

Figure 2.7 – AAPL stock price. Archived image retrieved November 2, 2022, finance.yahoo.com via web.archive.org

Notice that the preceding screenshot contains 16 metrics, including **Market Cap**, **P/E Ratio**, and **Volume** all on the left-hand side, while the following screenshot shows only eight – and they have moved:

Figure 2.8 – AAPL stock price. Archived image retrieved November 14, 2022, via live site finance.yahoo.com

Figure 2.8 shows **Earnings** in bold as a link to the right of **Chart**; these options used to appear in the bottom right on the main page.

Putting aside the problem of checking the graphs, this leads us to three maxims defined by Matt but published for the first time right here:

- **The maxim of documented testing**: At the end of every human-run, pre-designed, documented test is a hidden expected result – *and nothing else odd happened*:

    - **The first corollary**: That assumption is particularly difficult to automate.

    - **The second corollary**: And if you try, without AI, you'll get a whole lot of false errors. (We use Danny Faught's suggestion of "false errors" instead of terms instead of false positive/false negative as we find that the latter terms lead to some confusion.)

- **The maxim of test automation**: Even if a test could be automated, the second time it runs, it fails to be test automation and becomes change detection:

    - **The exception**: High volume empirical, data-based tests, or simulate them by injecting *randomization*. You'll need some automated *oracle* to know what the right answer is. One such oracle is the previous version of the software.

- **The automation decision dilemma**: When it comes to a computer running unattended and producing results, the tool can likely check everything for errors (and it becomes change detection) or it can check specific things (in which case it ignores everything else). Finding a middle path requires a future knowledge of what might change that would be wrong, divined as different from what might change that would be right. As it turns out, it is very difficult to get a computer to have this pre-calculated or *a priori* knowledge.

The intersection of these rules creates particular problems for software maintenance.

This section was introduced as the "maintenance problem" for good reason. A simplified test approach is going to miss a great deal of defects. Like… a lot. Even a simplified *smoke* test for the Yahoo! Finance page we just looked at is likely to fail miserably when the site is redesigned. If you go to the *wayback machine* and compare them, the site wasn't even re-designed. Instead, the data was put in different places. The programmers likely have each container that holds data expose itself as an **application programming interface** (**API**) that generates a web page, then have a sort of master web page that plugs those APIs in like Lego bricks. This is a wonderful, post-modern development strategy that can make changes fast.

The problem is that the test maintenance can't keep up.

Think about this for a moment. Most people perform test automation because the human test burden cannot keep up with the changes, yet any test automation effort would cause all deliveries to stop while the tests are re-recorded and turned green. In the best scenario, this is a coordinated effort with multiple disciplines, done iteratively, with a net impact of only slowing delivery down by 10% or so. In the worst of worlds, the test tools that all fail are thrown away. Instead of running them, humans do a mad, slap-dash job and the code goes out. 6 weeks or 6 months later, some consultant is called in to help with a new automation initiative. The consultant asks about the "old tests" from the last time they were there, and no one remembers.

If you've read this far, you know this statement is not academic – it has happened.

The dangers of comprehensive tests

More comprehensive tests are worse because they break more often and cause continuous delays. The more time that passes between the code being checked in and automation being run, the more changes that are introduced between runs, and the more the code will break. This causes a problem we call *automation delay*. This is the delay that's caused by test automation that fails and needs to be checked, corrected, and re-run.

When people pay to introduce test tooling, the last thing they are expecting to hear is *"For the tests ran, we need about a half day to debug them, fix them, and re-run them, and then we can tell you where the software is at."* In some organizations, it is much more than a half day.

Plus, the test will miss some errors. Here's a real screenshot from a real customer from a few years ago, where, in offline mode, the tool printed the "offline retry in X seconds" message, where X would keep doubling for a bit – but the programmer made a typo, so the digital formatted number instead appeared at "%ss." What's most interesting here is that this only appeared in the menu on mobile devices. If a programmer were to make the effort to automate this check, they would likely code the check to make sure the correct message appeared somewhere on the screen. That way, if the message moves, there is no false error. Sadly, the correct message *does* appear somewhere on the screen. It is unlikely that most straightforward tooling approaches would find this error:

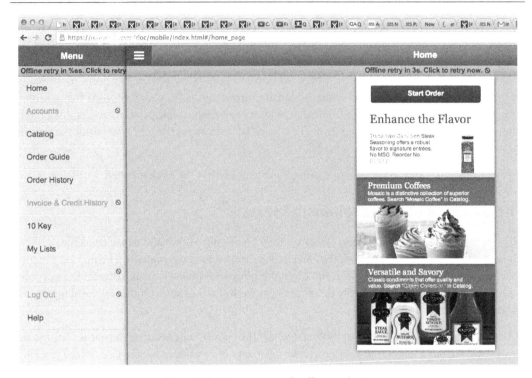

Figure 2.9 – Home page of coffee products.
The intent of this screenshot is to show the maximized layout; text readability is not required.

To be fair, there are solutions on the market that at least moderate these problems, which we'll mention when we talk about rules for automated checks.

Speaking of solutions, let's talk about money.

The money problem

Imagine for a moment that you are leading a software organization that does not have any of this fancy-schmaltzy test tooling. The human test process is too slow; it is taking too long. Anytime you want to perform some testing, it takes you 2 weeks to sweat out a release. As a result, you've slowed down the release cadence, which means once it is time to get to regression testing, the code is in really bad shape.

Perhaps your organization isn't like that and does better, and that's fine. We haven't found an organization we've worked with yet that can't get to at least a 1-day human regression pass – but still, perhaps that is too infrequent. Perhaps you want results on every build.

So, you decide to start some sort of test tooling effort, perhaps through the user interface. Fantastic.

Who is going to do it?

If you have the testers do it, say, half the time, then it'll take a very long time to make meaningful progress on the tooling. Meanwhile, the test process itself will take twice as long. You started this thing because the test process took too long! An option to "fix" it is to have the group spend less than half time on test tooling. In our experience, if a subset of the team is spending less than half their time on tooling, it is unlikely any meaningful progress will ever happen.

Having humans who focus on testing create automated tooling introduces a second problem, in that these people are not professional programmers. If the tool involves writing code, the testers are likely to create code that is greasy, squeaky, and creaky. They will run into places where it is hard to automate, and, without oversight, simply skip those elements. Yet the bug finder heuristic applies: *The harder it is to set up and run conditions for a test, the more tempting it is to skip, which also means the more likely it is to have bugs that matter hiding in it*. This is because complex things are hard to figure out. If it was hard for the person testing to simulate, it was likely harder for the programmer to figure out. Hard-to-figure-out things have unintended consequences and rules that lead to defects.

Testers without training in programming and patterns are likely to create *Big Ball of Mud* (`www.laputan.org/mud/`) automated tests. They'll run acceptably, for a while, until something big changes. Then, updating the tests will be slow and painful and the team will be tempted to throw the tests out, or "update them later."

Who will do the work?

You could have the programmers write the first draft of the tests. With the right framework and the right-minded programmers, this is often a very good choice. When we've seen this done successfully, the team usually creates tests in the same language as the production code, puts it in the same place in version control, runs the tests on every build, and considers "all tests pass" as a requirement to begin human exploration.

This is still a tradeoff; most programmers do remarkably poorly on the palindrome problem we introduced in *Chapter 1*. We suspect that this is because of the difference between a constructive mind (how do I make it?) versus a critical mind (what could go wrong?). We do think it is possible to train programmers to do both; this book can help here.

Sadly, not all teams are willing or able to pursue having programmers as automated test creators. For one thing, it means slowing all development down considerably. Some executives are simply unwilling to consider it; some programmers are uninterested. In some cases, the programming languages or the build process don't support the style we described earlier. In any event, it isn't hard to imagine an executive saying "*You don't get it. We need the test automation because testing is too slow. That slows down delivery. The "fix" you propose is to make my programmers slower. That's a non-starter.*"

We have heard these lines from executives in the past.

The next step, which is to not slow down the test and not slow down development, is to hire some other group to build up enough tests that the code can be released without (as much?) human exploration. These are usually programmers/testers, sometimes called **software developer engineers in test (SDET)**. These SDETs are often not strong enough programmers to get production programming jobs and are hired as contractors. Generally, they'll come in and slow everyone a bit when onboarding, and then they'll spend 3 to 6 months building tooling. Eventually, they release a "smoke" test that covers the important cases and will find the big, obvious bugs. One company Matt worked with did this, and, after 9 months, the most common problems were things such as "the test environment is down," or "this or that database is down," problems any person would identify in a few seconds.

When do we see results?

It likely takes a year of work for management to see any significant reduction in the length of the build/test/deploy process. At the end of that year, management is probably paying 20% more for development costs overall and 50% more for testing. Turning their head sideways and squinting, the same executive who yelled at the team to do automation and championed the funding is heard to ask "*What if we had just hired a couple more testers for half the price?*" This is a good case. In a bad case, after a year, the executive sees no significant improvement in performance, goes somewhere else to preach their new gospel of automation, and the new-hire Vice President of Development "saves" the company a million dollars a year by not renewing the contracts of the SDETs. After a few weeks, tests start to fail that no one understands; eventually, they are commented out and forgotten.

It does not have to be this way. Yet we hope, by now, you see how it *could*. The rest of this book is on helping you avoid the landmines. Or dog doo-doo. Or... hide your battleships?

In any event, a great deal of test code tends to be created – not a simple find-element/click/find-text, but instead algorithms. For example, if a book will be delivered in 4 business days, the tool will do more than need to find *sysdate+4* – it will need to find the day that is 4 days away, not including holidays and weekends. Eventually, the test steps become complex enough that they need code. Conditionals, loops, dates, weekends, holidays, new account creation, server names, variables, independent calculation of what the subtotal and tax "should" be – all these imply code.

When the test registers an error, we have to figure out what happened and what the steps were. Instead of straightforward linear, we need to debug. Suddenly, the tests need tests.

A common response to this is the idea that automated checks should be incredibly linear straightforward, step – step – step – inspect. Repeat.

Lessons from the fundamental issues

The preceding examples are mostly modeled as end-to-end testing, where all the components are exercised as one system. In *Chapter 4*, we'll discuss how to build end-to-end tests, which are easy to debug, structured to easily change, and even so readable to be a documentation aid, explaining how the software should behave. For now, we'll talk about overcoming the other weaknesses.

It's easy enough to throw up our hands and say that unassisted evaluation of the software by a tool is a bad idea and walk away. We have peers who have said similar things; some call them the "anti-automation brigade." By now, you probably realize that at least some contexts exist where this debate is worth having.

This debate can also help us find ways to overcome these fundamental problems:

- **Visual testing**, for example, is the received term for a style of testing that compares window captures from just portions of a screen, combined with an easy "Click A for a bug, click B for not-a-bug and elevate this new screen as the new standard."

- **Crowdsourced testing** is a way to scale humans to cover large combinatorial problems. After all, if you press a "test" button that goes back to 100 people who all test the software and report answers within 1 hour, is that all that different from "automation?"

- **Codeless test automation**, first popularized with record/playback tools, may finally be coming into its own with the new standards in APIs

- **Multiple independent deploy points** eliminate unnecessary coupling between components, which makes large-scale regression testing a thing of the past

- **Browser compatibility tests** run the software in many different browsers and simulated devices, allowing one person to easily look at many screenshots in seconds to identify rendering problems.

- **Grid-based testing** makes it possible to run many tests at the same time. To do that, the tests need to be able to run independently in any order – something we'll discuss in *Chapter 4*.

- **Test instrumentation** makes it possible to associate code with the tests that exercise it and run only a small subset of all of the tests when a code change occurs.

Each of these ideas can reduce the burden of our fundamental problems in test automation. Only the largest of organizations can do them all; even then, they likely won't be implemented at the same time. The important thing is to identify problems with test tooling as it develops and to adjust the strategy so that it matches.

Mike Cohn, an early scrum leader, is widely credited with the idea of a test automation pyramid – that is, a triangle with a large number of *unit* (low-level) tests at the bottom, a smaller amount of *integration tests* in the middle, and very few *end-to-end tests* at the top. The figure has no slope to the sides and proposes no way to measure them; it is more designed to point out that end-to-end tests are slow, brittle, expensive to write, and problematic (you did notice this chapter's title, right?) while developer tests are easier to write. Therefore, they write many unit tests.

The test pyramid has been under fire for some time as people look for more precise models. Noah Sussman, an early adopter of DevOps, CI, and test automation at Etsy, proposed a testing filter. Here's how Noah thinks about it:

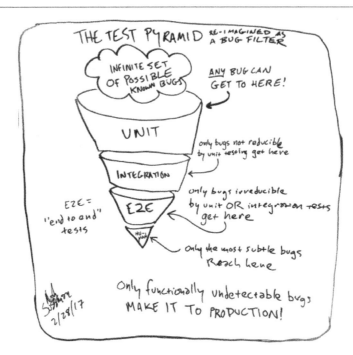

Figure 2.10 – Noah Sussman's Test Pyramid Revisited; used with permission

Noah's ideas are compatible with our work on combinatorics in *Chapter 1*. The programmer's unit and integration tests show the software does what the programmer expects. The end-to-end tests, likely defined by a group, demonstrate and help define the requirements. Thus, the things that slip through to be found by a human tester are the undefined, the unexpected, the odd, the "nobody thought about that," and so on.

This model is an ideal to get to. Certainly, many organizations have a different reality, including ones where there is a giant hole in the bottom of the filter where the bugs fall out.

Our job is to plug the holes.

Summary

Instead of talking about *how to do* test tooling and automation, this chapter covered the things a naive test toolsmith might discover in their first few years of work – at least, we hope they might discover them. As the saying goes, there is a difference between 10 years of experience and 1 year, repeated 10 times. Those problems include the depth of all that testing is (we tend to only automate part of the effort) and that defects tend to be unique, so repeated regression tests have only marginal value. We also discussed test maintenance as a hidden cost and how testing tools tend to either over-report or under-report defects.

Finally, we introduced a handful of patterns to, if not solve, at least decrease the pain of these problems.

While this chapter focused on exercising the software at the highest level, the next chapter will start at the lower level and move up. We call this programmer-facing, or the programmer's approach view of testing.

3
Programmer-Facing Testing

Programmer testing, also called developer testing, ensures that the software can at least do what the programmer expects it to do – one time. This has benefits outside of testing – for design, to create effective user interfaces, for maintainability, and benefits. To explain programmer-facing tests, this chapter covers the following topics:

- The programmer's view
- Unit testing
- Test-driven development
- Unit tests and unit code design
- Mutation testing
- Testing Web APIs
- Testing functional and legacy code from the programmer's perspective

This chapter ends with a practical exercise, or Kata, so that you know how to create unit tests in whatever language you are most capable of working with. The worked case examples were completed using Ruby.

Technical requirements

You don't need to be a programmer to read this chapter. Non-programmers might get the most out of this chapter because, by the end of it, they will learn many programming concepts. Programmers who read this chapter can gain an understanding of the topics. Ruby programmers can type in the examples and run them themselves. We've put the examples on GitHub in the *Chapter 3* folder: `https://github.com/PacktPublishing/Software-Testing-Strategies`.

Matt wrote an introduction to Ruby here – it should at least allow you to get the language that's been installed and understand the basics: `https://web.archive.org/web/20220523090912/https://www.cio.com/article/253100/development-tools-getting-started-with-ruby-a-tour-of-the-scripting-language.html`.

Take the examples as deep or as shallow as you like; you'll get that much value out of it. Consider typing the examples by hand and working through them to understand their differences, because this will make a difference. The best experience is likely typing in the examples and running them; we've included instructions on how to install Ruby in a sidebar.

Programmers working on the examples will have to have an appropriate programming language compiler, interpreter, text editor, and so on. While we will attempt to introduce concepts, knowing at least the fundamentals of how REST APIs work will greatly increase the chance that you will be able to take action in the *Testing APIs* section, as will an understanding of HTML and JavaScript make functional testing easier.

The programmer's view

It's common to think of programmer (automated) tests in terms of unit (smallest piece), integration (components interaction), and system (the entire application or business process). As the piece that's being tested becomes smaller, it tends to run faster, with less setup, change less often, and be easier to reproduce.

In the early 2000s, Mike Cohn and Jason Huggins independently came up with a vision for this called the test automation pyramid. A popular view of this pyramid, as imagined by Seb Rose (`https://cucumber.io/blog/bdd/eviscerating-the-test-automation-pyramid/`), is shown here:

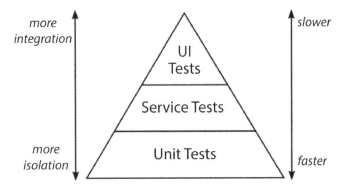

Figure 3.1 – The traditional test automation pyramid

Image source: `https://martinfowler.com/articles/practical-test-pyramid.html`

The purpose of the pyramid, according to Cohn, was to shift the focus and emphasis from end-to-end user interface tests, which are easily done by a human, yet slow and brittle, to the faster, more independent tests best done by a computer. You'll notice that there are no exact measurements; no one talks about the slope or angle of the pyramid. Even if we did, comparing a unit test that checks eight lines of code to an end-to-end test that goes through a complete order flow in a web browser seems like a *Sisyphean* task.

> **Note**
>
> In Greek legend, Sisyphus was the man in Hades cursed to spend all day rolling a boulder up a hill that rolled down every night.

Think of the pyramid as an illustration, a word picture urging you to get the unit tests right first, and you should. We'll see why next.

Testing and reliability

Imagine for a moment that it is possible to measure the reliability of a *method*, or *unit*. The unit is the smallest bit of code that can be tested independently. Reliability is the percentage of time the method will be called and create a proper result. Don't worry about how; instead, imagine that we could do it.

Let's say the typical reliability of a component is 90%. This is reasonably bad; 1 out of 10 calls to the method results in some type of failure. Now, think about what it means to test the software end-to-end – a typical end-to-end test might call 20 different units. Engineering tells us the total reliability of the system would be equal to 90%, raised to the power of 20 – that is, 0.9^{20}, or else 0.9*0.9*0.9*0.9*0.9, times 15 more zero-point nines. The net reliability of such a system is 12.15%. You can do your own math in a spreadsheet and make your own assumptions. The point is that a "decently good enough individual unit," repeated a large number of times, creates an unreliable system.

The "fix" for reliability is to massively increase the reliability of the individual units. 99% to the power of 20 has a net reliability of 82%. 99.5% gets us to 90%, and 99.9% gets us to 98% net. Of course, we can misunderstand the requirements between components (integration) or just misunderstand the customer's wishes (system), so we still need some ways to check for and reduce those risks.

Before we dive into unit testing, let's look at a different architectural view to understand a programmer's approach to writing tests. Then, we'll examine an "untestable" program and how to break it into units.

Note that one of our reviewers, Amit Wertheimer, points out that software does not wear out or break. When we speak of reliability as a percentage, we are not speaking that way, as an automobile. Instead, we mean that some percentage of the time the customer is trying to use the software, they encounter a bug that blocks their progress.

The hexagonal architecture

Some programs don't have units. Instead, they are a big ball of mud (www.laputan.org/mud/mud.html#Abstract). Alister Cockburn's hexagonal architecture (http://web.archive.org/web/20230418161402/https://alistair.cockburn.us/hexagonal-architecture/) suggests a way of thinking about software architecture that prevents the mud. It also provides us with a way of thinking about tests:

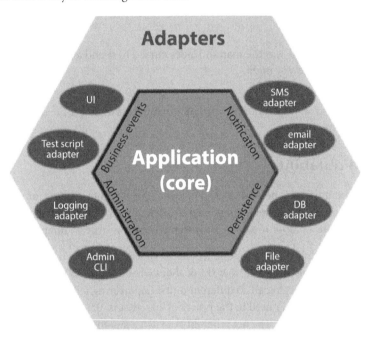

Figure 3.2 – Alister Cockburn's hexagonal architecture diagram

In *Figure 3.2*, the code application is code, living and running inside a machine. External elements such as a screen, database, or web request that want to interact with the application do so through a port, with the programmer writing *adapters* to take input or send output. That makes it possible for us to replace, say, a database adapter with a simple class that gives pre-defined results. In testing terms, a unit test is, well... a dot. It works on the smallest possible piece of the architecture, inside of the application. An *integration test* is a line that might or might not touch an external boundary. When an integration test touches one boundary, the line likely does not cross over into others. If the code itself forces this, then the second component is likely mocked, stubbed, or fake. When that second line is not mocked, stubbed, or faked, we probably call it a *system* or *end-to-end test*.

If you know the guts about how web pages (HTML, JavaScript, CSS) and modern mobile applications are created, you will likely realize that the hexagon is a model. All models are imperfect, and some are useful. In particular, programmers can write code to try to make it fit this model, which will make the code more testable. Testable code, at the tiny micro-unit level, can be one key to reliability. We like the hexagonal architecture so much that we wanted to show it twice. Here's a second, older example, taken from Allister's writing:

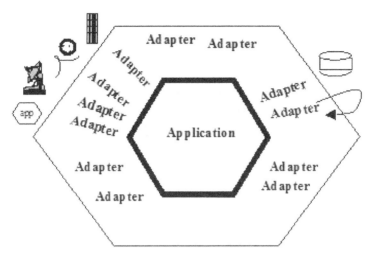

Figure 3.3 – An older example of the hexagonal architecture.
This image is only for representation purposes.

Note that adaptors can have their own unit tests. Later in this chapter, we'll discuss mocks, stubs, fakes, and service virtualization.

For now, let's look at a very simple program with an implementation that "cannot" be unit-tested, and then talk about how to make it testable.

> **Code along if you'd like**
>
> The example in the upcoming section is in Ruby. Unix, Linux, and Mac come with Ruby installed. Simply run this from the command line: `ruby (filename).rb`. Windows users will need to run an installer. You can find simple Ruby installer at `https://rubyinstaller.org/`. The Ruby code below was tested on Ruby 3.0.6.

Introducing FizzBuzz

When we interview programmers who will write code to help with testing, we like the exercise FizzBuzz. The exercise requires the programmer to understand conditionals (which are `if` statements), looping, and the modulus operator (which is the remainder in division). Let's see what a typical assignment might look like.

In the children's game of Fizzbuzz, players rotate, keeping a count that starts with one. If the next number is divisible by three, players say "Fizz." If it is divisible by five, they say "Buzz." If it is not divisible, they say the number. The goal is to write a computer program that runs on the command line and takes in the number to count up to in FizzBuzz math, then puts the output on the screen.

Matt wrote up an implementation of FizzBuzz in Ruby. Instead of the most powerful constructs of the language, he used the ones that were easiest to read. The following output could be "tighter," by far, but it was designed to be readable by nearly all audiences. The examples for the rest of this book will try to match this style. For a book with a more powerful Ruby style that also includes tests, we like **Poodr**, or *Practical Object Oriented Programming In Ruby*, by Sandi Metz. That book also has good coverage of testing concepts. If you aren't a Rubyist, our GitHub repository contains examples in Python.

> **GitHub**
>
> For now, here's the heart of the code; the entire program is available on GitHub at https://github.com/PacktPublishing/Software-Testing-Strategies/blob/main/Chapter03/ruby/FizzBuzz01.rb.

This code takes a command-line argument for how high to count, checks to make sure that it is valid, and then spits out numbers. The heart of the program is nine lines of code:

```ruby
count_to = ARGV[0].to_i;

if !defined?(count_to) or count_to<1
  puts "Use: FizzBuzz01.rb (count)\n"
  puts "Where count is a round number of value one or higher"
  abort("");
end

for count in 1..count_to do
  if count % 3 == 0
    puts "Fizz"
  elsif count % 5 == 0
    puts "Buzz"
  else
    puts count.to_s();
  end
end
```

It's worth noting that Matt created four syntax errors just by re-typing the code into this book. Here's what happens when it runs on a Mac, selecting an output from 1 to 12:

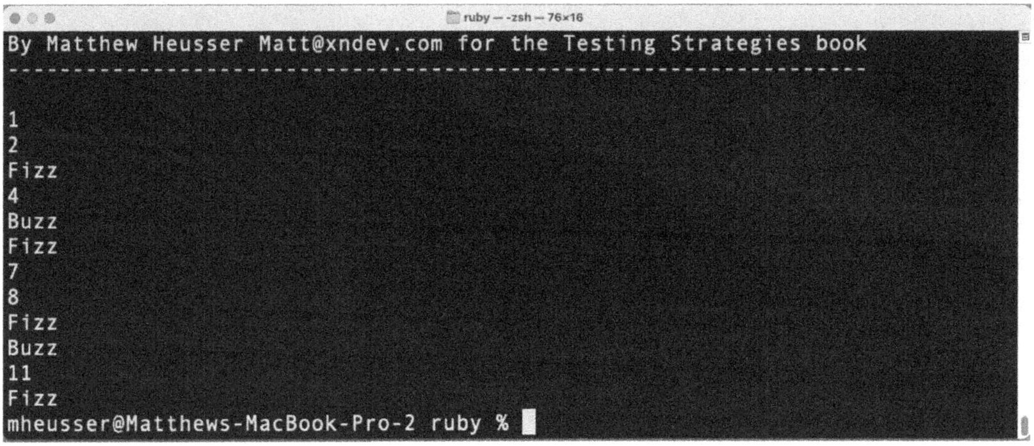

Figure 3.4 – Fizzbuzz output from Matt's laptop

If the four errors just to write a dozen lines of code doesn't give you pause, the program has a significant defect in it. Can you see it?

You won't see it in the output. I'll wait. Go read the code.

Okay. Here's the problem.

The numbers 15, 30, 45, and 60 are all divisible by both three and five. The preceding program will divide 15 by 3, decide it is "Fizz", and exit. We need something more robust.

The obvious problem with FizzBuzz is that it has problems. The programmer will have to set it up, run it, and check the output. If they find another problem, the programmer will need to make another change and run it again. This change-run-check dynamic is sometimes called *debugging*. It is the only way to run the program because the business logic to calculate the results, the input, and the printing are all combined into one "unit."

At the time of writing, the only way to test this is from the customer, or user, perspective. That isn't the end of the world as it is only nine lines of code – but as programs get larger, debugging becomes more and more painful. It would be better to compose our software of smaller, independent units that work a much larger percentage of the time. That's where unit testing comes in – but for it to work, we need to create code libraries that can be independently tested.

If a program can't be independently tested, separate from the user interface, some people call that untestable. We don't go that far as our hands and fingers seem to work just fine.

Still, unit tests allow us to get into the program so that we can define how it should work. They work as living documentation for the expectations of each component. As discussed earlier, a program that has 20 units that are 95% reliable, for some definition of reliable, is going to be massively more reliable than one where the units are 70% reliable.

Fizzbuzz needs unit tests.

So, let's define a unit, unit *testing*, and fix this thing.

Unit tests

Michael Feathers gives a description (`https://www.artima.com/weblogs/viewpost.jsp?thread=126923`) of what a unit test is not. According to Feathers, "*If it talks to the database, it talks across the network, it touches the filesystem, it requires system configuration, or it can't be run at the same time as any other test*", then it is not a unit test.

Unit tests defined this way will run incredibly quickly. They can run in parallel. They can be set up entirely in memory. Some testing schemes look at your code as you type and figure out what you touched, re-running unit tests. Others do that on check-in.

To help you learn how to perform unit tests yourself, we'll write FizzBuzz with unit tests in Ruby, using a Ruby test framework called `MiniTest`.

First, Matt used an open source tool he wrote called **KataGenerator** (`https://github.com/heusserm/katas/blob/master/katagenerator.rb`) to lay out the tests. **KataGenerator** takes a single word that describes the program to set up and creates it. The program creates a main program, a library directory, and a test directory, with a library and test file. Here's the directory's structure:

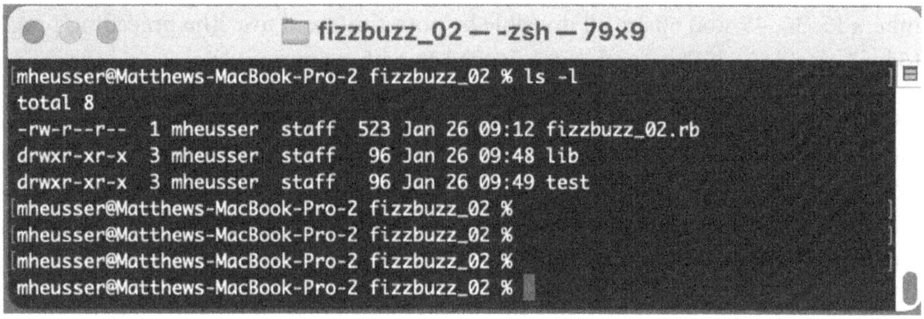

Figure 3.5 – FizzBuzz directory structure

Here's the source code for the main routine:

```
#fizzbuzz_02.rb

require_relative 'lib/fizzbuzz_02_lib.rb'
fizzbuzz_02=Fizzbuzz_02.new()
```

As you can tell, the program is "hollow." All it does is create the `fizzbuzz` (lowercase is the instance, a capital first letter is the class) object and call `new` on it. At this point, we have two directions we can go: either try to get the program to do something or build up some business logic. In the second example, we'll do the classic programmer thing and get it running.

The program will now have three pieces:

- **The main routine**: This creates a `fizzbuzz` object and asks for the entire text output of what is passed in on the command line.

- **The library**: This has two methods. `calc_invididual_buzz_result` will take a number and return the text for the translation, while `get_total_result` will loop from one to `loop_max` and add the results of the call to `calc_invididual_buzz_result` for that number.

- **The tests**: These are custom tests for the individual and total functions.

For the initial build, we just make the software work with the number 1. Here's our new main routine:

```
require_relative 'lib/fizzbuzz_02_lib.rb'
fizzbuzz_02=Fizzbuzz_02.new()
output = fizzbuzz_02.get_total_result(count_to);
puts output
puts "\n";
```

Here's the guts of the library:

```
def get_total_result(loop_max)
  return "1\n"
end

def calc_individual_buzz_result(input)
  return "1\n"
end
```

Here are the core elements of the `test` file in the test directory:

```
def test_calc_individual_result
  playing = Fizzbuzz_02.new()
  result = playing.calc_individual_buzz_result(1);
  assert_equal("1\n", result);
end

def test_entire_result
  playing = Fizzbuzz_02.new()
  result = playing.get_total_result(1);
  assert_equal("1\n", result);
end
```

This `test` file is new and different. It will create a `Fizzbuz_02` object in memory, call the method, and expect the output. The `assert_equal` method checks if the first value matches the second.

We can even run it from the command line:

```
➡  test git: (main) ✗ ruby fizzbuzz_02_test.rb

Run options: --seed 52435

# Running:

...

Finished in 0.001213s, 2473.2069 runs/s, 2473.2069 assertions/s.
3 runs, 3 assertions, 0 failures, 0 errors, 0 skips
```

Each dot, or period, is a passing test.

What we've done here is create what Michael Feathers calls *seams* in the application – that is, places where there is a split between objects, where the objects can be treated separately. In the hexagon architecture, these are called "ports and adapters." With our first example, to test the program, we had to test the entire program – there were no "seams." Minitest allows us to run just one small sub-method and examine the output. It is, in a way, sort of like Jeff Klein dumping the assembler output so that we could figure out what is going on.

Okay, it's not like that at all, but the metaphor works. By running just a tiny bit of the application at a time and peeking into memory, we can now isolate problems. This is what we are about to do.

Now that we have the basic components working, it's time to write some actual functionality.

Here's the total count function:

```
def get_total_result(loop_max)
  result = "";
  for count in 1..count_to do
    result = result + calc_individual_buzz_result(count);
  end
end
```

Here's the individual function:

```
def calc_individual_buzz_result(input)
  if input % 3 == 0
    return "Fizz"
  elsif input % 5 == 0
    return "Buzz"
  else
    return input.to_s()
```

```
        end
    end
```

Now, in theory, this should all still work according to our "just one" test, so I reran the tests. It did not work. See if you can understand the problem; I'll put the relevant bit of the output here:

```
.F

Failure:
TestFizzbuzz_02#test_entire_result [fizzbuzz_02_test.rb:20]:
--- expected
+++ actual
@@ -1,2 +1 @@
-"1
-"
+1..1

bin/rails test fizzbuzz_02_test.rb:17

Finished in 0.015063s, 199.1635 runs/s, 199.1635 assertions/s.
3 runs, 3 assertions, 2 failures, 0 errors, 0 skips
```

The test expects the carriage-return/newline character, \n at the end. Thus, if the number is not divisible by 3 or 5, the code would read as `return input.to_s()+"\n"`. There is also an error in `get_total_result` where I am missing a return statement. The tests cause both of these!

With the code running, I am off to write more tests, and I'm going to do something terrible – that is, I'm going to run the whole program for the number 12, see if it is right, and, if it is, reverse-engineer it back into a test. It works:

```
➡  fizzbuzz_02 git:(main) ✗ ruby fizzbuzz_02.rb 12
FizzBuzz02.rb
By Matthew Heusser Matt@xndev.com for the Testing Strategies book
---------------------------------------------------------------

1
2
Fizz
4
Buzz
Fizz
7
8
Fizz
```

```
Buzz
11
Fizz
```

➡ `fizzbuzz_02 git:(main)` ⊠

I copy the values from the list to memory, then paste them into the code, replacing the real newlines with \n, the code for newline. My new code looks like this:

```
test_string = "1\n2\n\Fizz\n4\nBuzz\nFizz\n7\n8\nFizz\nBuzz\n11\
nFizz\n"
result = playing.get_total_result(12);
assert_equal(test_string, result);
```

And my tests pass:

```
Finished in 0.001051s, 2854.4244 runs/s, 3805.8991 assertions/s.
3 runs, 4 assertions, 0 failures, 0 errors, 0 skips
```

It is time to write a test that fails – or, for fun, a whole bunch of tests, some of which will fail:

```
def test_calc_individual_easy
  playing = Fizzbuzz_02.new()
  result = playing.calc_individual_buzz_result(1);
  assert_equal("1\n", result);
  result = playing.calc_individual_buzz_result(8);
  assert_equal("8\n", result);
  result = playing.calc_individual_buzz_result(301);
  assert_equal("301\n", result);
end

def test_calc_individual_fiz_or_buz
  playing = Fizzbuzz_02.new();
  result = playing.calc_individual_buzz_result(3);
  assert_equal("Fizz\n", result);
  result = playing.calc_individual_buzz_result(5);
  assert_equal("Buzz\n", result);
  result = playing.calc_individual_buzz_result(6);
  assert_equal("Fizz\n", result);
  result = playing.calc_individual_buzz_result(10);
  assert_equal("Buzz\n", result);
end

def test_calc_individual_fizzbuzz
  playing = Fizzbuzz_02.new()
```

```
    result = playing.calc_individual_buzz_result(15);
    assert_equal("FizzBuzz\n", result);
    result = playing.calc_individual_buzz_result(300);
    assert_equal("FizzBuzz\n", result);
  end
```

Now, I will fix the code:

```
def calc_individual_buzz_result(input)
  result = ""
  if input % 3 == 0
    result = result + "Fizz"
  end

  if input % 5 == 0
    result = result + "Buzz"
  end

  if result == ""
    result = input.to_s();
  end

  result = result + "\n"
end
```

Finally, I can rerun the tests, which now pass.

Ironically, on the way to get to the preceding code example, Matt made three significant errors. First, he had buzz and fizz typed in lowercase accidentally. Then, he had 'if result = "" ' – the single equals sign was an assignment. Thus, it forced the result to be empty and added to it, destroying the previous Fizz and Buzz-ified value. The third time, he forgot to save the file before running the tests. These would all be painful to debug end-to-end but took seconds to fix because the code was isolated.

Someone pursuing a "pure" **test-driven development** (**TDD**) approach, which we'll define next, might argue there should be one assert per test method. In Minitest, having more than one assertion per test method is a problem because any individual test will "bow out" and fail after any assertion fails. If there is more information to be gained from other failures, it will be lost until the code is fixed. To mitigate this, we broke the code into a few test methods. At runtime, the compiler will be smart enough to know that any method that starts with test_ should run.

The test file itself is also structured as a class, with an init method. It might make more sense to make playing a class-level variable so that it is only initiated once.

In not that much time, we've created a class that performs testing and a way to do it at the unit level.

Let's talk about how to do this in a test-driven fashion.

TDD

The earlier approach resulted in a code base with some tests. Essentially, Matt wrote the plumbing code to return the simplest possible result ("1," the result of the parameter 1 passed into FizzBuzz), then wrote the code to make Fizzbuzz "work," and then wrote tests to check it. That's better than nothing, but there is no real confidence that the tests cover the important permutations of the software. With Fizzbuzz, the code is trivial. `get_total_results` has one loop. You can cover all the code in one test. `calc_individual_buzz_result` has three `if` statements; you can cover all the code in three tests and all combinations in four.

TDD is a discipline where, before a new line of code is created, the programmer creates a failing test. In our FizzBuzz example, that would mean creating a test for an input of 2, implementing the code, creating a test for "3" (fizz), implementing the code, creating a test for "5" (buzz), implementing the code, implementing a test for "15" (FizzBuzz), and so on. TDD comes out of a family of unit test frameworks called **xUnit**, where x is usually an abbreviation for the programming language. xUnit comes from an object-oriented approach, meaning programmers write a collection of tests for an object. The name of the test works as a descriptor of the test, and each test has one assertion. Here's what the tests might start to look like TDD style:

```
def test_calc_fizz
   playing = Fizzbuzz_02.new();
   result = playing.calc_individual_buzz_result(3);
   assert_equal("Fizz\n", result);
end

def test_calc_buzz
   playing = Fizzbuzz_02.new();
   result = playing.calc_individual_buzz_result(5);
   assert_equal("Buzz\n", result);
end

def test_calc_fizzbuzz
   playing = Fizzbuzz_02.new();
   result = playing.calc_individual_buzz_result(15);
   assert_equal("FizzBuzz\n", result);
end
```

The *loop* for programming in TDD is called **Redbar/Greenbar/Refactor**, after the color of passing (green) or failing (red) tests. Thus, the programmer writes the test for the feature that hasn't been implemented yet (if the remainder of dividing the input by 3 is fizz, add fizz), sees it failing, adds the code, and now sees it passing. Once the code is passing, the programmer can improve the design of the existing code, or refactor it. It is frequent, for example, to start with something like a `get_total_results` method and realize that the method loops over the contents of an array, doing the same thing each time. The programmer can then pull the code of the inner loop into its own method without changing the system's behavior.

Over the years, we've slowly seen unit test and refactoring tools added to popular **integrated development environments (IDEs)**. Highlight the code, right-click it, click through a menu, and suddenly your code has been moved to a place where it is small, modular, and testable. For a few years, there was a cottage industry of tools that were plugins to IDEs such as **Microsoft's Visual Studio** or **IntelliJ** to enable unit testing and refactoring. Today, for the most part, IDE developers have swallowed these ideas and implemented them. Entire categories of "errors," such as compile-time and syntax errors, can go away with a good IDE. What surprises us the most as consultants in this space is how little and how poorly they are adopted. These things are not like a light switch you turn on or off. Instead, they are features that take a little skill to develop.

TDD is much the same way. Covering it well would take a book – and there are a few. Our goal here is to give you the flavor of it, plus the tools to learn on their own. Another goal of ours is to understand the consequences of pure TDD – and it does have consequences.

Consequences of TDD

As we saw in FizzBuzz, for code to be testable, we need to take it out and turn it into separate methods, each that does something specific and defined. The tests provide that definition – given this input, expect this output. They have to run independently; they can't be based on what is in a database at a given point in time. They can't be overly complex or require a great deal of setup. By creating the software one passing test at a time, the programmer has a system of forces that make writing complex software difficult. Getting TDD to work with existing code is a topic we'll discuss later. For now, it is enough to know that TDD pushes the programmer toward small, independent modules.

That means more code.

A lot more code.

The unit-tested version of FizzBuzz has 37 source lines of code, and that is only a library of code. The core implementation of the no-unit-tests version is seven lines of code. Likewise, Matt's test-driven kata of Conway's Game of Life (https://github.com/heusserm/katas/tree/master/game_of_life) is roughly 280 lines of library code; a "tight" Ruby implementation might be half of that.

For that matter, the tests for the *Game of Life* implementation are twice as much code as the production code. To write the 280 lines of production code in *Game of Life*, Matt had to write 50 unit tests with around seventy assertions, which represent well over 600 lines of code.

In other words, in this example, the TDD approach generates twice as much production code as needed, plus four times the test code.

In general, we see this as a very good thing. Clean, well-separated, independent subcomponents that can run in isolation will save you money in the long run. They can be very helpful for maintainability. They will also tend to push the testing problem up. Once you've solved for unit tests, you still need to solve for everything else.

These examples are unit tests -- they just testing the dot inside the hexagon. Integration tests could connect objects in memory, or even connect to actual systems, such as a database. End-to-end tests could drive a web browser. These add even more code. In some cases, it is possible to have software that is essentially all business logic, such as a Fahrenheit to Celsius converter, that is tested three to four times, all redundantly. In other words, the TDD unit tests test the little method and all the reasonable combinations, the integration tests do the same through the API, and the end-to-end tests do the same through the web browser. That approach can get silly.

TDD started with Kent Beck, and his **sUnit** framework for **Smalltalk**, back in 1995. Kent would go on to create **Extreme Programming** and make TDD a core practice. In 2010, with 15 years of experience, Kent did a screencast for **Pragmatic Programmers** where he did not suggest a new test for every single code change – instead, he suggested a handful of tests to drive out the design in a class. Another early influencer of Extreme Programming was Ron Jeffries. When we debated this topic a decade ago, Matt pointed out that Kent Beck no longer dogmatically performs **Redbar/Greenbar/Refactor**, and Ron replied with, essentially, "Maybe so, but ask yourself this question: are you Kent Beck?"

Put differently: to master TDD, start by doing a lot of it. We've placed an exercise at the end of this chapter, the *Roman Number Kata*. If you are a programmer, try reading this whole chapter to understand how to begin to write in a TDD style in legacy code. Perform the Roman Numeral Kata a few times. Improve the quality of your code. Eventually, you might reach a place where you interleave code with tests as you develop – but don't start there.

Unit test and unit code design

Remember that first example – FizzBuzz. It took values from the command line and spat results out to the screen. To test it, we would have to test the entire system as a system. To automate that, we could do… something. It is possible, for example, to write a program that calls FizzBuzz from the command line, passing in inputs from a file, writing the results to a file, and comparing actual to expected results. That is what most customer-facing test automation looks like. That kind of automation is clunky, awkward, and painful.

Or, using the hexagonal model, we can break the line into independent components and test them. You saw this in the FizzBuzz example, where we essentially had three elements.

The main routine is as follows:

1. Accept input, call `get_total_result`, and print it.
2. `Get_total_result`; loop from 1 to input, `calc_individual_result`, add to the total, and return it.

3. `calc_indvidual_result`; the business logic of divided by 3, divided by 5, or return value, goes here.

This works well for trivial examples that are started from scratch. Legacy code tends to have the following aspects:

- "God" objects that mix data and algorithms
- Connections to databases, sometimes with database names hard-coded
- Writing to filesystems
- Calls to external APIs that might or might not be production systems
- Extremely hard to set up objects
- Objects that "load" from a database

All these things conspire to make it difficult, if seemingly impossible, to isolate code to test it.

In his book, *Working Effectively with Legacy Code* (`https://www.oreilly.com/library/view/working-effectively-with/0131177052/`) Michael Feathers suggests finding *seams* for code – that is, logical ways to break methods up. The most common way to do this is to add new functionality as an independent method and test just that method. When you approach the edges, such as writing to a filesystem or the screen, you can act like our FizzBuzz example – make a calculator method and test that. Sometimes, the program interacts with a database, doing different things depending on what it finds. What then?

Joe Armstrong, the creator of Erlang, once explained that this is a natural consequence of a sort of naive adoption of **object-oriented programming** (**OOP**). As Armstrong put it, "*Because the problem with object-oriented languages is they've got all this implicit environment that they carry around with them. You wanted a banana but what you got was a gorilla holding the banana and the entire jungle.*" (Joe Armstrong, 2020, *Banana Gorilla Jungle – OOP*, `https://medium.com/codemonday/banana-gorilla-jungle-oop-5052b2e4d588.`)

In practice, when these problems surface, the programmers will simply abandon TDD. This is especially true if anything less than the entire team is brought into the work as the non-TDD team members will appear to make progress while "breaking the build" for anyone running tests before checking in code. As less and less of the code base contains tests, there will be more and more debugging, uncertainty about what code is executed, and, ultimately, attempts to "test quality in" by using the system end-to-end.

Our friends in the software quality world will say, "You can't test in quality." Strictly speaking, this is true – testing only shows the presence of (some of the) errors. In practice, however, there is a software method we call "code, test, debug, fix, recode, retest, redebug, refix, rerecode, reretest…" Another term for this is "Code it (at least) twice," which involves delivering software that might barely be good enough late. Half of these problems come from poor components; the other half comes from a lack of understanding of the requirements.

The alternative is to make clean lines between components, which, again, is where naive OOP tends to fall. Again, you want to test the banana, but you will end up needing to create the entire jungle. In real software, that means you need a real database to run a unit test, that database needs to query a full data warehouse with predictable data, and suddenly running unit tests takes hours plus expensive cloud resources.

The common solution around this is a set of patterns called *test doubles*, using the example of a video game.

Using test doubles to create seams

Most of us are familiar with video games that can save the state – the player's statistics. These include their level, experience points, class, equipment, and so on. That class is likely stored in an object that includes both data (the statistics) and an algorithm. A simple enough algorithm reads from a disk or database. In a naive implementation, a programmer would not be able to separate the two. The lowest level of automated test might be by calling the `write_to_db()` function and then executing a query on the data to see if the database is populated correctly. Again, this will be a slow test – dozens to hundreds of times slower than one that could run in memory. To run it, we have to have a real database running and, if there is an error, we would need to work to debug, to figure out where the problem is and isolate the error. This style of thinking also leads to multiple implementations of the same feature as we might need a `write_to_cloud()` feature when we migrate to Amazon Web Services, a `write_to_API`, and so on.

In an object-oriented system, we likely represent the database represented by an object. There might be a base database object, and then children classes from it to write to every major database, such as **Sybase**, **Oracle**, **Microsoft's SQL Server**, **IBM's DB II**, and so on. Given a base class, it is possible to create a subclass of the database that does nothing at all. A stub might return the same value every time, say a success flag. A mock, on the other hand, might have some predefined behavior, returning success under some conditions and failure under others. A mock can also record how many times it is called. All of these fall into the broad category of **test double**. When testing an object that connects to other objects, the programmer passes the test double.

Let's talk about how that works.

At runtime, our program calls the `user->write()` method, including a `writer` object. The `writer` object includes the strategy to use (DB, database, or API), along with the actual connection. Here are the steps we follow to peel apart our program and test the internals as units:

1. To test the main classes, we mock out the writer object and ask, "When write and read are called, how often are you, the writer called, and with what data?"

2. To test the writer, we mock out the database connection and ask what information is sent to the database object. In this case, it would be `INSERT` or `SELECT` statements to load an object.

3. A strategy pattern takes information and returns objects. In our case, it might take the text name of the object and the connection information. For a database, this might be `MS SQL SERVER` and a connection string. For a text file, this might be `Text file","C:\Matt.txt`. To test the strategy, pass in information, get the object back, and ask the object about itself.

Using test doubles in this way results in code that is separate and can be tested separately. Sometimes, the code already exists, and you have the whole jungle problem. Other times, you just don't have the base classes in the right foundation. Most modern programming languages today have mocking libraries that are free or freely available that allow you to swap out objects with mocks at runtime.

It's worth noting that one of the first public uses of mocking was for a cache. With a cache, you have a small amount of commonly used information somewhere (perhaps in memory) and access to much larger but slower information somewhere else (perhaps on disk). If the cache wasn't working correctly, it might always read from disk, which would "work" but eliminate the value added by the cache. In this case, whether the `read_from_disk()` method is called is important; it should not be if the data exists in memory. Thus the "how many times were you called and how" recording functionality of a mock becomes a part of the testing process.

Mutation testing

In *Chapter 2*, we talked about code coverage – that is, by running the tests while measuring, we can determine how much of the code is covered by the tests. That example was by metaphor, of a dog park. We can, however, look at the actual lines of code and ask if they are executed when the test runs. The number of lines of code executed divided by the total lines of code is the statement coverage. There are problems with this approach that we'll discuss in *Chapter 9*, but we hope you can agree that having such a number is generally better than nothing. Speaking of ways, there is another, slightly tricky way to see how sufficient unit tests are. We could change the code itself to perhaps compile, yet intentionally break. For example, we could change hard-coded `TRUE` statements to `FALSE`, remove a line of code that includes a method call, change the order in which parameters are passed into a method, and so on.

This involves changing the production code in memory at runtime. In theory, if we break the code in this way, some tests should fail. Thus, we mutate the code and see if it fails. Mutation testing may be more popular on interpreted languages, and projects that break down easily into small sub-projects, as it can be memory and CPU-intensive. We increasingly hear about its use.

As luck would have it, a mutation library, called `mutant`, exists for Ruby/Minitest, which is the test library we used for FizzBuzz. Code that uses it must either use an open source license or pay a fee, but there is a sample program, `auom`, that you can play with at no cost. To configure the library, you need to add a bit of code in the `test` module that tells the compiler what the test code is covering, download the mutant library, and run the tests with the bundler.

Note what this will do: It will run the tests against one version of the code, then change the code, and then run it again and again while looking for errors. The larger the methods, the more interconnected they are, the more exponential the number of tests run. The example for `mutant`, `auom`, is 225 source lines of code, not including comments. Here's the result of a test run, which generates 798 mutations and takes about 8 seconds on a high-end MacBook computer:

```
warning: parser/current is loading parser/ruby30, which
recognizes3.0.5-compliant syntax, but you are running 3.0.4.
Please see https://github.com/whitequark/parser#compatibility-with-
ruby-mri.
Mutant environment:
Matcher:             #<Mutant::Matcher::Config subjects: [AUOM*]>
Integration:         minitest
Jobs:                8
Includes:            ["lib", "lib"]
Requires:            ["auom", "auom"]
Subjects:            23
Total-Tests:         90
Selected-Tests:      90
Tests/Subject:       3.91 avg
Mutations:           798
progress: 136/798 alive: 0 runtime: 1.01s killtime: 1.04s mutations/s:
134.67
progress: 244/798 alive: 0 runtime: 2.01s killtime: 2.41s mutations/s:
121.25
progress: 342/798 alive: 0 runtime: 3.02s killtime: 3.95s mutations/s:
113.09
progress: 423/798 alive: 0 runtime: 4.04s killtime: 5.21s mutations/s:
104.79
progress: 533/798 alive: 0 runtime: 5.04s killtime: 6.01s mutations/s:
105.79
progress: 648/798 alive: 0 runtime: 6.05s killtime: 6.80s mutations/s:
107.06
progress: 754/798 alive: 0 runtime: 7.06s killtime: 7.39s mutations/s:
106.74
Mutant environment:
Matcher:             #<Mutant::Matcher::Config subjects: [AUOM*]>
Integration:         minitest
Jobs:                8
Includes:            ["lib", "lib"]
Requires:            ["auom", "auom"]
Subjects:            23
Total-Tests:         90
Selected-Tests:      90
Tests/Subject:       3.91 avg
Mutations:           798
Results:             798
Kills:               798
```

```
Alive:           0
Timeouts:        0
Runtime:         7.56s
Killtime:        7.62s
Overhead:        -0.80%
Mutations/s:     105.57
Coverage:        100.00%
```

Commenting out two tests, the coverage dropped to 98.7% and the software generated an error. Here's what the error looks like from the command line:

```
minitest:AUOMTest::Binary::Multiply::Unitful#test_unit_denominator_
addition
evil:AUOM::Algebra#*:/Users/matthewheusser/Desktop/code/auom/lib/auom/
algebra.rb:74:00214
-----------------------
Killfork: #<Process::Status: pid 83111 exit 0>
Log messages (combined stderr and stdout):
[killfork] Run options:
[killfork]
[killfork] # Running:
[killfork]
[killfork]
[killfork]
[killfork] Finished in 0.001970s, 4568.5280 runs/s, 55329.9497
assertions/s.
[killfork]
[killfork] 9 runs, 109 assertions, 0 failures, 0 errors, 0 skips
@@ -1,6 +1,6 @@
  def *(other)
    klass = self.class
    other = klass.convert(other)
-   klass.new(other.scalar * scalar, numerators + other.numerators,
denominators + other.denominators)
+   klass.new(other.scalar * scalar, numerators + other.numerators,
other.denominators)
  end
```

This may be difficult to read, but that makes sense: all mutation testing can tell you is that it changed some code and that the change did not result in a failing test. That's very different than knowing the code needs a test for integer-math in the unitful method of the Algebra class.

Note that in this example, *coverage* might be more accurately described as the number of mutations that would be caught by a unit test run.

Given the time it takes `mutation` to run, teams may be better off running it overnight or running it as part of a pull request, before the merge, instead of running it as part of a build pipeline. In *Chapter 2*, we talked about more traditional measures of test coverage:

PYPL Index (US)

Jun 2022	Programming language	Share
1	Python	29.53%
2	Java	17.06%
3	JavaScript	8.56%
4	C/C++	6.49%
5	C#	6.31%
6	R	5.83%
7	Objective-C	3.43%
8	Swift	2.89%
9	PHP	2.85%
10	Rust	2.33%
11	Ruby	2.25%
12	Matlab	2.06%
13	TypeScript	1.98%
14	Go	1.85%
15	VBA	1.11%
16	Scala	0.79%
17	Lua	0.79%
18	Julia	0.77%
19	Kotlin	0.7%
20	Visual Basic	0.59%
21	Perl	0.41%
22	Groovy	0.4%
23	Haskell	0.27%
24	Abap	0.24%
25	Cobol	0.23%
26	Ada	0.11%
27	Dart	0.11%
28	Delphi/Pascal	0.05%

Figure 3.6 – The PopularitY of Programming Language (PYPL) index

In this chapter, we treat testing methods, classes, and classes that create other classes roughly the same. There are some data structures and algorithms, such as trees and searching, where testing a node/leaf is less valuable than testing the entire structure. Learning when to use test doubles and when to not might be best learned by experiment. All that changes, though, when you hit a hard boundary, such as a disk or network. In our era, the glue between major subsystems is the API, specifically the Web API.

Web APIs from a test perspective

Generating a web page used to be the result of a single computer program. We'll call this "20th century web development." In that style, with a programming language such as PHP, the user could fill in a form, click **Submit**, and the program would add that new catalog to the recipe book and re-display the page. Some programmers might still take that approach. According to the PYPL index (source: `https://statisticstimes.com/tech/top-computer-languages.php`) of USA-based programming languages, PHP is the 9th most popular programming language, and 2.85% of development uses PHP. Factoring in that not all programming is web development, and not all 20th-century web development uses PHP, we can see that 20th-century web development is still significant today.

If you think about it, this style of web development is the same big ball of mud we broke apart to test FizzBuzz – that is, all the code is together; if we want to test it, we need to functional test it. Modern web development, in comparison, puts "seams" in the software using APIs.

This style of development separates the frontend (HTML, JavaScript, and CSS) from the backend. Frontend developers write the user interface code to draw the screen, call a REST API, and get the results back, likely in a hash-array data structure called (**JavaScript Object Notation (JSON)**). The JavaScript can then loop through the results and create a table on the web page – for example, for search results for employees with a specific name.

On the customer side, if the tester finds an error after a click, they can turn on Chrome DevTools, see the network diagram, and click on the JSON to see if what was sent was correct and if what came back is correct JSON, as shown in *Figure 3.5* (source: **Chrome Developer Tools**; website: www.xndev.com):

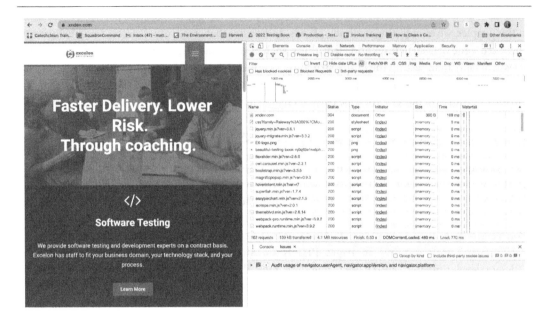

Figure 3.7 – The "Waterfall" diagram shows every file that's been downloaded and every network interaction as a page loads.
The intent of this screenshot is to show the maximized layout; text readability is not required.

Building a modern application means stitching together the various APIs to be called at the correct time. An eCommerce website might have APIs for logging in, displaying profiles, editing profiles, searching, displaying products, checking out, order history, and so on. This strategy limits the functionality under development to one piece at a time, making the entire application a puzzle using JavaScript as the glue.

The good news about Web APIs is that they enable next-generation software development. The same APIs you use in your web application can likely be reused for the native software of your cell phones and tablets. Once they exist, writing a native Windows, Mac, or **virtual reality** (**VR**) (Oculus) application becomes much easier.

Web APIs are essentially just web links, sometimes with data attached or returned. In theory, testing an API is as simple as writing a little program to call the API and check the results.

In practice, most Web APIs require logging in. Because the web is stateless, the APIs need to pass some sort of unique number, likely a session token, back and forth, to make sure that the username, shopping cart, and so on are consistent. That means testing whether the API is consistent in terms of first logging in, getting the session ID, and passing it into subsequent work.

Testing a complex web application can be more complex still.

Web API testing strategy

APIs tend to run across a network, reading and writing to databases. That makes a typical API test 10 to 100 times as fast as a unit test. Indeed, where the mutation tests could run about 800 tests in about 8 seconds, a "fast" true API test that went all the way to the database and back that took 1 second might be fast. The test tooling pyramid helps here, suggesting fewer API tests. System and test design can help us here as well. Here are a few heuristics, or guidelines, for designing web API tests:

- Try to isolate components as much as possible.

- When an API calls an API that calls an API, and so on, in a chain, you can mock out the dependencies using service virtualization.

- To test business logic and various logical classes of tests, mock out the database or the other APIs.

- To check the entire dependency chain (a line from one end to another in the hexagon), write a small number of tests. These are a success condition and some obvious failures – for example, a read (no user with the name Joe Schmoe), write, read (now there is) delete, and re-read (name does not appear) pattern or a database error, such as a duplicate, and perhaps an invalid user information. Other permutations such as "no last name generates error" can likely be tested as business logic.

- Tests should be able to run independently and in parallel. That means creating a new user per test, the ability to clear databases on demand, sometimes having pre-known expected search results, a guarantee that the currently-running tests will not poison your search results, and other techniques we discussed in Chapter 7, *Test Data Management*.

Managing users, sessions, search results, JSON, and so on can become complex. In some cases, the JSON that comes back that is expected will be very similar yet vary a little bit. `date`, `orderID`, `customerID`, and so on may change on every test run, yet be predictable. Alternatively, you may get the same blob of JSON data back every time but changed ever so slightly, so you want to build up a variable with the data to send or the expected result.

There are a handful of tools, some commercial, some free, and others open source, that allow the user to do this while creating test cases, code libraries, and suites. Generally, the suites consist of many tests – you might have a search suite, a product display suite, an all-the-fast-tests suite, a just-the-important-tests suite, a "smoke tests" suite that checks everything but just a little bit, and so on. At the time of writing, we are familiar with **Postman** (free/open/in the cloud with upsales), **SoapUI** (free, commercial, native to your laptop), **ReadyAPI** (the commercial version of SoapUI, with more tools for service virtualization), and **Subject7** (the commercial, web-based Cadillac of such tools). Most of the tools have a free trial.

Finally, consider true contract testing – that is, the tests act as a contract for what the software "should" do. Tools such as **PACT** can analyze your consuming applications (your "customers") to create tests that simulate what the consumer expects when they are called. This tends to focus on the form of the JSON that's returned, to make sure every element is present. That way, if a programmer drops the "city" because they provide "zip code," which is redundant, if some customers expect "city," the software can find the problem in the build/test run before the code is promoted to production.

Testing functional and legacy code

As we continued with this chapter, we got away from the "dots" on the hexagon and more to lines that run end-to-end. Increasingly, these look like things a customer could understand. As APIs start to look and feel more like actual business functions, it becomes possible to express tests as a table that customers can understand and run. Once it is possible to express functionality in terms a customer can understand, it might make sense to expose it to the customer so that they can see the tests as living documentation. We'll talk more about this in *Chapter 4*, where we'll cover customer-facing tests. Eventually, this may blur the line between developer–facing and customer-facing testing. *We are okay with this.*

Most of this chapter discussed tests as artifacts – that is, as bits of code. We think of a test as a living exploration of software. Remember that a test written down, institutionalized, and run over and over, is more like change detection than testing. It is a test the first time we write it, all while we think consciously about it, thus making TDD an apt name. We've mentioned this here because we don't want you to forget about the power of "what if."

This means creating little tests in code that run once and get thrown away – "poking" an API with a tool five or six times before creating one test you institutionalize. That is to say, unit testing, API testing, TDD, and functional developer-facing tests can all have an exploratory feel.

Finally, we'll provide a programming exercise so that you can create unit tests.

This next example looks at a way to change Roman numerals into Arabic numerals in a process called a "coding kata."

A Roman Numerals Kata

A Kata is a programming exercise we do to obtain mastery of a programming language, programming patterns, or technique. Matt has a modest set of his checked into GitHub, mostly in Ruby (`https://github.com/PacktPublishing/Software-Testing-Strategies/tree/main/Chapter03/ruby/romannumeral`).

To learn unit testing and TDD, we suggest the Roman Number Kata. The program itself is straightforward – write a console application that takes Roman numerals as input and outputs the Arabic ("regular, decimal") number.

Roman numerals generally move left to right, with the largest number on the left. Here's the high-level translation:

- I = One
- V = Five
- X = Ten

- L = Fifteen

- C = One hundred

- D = Five hundred

- M = One thousand

To repeat a number, just add it to itself. III is "three." However, when you get to one before the next number, things get tricky. You generally use a one in front, reversing the usual left-to-right order. Thus, IV is "four," IX is "nine," and IL is "forty-nine." XL is "forty;" CD is "four hundred." There are plenty of Roman numeral translator tools online for free, providing an easy Oracle to check correctness.

To learn TDD, try implementing the Roman Numeral Kata for yourself, with a test framework, in your favorite programming language. If you'd like a tool that takes in the name of an object and then creates a Ruby structure for a kata, with the object in a library, a test directory, and a runner executable, consider **The Kata Generator** tool: `https://github.com/heusserm/katas/blob/master/katagenerator.rb`.

Summary

This chapter focused on how programmers approach software testing, which tends to be bottom-up – that is, programmers build the software, bit by bit. If they can find a reason to have confidence that the individual bits fit together well, then there's a chance the entire system can work effectively. However, if the individual parts do not work well, the entire system will be hopeless. To do that, we talked about developing components that can be tested in isolation, calling the separation between the components a "seam."

We also described the hexagonal architecture, which is a way to think about how those components interact. Once we can isolate what a small developer "unit" is, we can describe unit tests, along with a particular discipline within unit testing called TDD. After explaining TDD, we covered ways to isolate the code to test one component, including the use of test doubles. This chapter included coverage of mutation testing and Web APIs and also put those together to begin a conversation about testing full functions – still likely below the view of the customer.

This chapter provided you with enough of an understanding of unit testing that you can apply it to any particular programming language, including working examples. Now that we've finished our programmer stroll, it is time to talk about driving the entire system with tools – what we call customer-facing test tooling.

Chapter 4 is all about customer-facing test tooling. We recognize that might be the Zeitgeist, the prevailing belief of the age. Yet we have seen so much money wasted in such poor testing-like activities that we have opened and closed this chapter with a word of warning. In the middle, if people insist, we provide our ideas about what works in test tooling. That includes combining the best aspects of person and machine, GUI automation patterns, specification by example, low-and-no code test tools, and batch and model-driven development. We hope to synthesize these ideas that "only humans can test" and "automate all the things" to create a message that is greater than the sum of its parts.

4
Customer-Facing Tests

In previous chapters, we introduced the idea that testing can be programmer-facing or customer-facing. We also defined testing as a technical investigation into the state of the software. For this chapter, our first problem is likely to be figuring out what the *test automation* portion of *customer-facing test automation* means. To accomplish this, we'll discuss the consequences of the idea and then list some patterns we have seen to make the approach successful.

In this chapter, we cover the following topics:

- A word of warning

- Human or machine—is it either/or?

- GUI automation patterns

- Designing your customer-meaningful test tool approach

- Specification by example

- Low-code and no-code test automation tools

- Batch- and model-driven development

The astute reader should finish the chapter with the ability to analyze a given user interface and determine methods to save time by offloading test effort onto the computer. They will likely not have a list of the specific technologies to work with their particular user interface technology. In our experience, if we tried, the list would be out of date before the book was available in print. We find the patterns more valuable and more constant.

Technical requirements

The examples in this chapter use programming concepts. To avoid getting too high-level and abstract, we'll use concepts from front-end programming, in particular, HTML, the language of the World Wide Web. The examples matter less, as you might be working in a different technology stack entirely. To the extent we use them, we attempt to provide cues so that those of you who are unfamiliar with HTML,

JavaScript, and **Cascading Style Sheets** (**CSS**) will be able to infer meaning from our examples. You will be guided to a style of solution that fits the skills and aptitude of your team.

A word of warning

A great deal of customer-facing test tooling is a huge waste of time. The awkward, clunky, slow, brittle test steps tend to break a lot, are hard to debug, and rarely find real problems that matter. When Matt and Michael look at our customers and peers over the past two decades, few of them have really internalized the lessons from *Chapter 2* of this book. There have been a couple of successes, but, on a bad day, we wonder if those are the exceptions and not the rule (`https://techbeacon.com/app-dev-testing/6-common-test-automation-mistakes-how-avoid-them`). Before we get started, let's think for a moment about how most customer-facing test tooling works. It drives a user interface from the outside, perhaps through the operating system or the browser, simulating what a human does. Imagine an autonomous vehicle that did that with external video systems bolted on. Servomotors and gears control the steering wheel, gear shift, brakes, and accelerator, while a laptop connects everything. Computer programmers write a program to *drive* the car. This might work as a prototype or proof of concept, but for mass production, anyone would integrate the automation into the vehicle—not bolt it on.

Customer-facing test automation is usually bolted on, suffers from all the problems outlined in our first paragraph, and learns none of the lessons from the second chapter. There is a real risk the reader will try to follow our advice and do a *slightly worse* job than they would have anyway when it would be entirely possible to test and deploy at the API level and test each component as a person.

And yet, we wrote this chapter anyway.

One definition of maturity is the ability to agree, intellectually, to two terms that disagree and move forward while holding agreement. F. Scott Fitzgerald put it this way: *"The test of first-rate intelligence is the ability to hold two opposing ideas in mind at the same time and still retain the ability to function. One should, for example, be able to see that things are hopeless yet be determined to make them otherwise."*

So, we have two statements:

- **Graphical user interface** (**GUI**) facing test automation is a silly waste of time
- Testing should be automated as an inherent good

> **Note**
>
> We get value from asking how these could both be true at the same time. Another term for this is the "Hegelian synthesis of thesis and antithesis." If you'd like a little test philosophy for the chapter, we recommend the entry for Hege's Dialectics in the Stanford Encyclopedia of Philosophy: `https://plato.stanford.edu/entries/hegel-dialectics/`.

Turning our heads sideways and squinting, we see that we don't really agree with either of these. Instead, we propose to synthesize them, replacing them with the idea that GUI-facing test automation is often a silly waste of time. So, let's take a careful look at how the customer uses the software to see if there are opportunities to use tooling to reduce human involvement to the extent that it makes sense.

Human Or Tooling—is it either/or?

When people talk about *test automation*, in particular *customer-facing test automation*, they likely mean a few specific things:

- When I, as a technical person, click a button:

  - This may cause The building and deployment of the software to occur

  - This may cause a refresh of the test code from version control

- The *tests* run against the build

- The tests report the status of the software

The term *test automation*, examined this way, might be more accurately described as unattended test execution, evaluation, and reporting. When people talk this way, they usually don't mean automated test design or selection. Likewise, the reporting is rarely good enough to give to programmers to fix. Instead, failing tests need to be investigated and adjusted based on the changing software. Sometimes the test code needs to be updated to match the changed production code and sometimes the test code is *flaky* (more on this in *Chapter 11*). Even if the tool found a true bug, it is likely that someone has to evaluate the defect in order to make a report clear enough for a programmer to fix.

What is described here is very different than the testing we learned in the introduction, *Chapter 1*, and *Chapter 2*. It does bear some semblance of a programmer-facing test suite, as seen in *Chapter 3*, but that test suite has limited utility. The test suite that we saw in *Chapter 2* is valuable in the creation of the code itself. In the overwhelming majority of cases, a user-interface test suite is bolted on after the fact. Such a test suite cannot even run, or *pass* until it is providing no value. For the test suite to run, it needs to have all the bugs preventing its run stomped out. If, for example, the login, search, and add to cart functions do not work, then the person creating the automated test has to report the problem, get the test fixed, report the next problem, and so on. Once the test actually exists, it will report success over and over until there is a regression problem, at which point it will report an error. Regression failures are only a small percentage of software code errors. Thus, a user interface automated test will add no value until it runs, at which point it will add no value until someone makes a change that makes the feature fail. Note that this example references a style of pre-defined test tooling where the computer drives a browser, clicking, typing, and expecting certain results.

Humans test differently. They are good at guessing how to break a user interface, and also good at noticing problems. Computers are generally stuck with two options:

1. If anything, I am specifically looking at a change, which is bad; I'll call it an error.
2. Don't look at that thing. The reason we need a regression suite is because programmers are making changes that might change things. This makes the second point a non-starter and will lead the first point to false error reports.

What the computer is good at is different than what a human is good at. This leads us to the classic debate found in the test automation literature for the past thirty years, which we can summarize as follows:

1. One bunch of people say, "We should just automate everything"
2. A second bunch of people say, "It's more complicated than that"

This book is in the second camp. As an analogy, unattended test execution and evaluation is a bit like trying to make a robot chop down a forest when integrating the tester and the machine could be as simple as buying a chainsaw.

If unattended test execution and evaluation is your goal, this chapter, along with the build pipeline materials, will help you get there. It is possible to get a machine to at least clear the biggest trees in the forest. For the entire job, you'll also want a human directing some work, and you require some tools to do that. Our goal is to give you everything.

So, let's start with some GUI automation patterns. To do that, we'll tell a story of a hypothetical company building automation on its own, making all the classic mistakes, and actually learning from them. Hopefully, you can learn from our mistakes and start with a better template for success!

GUI test automation patterns

This section will discuss classic unattended test execution, evaluation, and reporting. A human, watching what testers do, might imagine the process as the tool walking through the user journey. Log in, search for a specific product, find it, add it to your cart, check out, and add a fake credit card in a test system. After that, check your emails to see if the order was sent and check the backend systems to make sure the card would be charged and the order would be delivered to the warehouse. This end-to-end test has at least eight major components:

1. A login page
2. A homepage
3. A search function
4. Product display
5. An add-to-cart function
6. Cart view

7.   A checkout process

8.   Backend inspection

If anything goes wrong, the software will stop. If it fails to log in, the software might work up until checkout, at which point it will render an error. If the search function encounters an error, the software will try to click the product link and fail, try to add it to the cart (when it is on the wrong page), and then try to check out (when there is nothing in the cart). In a system where each component is 95% reliable, meaning it only demonstrates an error every twenty changes, the entire system is as follows:

Number of components	Percent uptime/success	End-to-end reliability
1	95%	95%
2	95%	90.3%
3	95%	85.7%
4	95%	81.5%
5	95%	77.4%
6	95%	73.5%
7	95%	69.8%
8	95%	66.3%

Table 4.1 – The end-to-end reliability percentage

That means that every three builds, there will be some kind of error. If the failure happens early, we'll need to wait for the whole run to fail, drive the software until the failure, and then figure out if it really is a failure. For example, if login fails, we'll see what looks like a checkout error because the software will behave differently, asking for a credit card for a guest checkout. A well-designed login test would catch this, looking in the upper-left corner for `Hello, Matthew`, but we might skip that in our haste to get the test done.

It's worth pausing for a moment on that. Say, for example, that login fails for this test because something else went wrong. Someone else may have been testing in the environment with that `userid` and chose to make it inactive. Now, when the test runs, the software shows an error, but you can still click on the homepage and have it load. The test author would need to create an assertion that a particular error, known in advance, did not appear. In practice, it is exceedingly rare for a test author to write *...and make sure this text does not appear on the screen.*

Human testers don't have this problem. They'll observe login failure and report it immediately. They'll notice a screen that doesn't look right and report it. In many cases, it makes sense for the human to model the user journey. For a computer, we can look at the journey like a program. The program consists of steps. Each step has a setup, execution, expectations, and teardowns. Thus, while a human can see the whole journey, testing end-to-end, computers are particularly good at running small, independent pieces, sometimes randomly. When we let the computer drive, we like to keep those small checks quick, lasting 2 to 30 seconds. That leads to the computer and the human doing different things, with different strengths and weaknesses.

To take the computer-driven approach we need some testability hooks. For example, we might want a way to create a logged-in user with a valid session cookie or set up a cart with items in it. This gives us eight different automated test cases.

Of course, each of these test cases is a feature and could likely become 5, 10, 15, or 20 tests. Each starts in a specific position, runs a specific operation, and checks something. Generally, we would add something to each test case, such as a tag with the feature name. A test execution run can run every test with certain tags, all the tests, or some percentage of them, perhaps in a random order. This is very different from doing one test at a time where each test runs the complete user journey.

This will require a fair number of features, from creating an account to finding the session cookie to inject items into the shopping cart to executing an order. Usually, this can be done through an API call, though sometimes a command. The point is to make the individualized setup time for each test one to six seconds.

Someone will say "Hey! That's not how humans use the software."

That is correct. We are not trying to test how humans use the software. We are trying to optimize the performance of the computer for *unattended* test execution, evaluation, and reporting.

> **Objection**
>
> Many of the examples so far have been about e-commerce; I have a fair amount of experience testing these sorts of applications. Social media websites and other websites have many features in common, such as login pages, search functions, and so on. Someone is going to point out that "real" e-commerce systems such as Amazon have tens of thousands of programmers, and that each feature can be tested independently. This kind of test suite I am describing is unlikely to exist, as each team only tests their work, there are five teams for each component, and a hundred more I have not described. I hope the reader will indulge in this oversimplification, which we mostly chose because we are all so familiar with it. The principles still apply to a large company, though the scope is different, and we will likely need the continuous delivery infrastructure described in *Chapter 5*.

Now let's talk about how to do end-to-end customer test tooling.

We'll describe in very generic, high-level terms how to build a test framework. If you take the following advice, you could make something yourself without any bells and whistles relatively easily. Alternatively, use the description to compare to commercial and open source tools to see how they stack up, but more importantly to design your work process.

Eliminating redundancy with domain-specific libraries

A domain in software is a fancy way of saying the specific thing you actually do. In **Quickbooks**, the domain is accounting. On `Realtor.com`, it is real estate. On **Amazon**, it is e-commerce. Within the specific domain, we'll have actions the customers can take. For accounting, that might be creating a new business, creating expenses or income, viewing the accounts that have expenses and income, creating journal entries for those accounts, and running reports such as profit and loss reports. There are also more generic domain elements, such as a user's profile, that are common to most websites. If your work isn't customer-facing, some of those might not apply.

If you've done much test tooling, you may be familiar with the experience that one small change impacts everything. For example, say the application lists your username in the bottom left-hand corner on every page and you build in a little check for every test in which that username is present on the page. Then, one day, someone in product marketing decides to use `Firstname space lastname`. Suddenly, a programmer has to search through hundreds of tests, either doing a search and replace or writing a computer program to change the values.

Using domain-driven development

To prevent this, we build up a series of methods into what is essentially a code library. That way, the change only needs to be made in one place. Make the change, rerun the tests, and then suddenly everything works. To find the methods, we use the actions the user can take, which are remarkably similar to those in doman-driven design (**DDD**). The actions the user can take are methods such as `Search`, `Save Page`, and so on (`https://martinfowler.com/bliki/DomainDrivenDesign.html`). Whereas DDD looks at the business domain, a `Page Object` model (`https://martinfowler.com/bliki/PageObject.html`) looks at what is actually on the screen. With `Page Objects`, the actions the user can take are methods and the data on the fields are the member variables of a class instance. `Page Object` models are a popular way to create an abstraction layer to drive a web page, which is what we are talking about here.

A `Page Object` is a little more object-oriented than our example. For now, we'll just make a login method like this:

```
Login(userID, password);
```

The method would assume a global variable that is the base URL. It would do something like the following:

1. Go to the login page
2. Wait for the `userID` field to appear
3. Type the user ID into the `userID` field
4. Wait for the `Password` field to appear
5. Type the password into the `Password` field

After we implement this code, the user flow could change: Those programmers keep writing new features! For example, password has a new required field: a dropdown to select the type of investment account. We can create an optional parameter that defaults to `Personal banking`, getting the tests to work with minimal changes.

Another way we can eliminate duplication is with object locators.

Eliminating redundancy through object locators

Links have text, buttons have names, and elements have locations within the hierarchy. A typical series of tests might have to find an object 10, 100, or 1,000 different times. One strategy is to try to keep the locators the same all the time. Google's password field is an input field with a name of `passwd` and has been for a very, very long time. Another option is to use an object repository.

With an object repository, we have symbols (such as `LOGIN`) that correspond to text in a specific language. A lookup table allows the code to find what should be displayed (see *Table 4.2*). At runtime, the symbols are loaded into a table, thus effectively looking for the same label we found the last time the code had to change. In C, C++, C#, and Java terms, these are global constants. This can actually help with internationalization, too. Imagine a lookup table such as this one:

Code	English	French	Spanish
LOGIN	Log In	Connexion	iniciar sesión
EDITPROFILE	Username	Editer le profil	Editar perfil
SAVE	Save	Sauver	Salvar

Table 4.2 – An internationalization example for common elements

We can now change the language on the server (or use a VPN to call the service from a different location), change the language of the tests, and run through the tests in a different language! Adding a new language to the tests means adding a new column to the table, which will probably be available from the translation team.

In the preceding example, the texts are links. There are a handful of different tools programmers use to grab an object to type into it. The same tools work to figure out what object to click. That can include the location of an element within the page (the third table row of the `div` inside of the `div` named `UserInfo`), the attributes of the element (the input named `password`), or even an image comparison to a file stored elsewhere. The older record/playback approach and commercial tools tend to use image comparisons more often, perhaps storing them in a document repository. That goes back to the days of Microsoft Windows, where some programming languages created user interfaces that were truly confusing to drive. One method was to look at the screen like a bitmap using **optical character recognition** (**OCR**) software to find the text on the screen, identify a match, and click it. Other software compared bitmaps. As a person creating tests, you would hover over an area of the screen and click to save the expected result. Those approaches are still common today, which we'll discuss later in this chapter in the *The tradeoff between assertion and image recognition* section.

Do you need conditionals, looping structures, and variables?

If statements and for loops confuse the software and cause debugging problems. Our goal is to get to simple, clean tests that read more like a set of instructions you might give to a person. When and if we need looping and conditions, we push them down into a code library.

You might need read-only variables. For example, you might have a function that creates a new userID that is a combination of the feature and some sort of unique identifier. The software can tell you the name of the user that is created, populating the variable. Then, you can check if that userID appears on, say, the profile page. As a second example, you might generate unique text to be searched that will not pollute other search results if the tests run without clearing the database. Likewise, you might insert randomness into the tests in order to find errors. With regard to *Battleship* from *Chapter 2*, this will cause your code to cover more spaces over time. Do this at the beginning by populating variables—just make sure to save them somewhere to reproduce the problem.

What we don't want is variables that change. It makes debugging painful. If you need to loop through a bunch of variables and build things up, save the generated names to a text file, put the file in version control, and load it at runtime -- or embed them as data strings in the file itself. If you absolutely must use looping or conditional, stick it in a code library that has unit tests and make the code very clean.

We'll take these ideas and provide an example that is a test script for a wiki, which is a type of editable set of searchable web pages. Wikipedia is an example of a wiki. The example has a fair bit going on, so we'll unpack it.

Everything with a dollar sign at the front is a variable or a symbol. On execution, the code looks up the symbol in the symbol table. Our only exception is link=, which is a unique-to-HTML locator string. Our four methods are load_timestamp (which creates a local variable), login, create_user, and search. This example will run tests one at a time, so a date_time stamp will be unique; if it is not, you may want to substitute this for some other method to keep things such as search results separated.

Command	Param1	Param2
load_timestamp	$START1	
load_timestamp	$START2	
create_user	$USERID	$PASSWORD
login	$USERID	$PASSWORD

check_element_pres-ent	$LNK_CREATE_NEW_PAGE	
click	$LNK_CREATE_NEW_PAGE	
wait_for_element	$TXT_NEW_PAGE_TITLE	
type	$TXT_NEW_PAGE_TITLE	New Page Heusser $START1
check_element_pres-ent	$TXT_NEW_PAGE_TEXT	
type	$TXT_NEW_PAGE_TEXT	This page contains data at $START2
check_element_pres-ent	$BTN_SAVE	
click	$BTN_SAVE	
search	$START1	link=New Page Heuss-er $START1
expect_num_results	1	
search	$START2	link=New Page Heuss-er $START1
expect_num_results	1	

Table 4.3 – A test to search for partial page name

It's worth noting that the example in *Table 4.3* is not fully optimized. It still mixes in some pure commands to a browser-driver tool. At the same time, a non-technical person could read it to figure out what is going on. We'll talk about making it better once you've digested it.

A more fully optimized test might create a user for every new test automatically and log you in (unless the first line suggests not to). It might grab a date stamp automatically, but you can always not use it. The test automatically logs the user in, creates 10 **generic unique identifiers** (**GUIDs**), and puts them in variables for us.

Here's a more advanced version of the same test:

Command	Param1	Param2	Param3
create_page	New Page Heusser $GUID1	This is a test $GUID2	
create_page	New Page Heusser $GUID3	Lots of data $GUID2	
search	$GUID1	1	link=New Page Heusser $GUID1
search	$GUID2	2	/link=New Page Heusser $GUID1[^A-Za-z0-9]*/ link=New Page Heusser $GUID2/

Table 4.4 – A test to search for partial page name and text

Note we've created the new `create_page` method. Meanwhile, the `search` function has two parameters now. Notice that a non-technical person could read this and likely infer the meaning of the tests. The technical users, at this point, are probably considering how to put all this together, so we'll include one possible interpretation for you.

For example, you might store this test in a spreadsheet and the code in a code library. The tool opens the spreadsheet and performs the first column as a command, with columns B, C, and D as parameters. In Ruby, Python, and Perl, you can execute strings with the `eval()` method. For other programming languages, at the very worst, you might need to use a case statement.

Matt did something similar in Ruby that loops through a file with comma–separated values to find tests:

`https://github.com/heusserm/katas/tree/master/temperature.`

```
def evaluate()
        CSV.foreach(@csvFilename) do |row|
            f = row[0]
                    expected = row[1]
                    comment = row[2]
                    output = run_program(f)
                    output = output.strip
```

```
                        is(output, expected, comment)
            end
      return (@count-@total_ok)
  end
```

In general, we don't recommend that people implement their own frameworks —instead, we present this to you a bit like a computer science student might study the assembly language. Understanding how things can be done behind the scenes can help the way you think about tools, even if you never go backstage. Our point here is not to create a program in Ruby that loops through spreadsheets – it is to consider all of the elements of the model when you pick your framework or write your own.

Some useful exceptions to consider

There are plenty of times you might want loops in your code libraries, such as when you build up test data. Or, you might want to perform a search a dozen times. You might want to put a hundred tags on a page, each one slightly different. We are perfectly fine with variables, conditionals, and loops in your code libraries. We are just two people with some ideas. These are not rules as much as guidelines. If all you need to do is create a dozen tests for a codebase that never changes and you want to cut/paste a bit and keep things all in Python, that's fine. But… if you are only making twelve micro-features that never change, we have to ask, why automate your tests at all?

The final worked example in *Table 4.4* is a good example of what a test might look like, but it does have problems. The implication is that we have created a code library to drive the user interface to create two pages. We want to test search, not test page create. Presumably, we have other tests to check that functionality. If we do things through the user interface, the setup might take four to eight seconds to run. That might be acceptable, but if we build up a more complex page, we'll want to have some way to create the pages extraordinarily quickly, either through a backend (if we run the tests on the server, perhaps a command line to load a file) or through APIs.

In practice, the tactic Matt and Michael would recommend is the Standard Data Seed. With a Standard Data Seed, we have a set of web pages that look similar to those a real customer would use. We then create tests to access all the read-only functionalities, including searches, with this loaded web page. New users all have access to this golden master workspace (unless we turned it off to test permissions) but can write unique information into their own workspaces. Read more about the Standard Data Seed in *Chapter 7*.

The tradeoff between assertion and image recognition

Figure 4.1 shows the **Excelon Development** homepage. It is the way things are "supposed" to look, at least at a certain screen resolution and on a certain browser at the time of writing. Our automation could take a screen capture of the entire screen, but then, when anyone changes anything, the software would log an error.

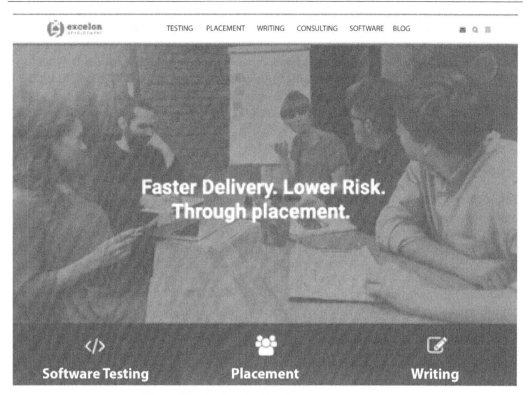

Figure 4.1 – The Excelon Development homepage

So, we could *just* validate the text. But if someone accidentally deletes an image from the server, say the < / > symbol in the bottom-left corner, we'd have an error we missed. Some of our peers have written comparison software to make sure every image is present (or better yet, that the pages referenced by external links still exist), but if someone changes the CSS class to an unreadable font size, the software still won't pick up on it.

Remember the Maxim of test automation: *Even if a test could be automated, the second time it runs, it fails to be test automation and becomes change detection.* The job of programmers is to introduce change! That means the programmer-test-automation-writer needs to decide how deeply to test the results. If they check at a superficial level, such as looking for a specific text to appear on the page, they may miss bugs. If they check too deeply, such as checking the font and location of all the text on the screen, they may get false errors. And there will be problems. Even if the programmers don't introduce change, things such as an upgrade to the operating system, browser, or graphics style of the company, the resizing of the device or browser, and a different-sized monitor (or simulator) can all cause images to differ by a few pixels. Those differences might be obviously non-problems to a human, but all a computer can do is flag them as test failures.

Software can help here. Some new-generation software, such as **Applitools**, can take a picture of a region of the screen and compare it to something that pre-exists. After a test run, a human can review the failures, marking them as correct and promoting them to become the new standard or as a defect. This blending of human and computer, using the best attributes of each, is the kind of thing that we recommend, but be aware that these are all tradeoffs. There is no magic. Even using a tool, the test creator needs to decide how deep the comparisons should be. Deeper comparisons will catch more errors… but also more false failures.

Designing your own system

This chapter began with our concerns with end-to-end test automation, stating that it was slow and brittle and that we had arguably seen more time wasted in the pursuit of tooling than time saved. Indeed, if your team can cleanly separate features and deploy them separately, you might be able to test and deploy each web page separately with humans, with no need for computerized inspection for regression.

If, however, you insist on going down this route, we wanted to provide our very best advice. So, consider the following:

- Abstract the code into functions.
- Abstract away the locators into objects with global names.
- If international, turn the names into a lookup table.
- Create tests that a business-facing customer could read and understand.
- Make them small.
- If you aren't testing it in this test, avoid the user interface for setup. Instead, create shims and hooks to make setup quick.
- Version control the customer-facing test tooling with the code if possible.
- Consider visual comparisons and how the code might change.
- Make tests small (less than thirty seconds) and able to run independently and randomly.
- Tests can be *tagged* along themes, making it possible to run all tests with that tag.

This strategy leads to a system designed for versatility. In the best possible words, when the company develops a mobile application, or whatever is next, you can re-use the tests by rewriting the underlying library they work with. If the code is a one-for-one replacement on functionality, it might just take even less, changing out just the code that manipulates the user interface and the class library.

How you actually implement these ideas is entirely up to you. **SelemiumIDE** gets you about 30% of the way there by itself, running in a browser. Some commercial companies can take this assemble-tests-like-Lego-pieces idea and implement it visually, creating the tests through the record/playback approach. You might decide to try something else entirely. We'll end the chapter introducing a couple of those "and now for something completely different" ideas.

For now, again, you don't have to do it this way. It might be worth reviewing *Chapter 1* to seriously consider and avoid these problems.

Next, we'll combine requirements, testing, and tooling to learn about specification by example, sometimes called executable specification.

Toward specification by example

The early **test-driven development** (**TDD**) literature observed that programmers don't like to do testing; they like to code. So, extreme programming and TDD made testing a programming activity. Around 2003, Dan North was teaching TDD with mixed success. He took the conversation further, stating that programming doesn't even like the word testing, but it does like the idea of defining and verifying behavior. So, he dropped the test in TDD, calling it **Behavior-driven development** (**BDD**). See more on BDD at `https://cucumber.io/docs/bdd/history/`.

More than just changing a word, Dan changed the way the tooling frameworks worked. In his initial article on **BDD**, North suggested that we replace words such as "test" in method names with "should", "expect", or "verify". Dave Astels, who had a conversation about this while the two were consultants at ThoughtWorks (`https://dannorth.net/introducing-bdd/`), created **RSpec** as a Ruby-based framework that spoke the language of *specification*, not *test*. Instead of a *test* in **RSpec**, behaviors are *described*. Where xUnit style tests *assert* things, such as with `AssertFalse`, `AssertTrue`, `AssertEquals`, `AssertNull`, and so on, **RSpec** *expects* things *to be* false, true, equal, null, and so on.

The following are two snippets of Ruby code that do the same thing. One is written in Rspec and the other in `Test::Unit`, a more classic unit test framework for Ruby. The code to be tested is `powerof`, which raises a number to a power:

The Ruby code in `test::Minitest` is as follows:

```
require_relative './lib/powerof.rb'

require 'minitest/autorun'

class TestPowerof < MiniTest::Test

  def test_powerof_positive_integer
    obj = Mathpower.new();
    assert_equal(27, obj.PowerOf(3,3));
  end

  def test_powerof_zero
```

```
      obj = Mathpower.new();
      assert_equal(1, obj.PowerOf(3,0));
   end

   def test_powerof_negative
      obj = Mathpower.new();
      assert_equal(0.25, obj.PowerOf(4,-1));
   end
end
```

The code in RSpec is as follows:

```
require "powerof"

describe Mathpower do
   describe "#positiveexponent" do
      it "multiplies the number by itself exponent times" do
         obj = Mathpower.new();
         expect(obj.PowerOf(3,3)).to eq(27)
      end
   end

   describe "#zeroexponent" do
      it "returns one" do
         obj = Mathpower.new();
         expect(obj.PowerOf(3,0)).to eq(1)
      end
   end

   describe "#negativeexponent" do
      obj = Mathpower.new();
      it "returns one divided by the number" do
         expect(obj.PowerOf(3,0)).to eq(1)
      end
   end
end
```

Programmers sometimes talk about **syntactic sugar**, which is code developed to be just a little bit easier to use. Wrappers and helper classes, iterator classes, and built-in complex objects are syntactic sugar. BDD was something different; it was semantic sugar designed to make programmers think intentionally about what they were building as they built it.

Take another look at the RSpec code. Notice how it seems to explain itself with something closer to words. This is the style that BDD moved toward thinking in terms of concrete examples. In the article in which Dan introduced BDD, he also introduced a language to think about requirements at a higher level. Dan's basic thesis was to make a story a micro-feature. By language, we mean something resembling English that can also be parsed by a computer. Sometimes this is called **Given When Then** or **Gherkin**. Here is his example (`https://dannorth.net/introducing-bdd/`):

Story tile:

*Title: Customer withdraws cash***

As a customer, I want to withdraw cash from an ATM, so that I don't have to wait in line at the bank.

Dan then breaks the single micro-feature down into examples, expressed using a subset of English called given-when-then:

```
Scenario: Account is in credit

Given the account is in credit

And the card is valid

And the dispenser contains cash

When the customer requests cash

Then ensure the account is debited

And ensure cash is dispensed

And ensure the card is returned
```

This Given/When/Then language is called **Gherkin**, and it allows the customer, business analyst, management team, and other non-technical people to express the requirements as a user flow with examples. The problem with Gherkin is that it is incredibly verbose and repetitive. The examples for how to turn Gherkin into code looked awkward and painful to code. Until they didn't.

Imagine taking the code block that we saw earlier and interpreting it, turning the spaces into underscores, and then executing the code. It should be easy enough to do. The Cucumber project came along and did exactly that, generating stub functions called `account_is_in_creedit`, `the_card_is_valid`, and so on for sample Gherkin. Once the programmers implement the stub code, the whole team can move the statements around to create all kinds of new combinations. Cucumber went much further than that, allowing the non-technical staff to enter numbers, and then converting those numbers into parameters. Thus, a non-programmer could take a block of text, cut/paste it, change the numbers, and rerun it in order to create new tests or set an expectation and find out what the software will actually do. Gherkin and Cucumber have other features such as tables, which allow the tester to re-use a test with different values and other forms of looping.

This allows for a new way of working: specification by example.

Specification by example

It's possible to look at the Waterfall model of software as essentially a set of translation activities. First, we get the requirements, which express "why", then we translate them into the specification ("what") and the design ("how"), then we build it, test it, and use it. In each of those steps, we just re-translate the software into the "language" of the person. Account managers speak in requirements, project managers speak in specifications, designers speak in design documents, programmers speak in code, and testers speak in test cases. **Rapid application development** (**RAD**), a fad of the 1990s, asked a really simple question: what if we got everybody in the same room and just built it?

Specification by example took a different approach to the same problem. With specification by example, we express requirements as examples. This could be Gherkin/Cucumber or it could be a tool such as **Fitnesse** (`docs.fitnesse.org/FrontPage`) that provides a more spreadsheet-like function. It might be an actual spreadsheet with a backend program that processes it. The point is that the whole team, including programmers, testers, customers, and designers, goes into a room to create examples of what the software should do before the programmers write the code. One term for this is "acceptance criteria".

The acceptance criteria don't tell us that a piece of work is finished, but we certainly know that if the acceptance criteria won't run, the feature is not done.

One easy way to look at examples is by minimum password strength. We expect that everyone is familiar with the password field that requires a length between this and that and typically must include both upper and lowercase letters, at least one number, and at least one special character. Sometimes the rules are even more complex, with no repeated numbers or numbers in the sequence. We expect most people to have been stuck with this at least once.

Let's assume the requirement is that the password must be 6–10 characters long, have at least one uppercase and one lowercase letter, and have at least one special character.

Scenario	Input	Pass or Fail?
Good	`Password!1`	P
Good - Capital not first letter	`helloDog!2`	P
Too Short	`A@c4`	F
Too Long	`GoodbyeDog$3`	F
No Special Characters	`Delivery4`	F
No Uppers	`deliv@ry4`	F
Good - Starts with special	`$alary123A`	P

Table 4.5 – A password requirement scenario

Imagine creating those as a group, sitting around a table, publishing the list, and making tests that fail before the programmers implement the code. Alistair Cockburn, the organizer of the *Agile Manifesto*, once compared this to knowing the questions in a test before reading the book. Alistair gave this as an example during his keynote speech at the Better Software conference in 2005; Matt was in the audience. That's the benefit of the coding process. On the design side, however, one could see an executive saying "Wait, `password` is a valid password? We need a dictionary feature!" or recognizing how painful a 12-to-14-character password requirement is. Imagine the team coming up with passwords that are pithy and fun only to find they are the wrong length. If the team is involved in creating this, someone may get the idea to use an open source password verification tool. Someone might ask what the actual standards are for passwords, perhaps saying "Can we just find someone else who has the same obligation to customers and use theirs?" or "Let's research what the competition requires. We don't want our system to be insecure and we don't want a password to be a barrier to entry." All of those examples are the sorts of things that just don't get figured out when the requirements are the simple one-sentence we started with. For that matter, after years of doing this, Matt and Michael find that ambiguities in English mean the requirements often mean different things to different people, which is a key source of bugs.

The following are a few things to think about for specification by example:

- **What level should the checks be?**: Writing GUI-level automation against acceptance checks is a great way to slow down performance. For the preceding case, creating an account might be limited to two checks, with the rest pushed down into the object that verifies the password.

- **Acceptance checks are not everything**: Acceptance checks tend to focus on business logic and business flows. They'll often forget to include what to do when the database is down, or race conditions, security issues, performance, multi-user issues - you'll still need to actually test.

- **Intent matters**: It's not uncommon to find out that a micro-feature is completely unusable but all the acceptance checks pass. More important than making a table of examples is the idea of communicating intent. When the feature fails to accomplish its purpose, the programmers need to say, "Yeah, you're right, we're supposed to end up with a logged-in user", not "Well, I guess you need to create another story for that." Examples that can be institutionalized as automated checks are the result, and the goal is a shared understanding of the work.

Specification by example is an attempt to describe what the software should do in simple terms that translate into code. Another approach is to drive the software under test with models, having the test tool transform it into code. Sometimes these are called low-code or no-code test automations.

Low-code and no-code test automation

For the past several years, it has been possible for someone in marketing to log into an app, add a spreadsheet or database, and create real working software. These tools are generally developed for phones and tablets ("mobile first") and grouped into low-code and no-code tools. In practice, they are often things such as a conference website or a college registration website. The more complex ones allow the user to actually build up a set of pages to walk through based on databases. You might use low-code tools to set up a workflow for brokers/agents/sellers/buyers on a home purchase or manage students who are applying to a university. Programmers who use these apps can create working software in an afternoon and a finished product in a week, which might otherwise take a programmer a month.

Since these tools exist for programmers, it seems intuitive that they exist for testers. One easy way to start is by taking a record/playback approach. That is, the tester clicks **Start**, drives the application through its paces, and clicks **Stop**. The tool turns those clicks into symbols, creates its object repository, and creates something more like a spreadsheet of actions, such as the tables we saw previously. The tester may need to add some validation, and *voila*! The test is complete.

It's a simple idea. It's an intuitive idea. We wish it worked; it would be easy.

Sadly, most of the time, there is a fair bit of work required to build up reusable components, deal with test data (we've got a chapter on that), make the test run multiple times, allow the tests to run independently, and all the other things that keep coming up in these chapters on tooling. For today, we'll say that, inevitably, to make sure the software produces the correct output, test tools need to do algorithmic work. Tools need to calculate when three business days in the future is and they need to be aware of leap years. They need to calculate the current date as text in a specific format or create a hundred users, each with a slightly different userID. Combined with the other issues, code test tools have a history of failure. We do have some hope for low-code tools. While we are reluctant to mention commercial tools by name, Matt has done some work with a tool called **Subject-7** that has passed many of the tests he put before it.

For full disclosure, Matt had a commercial relationship with Subect-7 that ended in 2021; it never exceeded 2% of his company's sales for a year.

In our final section on the style of tooling, let's talk about high-code customer-facing test automation.

Batch- and model-driven test automation

In *Chapter 1*, we discussed high-volume test automation. In the case study, we had a system with no user interface. What the system did was take from text files to populate a database. When Matt was at the insurance company, he wrote a number of these **extract, transform, and load** (**ETL**) programs, sometimes just *extract*. For example, say an executive wants a list of all the customers who have Diamond status. There is no user interface or "state", just a data file to look at. The simplest method for independent reporting is likely to have someone else pull the data and compare the answers, combined with a random sampling. Sometimes this approach is called "write it twice." At the insurance company, for example, there was an independent reporting team, and they might write a second database query to answer the question. The results of the queries could be compared and, as long as the text file matched the results, the team could have some confidence the answers were correct.

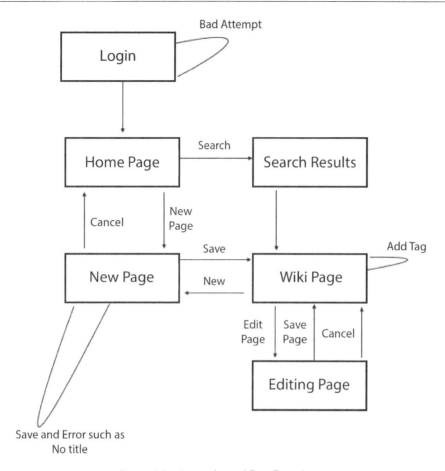

Figure 4.2 – A sample workflow flow chart

That sort of thing seems obvious and unnecessary, yet when you get to calculating complex points programs or insurance coverage, the queries can become very complex. By storing the query in a file, along with the test, it can sometimes be possible to write test automation. When a newer programmer comes along and changes the query, they'll get an error. This is good because it will force them to double-check and have someone adjust the *test* of the query to match.

You may be asking what that has to do with customer-facing testing.

Model-driven test automation applies some of these ideas to user interfaces. Say, for example, we are testing a wiki. A wiki has several different core pieces of functionality: you can create a new page, edit a page, tag a page, comment, search, and so on. However, each functionality only appears in a certain place. You cannot, for example, add a tag from the **New Page** screen, as the page does not exist yet. Once you understand all the options, it is possible to create a model of the application, such as the overly simplified one above. Another term for the model is **finite state machine** (**FSM**).

Once we've defined the FSM, we can create a model for what a wiki workspace looks like (a workspace would contain an array of pages with data) and a model for how to use the tool. Then, we can create a computer program to take random walks through the software.

Here's some pseudo code to do just that. We'll know the state and take action based on where we are. It's written in something close enough to English that both programmers and non-programmers can appreciate it:

```
CONST LOGIN = 1
CONST HOME = 2
CONST SEARCH_RESULTS = 3
CONST PAGE = 4
CONST EDITING_PAGE = 5
CONST NEW_PAGE = 6

Integer state = LOGIN;

Loop from 1 to number of runs using variable count
{
     If (verify_state(state) is false) {
print an error;
      increment the success count;
} else {
Increment the success count;
}
take next step based on state
{
        LOGIN:
            state = take_action_from_login();
        HOME:
            state = take_action_from_home();
        SEARCH_RESULTS:
            state = take_action_home_search_results();
        #...
        # handle all the actions
    }
}
Print the success and failure count;
```

Now let's look at the login handler, which takes one action and figures out where the software "should" be:

```
method take_action_from_login returns integer
#result is what the state should be
{
     action = generate_a_random_number(from 1 to 4)
     take next step based on action
     {
          1:  #This will be successfully log in
               login(good_username,good_password);
               return HOME;
          2:  #Leave username and pwd blank
               login();
               assert_error("Sorry, username cannot be blank);
               Return LOGIN;
          3:  #Get username wrong
               bad_username = generate_random_good_password();
               login(bad_username,good_password);
               assert_error("Sorry, username or password is
incorrect");
               return LOGIN;
          4:  #Get password wrong
               bad_password = generate_random_bad_password();
               login(good_username,bad_password);
               assert_error("Sorry, username or password is
incorrect");
               return LOGIN;
     }
}
```

Hopefully, those two examples give you a flavor of how this could be built. Taking random walks through the software for hours, days, or weeks combined with random inputs and outputs could generate a massive amount of coverage for little cost. Described correctly, this kind of work can even be customer-facing. Harry Robinson probably did the most approachable work in this area.

While model-driven testing solves a large number of important problems via coverage and testing, it does seem to have a slow adoption curve. Figuring out how to use it requires a different approach and a different way of thinking. Many people and organizations seem to be reluctant to use it, and they often only do so after a traditional approach. If the big bugs are hammered out in a wiki before trying a model-driven approach, then the model-driven approach will have more marginal value by definition.

This chapter is completely wrong

If you took a stopwatch and looked at what a skilled tester does, actually executing the test is only a small portion of the job. As mentioned previously, test execution automation doesn't include test design. Test design, however, can be assisted with tools. The consultant Michael Bolton recently wrote about ways to automate parts of the test design process (`https://developsense.com/blog/2023/01/test-tools`).

In test design, we use tools to help us achieve the following:

- Produce test data [tools like spreadsheets (why are some testers so eager to diss Excel? It's like a Swiss Army knife for testing); state-model generators; Monte Carlo simulations; random number generators].

- Obfuscate or cleanse production data for privacy reasons (data shufflers; name replacers), generate interesting combinations of parameters (all-pairs or combinatorial data generators), and generate flows through the product that cover specific conditions (state-model or flow-model path generators).

- Generate interesting combinations of parameters (all-pairs or combinatorial data generators)

- Generate flows through the product

- Visualize elements of the product (mind-mapping tools, diagramming tools)

Bolton went on to make four more similar lists for product interaction, evaluating the product, recording and reporting, and managing the testing workflow. Bolton argues that there is much more to test tooling than having the software load a page, type some things, click something, wait for a page to load, and compare with some expected result. We strongly agree. Michael Bolton makes some important points, which, arguably, makes this chapter incorrect. At least, there is a danger that this chapter pushes the reader in the wrong direction, focusing on the accident (the automation tool and the execution) instead of the essence and finding defects and other information that matters and reporting them well.

Our goal with this chapter was to give you real advice on how to structure effective test tools. Sadly, most of the projects we have seen have been littered with the bodies of ineffective tools, are broken, or are no longer working. Too often, the lesson learned is that "[last tool] or [last tester] was terrible, everything will be great now with [new tool]." So, we fenced in the top and bottom of this chapter with a warning. Beyond that, remember that this book does have a few hundred pages, and this chapter a few dozen.

To borrow a line from the fictional General E.Z. Black in the novel *The Captains*, "*If you can keep that in mind, we're sure you'll get along just fine.*"

Summary

This chapter introduced customer-facing test tooling. After a warning about the failure rate of such approaches, we dove in, explaining the patterns that make good user interface test tooling, how to move toward specification by example, and model-driven and low-code test tooling approaches. This should have given you several patterns for test tooling, along with the ability to analyze your existing software and select the best tooling approach: including no tooling at all.

So far, we've only talked about testing the features of the software. Type in some values and make sure you see a specific result. That doesn't deal with the issue of multiple simultaneous users, foreign languages, the speed of the results, security, and so on. We view all of these as risks to the product, which may be within the scope of this book. In *Chapter 5*, we talk about these more specialized forms of software testing.

5

Specialized Testing

Often, software testing emphasizes the *fit-for-use* scenario, and rightly so. However, the fit for use for one person is far different than the fit for use for dozens, hundreds, or even millions of simultaneous users. Also, there are situations where individuals will not be able to use the software as originally designed or intended. This can be due to situational or environmental reasons, or it could be due to a disability the user has. Not everyone speaks the same language or uses the same alphabet. Some software requires rigorous vetting and certification before it can be released due to its sensitive or life-and-death nature. Additionally, there are bad actors out in the world who intentionally look to subvert software and make it into a tool for scams and other criminal activity. To that end, it is important to look at and consider a variety of specialty areas within testing.

In this chapter, we'll explore some of the most important and widely used types of specialized testing:

- Performance and load testing
- Security testing
- Accessibility testing
- Internationalization and localization
- Continuous integration
- Regulated testing

Each of these areas has its unique challenges, methodologies, and tools. So, let's get into it.

Technical requirements

There are a variety of applications and tools that can be used to help with specialized testing. Each area will have unique requirements. Load testing will use JMeter, which can be retrieved at `https://jmeter.apache.org/download_jmeter.cgi`.

Understanding load and performance testing

I'm grouping these two items here because they are related to each other, but they are not the same thing.

Load testing is a type of performance testing, in that we assess the behavior of an application under normal conditions and then with increased loads of data. The purpose of load testing is that we can identify how well an application or system will perform when a high volume of users (or transactions) interacts with the system. The main goal is that the system does not crash, slow down, or cause the users to not be able to complete their objectives. Load testing helps identify performance bottlenecks, slow response times, system crashes, and more that occur under high user loads. Load testing is important for capacity planning, scalability, and system stability.

Performance testing, on the other hand, goes well beyond load testing to determine how well a system performs. It includes looking at various pieces of user activity and different types of system configurations. Performance testing includes load testing as well as other types of testing, such as **stress** (testing the system's ability to handle extreme loads), as well as **endurance** and **soak** (testing the system's ability to perform over an extended period). Performance testing identifies performance issues that could affect the system's functionality or user experience and helps highlight areas where we can optimize the system's performance.

Getting to know the basics of load testing

Load testing requires creating realistic test scenarios that simulate the expected usage of the application or system. A beginning tester should know how to define user actions, user data, and test data for a load test scenario.

In addition, we want to create load models. These are made so that we can allocate a certain number of users or transactions to run. There are variations to load models but three common ones are as follows:

- **Step-up**: This involves gradually increasing the user load on a system over time. This is done by starting with a small number of simulated users and gradually adding more users until the desired level of load is reached. The goal of step-up load testing is to identify the maximum user load that the system can handle before performance issues occur.

- **Step-down**: This involves gradually reducing the user load on a system over time. This is done by starting with a high level of user load and gradually reducing the number of simulated users until the system is back to a normal or baseline level of load. The goal of step-down load testing is to identify how the system performs when the load is reduced and to ensure that it can handle sudden decreases in user load without issues.

- **Constant load**: This involves maintaining a constant level of user load on the system over an extended period. This is done by simulating a specific number of users and maintaining that level of load for a set duration. The goal of constant load testing is to evaluate how the system performs under sustained user loads and to identify any performance issues that may occur over time.

Let's take a look at some common load-testing tools and see how we might put some of them to work in practice.

Setting up a load test

A variety of tools can be used for load testing. Here's a short list:

- **Apache JMeter**: A popular open source tool that is widely used for load-testing web applications
- **Gatling**: Another open source load testing tool that is popular among developers and testers.
- **Locust**: A Python-based open source tool that is easy to use and highly scalable
- **Taurus**: An open source tool that provides a simple way to create and execute load tests
- **k6**: An open source tool that is designed to be developer-friendly and highly scalable

Since there are so many options and only so much space, I'm going to focus on JMeter. Download JMeter and install it on your system of choice (Mac, Linux, or Windows). Once you've downloaded it, follow these steps:

1. Open JMeter and create a new test plan by selecting **File | New** from the **Menu** bar. Right-click on **Test Plan** and select **Add | Threads (Users) | Thread Group** to add a new **Thread Group**:

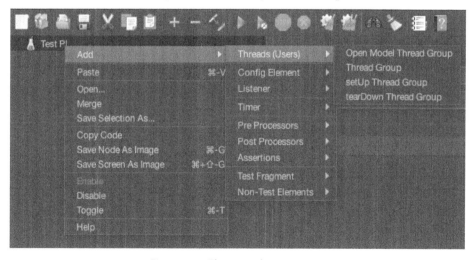

Figure 5.1 – The menu bar in JMeter

2. In the **Thread Group** panel, set **Number of Threads (users)**, **Ramp-up period** (time taken to start all threads), and **Loop count** (number of times to execute the test plan):

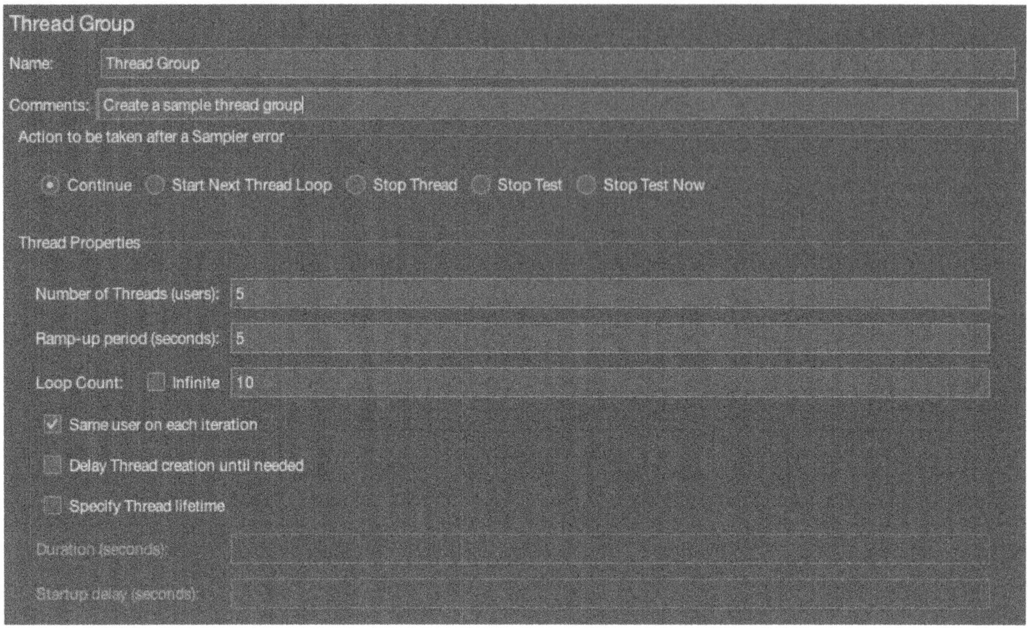

Figure 5.2 – Setting up a Thread Group in JMeter

3. Right-click on this **Thread Group** and select **Add | Sampler | HTTP Request** to add an HTTP Request sampler.

    In the **HTTP Request** panel, enter the URL of the website or web application that you want to test.

4. You can also configure the HTTP Request sampler with additional settings, such as parameters, HTTP method, headers, and body data.

5. Right-click on **Thread Group** and select **Add | Listener | View Results Tree** to add a listener that will display the test results.

6. Start the test by clicking the **Start** button or selecting **Run | Start** from the **Menu** bar.

7. JMeter will start sending requests to the specified URL and display the test results in the **View Results Tree** listener:

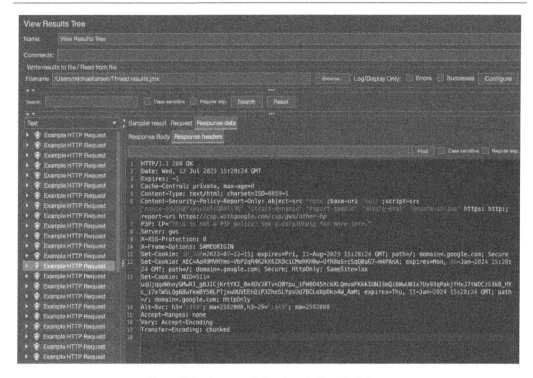

Figure 5.3 – Output of View Results Tree in JMeter

8. Analyze the test results to determine the performance of your website or web application under load.

From here, you can explore additional features and settings in JMeter to create more complex and realistic load tests.

Again, while load testing is a subset of performance testing, load testing generates several useful performance metrics, such as response time, overall throughput, and error rate. By examining these metrics, we can identify potential bottlenecks.

Load testing can be practiced on any system but for it to be useful, the test system needs to accurately replicate what is in production.

Caveat

Load testing is an aggressive form of testing and traffic generation. It can have a huge effect not just on the system under test, but also on the network it is running on and the overall performance of that network for all of its users. Do not just randomly select a site and throw traffic at it. This could be classified as a **Denial-of-Service** (**DoS**) attack (more on that in the *Exploring security testing* section) and it could potentially result in a visit by law enforcement.

In other words, *BE CAREFUL WITH THIS BECAUSE HERE BE DRAGONS!*

Some websites have been set up specifically to allow for load testing practice. These sites are often used for educational purposes. One of the most well-known is `http://httpbin.org`.

This is an open source project that allows users to send HTTP requests and inspect the responses. You can use JMeter to send requests to `httpbin.org` and analyze the responses, practicing various aspects of configuring JMeter. Since it's designed for this purpose, you won't be disrupting any real-world services or users. Another site that could be used for this is `https://blazedemo.com/`. This is another site that has been set up to allow users to practice setting up their tools and scripts so that they can test examples without this having an impact on external users.

Exploring security testing

If you are looking for a place where testing must be on the cutting edge of what's happening, look no further than security testing. Threats to digital systems have never been so pervasive. Hackers and criminals, scam artists, and phishers are getting more sophisticated every day. To that end, organizations are actively looking for people able to not just test against threats but to look ahead and help find ways to harden systems and protect organizations. If that sounds exciting, security testing may be right up your alley.

Security testing, put simply, is the process of identifying and mitigating potential security risks in a software application or system.

Security concepts

If we want to get involved in security testing, it's important to be aware of the following aspects:

- **Confidentiality**: The prevention of disclosing information. Confidentiality testing helps to confirm that sensitive information such as user credentials, personal data, and financial information is only accessible by authorized users.

- **Integrity**: Protection of information from unauthorized changes. Integrity testing focuses on making sure the accuracy, consistency, and completeness of data are not altered in any way by unauthorized users.

- **Availability**: Authorized users have access to the system and its data when required. Availability helps confirm that the system is operational and that users can access it without any barriers.

- **Penetration testing**: This involves simulating a real-world attack on a system to identify potential vulnerabilities. The goal is to identify weaknesses that could be exploited by hackers.

- **Vulnerability scanning**: This involves performing automated scans of a system to identify potential vulnerabilities. Vulnerability scanning tools scan the system for known vulnerabilities, misconfigurations, and weaknesses, and then present a report to show which known attack areas our applications are vulnerable.

- **Security auditing**: This is a process that reviews the system's configuration, design, and code to identify potential risks. Security auditing helps identify risks and provide recommendations to mitigate them.

- **Threat modeling**: Here, we identify potential threats to a system and assess their impact. We want to identify potential security risks and provide recommendations to mitigate them. Threat modeling is typically done in the design phase of the software development life cycle.

There are a lot of ways that a *bad actor* can interact with our systems, so let's look at some security vulnerabilities that we may find ourselves dealing with.

Checking out common security vulnerabilities

There are many ways that a hacker or bad actor could attempt to exploit or compromise our systems. Some key areas are as follows:

- **Malware**: Malicious software that is designed to damage a computer system or network. Malware can include **viruses**, **Trojan horses**, **spyware**, and **ransomware**.

- **DoS attacks**: An attempt to overwhelm a system's resources, making it unavailable to users. DoS attacks can cause system downtime, data loss, and financial losses.

- **Phishing attacks**: Phishing is a form of social engineering that tricks users into divulging sensitive information such as usernames, passwords, and financial information. Phishing attacks can lead to identity theft, financial fraud, and data breaches.

- **Injection attacks**: These exploit vulnerabilities in software that allow untrusted or unauthorized user input. They allow attackers to execute malicious code on systems or access sensitive data.

- **Unauthorized access**: This refers to an attacker gaining access to a system or network without proper authorization, which can lead to data theft, data loss, and system damage.

- **Insider threats**: Not all bad actors are on the outside. Some attacks can come from inside an organization. Employees, contractors, or partners may have authorized access to a system and get access to things they should not be privy to.

These examples merely scratch the surface of the possible areas that a *bad actor* may choose to try to exploit our systems. It's always a good idea to keep these areas in mind. Next, let's look at ways we can keep informed about security threats.

Learning about industry standards

Several organizations actively publish and discuss security threats and how to mitigate them. Here are a couple worth learning more about:

- **Open Web Application Security Project** (**OWASP**): OWASP is a not-for-profit organization focused on improving the security of software. OWASP provides tools, guidelines, and processes to help develop software more securely. In particular, OWASP publishes a list of the *Top 10 Web Application Security Risks* (`https://owasp.org/www-project-top-ten/`), which is widely used as a reference for security testing.

- **National Institute of Standards and Technology** (**NIST**): A United States government agency that develops and promotes technology, standards, and processes for a wide range of fields, including cybersecurity. NIST publishes a wide range of guidelines, frameworks, and standards related to cybersecurity, including the Cybersecurity Framework (`https://www.nist.gov/cyberframework`).

By understanding these standards, testers can improve their testing methods, and aim to address the most critical risks. Cybersecurity threats are constantly evolving, and these sites are regularly updated to reflect the latest recommendations and guidelines.

Investigating some security testing tools

There are numerous tools available that can help with developing tests and automating the process of finding vulnerabilities in software. To that end, here are a few well-known and freely available examples:

- **Burp Suite**: This tool helps automate the process of testing for vulnerabilities in web applications. It includes a proxy server, scanner, and web spider/crawler. Each of these can help identify security vulnerabilities such as injection flaws, **cross-site scripting** (**XSS**), and broken authentication and session management. There is a Community Edition as well as a Paid License version.

- **Metasploit**: This is an open source framework that's used for developing and executing exploits against software vulnerabilities. It includes a range of tools, including a network discovery module, a vulnerability scanner, and a payload generator, which can be used to identify vulnerabilities in a system or network.

- **Kali Linux**: This is a Debian-based Linux distribution that's designed for penetration testing and digital forensics. To be clear, this is more than just an application – it is an entire Linux distribution/operating system. It includes Metasploit and Burp Suite, as well as other tools such as Nmap, Wireshark, and John the Ripper.

> **Caveat**
>
> Much like the load testing tools mentioned previously, these tools can be exceptionally helpful in the hands of experienced users and dangerous in the hands of inexperienced users. It is always wise to set up a sandbox system inside of a virtual machine or some other isolated network to learn how to use these tools. Do not apply these tools to production systems unless you are fully aware of what you are doing.

Security testing is a broad and interesting field and, as stated previously, the potential to play with fire is great. Again, if dealing with a dynamic and ever-changing landscape interests you, security testing may be right up your alley. Next, let's have a look at accessibility, an area that affects a large percentage of people. Technically, it will be an issue for all of us if we are lucky to live long enough.

Delving into accessibility testing

There are many users of the various applications we create and deploy that, through no fault of their own, will struggle to use it as intended. Often, this is because of a physical disability such as blindness, being deaf, cerebral palsy, or dyslexia. Each of these represents an example of a particular area of disability (visual, auditory, mobility, and cognitive). Roughly one in five people have some form of a primary (meaning consistent) disability. By not creating ways for people with disabilities to access and use our systems effectively, we are locking 20% of our potential customers out of our applications. To put this into perspective, if we are lucky to live long enough, every one of us will experience at least one primary disability, if not multiple disabilities. To that end, accessibility is a very worthwhile area of testing and advocacy.

What is accessibility?

Accessibility refers to the *intentional* design of products, devices, services, vehicles, or environments in a way that enables people with disabilities to use them effectively. It encompasses the concept of accessible design and the practice of accessible development, which aim to provide both *direct access* (meaning unassisted access) and *indirect access* by ensuring compatibility with assistive technologies, such as computer screen readers. In simpler terms, accessibility is about creating inclusive experiences that empower individuals with disabilities to fully engage with and benefit from the designed solutions.

Put simply, accessibility is making sure that people with disabilities have the ways and means to gain access to and use our products. Typically, this means using methods that will allow them to use our services and our applications in ways that normative users may not need to. Examples include images on pages, which would require a description for a non-sighted user. Closed captioning is important for people with auditory disabilities so that they can read what they cannot hear, while making it possible to provide high-contrast layouts can help those with low vision or color blindness differentiate between text and backgrounds.

Advocating for accessibility

In many ways, accessibility requires more than just testing ability. It also involves taking the time and making the effort to advocate for people who often cannot speak for themselves. As an accessibility tester, I often have to challenge the expectations and methods of software development teams and encourage them to see beyond just a basic level of compliance.

Here are some ways to be an advocate for accessibility:

- Learn about different disabilities, accessibility standards, and laws related to accessibility. Familiarize yourself with assistive technologies that can help people with disabilities access information and communication.

- When you encounter barriers to accessibility, speak up and share your concerns with the relevant person or organization. Explain the importance of accessibility and suggest possible solutions.

- Work with others who share your passion for accessibility. Join advocacy groups or connect with disability organizations in your community.

- Be an *#A11y*; this is a common hashtag that is used to discuss and advocate for accessibility. **A11y** is shorthand for **accessibility**, and the 11 represents the letters between the "a" and the "y." This also associates the A11y acronym with the word *ally*. As an ally, you can support people with disabilities by amplifying their voices and advocating for their rights. Listen to their experiences and needs. Amplify their messages.

- Encourage designers and developers to prioritize accessibility in their work. Make sure that accessibility is considered in all aspects of design, including websites, apps, and physical spaces.

There is also a related discipline called *inclusive design* that goes hand in hand with accessibility. Let's take a closer look.

Investigating the distinctions between accessibility and inclusive design

Accessibility and inclusive design are related concepts, but they have different focuses and approaches. Accessibility refers to designing products, services, and environments *to ensure that people with disabilities can use them*. It aims to remove barriers that prevent people with disabilities from accessing information, communication, and physical spaces. More to the point, accessibility focuses on providing the ability to interact with a person's assistive devices, such as screen readers, dictation programs, closed captioning, joysticks, blow tubes, and so on because these users require these devices to access information and interact with sites.

Inclusive design, on the other hand, refers to designing products, services, and environments that can be used by everyone, *regardless of their abilities or disabilities*. It aims to create products and environments that are usable, understandable, and enjoyable by the widest possible range of people. Inclusive design often involves involving people with diverse backgrounds and experiences in the design process to ensure that their needs and perspectives are considered.

Learning about the WCAG standard

Most countries have laws and standards relating to accessibility and the ability of people with disabilities to gain access to services. The **Americans with Disabilities Act** (**ADA**) in the United States and the **Accessibility for Ontarians with Disabilities Act** (**AODA**) in Ontario, Canada, are examples that require software products to be accessible. While it's important to understand the laws that apply to each country, rather than have to focus on each of the different countries' rules, there is a standard that acts as a global repository that most countries look to. That standard is the **Web Content Accessibility Guidelines** (**WCAG**), for which the guidelines can be found at `https://www.w3.org/TR/WCAG21/`.

WCAG provides a set of standards and guidelines for ensuring that web content, including software products, is accessible to people with disabilities. By following these guidelines, software testers can help ensure that their products are usable by the widest possible audience, including people who have visual, auditory, motor, or cognitive disabilities.

By testing for accessibility and following the WCAG guidelines, software testers can help create a more inclusive and equitable digital world.

Investigating some accessibility testing tools

There are a variety of free or inexpensive tools available that can help people test for accessibility in software products. Here are a few examples:

- **WebAIM's WAVE**: This is a free online tool that checks web pages for accessibility issues based on the WCAG standard. It provides detailed information about the issues and suggestions for how to fix them.

- **aXe**: aXe is a free accessibility testing tool from Deque Systems that can be used on web pages, mobile apps, and other software products. It provides detailed information about accessibility issues and how to fix them. It runs in the Development Tools section of most browsers.

- **Non-Visual Desktop Access** (**NVDA**): This is a free screen reader for Windows that can be used to test the accessibility of software products. It allows users to navigate websites and software using only the keyboard or a braille display. There are other free versions available for other operating systems. **VoiceOver** is built into macOS.

- **Color Contrast Analyzer**: This is a free desktop tool that checks the color contrast of text and background elements on a web page or software product. It helps ensure that text is readable for people with different levels of visual acuity.

- **AccessLint**: AccessLint is a free tool that integrates with GitHub and checks pull requests for accessibility issues. It provides detailed information about the issues and suggestions for how to fix them.

An important thing to remember when testing and advocating for accessibility is that there are standards that may work well for one group of people but perhaps not as well for others. It is entirely possible to make a site completely WCAG compliant at the highest levels and still be difficult to use for some people. Often, there is a judgment call that goes into what is compliant and what is not. In some cases, we must be thorough and complete, whereas in others, we must strike a balance so that the broadest group of people can use their assistive technology effectively. If advocating for and speaking up for people who struggle to use the systems as designed is appealing to you, accessibility is an area of testing that is always looking for people to get in and participate.

Now that we have a handle on accessibility and ensuring those with disabilities can work with our applications, we also want to make sure that people all over the world can use them as well. To that end, let's take a look at internationalization and localization.

Internationalization and localization

Do you ever wonder how on-the-fly translations work... or maybe don't? Do you wonder if the menu items you have worked so hard on the design for will appear correctly if they are translated into Korean, Thai, or Arabic? If questions like this keep you up at night, there may be an internationalization or localization testing role in your future. Seriously, though, what are these two areas and what do they mean?

Internationalization (often abbreviated as *i18n*) refers to the process of designing software products so that they can be adapted to different languages, cultures, and regions. This involves ensuring that the software can handle different character sets, date and time formats, currency symbols, and other cultural conventions. Essentially, internationalization involves making the software "global-ready."

Localization (often abbreviated as *l10n*) refers to the process of adapting software products for a *specific* language, culture, or region. This involves translating the user interface, documentation, and other content into the target language, as well as adapting the software to comply with local conventions and regulations. Essentially, localization involves making the software "locale-ready."

Preparing for internationalization and localization

Before you can test for either internationalization or localization, you need to understand the specific requirements for the target language, culture, or region. This may involve researching the target audience and their preferences, as well as understanding any local regulations or standards:

- **Character encoding**: Different languages use different character sets, and it's important to ensure that the software can handle them all. Test for character encoding by entering text in different languages and scripts, ensuring that the software displays and stores the text correctly. Confirm that characters fit inside their respective containers and spaces.

- **Date and time formats**: Different countries and regions use different date and time formats. Confirm that the software can display and store them correctly.

- **Number and currency formats**: Check the various symbols that are used to denote currencies in different countries. Ensure that the software can display and store them correctly. If currency conversion is part of the process, make sure the numbers add up.

- **Bi-directional languages**: Some languages, such as Arabic and Hebrew, are written from right to left. Test with bi-directional languages to ensure the software can handle them correctly.

This is a lot of things to keep track of. Let's look at some tools that can help us do exactly that.

Investigating tools for internationalization and localization

For both internationalization and localization, there are a variety of areas that require keeping track of and identifying if they are displaying correctly. Here are some tools that help achieve this:

- **Google Translate**: For quickly examining characters and translating key phrases and examples.

- **UnicodeChecker**: For checking the Unicode support of your software application.

- **BabelEdit**: A translation and localization tool that can help you manage and edit translations for your software. A license will cost about $40/year but you can try a free version for 7 days.

- **Apache OpenOffice**: An open source office suite that supports a wide variety of languages and can be used to test internationalization and localization.

- **GNU gettext**: A software localization tool that can help you extract translatable strings from your software and manage translations.

In the next section, we are going to look at an area where software testers can often provide a lot of benefits – that is, the process of building and deploying software. Let's have a look at **continuous integration** (**CI**) and the options we have available to implement and interact with it.

CI

CI is a software development practice that allows software developers and software development teams to check their code into a shared repository, automatically building and running tests on both existing code and code changes. This helps ensure that changes do not introduce new issues. Ideally, the tests in the CI system will run and if they all pass, the software will be ready to be deployed.

CI and the pipeline

When discussing CI, the concept of a **pipeline** is helpful to visualize the steps. Think of a pipeline in the literal sense. You might have to connect a variety of pipes in a plumbing fixture to get water to go where it needs to. The pipeline in a CI context is when we stage and string together a variety of scripts and processes to move along between the steps necessary to get from code check-in to delivery of software to a destination platform(s).

The typical stages in a CI pipeline are as follows:

- **Build**: Compiles the code and creates the necessary executables and packages needed to run effectively

- **Test**: Automated tests are run to confirm that code changes are working correctly and have not introduced regressions into existing code

- **Integration**: Merges our changes and tests those changes against the rest of the code base

- **Deployment**: Pushes the changes to a testing, staging, or production environment

Ideally, in a pipeline application, each step is run automatically. If, at any point in the process, an error is detected, the pipeline will stop and report the failure.

Getting involved with build management as a tester

As a software tester, CI is a great place to become involved in the overall build process and the scripts and steps necessary to create a successful release. I have worked on teams where I was the person who managed the CI server, application, and scripts.

CI can be as simple as an application running on a single system, or it can be set up in a cluster with multiple machines and tests running in parallel to save time.

The biggest benefit of CI is that you can automate a set of important tests and reduce the time to test your code changes. This does not guarantee that the code is bug-free but it does help you identify the critical areas you must be sure are in working order to allow a release to go out the door.

Investigating CI tools

There are a variety of CI tools that can be set up and experimented with. How they are set up will depend on the environment that you have and how software is deployed at our organizations. Here are a few examples:

- **Jenkins**: Jenkins is a popular open source CI tool that's available for a variety of platforms. It can be set up to run independently or in a client-server arrangement where multiple guest systems can be spun up and managed to run tests in parallel. You can download Jenkins from `https://www.jenkins.io/`. Additionally, a popular plugin for Jenkins is **Blue Ocean**, which is available directly through Jenkins.

- **CircleCI**: A cloud-based CI tool that offers a free trial (`https://circleci.com/`).

- **Travis CI**: A cloud-based CI tool that offers free accounts as well as subscription plans (`https://travis-ci.com/`).

- **GitLab CI/CD**: An open source CI/CD tool that is integrated with GitLab, a popular Git repository management platform (`https://about.gitlab.com/`).

CI is an area where many testers can add value, learn about software development, and be key contributors to the process. By regularly integrating code updates, automatically running tests on those code changes, and managing the deployment process, software testers can actively be involved and help make the processes work better, often leading to development work if desired.

Regulated testing

In many industries, a bug may be an inconvenience or perhaps delay something a user wants to do. Still, the results of such a bug would hardly be considered life and death. In some industries, however, death could be the consequence if a bug slips through. Think of the software that controls jet aircraft or marine shipping vessels. Think of medical devices. In financial software, if a bug were to be introduced, this could have catastrophic financial implications for an organization. These are areas where a much higher standard is applied and thus, regulations are in place to ensure that these organizations are offering the safest possible product with a minimal chance of failure.

Navigating regulatory requirements

Regulatory requirements typically spell out the types of testing needed, the documentation that must be written and followed, and the exact steps that must be followed to comply. The US **Food and Drug Administration (FDA)** uses **IEC 62304** (`https://www.iso.org/standard/38421.html`), which defines the life cycle requirements for medical device software.

As a software tester, it may be required that you obtain specialized training and certifications. While it would be difficult to anticipate every option, some of the more common certifications might include the following:

- **Certified Software Tester (CSTE)**: This certification is provided by the **Quality Assurance Institute (QAI)** and is specifically developed to certify software testers working in regulated industries

- **Certified Software Quality Engineer (CSQE)**: This certification is provided by the **American Society for Quality (ASQ)** and is specifically designed to cover the knowledge and skills of software testers and quality engineers working in regulated fields

Research the requirements necessary for the industry of interest. Likewise, understand which certifications may be required and also recognized by employers in the regulated field you will be working in.

Regulated testing is a critical part of the software development process in certain industries. Make no mistake – errors or bugs in these industries could mark the difference between life and death.

Summary

In this chapter, we provided a high-level survey of other testing disciplines that a software tester could specialize in. Frankly, each of these areas is deserving of their own chapters and conceivably entire books could be written on each (and have been). There are many areas in which software testers can branch out and explore their interests, even if it's just to gain a little bit of familiarity with each. How far we go down each rabbit hole is entirely up to us.

In the next chapter, we will take a look at the various ancillary skills that a tester will need to know to be effective. This includes making bug reports, developing and defending test plans, writing and understanding test cases, making projections, and, yes, working with and understanding metrics as they relate to testing.

6

Testing Related Skills

So far, this book has focused on test design and execution. Those things are important, but it misses out on some important things, such as how to recognize a problem. Once we understand there is a problem, we need to communicate it as a problem to someone else in a way that stands up to scrutiny. You can argue that finding bugs and communicating why they need to be fixed is these are simple, even obvious… yet if that is true, why is so much software so buggy?

To be effective, the testing activity needs to find risks to the project and communicate them in ways that make change happen. Those things will vary depending on many factors, such as the company's culture, the people receiving the news, the amount of pressure they are under, and so on. That means there is no "one true way" to communicate. Instead, communication is a skill. You'll have several tricks in your toolbox, then try more of what works. In this chapter, our goal is to fill up your toolbox and give you a few examples of how to implement it.

To do that, this chapter will cover the following topics:

- Recognizing bugs – how to find them
- Communicating problems to stakeholders
- Planning and documenting the work
- Measuring work, progress, and work effectiveness – metrics
- Influencing change

Technical requirements

This chapter will refer to the idea of tracking our work and collecting information about that work. How you do that, we don't care. A particularly high-functioning team with high trust might just put sticky notes on a board, use a marker, and use running, tested features as the primary measure of progress. At the time of writing, it is far more common to use a tool such as Jira, Trello, or Microsoft Teams to track work and then perhaps export the data into a spreadsheet to gather the metrics. This book will provide solutions for both extremes and most people in the middle. Having access to these tools so that you can gather the data yourself will allow you to internalize the lessons of this chapter, and it is likely to provide key information to decision-makers. Having access to those tools and reviewing them could help demonstrate the validity of our ideas. On the other hand, a lack of these tools may help you realize what you are missing.

A few years ago, Matt provided some training to a team that reported bugs and no one seemed to care. The testers were in a different location than the developers, so the bugs were tracked in a database that no one was looking at. In this software system, it was possible to sign up, enter an invalid credit card number, and get access to the service. You could simply make up a credit card number and get access. The testers presumed that maybe the service was soft-launched to friends and perhaps credit card processing was not "hooked up" yet – they guessed. This story seems far-fetched, yet micro versions of this problem are incredibly common in software.

The team got things half right – they found the bugs. That is the start of this chapter. The second half, which involves setting expectations, communicating, and creating feedback that inspires action, is something they missed.

Our goal with this chapter is to provide you with the tools to avoid ever being in this trap.

Finding bugs

The common way of thinking about testing, or perhaps the loudest, leftover from the previous century, was to "plan the work and work the plan." People doing testing would run through a sequence of steps, and the end would have an "expected result." If those two don't match, file a bug. Seems pretty easy, right?

Except it never seemed to work out that way.

Instead, the person doing the work would just try to follow the steps, and they wouldn't work. Report the bug, wait for a new build, then try to recreate where they were in the procedure. We wrote "seemed" earlier because that was the past. Today, many of our customers have broad general success on the first pass with their software. The problem is that idea of an "expected result." As we mentioned in *Chapter 1*, every documented test with an expected result has a hidden second assertion "...and nothing else odd happened." If you have any of these sorts of step-step-step-check documented tests along with a bug tracker, you can compare them to see how many bugs that emerge come from the expected result. In our experience, it is precious few.

So, where do bugs come from? By this, we mean, how do they reach our awareness?

Someone notices something that seems wrong to them.

Most of the time, most people don't make an intentional study of how problems are noticed. If a word is spelled incorrectly, the person likely has a mental model of what the correct spelling is. "We know it's wrong," they'll say. Once we dig into more advanced user interface issues, such as how to handle line breaks with no spaces, resizing windows, or the results of complex equations, such as the algorithm to recommend books or movies, the exact process of how you figure out what is "wrong" become more important. Instead of a single right and wrong, we tend to look for a series of imperfect ways to identify a problem. The term we'll use for that is **Oracle** – not the database, but more like the ancient Greek soothsayers who would give wisdom. Oracles are not requirements, and they might not be perfect. Pasting this book into a spell checker, we might use several terms such as DevSecOps that trip the spell checker, yet they are correct. Still, spell check can be a helpful way to find problems.

Oracles in software testing

Requirements: The focus and default assumption of the overwhelming majority of writing about testing is the requirements. These can be the shared mental model of the team members, written down in a document, or even encased as examples to be automated. One place often overlooked for test ideas is the documents themselves. Often, they will have tables with features separate; what happens if you use different features at the same time? For example, the user interface allowed Matt to turn up the heat and the air conditioning at the same time in his 1993 Ford Escort, though this was not good for either system.

Dictionary, standard, or society: Most of us "just know" that there are 12 inches in a foot. We don't need to look it up. Likewise, we can look at a screen and "just know" that it looks wrong. For example, if you were to save a word with a special Spanish character, such as "café," and the result looked like a box with a dot in it, you would "just know." That's a failure of internationalization, as we discussed in *Chapter 5*. The most commonly accepted standard in software testing is probably the oracle of comparable products, which we'll discuss next.

Comparable products: Modern Office productivity applications have a familiar menu, with **(F)ile** appearing first. The **(F)ile** dropdown has **(N)ew**, **(O)pen**, **(S)ave**, **(P)rint**, and **(E)xit** in that order:

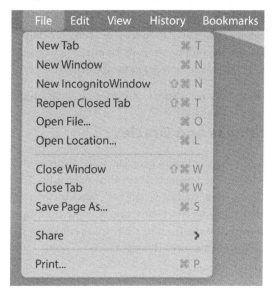

Figure 6.1 – Typical File menu

We expect this because every application behaves this way. One term for this is the comparable products Oracle – that is, when things look wrong because the software does not behave like other software. A video application should play when you click on it, pause when you click again, and react to the space bar to the same effect. If the software doesn't behave like similar products, it could be a conscious choice – some amazing innovation – but then we would expect our requirements to override this.

> **Note**
> Today, even Mac Pages follow the same Microsoft User Interface Standard.

Blink testing: It was Malcolm Gladwell who wrote *Blink: The Power of Thinking without Thinking*, which provides examples of human insight with limited information. The candidate software tester and consultant Michael Bolton formalized that into an Oracle. You might perform blink testing by looking at log files or looking at random text output, finding that, for example, there are no special characters (or too many special characters, too many numbers, and so on). Blink testing happens by zooming in and zooming out.

Another program: In model-driven testing, we might create a bit of code to perform the same transformation as the software under test, feed both inputs into both programs, and compare the output to see if there is a problem.

History: Perhaps the simplest oracle is to compare what the product did yesterday to what it did today. If the difference was not expected (and cannot be inferred) from the intended changes, then the change is accidental.

Some of the most thorn test problems we've encountered are when there is no good definition of what the software should do. Executable tests can come to our rescue here, because, at some point, some person (with authority, we hope) defined that under these complex transformations, given this set of inputs, there should be this specific output. Perhaps, as our reviewer Jeffrey Nadelman suggests, we should call this the Oracle of *executable running automated checks*.

Sometimes, our Oracles fail us because we are looking for problems in the wrong place.

Inattentional blindness and Oracles

Let's talk about how we find things using an exercise. Before you read on, if you can, go watch an inattentional blindness video on the internet. At the time of writing, YouTube has the *Inattentional Blindness – How Many Passes* video available (`https://www.youtube.com/watch?v=z-Dg-06nrnc`). In that video, there are two teams, one in white clothing and the other in black. The challenge is to see how many passes the team in white makes in about 12 seconds. To make sure we keep things as a surprise, I'll inject a figure. This figure has no point – it just breaks up your reading to give you time to watch the video:

Figure 6.2 – Image added to prevent spoilers. Credit: Juliana Heusser (Matt's daughter)

Source: Hand drawing, Juliana Heusser, work for hire

Whether you watched it or not, it's time to talk about the video.

The apparent goal of the 12 seconds is to count the number of passes. This is not that different from following a "test script." Then, the video surprises you: did you see the person in a bear suit who dances across the stage? After doing this exercise with thousands of people on a few continents, we've yet to see someone say, "Oh yes, I saw the bear."

In software testing, the bear is a bug – or at least, it is the hint that something might be worth investigating. It is a bug we didn't find because we were too busy following a set of instructions that pushed us down a specific path. This tells us that documented test steps might hurt our ability to see the entire system as a system. Testers tend to get tunnel vision and only check the "expected result." This means paying attention to how bugs are noticed becomes more important, as does recognizing the limits of click-inspect style automation. Speaking of which, for click-type-click-click-check automation, the bear video is not so much an analogy, but more of a direct match of what the software is doing. Step comparison test tooling will never say "That's odd," "Huh," or "That doesn't look right." *Chapter 2* ended with a few ideas to decrease that risk, to blend the human and the machine, such as with visual testing.

There are a few ways to deal with inattentional blindness. One is to review the same software several times, from different perspectives. On the first pass, you might model the use journey and on the second create odd and invalid conditions to trip errors. Likewise, one pass might be the scripted, defined steps (or have the computer do that with tooling), while a second pass is more exploratory. Alternatively, you might perform mixup testing (*Mixup testing, a cross-team testing activity between scrum teams* – a session at Øredev 2012 (`https://archive.oredev.org/oredev2012/2012/sessions/mixup-testing-a-cross-team-testing-activity-between-scrum-teams.html`), where team members test software they are not working on, and unfamiliar with, to test with a beginner's mind.

Through testing, we can exercise that the software and the bugs show up, but nothing happens unless we notice and take action. Studying oracles can help you identify when there is a bug – something that bugs someone that matters. Before we get to bug reports, let's talk for a moment about how we define bugs.

About the word bug

In this book, we use the term *bug* intentionally, in that it is something in the software that bugs someone and that is worth talking about. It might be an annoyance not worth fixing, or the fix might be trivial. The problem might block work, such as a serious login bug, or there might be an obvious and easy workaround. A bug might be a missing feature. Defects, on the other hand, imply a certain kind of error, a lack of conformance to the specification (or requirements). In our experience, using the term "defect" implies a mistake, or error, likely made by a programmer. This leads to an argument about what is, and what is not a defect. We haven't found a lot of value in those discussions. Instead, today, we are more interested in whether this should be changed (fixed) or documented in any way.

We'll talk about bug reports next.

Writing bug reports

Some of the teams we work with have stopped writing bug reports. They don't track bugs. Instead, the developer-tester pair discovers the problem while they are working together and implements the solution. In some cases, someone creates a failing automated check, perhaps in a framework. In that case, the fix is to get the check to pass without causing anything else to fail. In some cases, the programmers do testing and just need to "fix it and move on." In others, the team sits in one virtual room, so the person who finds the problem just walks over to the person (pair, tri, or mob) responsible, explains it, and the issue gets fixed. Many would argue this is the modern way to do software development – that is, to collapse testing into development so that the two are indistinguishable. That is fantastic; we are happy to support it.

And we still think you should learn how to write an effective bug report.

At its heart, a bug report is a way to communicate something less than ideal. It bugs someone that matters. This can happen verbally when we tell someone else the problem, or in writing. Practicing how to do it well in writing, learning to get specific, and developing a habit of taking screen captures photos, and movies – these things will have value in any way problems are communicated. The risks are a little different when we communicate verbally as conversations tend to be more vague yet provide better opportunities for feedback. Bug reports, however, give easy opportunities for improvement. If your company tracks them, take a lunch hour and look back over the past hundred bug reports and see which ones were fixed. In most cases, we can predict the future of the bug by how it is written. Bug reports that are vague and put any work back on the fixer to investigate are likely to be either closed as unable-to-reproduce, works-as-designed or perhaps result in an incredible back-and-forth between development and whoever did the reporting.

Again, we define a bug as "something that bugs (or bothers) someone that matters." It is common for a junior tester to find something that bothers them – but they are not the person who decides it gets fixed. As our colleague Jeffrey Nadelman rightly points out, this can be demoralizing. Our hope with this work is to help you understand what will matter to the decision-maker and to articulate it in ways that matter. More advanced workers may "take on the mind" of the decision maker, becoming a bit of a mini-product owner themselves.

Bug reports are especially important for companies that do **user acceptance testing** (**UAT**). By UAT, we meant that the software is built for a particular kind of customer (the user) and the company brings that role into the process. Unless someone in the room helps them write bug reports effectively, the result will be vague information that isn't helpful. We, the authors, see bug reports as a mechanism for improving the quality of the software. Without that, the process is a waste of time. This is how many people feel about UAT… because their bug reports are bad.

In some cases, bugs will escape into the field. Even if the team consistently catches all problems before they escape to production, a new browser version or operating system may change behavior and create a bug. In that case, if the report coming in is not effective, the software might not get fixed until the problem is reported again… and again… and again.

We must write them well.

Effective bug reports

Here's a simple template for a bug report:

1. **Pre-conditions**: Environmental variables, what is in the database, and setup. If you find a problem on a particular browser, say Mac/Safari, put that here.

2. **Setup**: What you did to get the problem to materialize, perhaps in numbered steps.

3. **Expected result**: What you expected the software to do.

4. **Actual result**: What the software did.

5. **Further reading**: If the result is anything but straightforward, consider attaching screenshots. If it is complex, consider making a video. Today, we would recommend the Windows snipping tool and **Techsmith's SnagIt** to gather these. Another option is to use your cell phone to take

an actual picture and attach it. If there are any problems with reproducing the bug, but you can get it to show up 70% or more of the time, list the hints and tricks here. Jeffrey Nadelman suggests running testing in brief sessions (likely 30 minutes or so) and recording the entire session. This will provide reproducibility from the beginning.

6. **Summary/title**: A simple, one-line explanation of the problem.

In practice, people will often skip all the details. We try to write the summary so that they can skip the body and do just fine. To do that, we listed the summary last. It might be wise to fill it in last.

To illustrate this, we've provided an actual (slightly obfuscated) screenshot from a website. What title would you give the bug?

Figure 6.3 – A mobile app miscalculates text

Let's look at some of the possible titles and how the tester might perceive them:

- **Numbers jumbled on the mobile version of the About page for a conference site**: The person checking might try to reproduce this on a tablet, not see a problem, and file it as unable to reproduce.

- **Numbers overlap/jumbled on (specific iPhone device) using Safari for the About page**: This might lead to an argument about the number of users for the iPhone, which versions of iPhones are supported, and if the company supports Safari.

    In practice, companies tend to have a minimum support version for devices (two or three devices back is common), along with supported browsers. When it comes to testing, we typically test in at least two browsers and try to test in a different browser than the production programmers are using. Still, as the browser market matures, we find there are fewer and fewer "browser compatibility bugs."

That leads to a summary more like this:

- **Numbers overlap/jumbled on a mobile for the About page (example/screencap iPhone 16 Pro)**: This tells the reader they can reproduce it, but it is not limited to that device

When we put this screenshot up on X (formerly Twitter) and asked for a good summary, one person responded with *"Column titles bleeding into each other,"* which we would update to *"Mobile: column titles/data overlap on about page (screencap from iPhone 16 Pro)."*

Imagine that the reader is lazy. They don't want to go through the reproduction steps. They want all the information in the title, and they want it now.

Why not give it to them?

Effective reproduction steps

Imagine that you are testing an online billing application. You click on the service date to see the "month" popup, as shown in *Figure 6.4*. Some of the dates are displayed as the written-word numbers, while 23 seeds are displayed as **2.3**:

Figure 6.4 – A text conversion error in a calendar feature

We'll provide two ways to write this up:

- **Summary**: Some numbers appear as words in the calendar for the service date (New Invoice).
- **Reproduction steps**: Using the current version of Chrome, create a new invoice, click on the calendar for the service date, and see some numbers displayed as words, such as the attachment.

Here's our second write-up.

- **Second summary**: New invoice laptop – some numbers appear as words in the month in the calendar dropdown for the service date.
- **Second reproduction steps**:

  I.   Log in as a test user – that is, `testuser@testaccount.com`.

  II.   Wait for the page to load.

III.   Click **Sales**.

IV.   Click **Invoice**.

V.   Click **New**.

VI.   Wait for the page to load.

VII.   Navigate to the **service date** in the first row of the first invoice line.

VIII.   Click **service date**.

IX.   Go to the **Month** popup.

X.   Move the month to August.

- **Expected result**: The calendar month popup looks as it always did.

- **Actual result**: Calendar days 1, 2, 11, 15, 20, and 21 appear as words ("one," "two," and so on), while 23 appears as **2.3**. (This is the error; there is a period between the two and the three.)

Hopefully, you can see that the second example is precise and more accurate but boring. Excessive details at the left of the summary will mean that all the bugs will tend to blur together – especially if there is limited screen space for display.

The "right" sweet spot between correct and "easy to read" will vary by team and by bug. In our experience, visibly wrong things are more likely to go with a simple explanation and a screenshot. As an exercise for your team, we suggest taking a real bug and having every team member write the bug up. Print out the reports, bring a marker, and ask the team members to vote for their favorite bug report. Then, sort and discuss what you think makes a well-written bug report. This exercise is described in some detail in Robert Persig's book, *Zen and the Art of Motorcycle Maintenance*, which has the subtitle, *An inquiry into values*.

For now, we suggest that you look into bug reporting as a goal-oriented conflict. People reading bug reports, however they are delivered, have a goal to ignore the report. They have deadlines and important things to do, and bug fixing will just slow them down. That being the case, they look for any excuse to not address the issue. These can include the following:

1. The bug report is too vague; I can't understand or reproduce it.

2. The bug report is too specific; it's boring, so it doesn't matter.

3. This only shows up in a (specific environment). That's not that important.

4. You left the environment off, and I tested it in a place where it does not show up. I'm unable to reproduce it.

5. This bug report has so many typos I can't take it seriously.

6. This bug report is too long; it's just a rant.

This makes the process of reporting bugs similar to Odysseus when he had to steer his ship between the twin monsters Scylla (who lived on a cliff with rocks) and Charybdis (who created a whirlpool). The perfect bug report is precise but not boring, unable to be misinterpreted, and expresses scope properly.

If your environment is prone to bugs that only show up on one platform, take 10 minutes to discover if the problem exists on other devices, form factors, operating systems, and browsers. If it does, you can still list where you found the problem, while indicating it appears to be common.

Pressure on the test reporting process

As we round out this section on bug reports, we'd like to zoom out and take a look at *ineffective bug reports*. The *Practicing politics* section, starting in *Chapter 12*, will contain stories of test efforts that were ineffective and did not create change. In most of those cases, the bug titles did not make a convincing enough case that the issue must be fixed. For whatever reason, the people reporting the bugs were unable to convince management that they mattered. Then, a week, a month, or a year later, when there was a serious customer problem, the finger snapped back to the people who were supposed to be paying attention to risks to the product – in particular, risks related to quality.

Poorly written bug reports also have a time-decay function. Today, exactly what is meant is clear because the team is knee-deep in the work. In the next sprint, it may take some debugging to understand a poorly written explanation. By next year, the team's composition may have changed, and the report might not make sense to anyone due to the lack of shared experience. The new team may not see the value in old reports because, well, they are not valuable to them.

All these forces combine to marginalize or eliminate the test effort. This force isn't new, is not unique, and is not going away. We hope that while the role might lose focus, people in the software process understand that with fewer testers or without a tester role, everyone on the team needs to study testing more. Agile and high-trust teams that don't document their bugs, choosing to "just fix them," run even deeper into the risk that they don't understand what is happening in the test process and have no data to validate assumptions, make corrections, or run experiments. Without that data, the other elements of testing, such as measurement, projections, and planning, become even more important, so we'll shift to those next.

Planning testing – cases and plans

The traditional test literature is full of these ideas of test plans. We like planning, but, to be honest… we've never really understood what those people are on about. So, we decided to put in some quotes about planning and then attempt to deconstruct their logic a bit.

"To fail to plan is to plan to fail"

Lots of people, but at least Renee Bullock, Summer 1995

"No battle plan survives first contact with the enemy"

Prussian Field Marshall Helmuth Von Molke

"Planning is invaluable, plans are useless"

Dwight D Eisenhower

"Everybody has a plan until they get punched in the mouth"

Mike Tyson

Hopefully, you see the point of all these quotes regarding the futility of expecting to stick to a plan. So, when people talk about "test plans," it surprises us. We'll break down what we think that means, how it plays out, what actually happens, and how to do that well.

Some people view testing as re-running all the test scenarios they've come up with. We'll call these scenarios "test cases." Generally, test cases check a particular micro-feature, and perhaps a large number of combinations.

The idea seems to be to have a bit of a library of test cases. Testers, or computers perhaps, can check out one test case at a time, and mark it as passing or failing. When they are done, they check it back in. Someone, somewhere, is tracking what is passing and failing. If bugs fall out of the case that need fixing, the test case fails. When the bugs are fixed, we re-run them. Testing then continues until all the bugs that need fixing are marked as fixed and the associated test cases pass or we run out of time.

The master test plan is, well... we don't really know what the master test plan is. It seems to be a document that ties together all the test cases, perhaps describing what other testing will happen by whom, and what kind of testing (perhaps security) is not performed, or is someone else's responsibility.

What we've described here doesn't match our experience. Worse, it doesn't seem to be what is happening in the projects where the leaders *tell us* that is what they are doing! So, let's spend a moment talking about what we see in projects.

Test cases in practice

Today, when people are using test cases, they may be testing a micro-feature. The test will be detailed, specific, and exhausting to write. It may be passed off from the author, who is moderately skilled, to a more low-skilled person. That test case is then used to test a micro-feature by hand. Someone may write tooling with the same name that does similar things, putting it into a regression test pack.

When it is time for the software to be released, the company typically has some kind of release process. If the change was only to one component (say an API), the API was tested and the API automated regression checks all pass, the change might go out immediately to be monitored in production. However, if there is no way to deploy just that change, and that change is mixed up with a bunch of other changes, then the change will be held to be released in a group, perhaps at the end of a "sprint." At the end of the sprint, the company has some sort of process of checking things, sometimes called regression testing. This could be a combination of tooling and human work.

It's difficult to draw generalizations, but we tend to see more success when the regression process is more of *walking the user journey*, and the feature testing ("test cases") is tighter around the specific feature and changes relating to that feature. This separates the style of testing for feature and regression testing. Likewise, when we've seen the user interface being automated, we frequently see a large number of small checks that run in seconds and check one particular thing. Once established, a tool can run these in a random order and perform redundancy and duplication.

It turns out that the heavily documented, written in English (not code), step-by-step test cases are expensive to write, go out of date quickly, and rarely produce much value. They do have value embedded in them, such as exactly what to click for a difficult setup. We call these "recipes," and we believe they should be part of the process; we'll cover how to build a better process in *Chapter 9*.

For now, know that people can mean a lot of different things by the term "test case," and those things can serve different audiences – a project manager's interest in test cases might be very different from a tester's. The same is true for test plans.

We do think that it is reasonable for people to want some measure of process. "Number of passing test cases divided by number of planned test cases" gives us a nice, easy percentage to talk about progress, the release time frame, and "doneness." The percentage of passing test cases can sound attractive to groups that go more than a couple of weeks between releases and have a reasonably long regression test period. But man, that is a lot of effort for not a ton of value.

Let's dive into metrics.

Metrics and measurement

As we write this, we find ourselves trying to navigate between two extremes. On the one side, we have the sort of naive optimism of irresponsible numbers. On the other, we have an open hostility to software metrics. As usual, the best option is a middle path.

For our purposes, a metric is a number with labels attached. The number three does not speak for itself, but if that were *three programmers are working on that feature*, then we have a metric. We speak in metrics all the time. For example, "We have 5 days until Friday, and we are planning on releasing Friday at 3 P.M." lists two different metrics. Metrics as we use them are, according to the Oxford English Dictionary, just a system of measurement. We measure things all the time. So, we don't want to reject metrics as a concept.

There is, however, a more subtle version of the word metric. This is the implication that is usually quoted: "If you can't measure it (turn it into a number), you can't manage it." We don't quite buy that. Most of the people we know decide it is time to get a haircut by looking in a mirror. A few schedule things on a calendar. We don't know anyone who would take a ruler to their hair to check the number of inches. In software, though, reducing to a number has an advantage. You can measure things, set a goal, and then come back periodically and look at the update. If things are on track, great. Congratulate yourself and play some golf. If they are yellow, then tell your underlings to get to work. If they are red, demand explanations and periodic updates.

Dashboards are a way to stay outside of the process, to not understand it, and yet look and feel like you are in control. It fails due to dysfunction.

Metric dysfunction

The simplest measurement schemes involve counting the number of bugs. Testers and analysts are rewarded when there are a large number of bugs; programmers are rewarded when the number is small. Project managers look to have zero open bugs or some low lumber so that they can make ship decisions.

Sadly, the simplest approach isn't the best as it invariably drives dysfunctional behaviors. Let's explain.

Every single time we've seen this scheme (including consulting assignments), that measurement scheme leads to testers creating a bug for not just every typo, but every arguable typo. Meanwhile, programmers expend effort on how this is "not a bug" or "not my bug" at least. Management may put pressure to get the bug count down, so people stop entering the data in the system. People pass notes through sticky notes, or, when working remotely, chat.

The desire to quantify drives useful information out of the system.

This happens with all parts of the delivery process, not just testing – this can include velocity, the number of users on the site, and the number of features completed per week. Matt once worked with a company that was counting the number of automated checks running per day (24 hours). Yes, the programmers were writing checks, but the manager also changed the code to decrease the delay between test runs every month or so to guarantee that the number went up.

Matt's graduate school professor, Dr Roger Ferguson, once said "A number is better than no number" – that a number gives people a place to start. That said, consider a system that had five spelling error bugs yesterday. Today, login is broken; no one can use the test environment at all. Would it be fair to say that quality improved because we decreased the number of bugs from five to one? Of course not; the idea is absurd. Yet to someone abstracted away from the process looking at a dashboard, that might appear to be the case.

Dr Cem Kaner, our mentor, calls this the problem of "construct validity," using a term that has meaning in the sciences. That is, no, it is not valid to count up several things. For example, we could count up the number of cash (paper) bills on a table, but if the amount of the bills varies, the number of bills wouldn't tell us much. If we rewarded teams by the number of bills, they could convert larger bills into smaller ones, creating the illusion of productivity. We've seen this in the number of automated checks example earlier. Dr Kaner probably described it best in his paper *Software Engineering Metrics: What Do They Measure and How Do We Know* (`https://kaner.com/pdfs/metrics2004.pdf`) – it's easy to come away from that paper sad and even depressed. Later in his career, Dr Caner would compare software to stock market investing, where publicly traded firms have a whole host of measures, all of which have problems. As the numbers are at least valid constructs, an investor who can consider a variety of metrics that balance each other out, and who understands them, will get a more informed view of the company.

Sifting through the data is one way to figure out *what is going on*. Another is to get involved in the workflow. If you can tolerate one more metaphor, a teacher doesn't need grades for their students – the teacher knows how their students are doing. The teacher produces grades for the parents, administration, and admissions officers. This is to give people from the outside an easy view and comparison. Metrics do that. As the levels of abstraction become higher and higher, as we go from the details of a single day to the team for 2 weeks for many teams for 3 months, information is lost. Our challenge is to provide the most information that is hardest to misunderstand in the smallest package possible.

We make a distinction between inquiry metrics and control metrics. If the defects are similar in size and damage, you might go into a requirements system and say that the team found 20 bugs this week, 20 last week, and closed 15 – it looks like the bug count is growing. You might even go back a few months and throw that number onto a spreadsheet to create a graph. However, when you update the graph every week and base promotion and raises on it, you shift from inquiry to control. With control metrics, people now have an incentive to change their behavior. Now, we'll start to see an argument about what is a bug, what is a feature request, and what the severity should be. People may start to see bugs and fix them themselves. We may see arguments that bugs closed as WILL_NOT_FIX should count as closed, and if you include them, the graph goes down. As a result, the quality slowly goes down.

> ### Sidebar – Jerry Nadelman on bug counts
>
> We found that bug counts were cyclical. When a new feature was started, the number of bugs was high. After a few days/weeks, as it progressed toward completion, the number of bugs found would decrease. If the metrics are important, then we must look at historical trends too. To us, the numbers of the first few weeks of a feature needed to be compared to only the first few of previous ones, and of course the same for ones later in the process. Without this, you would see a continual up-down-up-down, and the metric would be meaningless.
>
> We also needed to check the bug counts against the point estimate of the story. More points meant more complexity, and we would expect more bugs. Finding 20 bugs would be no big deal for a large story, but finding 20 bugs in a story that had low points and should be done in under a day would be a huge red flag.

This chapter's goal was to get you to pause and consider how a measurement program could send you in the right direction. We are all for inquiry metrics, but don't stop there – validate them. After listing the bugs that have been opened in the past 2 weeks, get a list of them. Figure out if, for example, the important ones are getting fixed or not – or the easy ones. If the important ones are getting fixed but the count is rising, how can we explain the impact on quality?

This was more of a "think" chapter than an example chapter. In Chapter 9, we'll be talking about examples of metrics for testing to stand up to scrutiny.

One common desire for metrics is to predict the future, sometimes called projections. That's worth a mention.

Project projections

The previous section gave two examples of projections – bug count over time and passing test cases over time. We aren't that excited about either of them. In an agile context, the goal is to resolve the defects worth fixing quickly; the only record of a bug might be a change in version control.

The word "projections" comes from "project;" we use this term loosely. When dealing with software quality, there are several projections you might want to make. These can include the following:

- How many people will be impacted by this change or defect?

- What is the revenue impact every day this is open? ("cost of delay")

- Besides direct costs of user-can't-do-feature, do we have indirect costs on user adoption, turnover, sales, and brand reputation?

- How much time will we be spending on find/fix/retest work?

- What is the return on investment of the next increment, compared to other potential efforts?

Amazon's claim that a 1-second delay in page loads leads to a loss of 1.6 billion dollars in sales annually is more than 10 years old (`https://www.fastcompany.com/1825005/how-one-second-could-cost-amazon-16-billion-sales`) If anything, more money could be lost in less time today.

Someone did that analysis.

There are tools today to analyze logs to find out this information. For Web APIs, that could be how long the average (mean), middle (median), and most common (mode) sets of replies come out. It might also be helpful to look at the slowest time to serve requests, such as the mean, median, and mode of the bottom quartile. Alternatively, we could just export the whole spreadsheet and look at the data.

In more traditional projects, you might find some way to measure what has been done and how often it fails to predict how many cycles you'll need to run to be done, as well as how long those cycles should be. With each cycle, the amount that's tested probably decreases. In the last run, if regression failures are a problem and we are unable to release just one piece at a time, then we like to go back to some of those early full-user journeys and re-execute them. The point is to use the bug reports, metrics, and analytical measures to balance everything out and predict outcomes.

First, we figure out what is going on. Then, we figure out what needs to change. After that, we figure out how to explain it. We will explore exactly how to do this in *Chapter 9* (on delivery models), and *Chapter 10* (the puzzle pieces of testing).

Influencing change

We can argue that testing is "just" a technical investigation to uncover quality-related information. That's fine, as far as it goes — but it doesn't go very far. If the test effort discovers problems, and those problems are well documented yet never read… nothing happens. The real value to the business of the test effort is zero. Perhaps the company gets lucky, and there are no "showstopper bugs," and the customers don't care. In that case, a rational executive should eliminate the testing budget. Or perhaps the company goes out of business.

Most of us don't have that problem, but we may have a problem where testing finds defects, and some get fixed, but not enough. Just as bad, the programmers don't learn from their mistakes, and keep creating the same kind of bugs, over and over again. This creates drag on the team. Some testers find this comforting as they will always have a job. One told us once that every release would have a large number of user interface bugs or changes. Using a record-playback automation script, everything would break. By re-creating the scripts (testing manually), our friend could find the bugs, wait for the fix, and fix them. The entire "automation" effort was redundant with human testing and didn't add value – but they would have a job so long as they wanted it. It didn't take them long to start their own company.

The "best" outcome for no-change testing is a forever job that turns you into a sort of non-thinker script follower. We don't believe that is very good. Beginning with *Chapter 12*, we'll start talking about the practice of politics – but a really good test-related skill to talk about in the meantime is summarizing information.

Summarizing information

Testers are directly in the information flow – we sip from the firehouse. Senior leaders rarely have the time or the attention to give into details that deep. If they did, that still would not give them what they need – high-level information to make a decision. Those decisions include the following:

- Is the software ready to go (today)?

- When will we be able to launch the advertising campaign?

- What needs to be fixed right now for us to call the software "good enough?"

- Is the new feature in good enough condition to demo at (name of conference)?

- Can we launch (a new feature)?

The old model was to put pressure on people to say things were ready to go. Then, when they were not, it was to criticize the people who were put under that pressure. We want a better way.

Context-driven testing presents the tester as an investigator and informer, not as a decision-maker. This means the tester doesn't say "Testing is complete," but instead "I tested for these six risks, found these problems, and don't see value in continuing." Those conversations can happen at the micro-feature level (with technical team members), at the regression test level (for an API, for a sprint), or even at the team-of-teams quarterly or program level. When we look at the overhead in some of the "large-scale" methods, we see an attempt to create this with roles such as "architect" or "release train engineer." Let's look at a simple text example of how to make such a summary for a fictional product, called *POWERTRAIN*.

After 4 hours of testing *POWERTRAIN*, we could resolve the following issues by the end of the day, release it as-is, or continue testing tomorrow. We recommend resolving and deploying. Our four largest problems are listed here; we expect that if we find additional errors, they will be smaller than this list:

- Regression on older versions of iPad/Safari, specifically models running operating systems before 2019. These are supported and usable, but in this version (Defect #2220), there are a series of usability issues with painful but intuitive workarounds. Safari/iPad users represent 0.25% of users by volume and 0.05% as a percent of sales. We did test other browsers.
- The fresh vegetable icon appears as a "broken icon" (Defect #2120).
- Combining a filter by five or more properties, plus advanced search terms (multiple ANDs or ORs), results in no results (Defect #2229).
- The comment field is limited to 2,048 characters (Defect #2225). The requirement is unlimited. It's worth noting that in the database, 95% of the comments are less than that length, and the error message is clear.

We expect that the programmers can fix this within the afternoon, and we can deploy the product tomorrow at 9 A.M. Our test effort was on search, product display, and the shopping cart, as these changed the most. We did a quick inspection of the reports and the control panel and created custom catalog functions. We could do 4-hour rounds on those areas, a deeper dive on the areas under change, or a plan to release.

The preceding example is a text summary, and if anything, it is a little "heavy." Future chapters will talk about how to use dashboards, mind maps, heatmaps, and other visualizations to show what is tested versus what is not.

The magic test report summary

The summary in the preceding section provided a few hidden cues; let's talk about them.

First, it presented management with options. "We could do this, we could do that, we could do a third thing." With one choice, people have no freedom. With two, they have a dilemma. With three, they start to believe they are in control.

Second, the summary presented that these were but bugs we found; if we had more time, we could probably find smaller ones.

Third, it explained what was not tested. This provides the decision makers with what they need to decide based on quality factors, but it also enables a simple head-feint. This means that if the bugs that are listed don't seem that bad if we can do without even fixing them, then we could go live now with less worry – after all, more testing will reveal more bugs we don't need to fix.

If there are more bugs, but they are in the areas we chose not to test (or only scratched the surface of), then we won't face the criticism "Why didn't you find these three issues?" Instead, we brought management into the conversation. They won't even ask the question, because to critique the decision is now to critique them.

Provide information to people. Let them be part of the decision, and they won't critique you later for it.

Sometimes, the organization will not listen to reason. They'll ignore your warnings that the product is a mess. The most carefully worded warnings will be ignored, and you won't be able to change the outcome.

You can still find good meaning in this. The next time it happens, the organization will have a chance to learn. When they state "*This project seems to be a lot like project POWERTRAIN*", you'll say, "*Was anyone else here for POWERTRAIN? Do we want to do that again?*"

If you want a career that involves testing, practice influencing change. Some of that is political – you need to realize that most decisions are made before the meetings, and if you try to change decisions in meetings, you may risk making someone else look bad.

The magic summary is a start. Practice it, with words or typing. Learn how much volume (text) your audience wants, and learn to adjust your amount of information to how much they can take in. Lead with the status, provide reasons for it, provide a comparison to things the reader will find relevant, and provide your reader with options to resolve it.

Frequently, people doing testing work are not given the authority to make decisions and then are criticized when, under pressure, someone makes a bad decision to release. We can't prevent this, but we can often help leaders buy into the decision and even, sometimes, help the organization learn.

Summary

In this chapter, we talked about the skills that are required to be effective at testing. This includes recognizing when something will bother people, reporting on those problems well, using numbers to tell a compelling story, and making projections.

The "change" piece of testing is often overlooked. Without it, testing is just "the thing we need to do so that we can put the software in production." Another often overlooked element of testing is the test data. In the next chapter, we'll explain why test data is important, and then provide you with some strategies to collect and manage your test data in ways that will roll with change, eliminate false errors, and reduce debugging time.

7
Test Data Management

Throughout our introduction, we talked about testing software: send this input, run this transformation, and expect this output. We talked about the state that the software is in, such as viewing the *home page*, but not the state of the data.

Consider, for example, testing adding a page with some text, followed by searching. The first time you run the test, everything works, but the second time, you get an error that the page already exists. You fix that by making the page unique, and the next time you run it, there is a different error – the number of search results has changed. Or, you may store user details, including their birthday, in the database, and after their birthday, all of a sudden the calculation for auto insurance costs is incorrect. We call this the *test data management* problem. This chapter is about how to solve it.

By the end of this chapter, you will have learned a variety of techniques to create, store, edit, delete, and restore the state of data. This allows testers to *drive* to an interesting place in an application quickly, so they can focus on testing, not on setup. It also makes it possible for test tools that create repeatable, reliable results. To accomplish that, we'll introduce the problem and discuss some common solutions, along with challenges.

In this chapter, we're going to cover the following main topics:

- The test data problem
- Automated setup scripts
- The standard data seed
- Synthetic users
- Pulling data from production for production refreshes
- Development, test, and production environments
- Regulatory issues in test data storage and management

Technical requirements

Test data needs to be saved, archived, loaded, version controlled, and so on. That, in a way, makes it very much like code. Our goal with this chapter is to aid the communication between programmers and less technical staff. Specifically, a tester who does not program might be able to create technical requirements for the test data that a product owner could prioritize as a feature for ongoing development. You'll also learn how to articulate the cost in terms of time investment if those tools don't exist. Programmers who read this chapter will understand the ideas and immediately be able to implement them.

The solutions in the chapter will tend to be high-level, programming-language-agnostic concepts. So, no specific programming language is required. An understanding of databases and SQL will be helpful. Teams that use key/value pairs and NoSQL databases will also be able to benefit from this chapter.

The test data problem

Throughout the book, we discuss different modes of testing, such as the extended user journey (actually using the software like a user) versus testing a specific feature as an isolated element. Often, we find splitting the automated checking up into these smaller pieces makes sense, while in other cases a human can add a great deal of value by looking at the entire system holistically. Joel Spolsky, an early blogger that we have been influenced by, wrote an article that appears to support this distinction, reinforcing the user journey. In this chapter, we'll add another layer of complexity to consider.

Here's a quote from Joel: *"Eating your own dog food is the quaint name that we in the computer industry give to the process of actually using your own product. I had forgotten how well it worked, until a month ago, I took home a build of CityDesk (thinking it was about 3 weeks from shipping) and tried to build a site with it.*

Phew! There were a few bugs that literally made it impossible for me to proceed, so I had to fix those before I could even continue. All the testing we did, meticulously pulling down every menu and seeing if it worked right, didn't uncover the showstoppers that made it impossible to do what the product was intended to allow. Trying to use the product, as a customer would, found these showstoppers in a minute." (*Joep Spolsky, 2001,* `https://www.joelonsoftware.com/2001/05/05/what-is-the-work-of-dogs-in-this-country/`).

This insight from Joel is certainly right, but it does leave something missing. The article does not explore why the features all seem to work when you run them one at a time but fail when they are taken as a group. One answer that comes to mind is something we'll call the problem of test data.

The software Joel was working on, **CityDesk**, was designed to allow users to publish web pages. They could edit the page, save it, and then publish it to the web. It was, in a way, an early content management system. Like word processors, they have what they display on the page, what they load from disk, and what things look like when they are published to the web (or sent to a printer). Along the way, they have the state, which is how the data is represented in memory, disk, or the database.

Model View Controller (**MVC**) is a dominant way of programming object-oriented code. In MVC, an object contains all the unique data in the application. When the user manipulates the screen, perhaps creating a new circle in a paint app, the controller manipulates the model, for example, adding a circle to the center (X,Y) of size A and color B to the model. The system can then call the view, which redraws the screen with the new or changed elements. Here's an example of how the model, view, and controller work together.

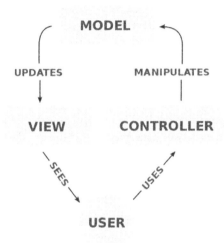

Figure 7.1 – MVC, per Wikipedia

Most MVC frameworks also have commands to save the file to disk or load it. In the case of paint, we'd want to save all the information about the circle. If the data were saved as a flat image, it wouldn't provide us with what we'd need if someone wanted to click on the circle and resize it.

Bugs can appear in any place where there is a change in state. The *state of the software* can be in memory or just executing code. In *Figure 7.1*, that would be the arrows, which are transitions that can change memory, display, and so on.

This book will refer to the data inside the model as the *state* of the model. The state will be different as the software is used over time. That means the view should be different based on the state. Most of the time, humans testing software can *figure out* what the *right* answer *should be* by mentally keeping up with the state as it changes. However, it is worth pausing for a moment to consider the implications.

In the preceding example, the VIEW function will draw the screen, filling in variables with the data that is in the model. That is, it will fill in first name, last name, and so on. The number of possible combinations of what is in the model approaches infinity. Even in a simple paint program with a small screen, say 400 by 400 pixels, a black oval that is 3 pixels in width could be of size 1x1, 1x2, 1x3, up to 1x400, and also 2x1, 2x2, 2x3, all the way to 400. That makes 16,000 combinations! Draw two circles, and we have 16,000 times 16,000, or 256 *million*, possible combinations for the first two ovals. Add color combinations, varying width, and other shapes, and we see different states can lead to radically different expectations.

This problem of combinations isn't limited to possible values in the model or possible ways the view can process the model. We have the same problem with the controller to model. If we add a circle to an image just once, it might work fine. We could also test adding a second shape a square, including save and redraw. All that could work. Consider a case where the programmer stores each object type in a different list data structure, and the `export->()` function for circles overwrites all the circles in the same place. We would only notice this error if we were to create an image with two circles, save and exit the application, and then load the image. Test scenarios that only draw one of each object (remember our Joel Spolsky quote early in the chapter!) would not manifest the bug, nor would drawing the circles and looking at the screen. We've seen this exact error in the real world in both telecommunication and insurance billing software. For the insurance billing.

If the state of the data, in memory and on disk, can impact how the software behaves, then we should be testing the software with a variety of data. We call this the test data problem, which is perfectly captured in the insurance example.

Test data and database apps

At an early 2000's STAREast conference, Harry Robinson was teaching Matt Heusser, one of the co-authors, about model-driven testing. At the time, Robinson was a Microsoft employee (he later worked at Google) specializing in Model Based Testing. Matt was working on a database, in an **Extract-Transform-Load** (**ETL**) program, and managed to pick up some hallway advice. The conversation went like this:

> Matt: "This is a simple data transform, Harry, it doesn't have state."

> Harry Robinson: "... that you know of."

Harry's point, that even programs that look like they don't have state likely have hidden transitions we might miss, was a good one. To understand this, we'll tell a story about a database application.

One program we worked on involved recalculating the amount of money people had spent out-of-pocket for medical insurance in a given year of a plan. This is called the deductible. The tester set up the data with medical claims that were below, at, and above the deductible, and then ran the interface to see the corrected numbers.

The software gave the correct answers and was put in production. The first day it ran, the program ran in 30 seconds. The second day, it ran in about 5 minutes. On the third day, it ran for about 25 minutes. On the fourth day, it took over an hour. In the second week, the program's queries were complex enough that they timed out the database, and we were called in to carry out a project rescue.

That entire project was a living example of the Robinson principle, that state matters more than you might think.

Databases in particular, however, have other problems. Consider a database that stores sales tax, by state abbreviation, in a table. To calculate the sales tax, the software takes the state address and does a lookup. There is also a different part of the software that allows the user to change the tax as, well, taxes change. If the people testing different parts of the application don't talk to each other, then the bills will come out *wrong* because the state sales tax is not what was expected. Table-driven functions can be much more complex than that. A clever programmer can often define a great bit of the business rules in the database itself, requiring only an INSERT statement to create new functionality, or UPDATE or DELETE to change existing functionality.

To succeed, the database needs to have known good data in it, so the output can be compared to some expected result. With table-driven results, programmers may need to include populating and changing the data as part of the test process. Lucky for us, that it is the focus of this chapter!

The simplest strategy for managing test data is probably to have a pre-defined set that can be loaded into the system at will. We'll call this the **standard data seed**.

The standard data seed

Many business software systems are essentially some permanent data stores combined with a frontend. The data has to come from *somewhere*, such as an API that calls a database. For our purposes, the backend could be anything. It might be within our control (a database of our customers) or outside our control. For example, **TweetDeck** is a tool that helps people view and plan their X.com posts. (Formerly known as Twitter). The tool was originally created by an independent software company. The *data* for that tool is data from X.com.

Now think about trying to test the tool. You'd want to log in as a certain user, search for certain things, and confirm they show up on the user interface – but that is reliant on X having the right data. Terms such as *3 days ago* would slowly age out; you wouldn't be able to confirm them. If someone else was using the same account, they might corrupt the data and give you different search results.

Enter the standard data seed.

What we call the *standard data seed* is predefined data, saved and version-controlled, that can be loaded into systems for every test run. In e-commerce, a standard data seed allows you to load up a user with a great number of orders, search the orders, and have a specific, predefined expected result. You can then add a new order, conduct a search that should find that order, see it at the top, conduct a search where you do not see it in the results, and so on. When the test run is over, you can delete the database, reload it for the next test run, and once again have *fresh* results.

Things get a little more complex with external services, but the concept is the same. Generally, companies find a way to use stubs, mocks, and fakes to simulate the external service in order to provide predefined results. Sometimes this is called *service virtualization*. Tools exist to run the software, capture and save the calls to thirty-party web services, and then stand up an alternative server to produce that pre-canned data.

Over the years, we have found a few things in common with successful standard data seed programs:

- **The ability to dump, clear, and load data**: To have a standard data seed, we need to isolate the data we care about, save it, clear the database, and reload it later. With a word processor, this might be as simple as using the save and load functions. In general, we find this functionality helpful not only for testing and development but also for operations, as it can streamline support and backups. We have worked with teams that did not have this in place, and instead typed in the same data, repeatedly, through the user interface for every major release. In one case, a consulting customer reported that they were spending 40% of their time on test data setup. A standard data seed might reduce that number to 5%. With the standard data seed in place, it is possible to run a *clean* test, knowing all the results that will come back; the user's name will not be changed, the search results will be predictable, the order history will be predictable, and so on. The data can also include the expected test scenarios. At **Socialtext**, this included data for two accounts, with a user that could only see one of the two. We expected search results to only show the data from the second account. This is a great improvement, but not perfect. If you have a great many tests, or testers, and you want to run them at the same time, one set of users could corrupt the data, causing another to get incorrect search results. The test process needs to be designed for this.

- **The ability to run tests simultaneously**: One way to ensure this is for each test to have its own server. This was unheard of just years ago, but modern cloud computing tools make this easy and possible. Another approach is to have multiple standard data seeds on the same server. Perhaps a standard data seed *group* of data can be imported into a separate directory, with the creator specifying the `userid` and `groupname` values. The elements of that group will only be visible to that user when they log in. When we have done this in the past, we've had the ability to generate a unique `userid` and `groupname` on demand as part of the setup process.

- **Consider dates**: As we said previously, with **TweetDeck**, there is a very real problem with data *aging out*. The solution is usually architectural: allow the software to accept an *as-of* date as a feature. That way, you can load the standard data seed data *as of*, for example, exactly one month ago. You can then store dates as *days since as-of date*, for example. Over the years, we've had to write middle-layer translations that take dates in a file and push them forward, creating a new file for import, so the imported data will be listed as from, for example, *three days ago*. This becomes important when testing accounting applications, quarterly reports, insurance applications where coverage dates matter, and so on. Our strong preference is to build the capability to change the date, sometimes called *time travel*, as a feature, instead of trying to work around it.

- **Version control**: The team will need a process for people to change the standard data seed over time. This can be very much like a code review process. The most effective way we have seen is for each team to own their own data, to communicate when changing the code internally, and to store it in the same version control system as the production and test code.

When we worked at **Socialtext**, the product was a wiki, which is an editable web page. The server was organized by accounts; accounts could have access to one or more **subwikis**, which were subdirectories. Users belonged to a primary account and could have rights to additional **subwikis**. The tool allowed administrators to export a wiki, which would be a text dump of the web pages and users, stored as a single *tarball*, which is a Unix collection of multiple files combined into a single file. Programmers could import the *tarball*, which would create the **subwiki**, and delete and re-add it on demand. The data needed to be big enough to make navigation and search meaningful, but small enough to load in seconds.

An interesting wrinkle in data seeding is when test data drives behavior. We will explore this next.

Table-driven – when test data drives behavior

Imagine a program that creates a bill for your cell phone. Once the program has all the items and subtotal in memory, it runs through two tables to look up and apply any state sales tax, along with any local taxes. These tables actually drive the behavior of the application. If the tables all have the same data during testing (assume all states have 5% sales tax), the software can run through every line of code and produce output that is correct. However, if no one ever changes the tables in the live database with the correct state tax – or, more likely, doesn't update them when the state tax changes – the software will suddenly have a bug.

We call these sorts of tables **lookup tables**. These tables can define what gets logged, what users have access to what information, and who has edit or delete rights. At one company we worked with, the tables contained **smart codes** to describe insurance products that were entered by hand. Sometimes they contained as errors.

If part of your application's behavior is table-driven, then a responsible risk management process could take a look at what is in the tables, how they change, what risks this creates, and how the testing process should address it. Having a standard data seed that is realistic and having a change-control process for the tables are two ways to mitigate (reduce) this risk.

The ability to import and export data in a standard data seed leads us to our second strategy: creating information quickly through commands, not the user interface. We call this a scriptable user and data structure.

Scriptable users and structure

Once we've tested creating users and accounts through the user interface, we likely don't need to do it again in the same test run. Yet, we may have complex tests, such as the account permissions example in the previous section, that require a lot of setup. One option is to write automation that isn't really testing anything, just creating accounts through the user interface. These checks will be brittle, meaning they break easily with small changes in the software. Brittle tests are hard to maintain because they confuse changes that don't matter with changes that do. This makes the software record a failure when it should not. Fixing the automated check will require re-running to failure, figuring out the new expectations, and changing the code, and running again. This extra work adds to maintenance costs. These checks also tend to be slow, because they actually load a real web page or run an application that connects to the server. Another option is to have some automatic way to create what we need quickly during setup. At **Socialtext**, instead of running through account creation through the user interface, we had a series of setup commands that might look something like this:

```
st-create account account%%unique%%visible
st-create account account%%unique%%invisible
st-create user user%%unique%%@socialtext.com --account
account%%unique%%
st-import –account account%%unique%%visible data-seed_1.tar
st-import –account account%%unique%%invisible data-seed_2.tar
```

It's a little much, but if you understand the preceding strategy, it is straightforward. We create two accounts, load them with data, and expect search results from only the first one. Then, we add the call to the `st-add` command to add the user to the second account and redo the search, seeing the results for both. The potential testing is, of course, infinite. We could have a third account, remove the user from the first account and redo the search, and so on. When permissions are removed from the first account, we'd expect to not see the search results from that account appear, as the user cannot access that account.

The examples in the preceding command-line code block imply a command-line option, which might mean executing code on the test server, but there are many ways to do it. It could be a command that runs a `SQL INSERT`, a command that makes an API call, or a half-dozen other ways. The important thing is to make it scriptable.

Creating accounts and users can help with testing software that has not been released yet. Once the system is in production, it is always possible the production data will look different and allow a new error to manifest. So, let's talk about a technique to run checks in production without causing problems.

Exploring synthetic users

Most of the systems we test have some concept of a user and a login. That isn't true for everything. Sometimes, systems are more like an online brochure or desktop application. Still, most software that is complex enough to warrant a book on testing has some sort of log-in concept. The purpose of having separate users includes isolating what that user can see as well as presenting custom and user-created content. That could be a list of orders, a shopping cart, credit card information, emails sent and received, public social media messages published, or the ability to scroll through messages published by others the user has access to.

This means User's have unique views into the system. They might create some combination of data that no one else can see. If by some miracle they report the problem without advanced tools, it is unlikely that it will be easy to reproduce. In addition, testers may wish to see things as users do in the live system, in order to test in production. In at least one version of **continuous deployment**, new versions of the software go directly to production, but will only be visible to users with the correct permissions – likely members of the development team. This allows the development team to see features in production and approve a *promotion* to production.

In order to use a synthetic data strategy, the software needs a special sort of user with elevated permissions. These test accounts need to do the same things a regular customer can do on a live account. In an e-commerce system, that would be login, adding to the cart, up to and including ordering, paying a subscription fee, and *not* seeing the software if the subscription is canceled. However, with synthetic users, the order should not be sent to the warehouse, a credit card should never be charged (though the Orders page would show that it was), importantly, any work should not show up in financial reports or user summaries. Things even trickier, in that way may want to have two false credit cards, on where the order appears to go through and another when it will be declined.

We call these test users in production **synthetic users**. Having mock accounts can be helpful to not only testers but also sales, marketing, and anyone who wants to give a product demo. While another common approach is to use a staging environment, we find staging environments are often not stable enough. Also, the ability to turn features on and off for classes of users using **feature flags** can be incredibly powerful and support testing/demo-ing in production. That also allows the team to roll changes back quickly without a complex deployment step.

Most of the examples so far have been about logging in to production as a test user. That user can have orders, but they should not appear on a report of sales, as they do not represent real revenue. Having a class of users that are mocks, thus cut off from reporting, external systems, and visibility to other classes of users can require additional work. Then again, it usually pays off for developers, sales, and support.

When programmers and vendors speak about **synthetic users**, they often mean something a little more nuanced. Specifically, they mean all the attributes we described previously, plus the ability to create (and delete) users on demand to use them as part of some kind of test automation in production. Usually, this test automation is much less testing and much more monitoring. For example, one company we worked with had a piece of automation that could open a browser, log in, let the home page load, run a simple search, log out, and close the window. The tool would then wait 15 seconds and perform the same process, over and over, on repeat. At every step, the tool would note the time, take an action, wait for the page to load, and log the time, action, and time elapsed in a database. This allowed the company to calculate the mean (average), median (middle), and mode (most popular of several ranges) times for a page load. It could also immediately notify support if the website went down or had a significant error.

Over time, the support team started to get complaints that the website was *slow*. Once it got back to the programmers, they could log in without any problem. The login tool showed logins were off by a bit, but not enough that most people would notice. At some point, someone looked at the data in hour-by-hour increments and found that logins were slow in the morning from 8 to 9 A.M, as well as in the afternoon, particularly around 1 P.M. The conclusion was business customers had to use the software all day but would be inactive overnight and at lunch, so the tool would force a new login.

As it turned out, as a security measure, the team had just rolled out a feature that forced logout after 30 minutes of inactivity.

In that case, the fix was as easy as extending the default logged-in period to 20 hours, plus adding a *stay logged-in* checkbox which extended the login to a week. This allowed users to balance their responsibility for private information with convenience, which we will discuss more when we discuss regulatory issues as follows.

Synthetic users can explore the production environment in a very similar way to test tools explore a test environment, reporting true end-to-end results, including timings and errors, and reporting back quickly. Those timings, errors, and results are easy enough to create as a graph that can be part of a dashboard to tell a company how things are going. IT operations have been doing these sorts of things for decades, but mostly, those reports are internal systems – disk space available, processing unit used, and how long processes are spending on the server. Synthetic users allow teams to test the live software from the outside in, as a real user would. The reports they provide are not themselves the technical investigation that is testing – but they can be powerful, value-adding tools.

Synthetic users tend to do things in production, such as order books or buy stocks. As we mentioned before, it is important that those actions don't actually trigger real events. A synthetic user might run on a loop in production, ordering books, but we don't want to ship 1,000 books a week, nor charge the credit card (which might itself be synthetic). The term for these transactions that go "almost," but not quite, end to end (and don't show up in reports either) is **synthetic transactions**. Both *synthetic users* in production and *synthetic transactions* can be an important part of a test monitoring strategy, which can influence quality. This chapter focuses on test data. In a way, synthetic users provide test data, as they can allow testers to see into live systems as a customer would. In some cases, the team may have special synthetic (live/production) test data accounts that need to be *kept around* because the insight they provide needs to stay consistent. However, they cannot provide the entire data picture. Another way to get the data is to pull it from production into a test environment.

Leveraging production refreshes

Sometimes, the work isn't user-interface-driven at all. Data processing groups often create reports or transactions (such as processing an insurance claim), or simply move data from one system to another, including ETL work. Insurance companies, banks, ERP software developers, and survey companies have this as their main business. Anyone doing fraud detection, distilling data, or carrying out data mining may also do this sort of work.

In that case, the company may want to simulate the production environment by copying data for the live server. Typically, this is done on some sort of schedule, such as every quarter, or with some *slice* of live data. This ensures the team is looking at the actual data, often in massive volumes.

Then again, imagine having a private medical issue and realizing that someone at your company in testing might be looking at your data. Or even someone viewing your bank account information or your credit score. In recent years, information risk, privacy regulations, and actually caring about customers have made this practice difficult. The *Understanding the regulatory issues in test data management* section later in this chapter will discuss these barriers; this section proceeds with the assumption that you've found a way to resolve them.

Production refreshes can enable all kinds of good testing. For example, say a data extract has a complex calculation of who has a certain kind of coverage and has reached their deductible. The programmer can take just that relevant part of the business requirements to a tester, who can create a database query to identify the exact users and what their output should be. The programmer can implement the data extract and then compare the two results. If the results are the same, that does not mean that the data extract is *correct*. It does not even mean that the programmer understood the requirements. It does, however, mean that for the existing population, two different people made the same reasonable interpretation of the requirements for the entire sampled population. When dealing with customer lists, claims, and transactions, this could be hundreds of thousands or millions of tests. Doing these sorts of tests for years, we found they were most likely to find situations the requirements did not cover, where there were a variety of conditions, and the English description simply did not say what to do under all circumstances.

Having access to production data also allows testers to look at things in the aggregate. For example, if the average customer's claims were $7,000 per year, but in a particular data extract they were only $900, that might be a clue that something was wrong with the extract.

For all this talk about migrating production (live) data to a test environment, we had better spend some time talking about environments.

Exploring development, test, and production environments

Spreadsheet programs that are stored locally don't need *environments*. You can run them anywhere. What you are coding in a spreadsheet is what you are coding as you code it, what you are testing when you test it, and what you have coded when you are done for the moment Once we talk about storing information somewhere and having server-side code, we need to consider the path of that code from programmer to the live server. The classic way to think about that is some sort of promotion path. We'll describe what this might look like in a few different ways; some of them may be more relevant to you than others.

Say, for example, that the application is a new and young website. It is small and fast enough that the code can run on the programmer's computers which is a similar version of Linux to the eventual live server. Most **continuous integration** systems today can produce an artifact that is everything you need to install to run the web server, or even a **container image** (such as **Docker**). The programmer can run the image locally for developer testing. The build/deploy system can promote it and install the build on a server, perhaps in the cloud. With one programmer testing their own work, we might only need local and production. Larger efforts may require one or more test servers, possibly two staging servers. One of these will have no third-party connections, while a second can actually tie out to test servers for the trading partners. Finally, we have production, which is the live system.

Each of these is more than a server; they are a mini network. Everything the company needs to run the software, from databases to web servers to monitoring and container orchestration, is together. These environments are often slow, brittle, and expensive.

One of the reasons we need environments is to have ready, predictable test data in the databases. For programmers and initial testing, blank databases will often do. Sometimes the programmers can just mock out all the external services. Later stages of testing usually require production-like environments, to make sure the services all *play together* in an integrated way.

The dev/test/staging/production paradigm tended to lead to an ever-increasing number of expensive-to-maintain environments. The arrival of virtualization, containers, and cloud computing made it possible to collapse the process while making environments available to anyone on demand. A company working in that way might have developer environments, staging, and production. Three challenges with on-demand environments are cost, time to create, and data. Classic **monolith** architectures are single applications that are completely self-contained, with a single code repository, building and deploying everything at once. They can be easy to get started but end up big, expensive, brittle, and hard to change. In addition, the data needs to be hosted somewhere. In practice, most companies either have a small number of databases that the development servers connect to or else have many canonical standard data seeds to pick from when the databases are created.

Another option for development environments is to know what you are testing in isolation and have a dependency tree, so it is possible to test just the things that your service is dependent on. This is a step in between testing a service in total isolation and testing the entire system from end to end. When we create test environments that have just the service and dependencies, likely using container orchestration tools such as Kubernetes, we call this "creating a constellation" test environment, like a constellation of stars.

Understanding the regulatory issues in test data management

The **Health Insurance Portability and Privacy Act (HIPPA)** does not specifically say that data cannot be copied to test, but instead states that only people who need access to the data should have that access. So, for example, someone in customer service should be able to access a current customer's information, to the extent that they are allowed to support that customer. Ultimately, is it up to the company, and their auditors, to determine how much test data is necessary.

Financial regulations are more stringent, including the **Payment Card Industry Data Security Standard (PCI DSS)** and **Personally Identifiable Information (PII)**. For reasons that are likely obvious, banks and insurance companies are not excited about everyone having access to the trifecta of full name, date of birth, and unique legal identifier. In the US, that identifier will likely be a social security number.

This creates a tension between testing and development, who are more effective with greater freedom, and security, who typically want to restrict permissions to the smallest subset possible.

Other possible regulations include the **Food and Drug Administration (FDA)** and the European Union's **General Data Protection Regulation (GDPR)**, along with voluntary certifications such as SAS70, SSAE 16, SOC, and ISO 9001. The voluntary certifications generally require a company to write down what they do, what controls they have in place to prevent fraud, how they will audit to make sure the process is followed, and then where the audit log is tracked. Sadly, companies often write these process docs as part of an idealized *the-way-it-should-be* process. People working in the system need to choose between breaking the rules or following them while doing less effective testing. Additionally, not following the regulations and privacy acts can cost a company a lot of money, as well as lead to customers losing confidence in the company's practices.

Some companies take a middle path, changing the data to be anonymous as it migrates backward. In the case of user data, that might be anonymizing social security numbers, changing addresses to other, valid addresses in a nearby area, changing names and birth dates – but keeping anyone over age 18 still over 18 and anyone under 18 still under 18 – and so on. Scrambling the data but keeping it good enough to be useful turns out to be such an effort that there are large, expensive software tools dedicated to doing it well. They may be worth considering, but our first piece of advice is to take a step back and read the regulations yourself. In our experience, most companies simply do whatever they did before that passed the audit. We don't want testing to be driven by regulations that might not really exist; we want to become the experts.

Part of becoming the expert is knowing what is really going on, which might include a **user spy** feature.

The user spy feature

Earlier, we mentioned synthetic users. A user spy feature is the ability to log in as a user, to see exactly what they see. If you've been following along, you will likely see how that can be a huge problem. Edward Snowden's whistleblowing was essentially complaining that the US government had built user spy functionality into social media that allowed people in his group to spy on anyone – and yes, people were spying on ex-girlfriends.

Yet, if the software is driven by user-created content, a user spy (or even user export/import) function can be incredibly powerful for support, testing, and development. One option is to log every spy session, audit it, and get permission from the customer before acting as a spy. Another is to anonymize the data as discussed previously, though in these cases the problem is usually with user data that is interpreted in some way as to look odd on the screen.

Increasing public pressure, as well as increased regulations around privacy, has caused companies to take a more careful look at the risk/reward tradeoff of the user spy. At the very least, it is possible to add architecture to log who logged in using a user spy, what account they spied on, when, and what actions they took. That log can be audited. Or you can make permission for the spy require two-supervisor sign-off, or record the user granting the permission, to include uploading the audio file, and so on.

Summary

Test data management sounds like the topic of a book you would read to help you get to sleep at night. It is not exciting. Yet actually knowing what to expect when a test runs is important. If we want to know what to expect, then we must predict what will be in permanent storage. This chapter discussed ways to know what is in permanent storage, such as having a standard set of data, making application setup scriptable, and creating test users in production. Other ways to get accurate test data include pulling data from production or managing the data that exists in development and test environments. Finally, we considered regulatory issues that might create additional challenges regarding test data. With this in hand, you should be able to create test plans that are immune to data corruption, failures due to tests *aging out*, and related problems. Not only that, but you will be able to identify problems with system architecture and test plans – and fix them.

With test data management well in hand, we have a decent view of what might be called *just* testing. That is, give us a build and we can test and provide test results. Now we will move on to look at how to scope our testing, how often to test, and where to test what version. To understand these things, we'll have to shift our focus from the business of testing toward the edges of it, where testing integrates with the rest of delivery. In the next chapter, *Chapter 8*, we examine the intersection of software testing and delivery by discussing delivery models.

Part 2: Testing and Software Delivery

In this part, we discuss integrating that into the overall development picture. Exactly how testing fits into Scrum, for example, is something the authors of Scrum never really talk about. They did this intentionally, as the idea of scrum is that the people doing the work decide how to do it themselves. As Scrum got more popular and began to enter use for marketing, HR, and children's chore lists, including technical how-to's actually became less and less valuable. Yet it seems foolish to have every team reinvent the wheel for themselves. So, we wrote *Part 2* first to describe the delivery models, then break down the testing of its component pieces, and re-assemble it to meet your delivery needs.

This section has the following chapters:

- *Chapter 8, Delivery Models and Testing*
- *Chapter 9, The Puzzle Pieces of Good Testing*
- *Chapter 10, Putting Your Test Strategy Together*
- *Chapter 11, Lean Software Testing*

Delivery Models and Testing

The previous chapters examined software testing as an independent process – that is, sitting down in front of working software and testing it in order to find quality risks. The **unit testing**, **TDD**, and **Specification by Example** sections in *Chapters 3 and 4* intertwined test and development a bit, but for the most part, we didn't talk about how the software got to its current state, what the team will do with the feedback, how the software is released, how testing deals with problems in the field, and so on. To borrow a metaphor, it is a bit like talking about nails and pieces of wood without mentioning hammers, measurement, design, and carpentry.

This chapter widens our scope to discuss how testing and testers interact with the wider world. It provides teams with the information to not only understand where they are, but where they want to go, how to get there, and how to optimize time spent risk management and other activities. In order to do that, we explore the various models used for software development in a testing context. Our intention is not to outline what is "right" or "truly Agile." As Alfred Korzbski wrote so well, *"The map is not the territory."* Instead, our aim is to help you understand the ideas that influenced how your team ended up where it is – along with some options to steer its future direction.

In this chapter, we're going to cover the following main topics:

- Waterfall
- Scrum and SAFe
- Extreme Programming
- Kanban
- Continuous delivery and deployment
- DevOps, platform engineer, and SRE

Finally, we aim to give the reader tools to explain the current tradeoffs in the delivery system; that is, to explain that we currently do X, Y, and Z, so we should expect A, B, and C outcomes. If the unfortunate tester gets push-back on that, well, that is what *Chapters 12-15* are for, a part of the book we nicknamed *"Practicing Politics"*.

For now, let's get on with talking about different ways of looking at software delivery, and how testing can change to enable those delivery styles. However, unless we can analyze the existing practices and have a wide variety of what should we steer toward, what does "good" look like?

Technical requirements

This chapter is all about software engineering processes. We'll cover some deep concepts in programming, but at a human-readable level. Those new to software engineering processes will pick up a great deal in terms of delivery ideas. Well-versed people may see the full software process explained from a test perspective for the first time. We expect they will derive the most value from the material on how to explain the process, customize it, and understand the tradeoffs involved.

To do that we'll start at the beginning, then move very fast. Our journey begins at the waterfall, or even before that, with code and fix.

Waterfall

The term *waterfall* is most popularly associated with Winston Royce's paper [`http://web.archive.org/web/20230511154936/https://www.praxisframework.org/files/royce1970.pdf`]. Back in 1970, Royce observed that the simplest model for software delivery was *code and fix*. Code and fix is what it sounds like – write code until you see a problem (likely a compile error), then code some more. While we laugh at this, it could be an appropriate style for, say, a complex spreadsheet where the customer, manager, and programmer are all the same person. That style might also work for a first-year computer programming assignment.

By the 1970s, software development was a big enough business to have programs supported by dozens of people. IBM's system/360, developed in the 1960s and 1970s, had hundreds of programmers on staff. Even for much more modest projects, managers started to ask what seem like reasonable questions, such as the following:

- How much will this cost us?
- When will it be done?
- What exactly are we going to get?
- Can you make sure the software has (for instance) single sign-on, password reset, pagination for long search results, or any other pet feature?
- When we get it, will it even work?

This book is focused on answering that last question, but by now you should have some insight into the others, along with some idea of the uncertainty that makes such questions hard. After first introducing code and fix, Royce's second concept was what has become known as the **waterfall**.

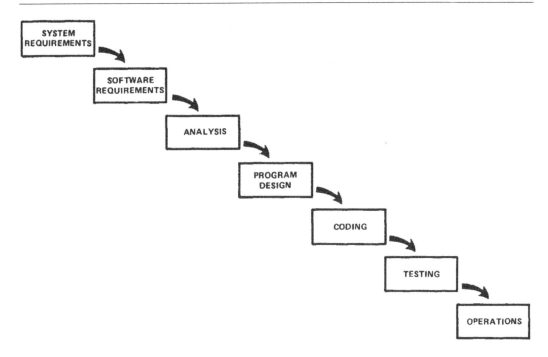

Figure 8.1 – Royce's "waterfall" diagram

The idea here is intuitive: Figure out what you will build, figure out how to build it, test it, and put it to use. The quote people forget is the words immediately following the diagram in Royce's original paper: *"I believe in this concept, but the implementation is risky and invites failure."*

Roger Ferguson, who taught Matt's software development management class at Grand Valley State University, put it this way: *The waterfall model fixes the schedule at the very beginning of the project, when the team knows the least about what they will build. It views success as conforming to a decision made early in the project by someone relatively uninvolved. The main benefit, then, of the waterfall, is that it makes management's job easy.*

This is true enough.

Schedule in hand, senior management can ask for progress. If things are going well, they can go back to golf. If things are yellow, management can point a finger and ask for more frequent updates. If they are red, management can ask for more frequent updates, create a sense of urgency, and apply pressure until someone tells them everything will be okay.

This is where testing comes in.

Notice that with every other phase of the project, someone can say the project is "on time." Requirements (what the customer wants, phrased in their language) become done because the day they are supposed to be done has passed. The same is true for the technical specification, which is the engineering-language description of what the software will do. Design documents end when the date occurs. Even programming can be "done," with the knowledge that buttons don't do anything combined with the certain knowledge that *other* programmers will have blocker bugs, so programming can continue during the testing phase.

It is during testing that we get the first real objective feedback that *this thing doesn't work*. It is the tester that will have to go to the project manager, absolutely committed to the July 1st release date, and say *"I know you want to release in a month, but I can't log in. If I try to search, I get an error message. I get an error when I change anything about my profile. The images for products do not appear. And ..."*

Only in testing do we get the objective feedback of what is really going on to steer the project. This is incredibly important and worth pausing on. Later sections talk about more modern ways to think about software delivery. In all of them, testing is moved to occur earlier and more often, and be more interleaved with software delivery. Many of these models offer an iterative approach, which gets a simple working system into use quickly to get fast feedback.

Royce didn't stop at the previous diagram, either. He quickly introduced the idea of "backwash", that the process could be insufficient and pushed back to the previous step. Later he admits that a defect found in testing might push the process back even further, perhaps to requirements. He suggests building a prototype that is thrown away – as a team is likely to throw away the first version anyway (`https://www.computerworld.com/article/2550685/the-grill--fred-brooks.html`). Eventually, Royce's waterfall paper [`https://www.praxisframework.org/files/royce1970.pdf`] ends up suggesting successive refinement. The example in *Figure 8.2*, from a process perspective, can be overwhelming and feel chaotic. Indeed, it looks a little like a model we would call "everything, everywhere, all the time." This zoomed-out example is vaguely inspired by the waterfall (see the square boxes) but each stage has a series of refinements, including prototyping and expecting change.

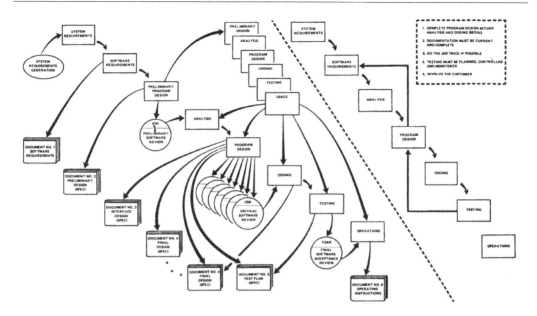

Figure 8.2 – The final process suggestion from the waterfall paper.
The intent of this screenshot is to show the maximized layout; text readability is not required.

We realize the preceding example might be a little unreadable in the book, and that sort of makes our point. Imagine some poor mid-level manager in the late 1970s, before the desktop computer was available, reading this paper and trying to figure out the software development process for their company, knowing their manager will ask the same questions about cost, schedule, and features. With a typewriter and mimeograph machine as the state of the art, and process documents in three-ring binders, it sure sounds appealing to just take the earlier diagram, write a description of every box, and call it done.

Everything that follows will be trying to balance out the problems the waterfall introduces.

We do not, however, mean to be too tough on waterfall-style thinking. We see it as having advantages, and even a place of its own in software development.

The advantages of and place for the waterfall

With waterfall development, testing looks like it only happens once. Yet if we could see inside the box called **test**, in most projects, it would be more like the following:

1. Test everything.
2. Figure out what needs fixing.
3. Wait for the fixes.

4.   Retest what was fixed, retest around what changed, retest core components, and anything else important.

5.   Figure out what still needs fixing.

6.   Wait for the fixes.

7.   Retest what was fixed, retest around what changed, retest core components, anything else important, and anything else you can think of.

8.   Figure out what still needs fixing.

9.   Wait for the fixes.

10. Retest what was fixed, retest around those things that were fixed (and so on).

Over time, the amount of retesting tends to shrink. When testing is done, we put the product in use and call it done.

If the software goes into ongoing development after operation use (sometimes called "maintenance" if the initial project is large and ongoing changes small), the team will need to find a new strategy for testing. This ongoing use more closely resembles the iterative development we describe next, because the team *makes changes, does some testing, and introduces new functionality*, on a loop for what is often years.

Our language in the preceding paragraph sounds critical, but we don't mean it to be overly so. This sort of approach can work just fine for a project built in a day, a week, or even a month. The smaller the discovery process and the less the market situation will change, the more the waterfall model makes sense.

Another early application for the waterfall model was to build software for hardware that did not exist yet. Not only did it not exist, but the hardware was much more powerful than anything that existed before, so it was not possible to run on a simulator. In these cases, writing designs on paper allowed the programmers to split up the work into components that interacted with each other over clearly defined interfaces. Once it was possible to program, the programmers could each take a well-defined piece, making parallel development easier. We've lost track of this today, leading to the branching and merging problems common in software development.

Before we leave the waterfall, let's spend a moment talking about the V-Model.

The V-Model

Earlier, we mentioned that testing at the end meant no feedback for the developers until then. The V-Model breaks down the testing process into stages. With the V-Model, first people surf the waterfall down into requirements, design, and implementation (code), then they climb out, with unit testing, integration testing, and system testing. With the V-Model, it is possible to write a "systems test plan" at the very beginning, a test plan for the design, and unit test the documentation. Here's a graphical example (https://commons.wikimedia.org/wiki/File:V-model.svg):

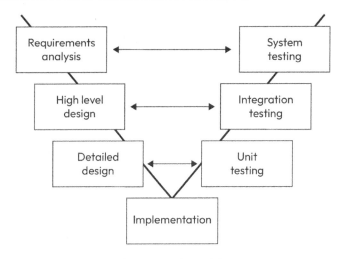

Figure 8.3 – V-Model

We think it's worth mentioning the V-Model. It's certainly a way of thinking about testing. We've just never quite seen things play out the way the document suggests. Our experience with real-time systems, such as aviation controls, is limited, but we have friends who have done this work and seem to make very good attempts to apply this model in a disciplined way. Still, it has the same fundamental problem as the waterfall, in that you build everything and integrate it at the end, hoping it will work.

In practice, the successful "waterfall" projects we've seen had prototypes at the beginning, things changing, developers unit testing as they went, and testers given large chunks of software early in the process to explore. The ideas that follow attempt to find a way to do better and test and integrate more often.

Iterative, incremental, and mini waterfalls

Remember, with the waterfall model, we don't really know how the pieces will come together until testing and integration. Modern engineering practices, such as **Continuous Integration**, can reduce this uncertainty – we can at least make sure that unit tests run, and the software builds along the way. Some teams want each little micro-feature to be well tested as the build progresses. That process is called **building in increments**, sometimes referred to as **incremental** delivery. For example, a team might list every micro-feature as a "story", and test each story along the way, perhaps adding some customer-facing test tooling into the build. With a waterfall approach, we still typically have some sort of final acceptance testing. If the team isn't careful, when it comes to the final testing, nothing really works, and the project is weeks or months behind. In addition, there is no value delivered until the end of the waterfall.

Iterative delivery, by contrast, involves listing the necessary features in order to create a simple working system – that is, all the features required to actually use the software, with the most important features first. For a job board, you might start with a list of jobs, without search functionality, where you simply email your resume by hand. From a business perspective, you could sell advertisements and job listings. From there, you can provide statistics on how many people click. Then hide email addresses and have people submit a resume, so you can track applications. Then create the ability for people to create an account and upload a resume, so they can one-click apply. After that, work on a search functionality, then the ability for employers to search through the existing resumes. In addition, people could have multiple resumes to submit depending on the type of job to help them highlight different aspects of their experience.

The most obvious way to enable this in software is by a series of **mini-waterfalls**. Every few months or less, the team moves through the cycle of gathering requirements, design, coding, testing, and deployment. Without sophisticated software engineering skills, the testing process tends to become more expensive and cause greater delays, as the team has more and more software to "cover" during testing. Mini-waterfalls made sense in the 1980s and 1990s, when software went out on physical disks in boxes, one release at a time. The leaders of the early 2000s grew up in such environments, and carried them into a very young World Wide Web, with physical servers. The main pain point with the mini-waterfall was testing, which led to a focus on tooling and automation of the test execution process, leading to the lessons we learned in *Chapter 2*.

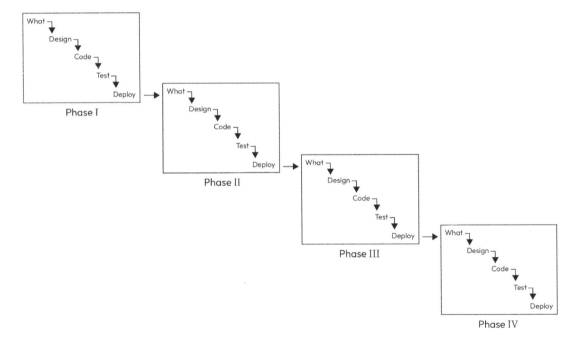

Figure 8.4 – Mini-waterfalls

A mini-waterfall approach is certainly **incremental**. If the software could be released after Phase I, then the approach was also **iterative**. With the Basecamp product, the parent company 37Signals took this idea to its logical conclusion. Basecamp had an initial 30-day trial, so the company released the product with no backend billing system or credit-card functionality (`https://medium.com/the-mission/how-basecamp-built-a-100-billion-business-by-doing-less-on-purpose-5f978ce6478c`). After all, they wouldn't need it for a month. From a business perspective, this allowed Basecamp to reduce time-to-cash by roughly one month.

As we discussed, the main issue mini-waterfalls have is a testing problem. Every step of the process can make the phases smaller and smaller. A "phase" could be as simple as adding a new column to a report. Yet the classic, human-driven, test-it-all-for-regression strategy will make the test process take longer and longer.

On the other hand, with our example of adding a column to a report, we know we do not need to test everything. If we have some way of looking at the code changes, recognizing the only change is in a report, and understanding the architecture, we might be able to test just the report and move on. Having the skills and discipline to understand how much needs testing is a focus of this book.

During the early 2000s, software that had been shipped on physical disks started to move to the internet, and new applications, including e-commerce, started to evolve on the internet. Just before that happened, a set of innovators started to create new kinds of software process, broadly called **Agile**. These processes were designed to support incremental and iterative delivery, but for different reasons. The first practice we'll mention, **Extreme Programming** (**XP**), took the programming world by storm but was hard for management to adopt. The second, Scrum, was easy to adopt at the management level, but did not have specific advice for testers. We'll discuss them both, how they can work together, what they mean for testing, and how much the software world has learned from them.

Extreme Programming (XP)

Extreme Programming, or **XP**, started out as essentially a thought experiment of what would happen if good things were taken beyond their usual limits. One term for this is to *crank the dials to 11*, which comes from attempting to turn speakers beyond their regular limits on a one-to-ten scale. Here are a few questions XP asks:

- If shorter delivery timeframes (mini-waterfalls) are good, what if we just organize the work into iterations of two weeks or less, and deploy at least every three iterations? (This goal was later shortened to every iteration.)

- If working closely with customers is good, how about we have an on-site customer as a team member? (For remote teams, this would be an embedded team member who is a customer/decision-maker, as opposed to a requirements document.)

- If code reviews are good, how about we have a continuous code review, with pair programming all the time?

- If testing is good, how about we unit test before we write the code, using **Test-Driven Development** (**TDD**)?

- If incremental work is good, how about we slice features into micro-features that a pair of programmers could build in a day or two? These would have acceptance criteria understandable to customers and that could be automated.

- If more frequent integration is good, let's run automated builds and all the unit tests for every story when it finishes on an integration machine.

- If having a programmer "own" a feature is bad, what if we simply have collective code ownership and allow anyone on the team to change anything in the code base at any time?

While there are twelve practices of Extreme Programming (`https://www.zentao.pm/blog/12-practices-to-fully-follow-in-extreme-programming-1315.html`), the preceding list captures some of the highlights. Looking back 25 years after it was introduced, some practices, such as continuous integration and unit tests, are now completely mainstream. Thanks to Scrum, which we discuss in the next main section, many teams have an embedded full-time person empowered to speak for the customer. The "coach" role is also common in software development today in a way it was not before XP. Perhaps most importantly, XP collapsed the waterfall, interleaving design, coding, and testing into one activity done by a programmer/programmer pair.

XP's focus on everyone-is-a-programmer has had mixed results, though most people doing testing are more technical today.

Before we leave XP, let's discuss the context – what problems was XP designed to solve?

The context of XP

The first major XP project was the Chrysler Consolidated Compensation, or "3C" project. With 3C, the Chrysler company was attempting to bring all their payroll systems into one. 3C was a command-line program that would read data from a database to create a text file that would be sent to a payroll vendor. Thus, 3C had no user interface. With no user interface, 3C was more an **Extract-Transform-Load** (**ETL**) data project (similar to the high-volume example in *Chapter 1*) than the kind of software we tried testing in the first two chapters. Thus, the creators of that project did not have to deal with the pesky user, nor the **event-driven** paradigm, where a user can bounce between features over and over again entering data that is unexpected or in an unexpected order.

It's also worth noting that 3C was an experiment with new methods, including **incremental** and **iterative** development. Prior to 3C, Chrysler used a waterfall approach, with perhaps a year spent with an outside vendor to write a requirements document. After a year, a second vendor might come in to change the requirements into a "Complete, Correct, Consistent" (another, different 3C) technical specification. That process might take eighteen months, as the second vendor might complain the first had done a terrible job. At that point, the internal programmers might be brought in to spend a year on design – invariably pointing out that the external vendors did not understand the company and they had to start over. After two years of design, coding could begin, which might take two more. At that point, the project was five or six years old. Whatever opportunity the company was hoping to capture may well have passed. When a new CIO or CTO or Vice-President came in or the company experienced a reorganization or new budget, the project might be cancelled. At that point, the project would have nothing to show for itself and have delivered no value.

With their desire to ship code every six weeks or less, the initial XP team was essentially in a race: *We are going to have deployed working software before you can cancel our project.* C3 was not the first attempt at a project of this magnitude, but it was the first to actually deliver anything. The first version of the software was not comprehensive at all. It did not do payroll deductions, did not process taxes, and only worked for employees at the corporate headquarters. For that matter, it only did payroll for hourly employees required to work forty hours per week or less, because it could not process overtime. As a result, the first version of C3 effectively only processed timecards for interns at the corporate office – but it did the entire process, not just loading the data into staging tables, but actually enabling an end-to-end business process to print timecards.

The systemic forces at play here are very different from the forces that created Scrum at roughly the same time. We'll discuss Scrum next, then Kanban, followed by modern technical approaches and how they reconnect to how they impact test strategy.

Scrum and SAFe

"Suppose you have a software development project to do. For each traditional phase, you can draw from a pool of experienced people. Rather than have several designers do the design phase and have several coders do the construction phase, and so on, you form a team by carefully selecting one person from each pool. During a team meeting, you will tell them that they have each been carefully chosen to do a project that is very important to the company, country, organization, or whatever. This unsettles them somewhat. You then give them a description of the problem to be solved, the figures for how much it cost in time and money to do similar projects, and what the performance figures for those systems are. Then, after you have gotten them used to the idea that they are special, having been specifically chosen to do an important job, you further unsettle the team by saving that their job is to produce a system in, say, half the time and money and it must have twice the performance of other systems. Next, you say that how they do it is their business. Your business is to support them in getting resources. Then, you leave them alone.

You stand by to give advice if you are asked. You get their reports, which come regularly but not as often or as voluminously as the waterfall model. But, mostly you wait. In something like the appointed time, out pops the system with the performance and cost figures you want.

Sounds like a fairy tale, doesn't it?"

This quote, from *Peter DeGrace and Stahl's* book *Wicked Problems, Righteous Solutions*, was a process they described in 1993 as **Scrum**. The book postulated a bit about what that might look like. It was three years later that Ken Schwaber and Jeff Sutherland presented their OOPSLA paper that formalized the process we know as **Scrum** today.

Here's a brief overview of **Scrum**. Like XP, it will be compressed, which involves some loss, but we'll try to hit the highlights:

- Software development work is organized into Sprints, of 30 to 90 days. With each Sprint, the team delivers an increment of working software.

- The work to be done in the sprint is organized in a list called a **Sprint Backlog**.

- Workers pull new work from the Backlog and work on it.

- Team members have a daily stand-up meeting to discuss how to accelerate the Sprint. This is sometimes called the **Daily Scrum**. At the Daily Scrum, team members typically discuss what they did yesterday, what they will do today, and if they were blocked by anything.

- At the beginning of the Sprint, the team has a planning meeting to discuss the Sprint goal.

- At the end of the Sprint, the team presents a demo to the customer of what they have built. The feedback from the demo is taken into the next Sprint. The team also does a retrospective on the previous Sprint in order to find ways to work better in the next Sprint.

- Scrum has three roles: Customer, Team member, and **Scrum Master**. The **Scrum Master**'s role is to make sure the team honors its working agreements, to facilitate the meetings, and perhaps do some servant-leadership for the team. This can include accepting obstacles from outside the team and working to resolve them.

The following diagram (*Wikimedia Commons*, `https://commons.wikimedia.org/wiki/File:Scrum_process.svg`) is an illustration of the Scrum process:

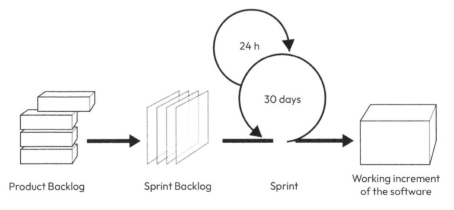

Figure 8.5 – Scrum

Notice that the Scrum process defined here is not really specific to software. Diverse teams today use Scrum to figure out marketing plans, cover the curriculum for college classes, and even organize chores for young families. That is an intentional aspect of Scrum: it allows people to define their own processes, and for the process to change anytime the team agrees in a retrospective.

Teams adopting Scrum often simply break their existing work down into mini-waterfalls, similar to *Figure 8.4*, where each phase is a Sprint.

The context of Scrum

Where XP was founded by teams trying to ship software before the project was canceled, Scrum was born out of the opposite problem – executives who changed priorities so often the team could get nothing done. Thus, Scrum was more *"leave us alone for ninety days to actually build something"* instead of *"let's compress our release schedule to stay within the funding decision loop."* XP focused much more on engineering practices and put the programmer first, while Scrum left it to the technical staff to decide their own practices, setting them free to do as they liked.

For some time, Scrum/XP was promoted by many, using Scrum for the project management aspects and XP for the software development practices. At one point XP was wildly popular, including a twenty-odd book series that existed at physical bookstores. For some reason, however, Scrum "won the branding war." That may have been better marketing, perhaps. We suspect that Scrum was simply easier to implement. Teams could work to short mini-waterfalls, attend Daily Scrums, and express requirements as stories without having to change job titles or descriptions. Pure XP, on the other hand, eliminated roles such as the business analyst and forced programmers to write code in pairs, something often resisted by both the programmers and management. It also required TDD as a discipline, along with coding discipline. Scrum became popular, but the idea of self-governing teams much less so. Instead, we got *stand-ups*, stories, and *Sprints* as the default way to do software development in the 2020s.

So far, we've mostly focused on two types of testing – at the micro-feature level (covering specific changes) and regression testing at the end (do all of these changes play well together? Did some new change break some old functionality, causing it to fall back, or "regress"?). Both Scrum and XP put pressure on the old ways of doing testing. With two-week Sprints becoming common, any regression test process would have to be complete in a day or two. Consider a test process that takes a day, followed by a day of fixing, a day of retests, and some final-final fixes and re-retests before deployment. Those four days are 40% of the Sprint, which totals ten business days – nine if a holiday is involved. Add a one-hour demo and retrospective on the last day, some planning and analysis on the first, and suddenly the team is only productive for 50% or less of the Sprint. In addition, while the code can get a little crusty and progress slowly, the potential effort of regression testing will continue to grow incredibly quickly. After a year of two-week Sprints, the team will have 26 times as much software to cover! Unless something changes, the cost of testing will continue to expand until it threatens the success of the project. There are two general strategies for this: either testing better, or changing the engineering process to reduce the need for testing in the first place. In *Chapter 10*, we will discuss strategies to "do more with less", aiming to do the most powerful testing in the smallest possible time.

By changing the engineering process, we mean interleaving analysis, design, coding, and testing, changing them into activities instead of phases. In addition, the team can either automate end-to-end regression checks, or perhaps eliminate the need for end-of-cycle regression testing – which we'll discuss under DevOps and SRE.

Scrum and XP did have one problem for senior executives, in that they were both designed to work at the same single-team scale, with everyone in one room for a stand-up meeting. Scrum made a small attempt to address larger programs with a "Scrum of Scrums", where each team sent a representative to a daily meeting. Still, for the most part, the two methods did not address how to organize large projects.

Enter **SAFe**, **Scaled Agile Framework for the Enterprise**, which in some ways descended from the **Rational Unified Process** (**RUP**).

SAFe and its context

Between the waterfall model and Scrum/XP, there was a major method called the Rational Unified Process, or RUP. The RUP was an advancement in that it was incremental, and it recognized requirements, design, coding, and testing as activities that interleave over time. RUP still had phases – **Inception**, **Elaboration**, **Construction**, and **Transition**. That is arguably an improvement over models that assume software projects spring from nothing and run forever in Sprints or iterations.

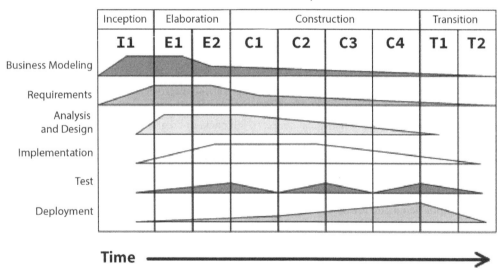

Figure 8.6 – The Rational Unified Process

Rational Software created the RUP; the software company was sold to IBM in 2003. The RUP was an implementation of the **Unified Process** (**UP**), an early **iterative** and **incremental** process. More detailed than the UP, the RUP could be described as a "giant toolbox." It's hard to argue against the RUP as nearly any software process can be described with it: most projects start, are worked on, and completed, and contain the activities in *Figure 8.6*. That said, it looks to us from the outside as if details of how to do RUP seemed to derive from theory, not practice, without much feedback from practice.

After Scrum, XP, and the Agile Manifesto (which we'll touch on later) came into existence, some of the key leaders from the RUP created SAFe. Like the RUP, SAFe is a *big toolbox* of ideas. The main benefit of SAFe is the idea that it can scale to large projects with teams of teams.

Where the main building block of Scrum and XP is the team, SAFe's building block is the Team of Teams, or **Release Train**. Just as each Scrum has a Product Owner, Scrum Master, and team, a Release Train has a lead **Product Manager**, **System Architect**, and **Release Train Engineer**. The Release Train has a **Planning Interval** (**PI**) that could be four, five or six two-week Sprints. PIs begin with a PI planning exercise for the entire Team –of Teams and end with demos presented back to the customer. In this way, SAFe is fractal – the next level takes several of the levels below, adds them up, adds new "triumvirate" roles, and adds the additional governance, metrics, and controls you would expect for a larger and larger budget.

It's hard to argue against SAFe because it encompasses everything. For implementation, teams can do Scrum, XP, or Kanban. The entire process is guided by Lean Thinking, which we apply to testing in *Chapter 11*. The "big toolbox" includes metrics, design thinking, built-in quality, team and higher-level Backlogs, team and technical agility, Lean-Agile leadership, core values, principles, an implementation roadmap…that's about half the high-level bullet points for "Essential SAFe." Each bullet point, of course, decomposes into a dozen more.

While the methods that comprise SAFe may *individually* each solve some specific problem in context, it is not clear whether they add up together to solve every problem for every large organization. Moreover, they seem to focus on processes and tools, which we will discuss later in this chapter. Ken Scwaber, the co-creator of Scrum, put it this way:

> *The boys from RUP (Rational Unified Process) are back. Building on the profound failure of RUP, they are now pushing the Scaled Agile Framework (e) as a simple, one-size-fits-all approach to the agile organization. They have made their approach even more complicated by partnering with Rally, a tools vendor. Consultants are available to customize it for you, also just like RUP.*

> *They are touting their processes and tools this week … They would be at the RUP conference, but there are none. They would be at the waterfall conference, but they are no longer. So, they are at our conference. Strange, but they had nowhere else to go. Try to be polite.*

This was intended as it reads, not just as a critique of the Scaled Agile Framework, but an attack on the legitimacy of the framework as an **Agile** method.

To understand the criticism, we need to discuss what *Agile* methods are and how to consider your context, to understand how to customize the process to fit your specific problems and constraints. That brings us to house-rules software development.

House-rules software development

A major challenge in all of these methods is the aspect of change management – that is, a team moving from how they developed software yesterday to this new way of working. Scrum is the most successful certification program of the methods we've discussed so far – the Scrum Alliance has given out 1.4 million certifications (`http://web.archive.org/web/20230527080619/https://www.scrumalliance.org/`) and Scrum.org over 800,000 (`http://web.archive.org/web/20230314185320/https://www.scrum.org/certification-list`). Due to this, most organizations we work with at least "talk Scrum", but that only provides high-level project management. It does not tell teams how to develop or test. When we talk to teams about how they work, we generally get one of two answers.

1.   "We developed our own in-house method, called *name-of-company* method."
2.   "It depends."

Of the two, we find "It depends" as the more frustrating. At more than one client, the conversation actually went like this:

> Matt: *"How do you do software delivery here?"*
>
> Worker: *"It depends on the product."*
>
> Matt: *"Let's just say for the product you're working on now."*
>
> Worker: *"It depends on the team."*
>
> Matt: *"Let's just say the team you working in now."*
>
> Worker: *"It depends on the feature."*
>
> Matt: *"Let's just say the feature you are working on right now."*
>
> Worker: *"It depends on the modification being made to the feature."*
>
> Matt: *"Let's just say whatever modification you are testing right now."*
>
> Worker: **Blank stare*.*

Methodology sounds like an old word; many people today are more interested in building tools to automate steps of the process (which we'll cover as our next major topic). Yet methodology answers questions about how things should be done. Without it, we improvise, getting a list of what should be built from somewhere, a deadline from somewhere else, and doing "some testing." With this approach, things get missed. Communicating "how we do things" keeps everyone on the same page.

Most importantly, having a "how we do things" tells people what is important. In addition to methods, some teams have ideals or principles. Given some principles that everyone agrees on, skilled teams can create their own methods. Two sets of principles we use in our work are the Agile Manifesto and Context-Driven Testing.

The Agile Manifesto

The Agile movement was launched at a small conference in Snowbird, Utah, in 2001. The event, originally titled "lightweight methods", was an attempt to unite several factions of people who were tired of the "documents, plans, and planning" approach to software. They saw software development as an evolutionary process of discovery, where people learned by doing. The authors decided on the term *Agile*, defining it as follows(`https://agilemanifesto.org`):

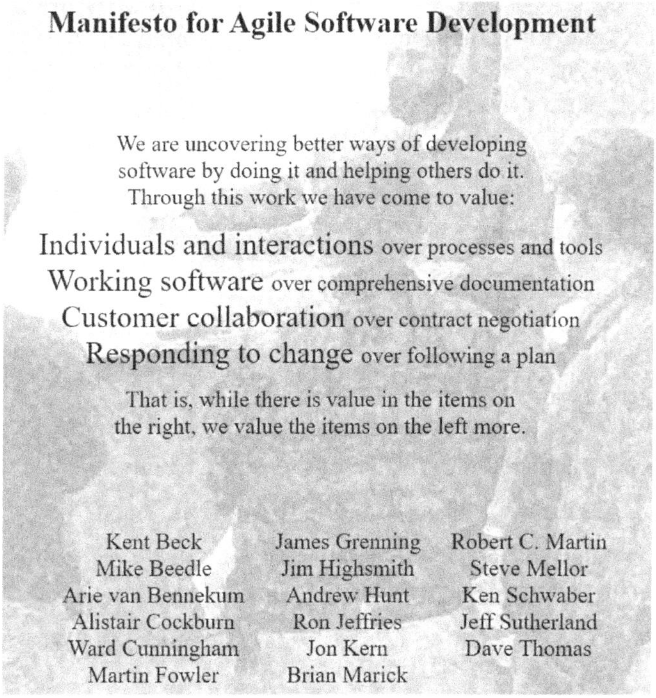

Manifesto for Agile Software Development

We are uncovering better ways of developing
software by doing it and helping others do it.
Through this work we have come to value:

Individuals and interactions over processes and tools
Working software over comprehensive documentation
Customer collaboration over contract negotiation
Responding to change over following a plan

That is, while there is value in the items on
the right, we value the items on the left more.

Kent Beck	James Grenning	Robert C. Martin
Mike Beedle	Jim Highsmith	Steve Mellor
Arie van Bennekum	Andrew Hunt	Ken Schwaber
Alistair Cockburn	Ron Jeffries	Jeff Sutherland
Ward Cunningham	Jon Kern	Dave Thomas
Martin Fowler	Brian Marick	

Figure 8.7 – Manifesto for Agile Software Development

2001, the above authors - this declaration may be freely copied in any form, but only in its entirety through this notice.

Notice that Agile is directly opposed to the idea of writing down exactly how every step should be done, "completely, correctly, and consistently," then turning the crank to transform the requirements into design, code, and testing, without having people talk to each other. **Agile** software development, with a capital-A, became known for a certain style of delivery, with story-cards, everyone working in the same room without partitions, everyone working on one project at a time, stand-up meetings, interleaving activities over phases, frequent delivery, and technical excellence. The event only had one person who self-identified as a tester, Brian Marick. Another tester, James Bach, was invited to the Snowbird conference but declined. James, Cem Kaner, Brian Marick, and Brett Pettichord would later create the context-driven principles (`https://context-driven-testing.com`).

Context-driven testing

The core idea of context-driven testing is that the situation drives the testing approach. The test strategy for a **Federal Aviation Administration** (**FAA**) air traffic control system might be very different than a video game. Even within a video game, one that is burned into a cartridge for single-player use would likely be tested differently than a multiplayer online game that can have many updates per day. In addition to how testing is done, context-driven testing says who is in the driver's seat – the person doing the testing. Thus, the person doing the testing owns their own work process; they have both the authority to decide the best ways to investigate risk, and the accountability to defend and explain it. (The employer can, of course, decide the investment in risk management isn't paying off and reassign or remove the person doing the testing.) The following are the seven principles of context-driven testing, along with some commentary:

The Seven Basic Principles of the Context-Driven School

1. The value of any practice depends on its context:

2. There are good practices in context, but there are no best practices.

3. People, working together, are the most important part of any project's context.

4. Projects unfold over time in ways that are often not predictable.

5. The product is a solution. If the problem isn't solved, the product doesn't work.

6. Good software testing is a challenging intellectual process.

7. Only through judgment and skill, exercised cooperatively throughout the entire project, are we able to do the right things at the right times to effectively test our products.

Illustrations of the principles in action

- Testing groups exist to provide testing-related services. They do not run the development project; they serve the project.

- Testing is done on behalf of stakeholders in the service of developing, qualifying, debugging, investigating, or selling a product. Entirely different testing strategies could be appropriate for these different objectives.

- It is entirely proper for different test groups to have different missions. A core practice in the service of one mission might be irrelevant or counter-productive in the service of another.

- Metrics that are not valid are dangerous.

- The essential value of any test case lies in its ability to provide information (that is to reduce uncertainty).

- All oracles are fallible. Even if the product appears to pass your test, it might well have failed it in ways that you (or the automated test program) were not monitoring.

- Automated testing is not automatic manual testing: it's nonsensical to talk about automated tests as if they were automated human testing.

This book takes a context-driven approach – that is, our aim is to give you a wide and deep toolbox from which to determine your own approach. We aim to accelerate your learning so you can make better decisions as you decide how to do your testing. If you lack discretionary authority in your day-to-day work, then arguably, you don't need this book. Your boss can just tell you how to do your work. But beware; if you don't own your process, you will forever be its victim.

Kanban as a house rule

Before we leave house rules, we want to mention Kanban. Inspired by the Japanese lean system of the same name, Kanban is different than most software in that instead of a push-based system (early phases push work to later), Kanban is a pull-based system. In fact, it could be as simple as a ticket-based system where team members pull and work on tickets one at a time, while limiting the work in progress. Teams can emulate Kanban by starting with Scrum, then dropping the concept of Sprints while moving planning, demos, and retrospectives to just-in-time.

Here's a sample Kanban board; the rectangles represent user stories.

Figure 8.8 – Kanban board

Source: *By Jennifer Falco - Own work, CC BY 4.0,* `https://commons.wikimedia.org/w/index.php?curid=132117320.`

Note that Kanban as defined here does not consider any sort of regression testing, or testing of any kind, really. The preceding small board collapses programming and testing into the single step of **Doing**. The initial program that defined Kanban (`http://images.itrevolution.com/images/kanbans/From_Worst_to_Best_in_9_Months_Final_1_3-aw.pdf`) was a maintenance team working on many small, non-connected applications and reports. When a report was changed, it could be tested and deployed independently.

Hopefully, by now, you are starting to see our main point: that software development processes solve a specific problem while introducing others. It is possible we do not have the problem the method addresses. Alternatively, the problems the method introduces could be greater than the problems they fix. In addition, testing already has the considerable problems we discussed in the preceding chapters. The chosen delivery approach will invariably create some risks. Testing can change its style to address those risks (see *Chapter 9*) or point them out and help the organization change. The context-driven principles and the Agile Manifesto may be able to help with that change.

Before we can close out delivery, we need to talk about continuous delivery.

Continuous delivery and deployment

While Scrum and Kanban enable teams to work on many small pieces independently, most architecture still harkened back to that "software build" tradition that came from physical disks. Yet by the 2010s, the dominant platform for new applications was the web. With the web, teams could update changes continuously. A bug that was found and fixed within hours would have a much smaller impact than a bug found, fixed, and redeployed two weeks later under Scrum. This allowed teams to take risks – if they could only develop an architecture to limit those risks.

One such architecture worth noting is that used by Etsy. The company used PHP, the "PHP Hypertext Preprocessor." PHP allowed programmers to embed computer code to change web pages as they were sent out. It is also interpreted, with each page a separate file. As long as the programmers didn't need to update a database or change a shared code library, it was possible for them to update just their own web pages without creating risk for other web pages. By building merge and deployment tools on top of its **Continuous Integration** (**CI**) server, Etsy made it possible for programmers to make and deploy an isolated change without a regression-testing cycle. Programmers could change a piece of code, deploy it, then go to a pile of monitors to see if that particular change was generating file errors, taking too long to load, and so on. This kind of work did require policies. For example, code that touched money or private customer information had to go through a more rigorous process, as database changes and libraries could impact other programmers. These approaches combined to become known as **continuous delivery** and had a major impact on how test/release was done.

One of Etsy's greatest advantages was their architecture; most larger organizations did not approve of PHP, or at least, were not willing to convert to it. By the mid-2010s, the internet was finding a new standard way to achieve continuous delivery, called **SOFEA**, or **Service-Oriented Front-End Architecture**.

With SOFEA, the standard web page looks much more like a template. A SOFEA HTML page might contain some layout and blank named fields for first name, last name, number of items in shopping cart, total price, and so on. JavaScript is used to call different APIs to find this information, then updates the **Document Object Model** (**DOM**) of the web page itself.

Under the SOFEA model, the web page, JavaScript, and CSS are just static text. The APIs are separate, typically microservices. Any programmer can update any of them; the deploy tool just needs to deploy one to five files together as a set. This can create some challenges with versions and deployments for larger teams, but those are solvable problems.

For our purposes, continuous delivery is a process where a single logical change to a system can be easily pushed to a test or staging environment. There may be a delay due to a human testing process in that environment, the need to sync with some other change, or for some other reason, then a person clicks "deploy" and the code moves to production. With continuous deployment, the build software pushes new code to production as soon as it passes the automated checks.

If you read that last sentence and thought "risk", you are not alone. Partly to address that risk and partly due to a lack of tooling, the sad state of the practice often involves days of delay between code completion and code in production – not exactly the original vision. To address this, advocates of continuous deployment invented entirely new categories of tools and infrastructure. For example, with configuration flags it is possible to run new code and old, side by side, only running the new code for users marked as testers or "beta" users. The broad term for the collection of those tools is sometimes called DevOps, SRE, or, increasingly, Platform Engineering.

DevOps, Platform Engineering, SRE

By the early 2000s, most new software development done was on websites, or else on company data centers. In both of those worlds, there were two sides: the developers who created changes, and the operations staff whose job was to keep the system stable. As the easiest way to keep systems stable is to prevent change, the two were often at odds with each other. The DevOps movement tried to align the incentives between the two, by getting operations on the same side as the developers, using the same programming languages, tools, and techniques, and often applying programming acumen to operations problems.

By 2011, continuous delivery was presented as a platonic ideal for software – eliminate regression testing by pushing just what changed and nothing else, all the time! Yet at the same time, software came from a single-build tradition that went all the way back to Windows and DOS applications.

In many cases, DevOps/Platform Engineering includes automating the build/deploy process and creating a continuous integration pipeline. Container software, such as **Docker** and **Kubernetes**, made it possible to create an image of the server software on every build, and for anyone to quickly create their own personal server with the current system plus just the change we are considering. A few of the risk management features enabled by DevOps are as follows:

- **Multiple deploy points**: If a programmer can deploy only the API that is to be changed, and that API has passing tests-as-contracts, it may be possible to deploy just that change.

- **Published metrics**: By showing performance on graphs at published URLs, developers can apply a change, then watch the monitors to see whether the page load or number of errors increases.

- **Blue/Green deployments**: This is where an entire bank of servers is loaded up with the new code, then the load balancer redirects traffic to the new bank. The old bank is kept around until the next deployment, enabling easy switch-back.

- **Configuration flags**: These allow software to run only under certain conditions. For example, a feature could be turned on just for employees, then also power users, and finally all users. The code checks whether the feature is turned on for that user, making it possible to switch the feature off by a simple database change in the event of a failure.

- **Integrated Build**: With integration of automated checks into the build pipeline and on-demand test environments, generally in the cloud.

All of these features change the risk picture. Some of them, for some changes, make it possible for the team to drastically reduce or eliminate regression testing as an activity.

Platform Engineering is a term for building the toolchain to enable self-service for test environments and production changes. **Site Reliability Engineering** (**SRE**) is a risk management role similar to testing but focused on observing the system in its entirety, including production monitoring.

Companies pursuing this last strategy (as discussed earlier) are often actively working to marginalize the value of testing through tooling and automation. That isn't an insult, but rather a rational strategy to reduce risk. People doing testing can work with these tools to discover value…or, if they are lucky, find a job elsewhere.

Summary

"Code (test) and fix" development creates an entire host of problems. We spent most of the chapter learning about adaptations people have made to reduce the risks created by code and fix. Reading the chapter, we expect you may recognize some practices from your own team, and, perhaps, recognize the problems the new practices introduce – or some that are missing.

The unfortunate tester looks at all these practices, and, hopefully, sees self-reinforcing ideas. In Extreme Programming, for example, the regression test suite produced by TDD combines with the second perspective of pair programming to decrease the risk of change. Refactoring, another XP practice, improves the design of the existing code, making it possible to build software as many small changes. Refactoring only works because of the TDD-built regression suite. And so on. And yet, XP was built without a user interface in mind and does not provide a deep strategy for UI testing. Scrum does not talk about how to do testing at all and runs the risk of mini-waterfalls along with an ever-growing painful regression-testing stage. Off-the-shelf Kanban does not even provide the time at the end of the Sprint for regression testing, while DevOps approaches tend to conflate automated checking with the kind of technical investigation only a person can do.

The context-driven tester (or at least someone wearing a "testing hat") has to look at what the team is doing, what the team thinks they are doing, and where the risks are. This chapter outlined where all of these concepts came from to provide you with comprehension, application, and analysis. In the next chapter, assembling the puzzle pieces of good testing, we'll go one level deeper, enabling you to complete analysis and perform synthesis – weaving a test strategy that adapts to the needs of the team. At least, that's our goal.

Let's go!

> **Note**
> This chapter compressed ideas that could themselves be a book into 1/5th of a chapter. Our goal was to distill the concepts to their essence. By definition, this compression had to be lossy, which we have mixed feelings about. On the plus side, with so little room, we believe the value per word is high.

Further reading

- *Wicked Problems, Righteous Solutions* was digitized by the Internet Archive in 2019 with funding from the Kahle/Austin Foundation and is available for checkout like a library book: `https://archive.org/details/wickedproblemsri0000degr`

- *The Scrum Development Process*, Ken Schwaber, OOPSLA Conference Report, 1996: `http://web.archive.org/web/20200926115254/https://scrumorg-website-prod.s3.amazonaws.com/drupal/2016-09/Scrum%20OOPSLA%201995.pdf`

9
The Puzzle Pieces of Good Testing

We can think of the software delivery style as setting us up for various kinds of risks. These could be simple bugs, strange bugs hidden in rare combinations of the software, performance and security problems, and anything in between. The delivery cycle might give us one opportunity to check things out before burning the software into a chip on a video game cartridge, or we might be able to update the software in seconds while maintaining uptime. This context of our work will indicate what pieces we need to assemble – and how to assemble them – to do good testing work.

A test case is not one of those primitives.

It is easy enough to rail against the test case as a structure, as a set of instructions on what to test along with an expected result. We see test cases as low value, yet people often fight for them. To the project manager, they give a sense of progress – looking at passing, failing, and percent complete, the project manager gets a sense of status. Anyone good at testing can figure out what to test, but the test case often has some bits of setup within it that might be complex and difficult to recreate; we call these recipes. There is also good general guidance on what the features are and how to test them embedded within the test case. By pitting many test case titles against the features of the application, we can get a feeling of how well the features are covered by testing work.

We propose breaking these concerns down and considering which apply to your team and how, then re-assembling them in *Chapter 10* so that you can build a test strategy.

In this chapter, we're going to cover the following main topics:

- Recipes – how to do hard things
- Coverage – did we test the right things well enough?
- Defects – what is the status of the software?

- Schedule – what do we test next?

- Strategy – what are our risks and priorities?

- Dashboard – how do we communicate what we know?

Technical requirements

The best way to get value out of this chapter is to consider the ideas while considering an actual, recent software project. By thinking about how the work was done (the accident) versus what needed to be done (the essence), you will be able to do a thought experiment about what could have been done. This means you will be able to achieve a higher level of cognitive work by analyzing testing ideas. Without that, you will be stuck more at the knowledge and comprehension levels. While there are no hardware or software requirements for this chapter, the ability to read simple software code will be helpful for the Coverage – did we test the right things well enough? section. The longest program in that section is nine lines of code, and we will provide a comprehensive explanation.

Our journey begins with understanding recipes.

Recipes – how to do hard things

One client we worked with had test cases stored in a test case management system. With that software, you could pick one project, get a list of test cases, and then get details about those test cases. For any release, you could create a "test run," and for every test run, you could mark the cases as passed or failed. By the time Matt arrived at the client, they were using an ancient client/server system whose version had just run out of support. The next version of the software would require a budget to upgrade. The operating system of the server was too old, so that would need to be upgraded, and the hardware was underpowered and out of date. Management performed a bulk export to Excel, threw the old test cases onto a network drive, and threw the test case management system away.

Nobody noticed.

To say that no one noticed might be a slight exaggeration. From time to time, someone on the team would be testing a particularly complex piece of functionality and not remember exactly how to configure things weirdly. For example, setting up an account in Spanish required setting a specific flag on a screen that might be forgotten. Sometimes, the test cases included database commands that would set up the accounts – **Structured Query Language** (**SQL**) commands to INSERT a row into the database, or a DELETE statement to clear out the last run followed by an INSERT statement. Over the next 6 months or so, perhaps once a month, someone on the team would not know how to perform a setup task, dig through the spreadsheets, and rebuild the recipe themselves. After about 6 months, we had rebuilt the core functionality and never referenced the spreadsheets again. All in all, the hard-to-reproduce value in those several hundred test cases was reproduced in perhaps 4 person days.

Given that this whole book is about seeking the highest value activities in our work, we suggest a subtle change in focus. Capture the most powerful, valuable pieces of things, with pointers to what to do next, and let humans figure out obvious things. That makes capturing recipes and storing and retrieving them a part of testing worth focusing on.

Defining recipes

For our purposes, we can define a recipe as follows:

A workflow or piece of functionality,

That is not intuitively obvious,

That if done improperly can yield an incorrect result in testing,

That, when performed, leads to an interesting observable state in the software,

That is worth writing down, keeping, and looking up.

Here is another definition:

The part of the test process you do so often, and is so complex, that it is both worth writing down and storing in some way that you and others will be able to find it and use it again later.

When we started talking about recipes, we called them *snippets*, because we saw no value in the test case except – oh, wait, that snippet we might keep. We are also very reluctant to introduce new metaphors. With an actual (food) recipe, you take standard ingredients, put them in standard equipment, apply a standard process, and have an expected result. A cook might change the mix a bit, particularly doubling or halving it, depending on the meal's needs. In software, we tend to call these things **design patterns**. They're a common solution that resolves a system of forces that can be combined to create software.

Design patterns are based on city layouts and construction, including ideas such as a portico or courtyard. They are generic things that you might want to use when building your town and correspond with generic things you might want to use when building software. Recipes, on the other hand, tell you exactly what to do to get a result that is expected. While it might be possible to leave the brownies in too long and burn them, a test recipe is precise enough that if something goes wrong, you've found a bug. As a result, we find that the term recipe maps a little better to these than design pattern.

What metaphors do for us is take something odd, different, and unfamiliar, and compare it with something familiar. If you've never boiled eggs or made boxed macaroni and cheese, we hope you'll at least be familiar with the idea. This idea of taking the key, important, non-intuitive things from the test process and putting them somewhere else, somewhere easy to look up and find, might not be possible. And yet many of us are familiar with the idea of a recipe book, a handy way of doing just that. We don't want to take this metaphor too far, and yet it can be helpful.

So, what exactly does a recipe look like? Let's look at some examples of sample test recipes:

- In a grocery store application, there's some SQL to find a fresh product that ships in 2 days or less and expires in 10.

- In a restaurant supplies application, there's some SQL to find cups, napkins, and bags that have a specific logo on them.

- In an enterprise social media application, it's specified how to create an account through the user interface that has access rights to a second account. Now, we need to expire that second account so that no one sees the search results, including overlapping accounts.

- In a complex insurance application, there are the rules for smart coding product benefits – the product number's second and third letters are the deductible, the fifth and sixth the co-pay, the seventh and eight the percentage up to the thousands as measured by the ninth and tenth number, and the eleventh and twelfth are the coverage beyond that number. There is SQL to confirm these numbers in the database.

- The process of changing the sales tax percentage for a given state.

- The process of clearing the claims for a given day for a given account number so that you can re-run for that day.

- The process of determining if a given `memberID` has coverage for a given date.

- Embedding our web-based product in `Microsoft SharePoint`, `SalesForce`, or `Quickbooks` as a widget, and so on.

- In a calculator, this might be a series of test ideas that do interesting things, such as push the calculator in exponential notation, where you have a number from 1 to 10 times 10 to a power. Another calculator recipe might be to add an exceptionally large number to an exceedingly small number, then divide, multiply, or add it to see if the number maintains the expected precision. These might come in a table of actions and expected results.

You can see how the last example might be a table with 10 rows that could also be expressed as 20 different test cases, each one page long. For people familiar with test cases, it might be helpful to think of a recipe as the part of the test case you want to keep. We find that recipe size is somewhere between 25% and 0.05% of the documentation involved in a "test case" approach. And, once you understand the concept of a recipe, you may start to see them all over the place.

Previously, we mentioned that a recipe is a tiny snippet of code. This is important because humans can figure out the rest. When you are faced with voluminous documentation that seems obvious and low value, our advice is to pause and reflect.

Sidebar – the value of your test documentation

Compression algorithms work in a specific way that might help assess documentation – that is, they process all the parts of a file, looking for terms and phrases that are repeated. The software substitutes each phrase for a symbol and then adds a symbol lookup table at the top. Thus, a 200-byte phrase repeated 100 times would become a phrase one time, plus perhaps 100 characters. Thus, that phrase in the file would be reduced from (200 bytes*100 times =20,000 bytes) to (200 bytes*1 time + 99 times *1 byte=299 bytes). The basic idea here is that in a test, redundant information adds no essential value and might take more time to flip through, load, and so on. In the preceding example, the redundant data could be compressed to something such as 10% of its original size, and much of what is left would be obvious things a human could figure out.

We can apply this method of analysis to more than just test documentation. A few years ago, a faction within testing tried to create an international standard, ISO 29119, for software testing. Access to the standard cost a few hundred US dollars, and you got a licensed copy with your name stamped on the side so that you couldn't give it away. We bought a copy. It is worth noting that volume 3 of the documentation is 127 pages long. The book has a series of types of documents, including *Organizational Test Policy*, *Organizational Test Strategy*, *Test Plan*, *Test Status Report*, and *Test Completion Report*, among others. There are dozens of these. Dozens. These have descriptions such as *4.31 test status report*. This report provides information about the status of the testing that is being performed in the specified reporting period.

These are low-value circular references. As an exercise, we cut and pasted the document into a text file and zipped it, achieving 81% compression, from 311K down to 60K. This is not a good thing.

The point of this sidebar was not to beat up on ISO 29119 – it was to say that redundant, low-value documentation has a cost. Not only does it take time to write and make it hard to find things, but it also becomes out of date quickly. Thus, you are either faced with being buried trying to update documents or declaring bankruptcy and just having a lot of documents that are out of date:

- In his book *Extreme Programming Explained: Embrace Change*, Kent Beck suggested a different approach by using a metaphor: *To travel light*. This involved thinking of software developers as nomads, where traveling light, without baggage, allows the team to move quickly. To do that, Beck suggested a few artifacts that are simple and valuable. His suggestion was automated checks and production code. Beck's focus was programmers, and he was thinking of tests as unit tests. Our recipe idea is similar, though – we only want to keep the reusable artifacts we will reuse.

Sometimes, when people look at recipes, they turn their heads and ask questions, such as "Shouldn't these just all be automated?", "Why are you putting SQL in our documentation wiki? it should be in Confluence", or "Isn't this completely redundant with technical documentation?"

Those are reasonable questions that are worth addressing.

Sometimes, the documentation simply isn't there. In those cases, we might have to create documentation for how the product works. In these cases, the best source of documentation about how the product works comes from testing, which can include automated checks as examples.

Shouldn't recipes just be automated?

Let's take one of our examples – that is, finding a live product ID to test against using a database query. The first time a tester does this, they might throw the query onto the web page that describes the feature (more about this in the Coverage – did we test the right things well enough? section). If the code is used by many people, it might go into version control. It might be easy enough to turn that into a computer program that produces the product ID on output.

Sometimes, though, testers will want to change the parameters, use different parameters, or get the second, third, or fourth results because they already used the first one today. They might want to change the sort order. One option is to keep the query in version control but link to it from the web page – which is fine. Our point is that there is no wrong answer. Do what is best for your team. Generally speaking, we have more success moving recipes in the direction of programming, but that is a wide generality.

Sometimes, the recipes don't look like code at all, but instead directions for setup or "how to test" a feature. It may be possible to script the setup as a command-line tool and link to it to fake out phone calls, as shown here:

```
setup_fake_calls      -d database_connection_string
                      -f from_number
                      -n number_of_calls
                      (opt) -t to_numbers_text_file
                      (opt) -sdt start_date_time
                      (opt) -eddt end_date_time
```

Sometimes, such a tool doesn't make sense.

Do recipes overlap with technical documentation?

At Socialtext, we built a product called **SocialPoint**; it was a SharePoint/Socialtext integration. In essence, Socialtext was exposed as a widget within SharePoint. Using the concept of a recipe for the setup, Matt created documentation for how to set up the tool on the **Feature** page for SocialPoint in the testing documentation wiki.

The tool was something we didn't need to test much – only when changes were made to it, new versions of SharePoint came out, or we were onboarding a huge customer and felt there might be a risk. Eventually, enough time passed that Matt forgot the ins and outs of the tool. When he found a problem, he called customer success and asked for help installing the tool in the test environment. They shrugged and explained they just followed the test documentation. If that didn't work, the tool was probably broken.

Getting your test documentation used outside of testing might just be a sign of success.

Our advice here is to not worry about it too much. Create test documentation for testers to be used by testers. In the event other people want to use it, that is a good thing. If there are remarkable similarities between the two, perhaps consider combining them.

This leads us to our next big issue: coverage. Over the years, we've started to work for a company to create a coverage map – that is, a feature map of the entire product. Arguably, this *should* be redundant with some other initiative or some technical documentation. We found that when we needed coverage maps, they did not exist anywhere else in the organization. By creating them, we had an artifact that filled a need and lived on, with value outside of testing. This was fantastic, but we built it because we needed it to describe coverage.

If our first primitive is a pile of recipes, we end up spending all our time sorting through the recipes, trying to find the right one. That is one of the reasons we need coverage.

Coverage – did we test the right things well enough?

Management asks if you've done testing. You say no, you need more time. *How much more time? Why? Can you answer?*

To develop an answer that stands up to scrutiny, we would need some measure of how wide, how tall, and how deep the space of the software was. However, from Chapter 1, we know that space is infinite.

Welcome to testing. As the saying goes, "Doing the impossible for the ungrateful." To some extent, we can do the impossible – at least, it can be helpful to think that might be possible.

All test coverage is based on some model. All models are imperfect approximations of the actual work. As such, they have limits. In *Chapter 2*, we looked at one imprecise, metaphorical model – that of the software of a dog park. We used the test as a walk through that dog park. It is possible to think of various parts of the park as features and produce some measure of how well each feature is tested on a scale of 1 to 10. This measure is open to personal interpretation; two features that are tested to the level of *2* would not have the same coverage as a feature tested to the level of *4*. One term for this is an *ordinal* measure.

Ordinal measures are numbers, such as "first, second, and third" place. They create a ranking. When we test using ordinal coverage numbers, we often create a scale, something like this:

- 0 – We have not looked at this function.
- 1 – We clicked the button once.
- 2 – We completed the highest level of the workflow.
- 3 – We tested the most common reasonable workflows.
- 4 – We tested the most common reasonable workflows and exceptions.

- 5 – We tested the most common, reasonable workflows and exceptions plus major external integration paths through this feature.

- 6 – The same as the previous point but we tested the uncommon flows and the corner-case, hard to set up interactions.

- 7 – The same as the previous point but over an extended time, diving in and out and back.

- 8 – We wrote down all our ideas, had a second team member independently produce test ideas, compared notes, and came up with more ideas.

- 9 – We had at least five people independently produce their ideas, conduct testing, and write their ideas down, after which we retested, shared our documents, came up with new ideas, and retested. We are exhausted.

- 10 – We have completely tested this feature.

As we know from *Chapter 1*, it should be exceedingly rare that anyone ever gets to a 10 for coverage. It might be possible, for, say, some of the smaller chips that compromise a computer's CPU, where the logic is burned into a board.

This was just a quick, dirty scale we produced, based on one of Matt's experiences. We suggest that any team using this idea create their own scale. Once you have a scale, another measurement is quality, which can be reduced to the classic green (good to go), yellow (problems but no showstoppers), and red (this feature is fundamentally broken) measures. It was James Bach who first published the idea that the combination of feature, coverage, and quality could be used together to create a simple visual dashboard that could appear on a whiteboard, something he called the Low Tech Testing Dashboard (`https://www.satisfice.com/download/low-tech-testing-dashboard`). Here's a sample testing dashboard based on a calculator function:

Feature	Coverage	Quality
Divide	3	
Multiply	3	
Subtract	3	
Add	4	
Equals	2	
Clear function	2	
+/- function	6	
% function	2	

Table 9.1 – A testing dashboard

The list in the left-hand column of the preceding table is not exhaustive. If the calculator were to run on a phone, it would miss out quite a lot, such as rotating the view on a mobile device, scientific notation, long-running transactions that can cause memory problems, starting and restarting the calculator, different mobile devices, sizes, operating systems – all the possible platform problems.

When this was first proposed, teams would work in the same physical location and write the dashboard on a whiteboard with markers. In the years that followed, multi-user online spreadsheets became popular, and it became possible to publish the dashboard to a flatscreen monitor mounted on a wall. Today, teams can share the URL. Let's imagine the difference between two conversations.

Conversation One:

Executive: "How's it going?"

Tester: "Oh, it's going. There are a lot of bugs."

Executive: "Well I need to know its status."

Tester: "I'm in the middle of this; I could check out the bug tracking tool…"

Executive: "Get to it. I need to know its status; when will you be done?"

Tester: "Oh, I don't know; about 4 days."

Executive: "We don't have that kind of time. Can you get it done today?"

Tester: "Uh…"

Conversation Two:

Executive: "How's it going?"

Tester: "Do you have the link? It's all on the dashboard. [Clicks tab and reviews] "Subtract" and "Add" are red. We haven't gotten very far in testing them this cycle. "Percentage" has some bugs and doesn't have much testing either. Everything else looks good but we haven't tested "Divide" and "Multiply" much."

Executive: "When will you be done?"

Tester: "I'd expect we get fixes tomorrow afternoon. Then, we need to give into those under-tested functions. I'd say about 4 days."

Executive: "That doesn't work for me. Can you get it done today?"

Tester: "You'll need to talk to the developers. If they can get us fixes for the known show-stopper issues today, we could retest in about 2 hours. Plus, when things roll out, we want to stick around for a while to make sure nothing is broken. I'd say we need to roll out by 3 P.M., which means we need fixes by 1 P.M., preferably noon. But look at these numbers [shares link over chat] – are you comfortable with those low coverage numbers?"

As you can see, the answers were essentially the same – 4 days should be compressed to 1, yet the second tester explained the coverage and risks in terms the executive could understand. They also put the executive in charge of the decision, making the test role simply providing information for the decision maker. This sort of measure is a later. Later in this chapter, we will discuss how to add a risk component to this discussion. For example, if equals and clear had not changed at all and the team was mature, a 2 for coverage might be just fine. If the features could be deployed separately, it might be possible to eliminate this regression-testing effort. Still, understanding the depth of the coverage can be helpful when discussing risk – what testing to invest in next.

The goal of this section was to introduce the idea of a human, qualitative measure to provide coverage for features. Teams can do this at many levels by making a list of major user journeys, such as checkout, and see how well they are covered, or major categories, such as insurance claims.

All the measures we saw earlier are subjective, human, ordinal, and qualitative. They are more like the number of stars a reviewer gives a movie. Code coverage measures, on the other hand, are hard and concrete, but they can still be misunderstood.

Precise code coverage measures

Chapter 3 introduced the idea of **statement coverage** – that is, the number of lines of code that have been exercised by tests divided by the total number of lines of code. Here's a simple program in C that is easy enough to build 100% statement coverage for. It is a little function that takes two numbers, dividing the first by the second, and returning a whole number result:

```
int integer_divide(int numerator, int denominator) {
    return numerator/denominator;
}
```

We can achieve 100% test coverage in one line of code, something like this:

```
ASSERT(integermath(2,2)==1);
```

As we can see, two divided by two is one. This is easy enough; now, we can call 100% of the lines of code.

Our test ideas might be a little more detailed – we might consider a big number divided by a small one, a negative numerator, a negative denominator, a small number divided by a big one, the limits of the size of integers, and so on.

In C, when we divide by zero, we are most likely to get an exception and the entire application will crash.

Statement coverage does not consider classes of input. Plus, there is another problem. Let's look at a code sample that is a little contrived. It takes an integer (whole number) for how much to calculate and does some calculations for either `allones` or `allzeros`. We'll use `//` as a comment and leave some of the details commented out:

```
void multiplemath(int numchars, bool allzeros, bool allones) {
    //create a memory pointer that is the size of
    //numchars in characters plus a terminator
    ptr = (char*)malloc(numchars*(sizeof(char)+1)*2);
    if (allzeros) {
        //Code A - not detailed - perform operations on ptr
        free(ptr);
    }
    if (allones) {
        //Code B - not detailed - perform operations on ptr
        free(ptr);
    }
}
```

We can get to 100% statement coverage with just one test – setting `allzeros` and `allones` to true. This will trip the error – that is, the code will try to operate on `ptr` after it has been freed and cleared of data. Another way to achieve 100% statement coverage would be to call the following:

```
multiplemath(1, true, false);
multiplemath(1, false, true);
```

These tests might "pass," giving us 100% statement coverage before triggering the error.

Beyond statement coverage, an additional measure is branch coverage. In this example, branch coverage would cover all the combinations of possibilities, executing the top branch, the bottom branch, both, and neither. Here's what the four calls would look like, though they would need tests wrapped around them to check something:

```
multiplemath(1, true, true);
multiplemath(1, false, true);
multiplemath(1, true, false);
multiplemath(1, false, false);
```

While `malloc` can handle negative numbers (they are just converted into positive equivalents), a `numchars` value of 0 could lead to a coding error in the routines. For that matter, the size of `int` in a Microsoft compiler is 2,147,483,647, while the max size of `malloc` is 16,722,568. So, the function could pass in a `numchars` value that is too large. And what is `* 2` for in `malloc`? Where did that come from? Code coverage can be helpful, but it is more likely a start than the finish line.

Closing out coverage

Often, the errors are not in the customer code at all. For example, a simple Windows program might look terrible when it is resized. This isn't about the custom code – it's a problem with the framework. This reminds us of the theory of error and platform problems we discussed in *Chapter 1*.

Statement and branch coverage offer precise mathematical models of how well the code is covered. They are much more likely better than nothing. But all models are imperfect. The only perfect coverage measure of software would be "input time and space combinatorial coverage," which is impossible for software where a human is involved.

The goal of measuring, or even thinking, about coverage is to help with our communication and decision-making. It's a primitive we can use to compose our solution. Coverage may be necessary, but it is not sufficient.

Defects – what is the status of the software?

Most people think of a list of defects as a to-do list. They must figure out what needs to be fixed, send them on to the programmers to fix, wait for a fix, get a fix, test the fix, test around the fix, and either send it back for another fix or move on to the next item.

But the bug list is more than a work queue. It is your ticket to the known status of the software. It is your ticket to improvement. Done well, an ordered open bug list is a quick view of a status – publish it. Looking at the recent list of bugs that have been opened and fixed can guide your testing – especially bugs that escape team-level testing and are found by customers. These give you a chance to figure out what is missing in your test strategy. Consistent bugs and defect categories that appear again and again offer two methods of improvement. First, you can add them to your list of common bugs and test that category with every new build. Second, you can bring them to the team to see if a process or code change can be made to fix an entire category of bugs.

For example, say the team consistently has problems validating email addresses and phone numbers. On every build, the tester kicks all kinds of bugs back. In programming terms, the programmers would create two new classes that inherit from the textbox and have the behavior they need, called `phonenumber_textbox` and `email_textbox`. Once the new classes exist, any other programmer could just reuse them. In very high-performance teams, this can lead to what Boris Beizer calls the pesticide paradox, where finding bugs becomes more and more difficult as team performance improves. Frankly, we don't see that as a severe problem. Test activity, over time, might decrease, or the people doing testing work might shift to other risks or other activities, or someone might transfer out of the department. High-performance teams, in our experience, usually change the platform, dependencies, and code all the time. They fix the frontend validation problems so that they do not need to be tested, and there will be a new mobile version of the software (or something else) to test soon enough.

That leaves the bug list as a sorted list, with the defect number, title, priority, and impact at the top. Users can sort the list by priority, and, perhaps, filter or resize it to a small window with a scrollbar. This list alone does not convey status –you might have entire swaths of the application that have not been covered. By knowing about coverage and the bug list, as well as some personal experience, it becomes possible to make a quick assessment of the status.

Schedule and risk – too many test ideas, not enough time

When people talk about testing as risk management, it is amazing how shallow the advice can be. From what we can tell, the advice is mostly "there is a risk that software will have bugs, so we test." When we agreed to write this book, it was with a commitment to not simply list things any reasonable person could easily figure out without this book. Instead, we wanted to push back on the ideas that seem obvious yet never seem to work – we wanted to reveal counter-intuitive truths.

Let's talk about risk management.

One way to approach risk management is to make a census of risks – that is, all the things that could happen. For each risk, you assign an impact, perhaps the dollar cost if the risk is realized, and a probability, from 0% to 100%. Multiply the two and you get a risk score. Sort by risk score and you get a sorted list of risks to track down.

Risk mitigation involves investing resources (time, energy, and money) in reducing the chances that risks will emerge. Say, for example, the top thing on the list is the possibility that a major investor simply will not like the software because of the user interface. The people doing testing are not particularly trained in usability, but they could do some research on the web, make a committed effort for a week, and provide feedback that might move the top risk down by a few percentage points. Doing the math, we can see that our effort could be spent elsewhere.

Of course, we do not know the percentage chance the risk can emerge, nor do we know the dollar-cost impact. And we certainly can't realistically assess the percentage points that the risks will drop as we test time. (In software testing, in some cases, we know we can drop to 0%, at least if done exactly as we tested. But what was the starting percentage?)

What we can build, most of the time, is a census of risks – that is, a list. Some projects are designed so that we can put a list in a spreadsheet. In other cases, there is a work-tracking tool. In any event, somehow, we end up with a sortable list. Assuming the test ideas have a bell curve of costs, we can work for a day, see how many we get done, and predict how long it will take to complete the entire list. Of course, when testing, we can always make the list bigger. Because we can always increase the list, we can usually work backward from the end date to find a *cut line* – that is, with the time we have, this is how much work we can do. The test ideas above the cut line get done, while the ones below do not. Management can move the priority of any test idea on the fly until we run out of time. If bugs do slip through and are below the cut line, that's not a problem; it is good governance!

One way to do this at the feature level is to agree on the feature and how critical it is for the team before work begins. We can do this by setting an expected level of coverage, from zero to nine, using our definition or the score matrix we mentioned previously. We can do this with both the human part of testing and how deep the tooling is. This is an attempt to adjust the test effort for risk – it's a start.

Before we leave risk and schedule, let's talk about another way to approach testing a large area of software under time pressure – iterative testing.

Iterative testing

Can you come up with a plan to test your software if you only have 5 minutes? How about only 20 minutes? 1 hour? 4 person hours? 1 day? 5? A test can expand to fit all, but can you scale it up or down to fit any particular timebox?

One approach we appreciate is taking a walk through the software in ever-increasing circles. As time expands, the depth of coverage in each feature (and the depth of complex user journeys) expands as well. For the calculator example that we saw earlier, 5 minutes might be enough to score "1" in each category, 20 to get to "2", 1 person hour to get to "3", and so on. There are plenty of exceptions: if the team is just testing one code change, testing might involve the bug fix and then expanding circles around the bug. Teams that do eCommerce might start with login, search, path-to-purchase, and create account, with several laps around those before expanding to anything else. The point is to be able to articulate how much would be tested with how much time. That changes the conversation from testing yes/no to "with 5 minutes, we can do this, with 20 this, with an hour that…"

Articulate that and we can finally get to strategy.

Strategy – what are our risks and priorities?

If you have gotten this far, then you recognize that there is an essentially infinite number of possible tests to run. Breaking the software into features, assigning a minimal test-effort value for the feature, making a list of the full end-to-end customer journeys… all of these things make the effort manageable. The 5-minute test plan and iterating around the product seem easy, but what do we do when there is just too much to test and some very limited time? One technique we'd like to mention here is RCRCRC.

Karen N. Johnson, a friend of ours who we have worked with, proposed a mnemonic – a memory device – for regression testing. She called it RCRCRC (http://karennicolejohnson.com/2009/11/a-heuristic-for-regression-testing/). This involves coming up with test ideas with short notice. Here are the letters defined, in her words:

- **Recent**: New features and new areas of code are more vulnerable

- **Core**: Essential functions must continue to work

- **Risk**: Some areas of an application pose more risk

- **Configuration-sensitive**: Code that's dependent on environment settings can be vulnerable

- **Repaired**: Bug fixes can introduce new issues

- **Chronic**: Some areas in an application may be perpetually sensitive to breaking

At one company we worked with, the team's usual 2-day regression test was compressed to a morning. We made a list of test ideas using RCRCRC and put them on sticky notes. Each note represented a test idea, something between 5 minutes and 25. Then, the team created a Kanban board with three columns: *To-Do*, *In Process*, and *Done*. The board looked as follows:

Figure 9.1 – A test in process Kanban board

Throughout the morning, the cards slowly moved from the left to the right, with management able to move cards, add new cards, and so on. Beyond *Done*, to the right, we could record bugs. At noon, we discussed the known quality of the bugs, the existing test coverage, our known gaps, and our recommendation to move forward.

When we speak of test strategy, we mean something like the dictionary definition – a plan of action or policy designed to achieve a major or overall aim. The test strategy ties together the forces in this chapter to explain what the testing function is doing, what risks and scope it addresses, and how it will get there. The example shown in *Figure 9.1*, and most of the examples in this chapter, are mostly of regression testing because the problem domain is so large and the time frame to do it is so compressed. In the next chapter, we'll look at the test strategy over time.

Dashboard – how do we communicate what we know?

In the *Coverage – did we test the right things well enough?* section, we mentioned the low-tech testing dashboard. Earlier in this book, we mentioned that having access to the most important bugs can yield a quick summary of the software testing process. The low-tech testing dashboard we looked at previously talked about coverage. We also mentioned the idea that a *census of risks* can drive quality. Other common components of communicating test information include the build status, the automated pipeline, and the history of the automated pipeline (what features frequently fail). This yields a potential test dashboard that is a single web page that continually updates itself. Some components of a test dashboard might look something like this:

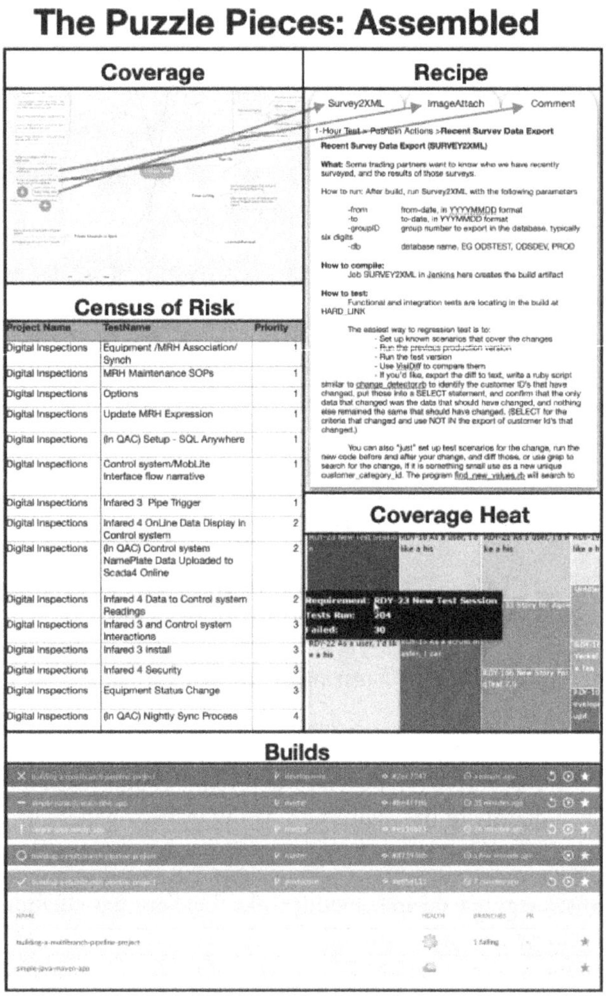

Figure 9.2 – Assembling the puzzle pieces to make a whole process dashboard. This image is only for layout representation purposes; text readability is not required

Let's look at a couple of real examples of heat maps we've built over the years:

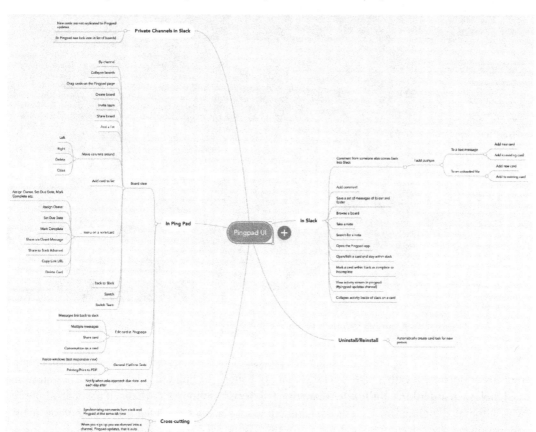

Figure 9.3 – A test coverage outline for PingPad created by Excelon Development that's been used with permission. This image is only for layout representation purposes; text readability is not required

In this example, we would copy the mind map for regression testing, then color the nodes red/yellow/green (for quality) and set different levels of darkness (for coverage). Another way to model it is with a more traditional low-tech dashboard for coverage and heat:

Features		Webkit	iOS	Android
	Q:7 C 9(matt)	Q:6 C: 8 (Sreejit)	Q:7 C 5 (Paurang)	Q:7 C 5 (Paurang)
	Q:9 C 3 (matt)	Q:7 C 5 (Sreejit)	Q:7 C 7 Sandhya	Q:6 C: 6 (Paurang)
	Q:6 C 8 (Sreejit)	Q:6 C: 7 Arun	Q:7 C 6 (Paurang)	Q:7 C 6 (Paurang)
	Q:9 C 6 (matt)	Q:8 C 7 Arun	Q:7 C 7 (Paurang)	Q:7 C 7 (Paurang)
	Q:7 C 5 (Sreejit)	Q:7 C 7 Arun	Q:8 C 7 (Paurang)	Q:8 C 7 (Paurang)
	Q:6 C 6 (subid)	Q:6 C 6 (subid)	Q:8 C 7 (Subid)	Q:8 C 6(subid)
	Q:7 C 5 (Sreejit)	Q:7 C 5 (Sreejit)	Q:7 C 5 (Paurang)	Q:5 C 7 (Paurang)
	Q:6 C: 8 (Sreejit)	Q:6 C: 7 Arun	Q:3 C 7 (Paurang)	Q:3 C 7 (Paurang)
	Q:6 C 6 (subid)	Q:6 C 6 (subid)	Q:6 C 6(subid)	Q:6 C 6(Subid)
	Q:7 C 8 Beth	Q:7 C 8 Beth	Q:5 C: 7 (Paurang)	Q:5 C: 7 (Paurang)
	Q:8 C 7Sandhya	Q:8 C 7Sandhya	Q:7 C 7 Sandhya	Q:8 C 6(subid)
	Q:7 C 5 (Sreejit)	Q:7 C 5 Arun	Q:8 C 8 (Paurang)	Q:8 C 8 (Paurang)
	Q:7 C: 1 (Subid)	Q:7 C: 1 (Subid)	Q:6 C 6 (Paurang)	Q:6 C 6 (Paurang)
			Q:2 C 10 (Sandhya) Account Preference	Q:2 C 10 (Paurang) Account Preference
	Q:3 C 5(Sreejit)	Q:3 C 5Arun	Q:9 C 4 (Paurang)	Q:9 C 4 (Paurang)
	NA	NA		

Figure 9.4 – A sample low-tech testing dashboard created for a client, anonymized

Bug/status could be an export from a bug tracking system, or, for more agile teams, perhaps an online, multi-user document with a high-level summary of issues. The build pipeline could be output from a CI tool, such as **Jenkins**, **Buildkite**, **Teamcity**, **Circleci**, **Bamboo**, or **GitLab**. Of particular interest with automated tooling is what tests are failing now, how many have failed recently, and how many frequently fail (flaky tests). Other elements for the dashboard could include automated gathering of RCRCRC information, such as the following:

- What files (if you have it, what features do they track back to?) have changed recently?
- What files/features have had recent defects files or been fixed against them?
- A tighter summary of the core functionality problems to be tested.
- Elements of the software that have recently been tested and have not changed.
- A list of configuration-sensitive components and test/change history.

The point of this dashboard is to create an instant summary of where you are in testing (coverage), the status of the defects (bugs), the number of risks covered (risks), and the risks that tools cover for us (tool and build pipeline) so that management feels like they have options. This changes testing from an "Are we done yet/why not" conversation to a conversation about where to invest time and effort. It also eliminates the "status" shuffle, where people write things down and give briefings, with information loss due to assumptions and forgetfulness, and then wait for meetings to make late decisions. Instead, this allows the decision maker to decide. As a bonus, after they decide, the decision maker now has to live with the consequences of the decision, as we discussed when we talked about risk – but they have a great deal more information. Thus, the question is not "Why didn't QA find that bug?" but instead "Hmm. It seems like we didn't invest enough time in *<feature_name>* testing to find that kind of bug. Should we change the amount of time we are investing? Should we test something else less?"

In internet terms, we could build this by creating a single web page that embeds other web pages inline. This can be done in HTML5 with an `iframe` construct. Many testing products have helped us move in this direction already. This section was designed to give you familiarity with this construct; in *Chapter 10*, we will talk about how to build a dashboard that works for you.

We'll look at more possible components for the dashboard in *Chapter 10*. For now, consider how much of a dashboard you have, what it would take to get started hobbling one together, and if it is worth the investment.

Summary

In this chapter, we covered some basic primitives of software testing. Recipes tell us how to test things that are not intuitively obvious. Coverage can give us a high-level view of the software, plus an understanding of how well we are currently testing, and the status of those components. Understanding coverage can help us understand if we are done, and where to invest the scarce resource of our time for what to test next. Coverage can help us make tough decisions such as "Are we done yet?"

Speaking of tough decisions, defects are a major source of information about the problems with the product and where to go next. The schedule for our testing determines a cadence; it needs to fit in with the rest of the delivery cycle. We considered the test strategy and how it evolves, specifically concerning addressing risks and priorities, including Karen Johnsons' RCRCRC heuristic. To communicate our primitives, we introduced the idea of the dashboard, which creates a visual summary of the primitives in action, along with ways to visualize that dashboard.

Christopher Alexander's pattern language formalized things that were already emergent in construction and city planning and gave them names – for example, the road crossing, the raised walk, and the courtyard. Alexander's patterns allow architects to speak at a higher level and have a shared understanding. Meanwhile, the reason the patterns emerged is that they solve a problem. Our goal was to do for software testing what Alexander did for construction. This gives us a deeper language to use – a set of solutions and an understanding of what problems they solve and what consequences they impose.

But what should that strategy be for your team?

We'll look at this in more detail in the next chapter.

10
Putting Your
Test Strategy Together

The previous chapter explored the puzzle pieces of testing. By the end, we had put them together, creating a potential dashboard to express the status of the software. Of course, that was only one potential dashboard among many, and our view of it was a conceptual one.

In this chapter, we will be looking at what we would consider *good-enough software*. When we have that, there is invariably some strategy already at play, which addresses some of the puzzle pieces that make up our testing process in some way. To be successful, we first need to figure out what is actually happening (the current state), as well as some ideal future state, and then address the gaps. That work needs to stand up to scrutiny. In other words, when a decision maker asks for ideas for how to move forward and wants to know "why," "how," and "when," you need to be able to explain. They need to believe that their questions are answered. That way, your new ideas can be implemented. Let's discuss how to do it.

This chapter covers the following main topics:

- How to analyze what is going on right now
- Expressing test ideas as a census of risk
- How to set priorities, including managing time, scope, and people
- Publishing and communicating your test strategy
- Moving from where we are to where we want to be

What are we doing now?

The Oxford English Dictionary defines strategy as *"a plan of action or policy designed to achieve a major or overall aim."*

When we talk about strategy, we mean the plan of action (plus policies) to achieve an aim. In our case, the plan of action will cover what we will do (and how we will do it) when testing software, with the goal of providing-makers with information about management's intent, so that the technical team, and even the person doing the testing, can make decisions on how to move forward. In other words, part of the strategy might be to push the decision-making activities into the team. This eliminates the need to wait for someone external to decide what to do when a bug is found. The more we can push decisions into real time and eliminate waiting, the more we'll improve system performance. When we write "decision making", that doesn't have to be a big thing; it doesn't need to be deciding what to build. It might be as simple as creating a set of rules of what bugs need to be fixed right now, such as no bugs. Eliminating waiting is one way to improve software delivery, something we'll cover in *Chapter 11, Lean Software Testing*.

For now, we'll create a strategy.

The easiest way to do this is with your own team in your own department. When we use a working example in this chapter, it will be loosely inspired by the work Matt and Michael did at Socialtext for over a decade. The Socialtext story is valuable because it shows not just a strategy but a conscious improvement in approach over an extended period.

Sadly, in our work, we've seen far too much starting of strategy and not enough finishing. In fact, we've seen consultants present on their one to three months of work at a company, work that seems so promising and presents so wonderfully. Then, we talked to the employees, only to hear how the work was thrown out and scrapped.

It's not just the consultants, but managers too. One of the biggest traps we've seen is in companies that need to pass some sort of audit, so they need process documentation. The managers create documentation about the way things *should* be, without any effort to change the system. A year later, when the auditors come back to see whether the company followed the process, well, of course, they didn't.

In the most egregious example, one manager stated that his team was going to begin conducting *ambiguity reviews* because the software requirements were ambiguous. It sounded like a promising idea. The manager printed off a checklist from a book and tacked it to a wall. The project managers who reported to him, under pressure to tighten schedules, were reluctant to add a new meeting that, if it worked, would lead people to get more precise answers, thus slowing the project down. The project managers looked to their manager to lead and he just… did not. The idea was never instituted as policy, was never put into any documentation, and simply faded away.

Declaring new ways to carry out software testing is unlikely to be successful. In fact, it stands in opposition to the context-driven approach favored in this book. With context-driven testing, the person doing the work is in the driver's seat on what to do, as well as how and when to do it. Management can express high-level goals; the person doing the test has to figure out the best way to accomplish those goals. In our experience, it might even be a bit more accurate to say that management makes a wish list, and the people responsible for testing see how close they can get.

When you make a strategy, our advice is not to talk about how things should be. Of course, that comes later. Instead, for now, write about how things are. If there are no standards across teams, use the team. Some teams support 100 different small interfaces, each one tested in a different way. For that matter, a major change, such as upgrading the web server the software runs on, might require a different kind of testing.

All that is fine, but we have to start describing how we currently test software somehow. Let's break off a piece of something (group-level process, team-level process, how to test one application, how we supported one change yesterday) and define it. To do that, we'll use the Lean Test Canvas – a technique Matt developed at Excelon Development.

The Lean Test Canvas

The Business Model Canvas started as a single page that expressed all the elements of a business model; where the money comes from, how the users receive value, what the company must purchase to deliver the value, and so on. It's interesting to note that the Business Model Canvas was designed for an existing business to describe itself and explore all aspects of a mature business. The next canvas, the Lean Canvas was designed for start-ups, more focused on what the next problem the business would encounter as it grew. Established businesses, after all, can have multiple product lines they may segment and advertise to different customers. Start-ups are more likely to try to find a single customer *archetype* to work with profitably.

The use of the term *Lean*, in this chapter, as well as *Chapter 11*, might be a bit confusing. In our case, we mean lean in the traditional sense (healthy, agile, no excess waste, and strong, as in lean food), the business sense, and in terms of the Toyota way of manufacturing, which is a method of focusing on continuing improvement. The *Lean Test Canvas* is a homage to all those ideas. At the same time, when we start improving testing, we often find there is some obvious *dead fish* on the table that no one can talk about. Hopefully, listing the test process on a single piece of paper will help you find that weakest link in the chain, that is, the thing to improve that will allow testing to improve.

The following example is a business view of testing; it is not a technology systems view. We will cover other approaches to put the puzzle pieces together in this chapter. For now, here is the Lean Test Canvas:

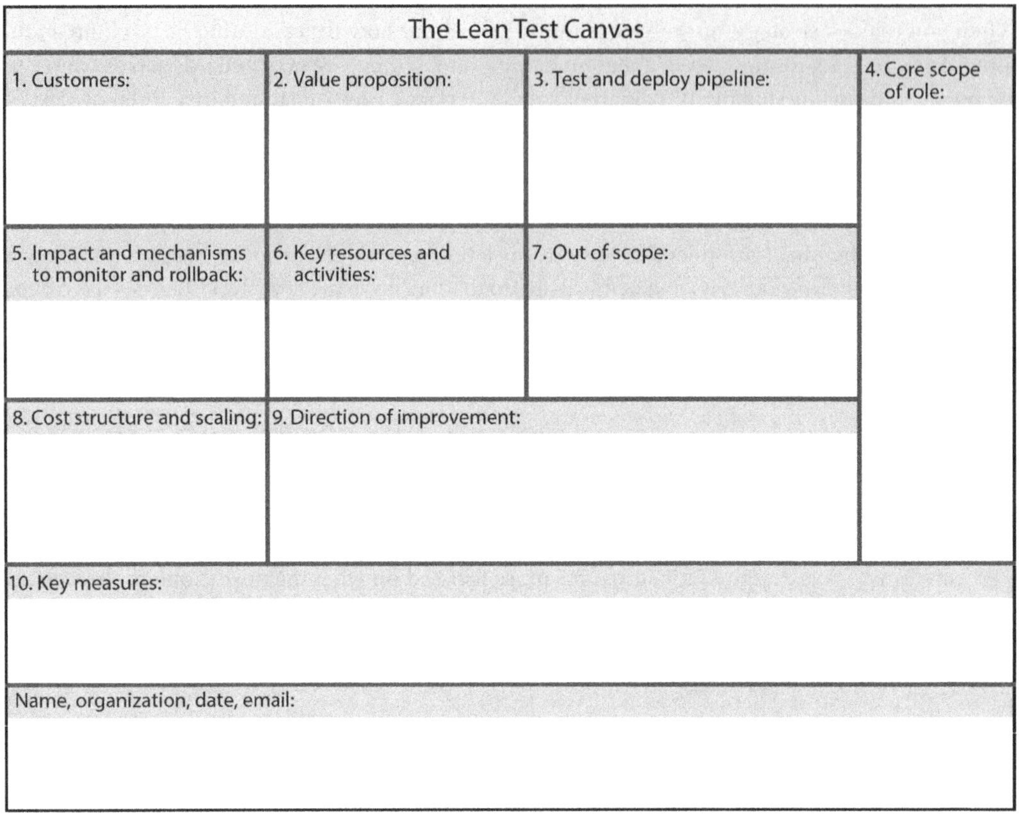

The Lean Test Canvas			
1. Customers:	2. Value proposition:	3. Test and deploy pipeline:	4. Core scope of role:
5. Impact and mechanisms to monitor and rollback:	6. Key resources and activities:	7. Out of scope:	
8. Cost structure and scaling:	9. Direction of improvement:		
10. Key measures:			
Name, organization, date, email:			

Figure 10.1 – The Lean Test Canvas (https://xndev.com/2014/11/the-lean-test-canvas/)

This document states how testing is done right now, for one team, component, project, or system. Ironically, if you give it to every member of a delivery team to fill out, you will likely get different answers. It is even possible that different roles all think some other role is responsible for something! Have management fill it out, and you may find expectations differ on how long things take.

Let's look at each element in the Lean Test Canvas, see what they mean, and then come back to see how to fill it out and publish it:

- **Customers**: This is not referring to the customers who will be using the application; these are the "customers" who will be testing the application. In a very high-maturity delivery team, it is possible the team itself is their own customer. That is, testing is so integrated into the work that all anyone external sees are running, tested features showing up routinely. On the extreme opposite end, testing could be a separate team, reporting to separate management. This team might have published **Service-Level Agreements** (**SLAs**) and written contracts; in their case, the customer is the person approving the checks. Some very complex programs have a **system testing team** that handles work that spans dozens of teams; they might report to senior management. In any event, the goal is to identify who the customer of your testing is.

- **Value proposition**: When someone asks, "Why do you need to do testing at all?" how do you answer them? This is an abbreviated version of the elevator pitch we'll discuss later. It needs to demonstrate some sort of return on investment – that $1 spent on testing will earn $1.25 in the year to come. Anything less and the company might want to invest in something else.

- **Test and deploy pipeline**: Once a program finishes its unit tests and pushes the code to version control, how long does it take to get the code to production? This could be several steps, each expressed in minutes, hours, or (shudder) days. Take the following example:

  I.   Waiting for code review approval and merge (less than 2 days)

  II.   Build and system-level tests (0.25 to 2 days)

  III.   Regression (weekly)

  IV.   Deploy to production (after regression runs)

Beyond unit tests, items two and three are where additional test tooling and automation live. The preceding example implies a regression test process, running every *sprint*. That right there might be the bottleneck for testing and delivery. Decoupling changes from the sprint can vastly improve throughput. More on getting rid of regression in *Chapter 11*.

- **Core scope of role**: This is a list of the kinds of risks that the team is responsible for. *Functionality, speed (of application), load, and speed of build pipeline* is a sample answer.

- **Impact and mechanisms to monitor and roll back**: A mobile application with a long build pipeline that needs to go to the Apple store might take a week to get a fix out; a Scrum team that puts bug fixes on the backlog might take two weeks to get a fix out. That means the time a bug lives in production could be very long, which means the team might focus on the mean time between failures.

- **Key resources and activities**: This defines who does the testing and what kinds of testing they do. List who is testing and what is actually done. Later, we can step back and ask what's missing.

- **Out of scope**: What do we not do? Some examples are performance, security, and accessibility testing. This is a double-edged sword. The team might feel relieved at not only not being responsible for performance testing but also putting that fact in writing. That means someone from outside might be called in to do the work, in a way that might be a serious intrusion. Also, it is possible that some executive will look at the list of what is out of scope versus in scope, and fail to understand the value of what is in scope. In that case, the executive might feel the group is adding no value. If the people who do the work are on the delivery team, this could identify a gap – for example, if everything is out of scope except for unit testing, well, who exactly will be doing all those other things? What will the consequence of not doing them be?

- **Key Measures:** The things the team needs to measure to know whether they are successful or not. Many teams don't really measure success as anything but "software delivered on time" when someone external creates the schedule. The usual result is testing is shortened, the software goes out buggy, and everyone wonders why. The alternative is to have other measures for software. Of the teams that have measures, many of those are naive, such as bug counts or bugs per line of code. We'll discuss measures more in *Chapter 11*.

- **Cost Structure and Scaling:** What we pay for testing relative to development, and what we would pay if we wanted to do more of it.

- **Direction of Improvement:** Once we have the measures defined, we decide which ones to improve next. More problems found, software delivered more quickly, reduced regression time, better visibility of coverage … which do we want to improve next?

Reading this, you may think you understand all of these, they are obvious. Yet having a personal understanding of these elements of testing is very different than having a single, cohesive view the whole team can understand.

Getting the form filled out can be more difficult than it might at first appear.

Getting the form filled out

As we have discussed elsewhere, people tend to think of testing in terms of their own roles. To a project manager with a waterfall orientation, testing should be a *stable*, *predictable*, and *repeatable* process, running on a cadence. To that project manager, testing is just an obstacle to release, a thing that needs to be done. That leaves testing as something that is easy to outsource. Programmers can see tests as either verifying that a component does what is expected (after-the-fact unit testing) or, perhaps, a guide to what *done* means, as in "the story is done when the automated tests run." Specialized testers in the context-driven tradition think of testing as a chance to provide information to decision-makers about the software's status and investment in risk management. Business analysts might think of tests as an addition to the requirements, as a sort of executable specification – and we could go on.

Notice that when our goal is to make testing a "stable, predictable, and repeatable" process, every role has a different concern that they see testing addressing. The point is to integrate them, to put the puzzle pieces together and to create a coherent strategy. Without a coherent strategy, the team is just doing whatever they are doing now. The point of the Lean Test Canvas is to get "whatever we are doing now" down so we can see what puzzle pieces are missing.

If the team is co-located, you could just print the template out and leave it around for a week or two. Try to create organic conversations. An alternative is to ask people to fill it out ahead of time as a team-building activity. The point is not to get to agreement; it is to find the disagreements, the misunderstandings, and the people who don't even agree on what they mean by the word testing. For example, **A/B split testing** is a typical marketing activity to help design advertisements to get more clicks, but it can also be used to change user interfaces to get customers to engage more on a website or mobile application. That kind of testing, combined with logs and reports, can provide quality-related information through technical investigation – so it is testing as we have defined it.

If you can use the process of getting the Lean Test Canvas filled out to figure out what the disagreements are and what is missing, that's a wonderful step in the right direction.

A second way to look at testing is your elevator pitch.

The elevator pitch

In our consulting work, we frequently meet people doing testing work who feel unappreciated and disrespected. Sometimes they use terms such as "second-class citizens" or complain about expectations. Personally, we, the authors, don't really have a problem with this. Software can exist without test specialists, but it cannot exist without programmers. We are pleased to be part of the story of creating the software and do not ask for more than that. Yet there is more to it than that. People complain in general if something unjust is happening and something is not right. Their role is not appreciated.

It is likely their role is not understood at all. Or, to put it differently, the other people in the organization only see their own puzzle pieces. The project manager just wants to sign off that *"testing is done"*; they do not want to hear about all these niggling obstacles. The product manager thinks the executable, predefined tests are simple. Programmers might see the testing as a source of extra work, or a list of annoyances.

One exercise we run is asking people to imagine for a moment that they have run into their group president, company CIO, or even CEO, in an elevator. The two of you are alone. To make conversation the executive asks what you do. Even better, they ask specifically about testing – they have heard testing is important, and you are a big part of that. *"How exactly,"* they ask, *"does testing contribute to business value? Shouldn't you get it right the first time?"*

How do you answer?

Running that as an exercise dozens of times, we find that many people cannot answer. Those that can often rattle off the kind of testing to do ("Functional!", "Performance!", "Load!"). Some give the classic context-driven answers of providing information to decision-makers – but notice that does not really tie back to business outcomes.

The answer here is highly context-dependent. You will need to understand what the business does, what the risks are, and how your quality-related information advances the interests of the business. Before we end this section, though, we'll share a story.

An elevator pitch example

Over a decade ago, back in 2011, our lead author, Matt Heusser, was on an extended test coaching assignment in an area of the Midwest called Michiana. Compared to other contractors, he was expensive; plus, he came in from out of town, so the company, which did large-scale data processing, had to cover travel expenses. Michael Drzewiecki, who was responsible for Matt's contract, came into the team room and saw the value he added. The work was due for renewal at the end of the year; bringing Matt back was a question of budget.

As affable and quick-witted as Michael is, he was still left with the elevator pitch problem. Outside of the team room, the company had no way to measure, or separate the value of, test excellence. That may be for the best; no one questions the value of testing an automobile so they can "cut" road testing and costs. Yet test coaching stuck out on the budget. Someone was going to ask if it was really necessary.

The week before that conversation, there was a very odd article on page A2 of the **Wall Street Journal** (**WSJ**). It turned out that a bug in a state department computer program told 22,000 people they had won the green card lottery when, in fact, they had not. Those people took to Facebook, which was just reaching worldwide use, and created a campaign demanding that the US kept its promise to grant them a green card, glitch or no glitch.

Matt took the page from the WSJ, put it on Michael's desk, allowed him to read it, and said, *"I keep your company off the front section of the Wall Street Journal. That is what I do."*

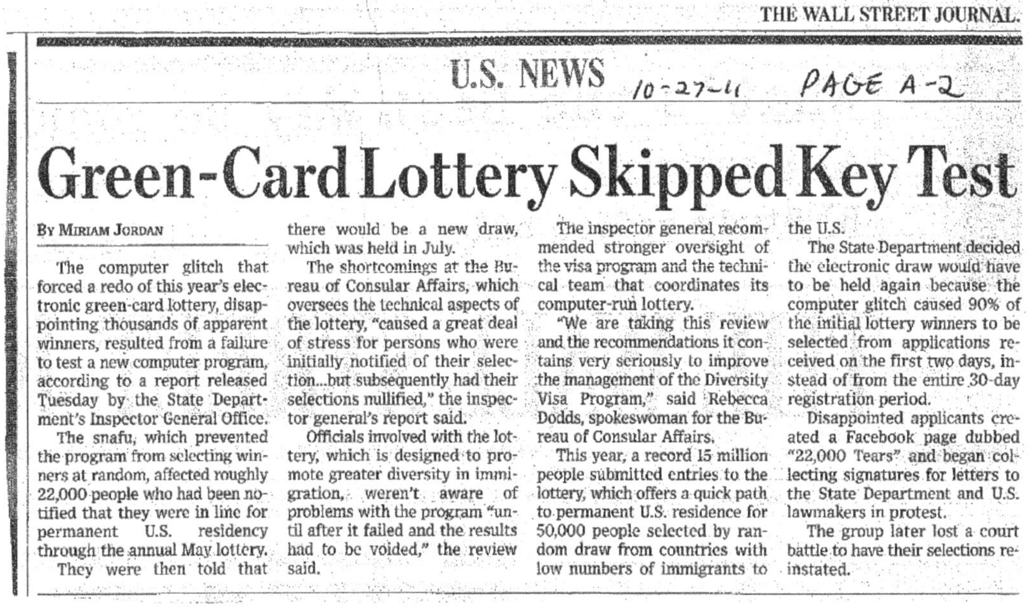
THE WALL STREET JOURNAL.

U.S. NEWS 10-27-11 PAGE A-2

Green-Card Lottery Skipped Key Test

BY MIRIAM JORDAN

The computer glitch that forced a redo of this year's electronic green-card lottery, disappointing thousands of apparent winners, resulted from a failure to test a new computer program, according to a report released Tuesday by the State Department's Inspector General Office.

The snafu, which prevented the program from selecting winners at random, affected roughly 22,000 people who had been notified that they were in line for permanent U.S. residency through the annual May lottery.

They were then told that there would be a new draw, which was held in July.

The shortcomings at the Bureau of Consular Affairs, which oversees the technical aspects of the lottery, "caused a great deal of stress for persons who were initially notified of their selection...but subsequently had their selections nullified," the inspector general's report said.

Officials involved with the lottery, which is designed to promote greater diversity in immigration, weren't aware of problems with the program "until after it failed and the results had to be voided," the review said.

The inspector general recommended stronger oversight of the visa program and the technical team that coordinates its computer-run lottery.

"We are taking this review and the recommendations it contains very seriously to improve the management of the Diversity Visa Program," said Rebecca Dodds, spokeswoman for the Bureau of Consular Affairs.

This year, a record 15 million people submitted entries to the lottery, which offers a quick path to permanent U.S. residence for 50,000 people selected by random draw from countries with low numbers of immigrants to the U.S.

The State Department decided the electronic draw would have to be held again because the computer glitch caused 90% of the initial lottery winners to be selected from applications received on the first two days, instead of from the entire 30-day registration period.

Disappointed applicants created a Facebook page dubbed "22,000 Tears" and began collecting signatures for letters to the State Department and U.S. lawmakers in protest.

The group later lost a court battle to have their selections reinstated.

Figure 10.2 – A scan of the article Michael Drzewiecki made in 2011

The company did not just do data processing; it sent more paper letters and emails out than the state department appeared to. Sending emails to the wrong recipients could lead to a leak of personal financial or health information; it could be disastrous.

Michael looked at the article, asked to borrow and scan it, and disappeared into the bowels of the organization to fight the battle of the paperclips, so to speak. Matt's contract was renewed with a 19% raise. He was allowed a month off between renewals; he took his family on a cruise. His travel rate was converted from photocopies-of-expenses-based to a single-day rate.

There are at least three ways to make a point. You can use anecdotes, as we did earlier. You can use statistics and numbers. Or you can use logic.

So, take some time and think about your testing elevator pitch. Remember, people doing the work tend to think about the work. People in middle management tend to think about the process. Senior management thinks about money. Tie what you do to money, or at least make it as obvious as our story, and you may have your elevator pitch.

The test canvas and the elevator pitch cover the business of high-level testing and its activities. They do not get at what we are looking for – risk, that is, how we track it down and what we do about it.

Let's talk about a list of things that could go wrong, for us to invest time into checking out. One might even call it a *census of risk*.

A census of risk

A census of risk is all the things that might go wrong. Some companies break this down into test cases and then describe every step. Another approach is to identify the risk, give it a "charter" or "mission," assign a timebox of 30 minutes, and allow the tester to explore the product with the intent to decrease risks along that charter.

We are going to disappoint everyone by suggesting neither approach.

The two approaches are not peers. Session-based test management, which includes time-based charters, notes, and debriefings, puts the tester in charge of finding problems. Our experience with paper, documented test cases is that they involve a great deal of typing, and most of the information is incredibly obvious. The parts that are not obvious often grow stale quite quickly. More than that, the test case approach reminds us of the walk through the dog park we took in *Chapter 4* – it covers the same input space repeatedly. That means less coverage over time, for any reasonable definition of coverage.

We suggest a more excellent way.

As it turns out, often, most of what matters in the test case is in the title. To a trained tester, someone of some intellect who has read through the preceding ideas and applied them, the title is nearly interchangeable with the content.

Here is an example of what a test case might look like.

Test Case: Basic Path to Purchase		
Step	Action	Expected Result
1	Launch website	Page loads
2	Log in as `testuser1@domain.com`	See "Hello, test user" at top left. Page loads. See the search box.
3	Click on search box	Cursor flashes on search box
4	Type in the name of a product	
5	Press <ENTER>	Search results page appears
6	Click on first result	Product display page appears; notice price
7	Click Add to cart	Shopping cart is incremented
8	Click Checkout	Selected item is added; price matches noticed price
9	Click Add new Credit Card Information	See credit card information appear
10	Use <link to wiki page howto> to fill in synthetic credit card information for test environment	
11	Click Order	Order complete appears; note order number
12	Wait 5 minutes, click orders page	Order now appears with correct order number
13	Check MRP system for order	MRP test system shows correct order

Table 10.1 – Basic test case example

Note a few things about it. First, it leaves some very important things off, such as how to find a product to search for, or what the search results should look like. Presumably, that is covered in a different test. Likewise, there are tons of things that we should, but are not told to, check for, such as what the appearance of the new credit card screen should be, what that user's shipping address should be, and so on. There are two things that seem important, how to fill in synthetic credit card information in the test and how to check the MRP system. To keep the example short, we've put this information somewhere else, such as the structure we'll call a recipe in *Chapter 9*. In most "test case" systems we've worked with, the test case would have the information we actually need, combined with information that is obvious.

Really, we could just call this a test idea: Path to Purchase. That's it. Store how to perform basic operations (logging in, how to figure out the URL for test websites, how to check the MRP system against our own, and how to find products to search for) in a recipe book and just store the test idea. This is a one-sentence description of what to test. We could collect all our test ideas in a much higher-level spreadsheet (or several) and call it a census of risks.

If we sound offended by the test case idea, it is because we are – at least a little bit. This style of storing information creates volumes of things that look important and valuable but really are not. They are painful to read, reduce the autonomy of the person running the test, and reduce the test coverage over time by forcing the same activity – all in the name of "predictable, repeatable" tests. Back in 2008, over General Tso's chicken at a Chinese restaurant during the first workshop on technical debt, Michael Kelly referenced test cases at the Conference for the Association for Software Testing as something that "doesn't come up much anymore."

The good news is we find them unnecessary. The bad news is that if you get rid of them, you need to replace them with something else. We suggest training the people doing testing and building a higher-level structure.

Defining a real risk census

What we are calling the census is essentially a list of things we might want to do something about. That could be exploring each element of the software independently (such as reviews for a product), or it might be a list of end-to-end user journeys (signup or path to purchase). The census will change over time; there might be a new browser version to track down over a weekend or a new mobile device form factor. Third parties that the software integrates with might offer new programs or end-of-life old ones. Or, someone might just "wonder what happens if" and list a half-dozen risks.

The point is that these are *emergent* risks, not covered by any unit test, tool, or type of automation. We won't run these on every build. One exception might be if we had no tooling or automation and a change in one place was likely to create changes in unexpected places. Instead, the census is a rolling list. We add things to it, run those checks to reduce risk, and cut the line, and move it to a different tab that represents risks reduced this week, sprint, or month. This rolling list can be a continuous activity, something we put an hour a week or so into. This is on top of whatever tooling and repeating tests we run. Here's the start of one census, based on data from a trading partner. We will talk about how to add measures for complexity, effort, and prediction in *Chapter 11*.

Project Name	Test Name	Priority
Digital Inspections	Equipment /DTA Association/Synch	1
Digital Inspections	DTA MxProcedures	1
Digital Inspections	Options	1
Digital Inspections	Update DTA Expression	1
Digital Inspections	(In QAC) Setup – SQL Anywhere	1
Digital Inspections	Cascade/MobLite Interface Flow Narrative	1
Digital Inspections	IRA 3 Pipe Trigger	1
Digital Inspections	IRA 4 Online Data Display in Cascade	1
Digital Inspections	(In QAC) Cascade NamePlate Data Uploaded to TOA4 Online	1
Digital Inspections	IRA 4 Data to Cascade Readings	1
Digital Inspections	IRA 3 and Cascade Interactions	2
Digital Inspections	IRA 3 Install	2
Digital Inspections	IRA 4 Security	2
Digital Inspections	Equipment Status Change	2
Digital Inspections	(In QAC) Nightly Sync Process	2
Digital Inspections	Delete TOA Equipment and Readings	2
Digital Inspections	(In QAC) IRA Configuration	3
Digital Inspections	Exclude IRA Data	3

Table 10.2 – A census of risk

Again, ideally, this is a rolling list. If we have to do a final check that everything works together before release, we can use a low-tech dashboard (such as in *Chapter 9*), or a *mind map*, as shown in the next section.

Notice the column on the far right notes priority. Assuming the priority is from 1 to 10 and this is a sorted list with the latest ideas injected periodically, it is possible that we will never get to the bottom. That is fine! Management decides the time and staffing to commit to addressing risk; management can adjust the priority. Over time, it is likely that the people doing the work understand the risk and set priorities right, but management can always review the published work and change the priority. That means management has "skin in the game." Instead of asking "Why didn't the test find that bug?" it is likely that what the test did was identify the risk and that the risk was not high in priority. To find time to do that, management would either need to add more time for testing or set the priorities differently. The tester can then pull out the list of bugs that were found and see what other risks they were related to. If management had increased the priority for "testing without IRA Data" without increasing the time, some other test would not have run. So, the question is, was the defect missed by excluding *IRA*

Data (which has a priority of 3) less important than the bugs found in *Options* (which has a priority of 1)? If the options bug is more important, then the system works as designed.

A published census of risk, then, is a tool to make the test effort for emergent risks transparent so management can set and adjust priorities. Once we learn how to project how much work we will get done (see *Chapter 11*), we can set a "cut line," which refers to the work we expect to get done before the next deadline. Management can then add resources, change priority, or extend the deadline.

Setting priorities, time management, and scope

The risk census discussed earlier gives one defined process that allows management to change the scope. We have talked about another – the low-tech testing dashboard. In all these examples, the team breaks the software down into features (or, in some cases, user journeys). Then, they make a list of things to test and ask management to advise on how deeply to test and the priorities. From there, with historical data, the team can predict how long the test effort will take.

Consider, for example, feature testing, which we have not covered deeply enough yet in this book. Most organizations think of testing as simply an activity that happens or does not. The subset of test ideas that are institutionalized as automated checks might just be the ones created by the business analyst or, most likely, the things the tester found easy to code up in the time available. Sadly, the automated check that is the most work to code (and thus skipped) is the one most likely to find a problem, because it was hard for the programmer to write as well.

Imagine a rubric for how deeply to test a feature – a level from 1 to 5, like coverage using the dashboard in the previous chapter. Management (perhaps this is deferred to the team) sets this, realizing that higher numbers will slow down progress. Periodically, the group gets together to discuss the impact of bugs slipping through. There can even be two numbers, one for exploration and another for what to institutionalize. Protected personal information, such as dates of birth and credit card numbers, could go through a more stringent process, which might even include a more complex change control and deploy process.

If the team has a high failure rate, and that rate is not correlated with the immediate work, they may have a regression test process. That process might look a lot like the census of risk – but it can be helpful to break the work down by feature. Several companies we've worked with have used mind maps to track the progress of regression testing or to document the quality of the level of testing.

In *Chapter 9*, we covered the idea of a testing dashboard for coverage. That model was a spreadsheet, with the rows as features and the columns as test environments. A mind map is similar but adds hierarchy. Starting with a central node, the features fly off the mind map, with sub-features or test ideas below that. While we've seen the most success using features, there are other ways to look at coverage, such as Karen N. Johnson's RCRCRC (`http://karennicolejohnson.com/2009/11/a-heuristic-for-regression-testing/`) or Rapid Software Testing's SFDIPOT (`https://www.satisfice.com/download/heuristic-test-strategy-model`). SFDIPOT walks the tester through Structure, Function, Data, Interfaces, Platform, and Operations. We find these models tend to work with dedicated testers on smaller units, while features give a wider view. On the other hand, it is possible that focusing on features can cause the tester to lose track of complex multi-feature use cases.

While it may be too small to read all the details, the example in *Figure 10.3* is a real example from a start-up company Excelon was consulting with recently. The four-person programmer team wanted to develop complex end-to-end GUI test automation by feature but had no structured test process at all. After a one-hour interview and exploration, we created this template, which we dubbed the "one-hour test." In an hour, we could explore the functionality of the app. As the application grew, this would become unwieldy, feedback would become slow, and we would need other methods for regression – but it was a visual start.

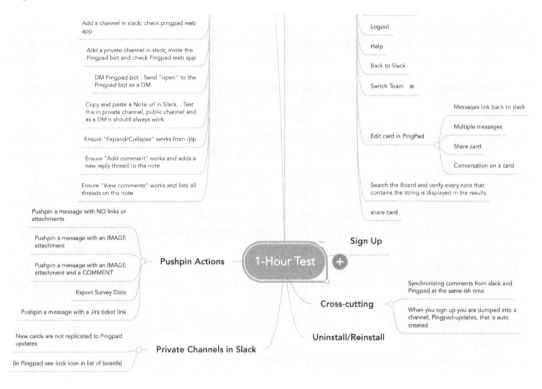

Figure 10.3 – A one-hour regression test mind map

To run the regression, we would copy the mind map and move through nodes, painting them as white for not run, red/yellow/green for status, or dark grey for skipped. To see how progress was going on regression testing, anyone could look at the image as it slowly converts to green or a more reddish hue. If there were fewer (or no) changes in a module, we could declare that a module gets less testing or is skipped. This was for a start-up with a small attack surface, with the GUI and API changing so often that automation was not the best use of time. Once the user interface became solid, the team might write automation and slowly cut the legs off the spider, so to speak. Eventually, all that is left might be the emergent risk, which might be someone's job to manage every day for 15 minutes to a few hours (or the team might rotate this responsibility, or everyone might test for five minutes. It's your strategy. These are just options).

The spider diagram was the last of a series of visual aids, designed to help the practitioner summarize the work, make it transparent, and make progress clear. By now, you should have several ways to point to how the work is being done, how long it takes for code to be tested, how to visualize the pieces of the application that are covered, and so on. All that is left is to talk about improvement.

Today's strategy versus tomorrow's goals

Starting with the lean test canvas, you might end up with a list of activities people do in various roles and the times they do them. That is not bad. The visuals from this chapter and the previous one try to tie that back to risk and priority. Hopefully, you can find some way to get started, by adding a shared spreadsheet for emergent risk, taking a long list of test cases and turning them into a summary or creating a mind map. One company we worked with started with a list of perhaps 12 major pieces of functionality in the application, each with 5 to 10 sub-items. At the start, they simply had to identify which team was responsible for what parts of the application. With over 100 full-time staff on the project, the process took nearly three months. The last month ended with senior executives hounding teams at the end to take responsibility for the unclaimed parts of the application. Once that was done, management had each team define the test process for each sub-bullet, which was stored as a wiki, or editable web page.

The act of defining the process will likely generate a bunch of "*does*" and "*shoulds*." Building a test environment *does* take so long and *should* take [a smaller time period]. Running the automated checks *does* take so long and *should* take [another smaller time period]. Automated checks fail so often but should fail less often. Automated checks run in a packet that takes 3 hours; instead, we should have 10 different deploy points, with each deploying separately and running checks in under 30 minutes.

Create a new test canvas with the way the world should be. Then start on a plan to get there.

We get it. Getting there is the hard part.

Don't worry. We've got half the book left to go.

Summary

In this chapter, we talked about assembling test strategy into something cohesive that can explained, along with the advantages of having a real, coherent strategy. You should now be able to consider an organization, analyze it, say "Oh, I see what is going on here," and summarize a test strategy easily – including the weaknesses.

The middle sections talked about a few particular ways to articulate that strategy, including the Lean Test Canvas, a census of risk, and a regression testing mind map. Those are not the only tools; in *Chapter 9*, we talked about Kanbans and low-tech testing dashboards, while *Chapter 5* briefly touched on continuous integration tools. By now, you have had broad exposure to many possible ways to organize the testing work (including model-driven and customer-facing test tooling) to create a single, comprehensive vision, capped off by the dashboard we saw in *Chapter 9*.

At the end of the chapter, we mentioned improving the strategy that exists. One simple way to do that is to look at the numbers, for example, the cycle time to get a change deployed, and to make that number smaller.

In the next chapter, we'll explore an entire theory of improvement, called Lean software testing, which provides tools to analyze which measures to improve next and why, what improving those measures will cost, and what the benefits will be.

11

Lean Software Testing

The previous chapters explained how to think about testing, document what you were doing, get a lay of the land, and understand your coverage. Once you have what you are doing today written down, you'll likely want to figure out how to improve it, set goals on what to do tomorrow, and measure and track improvements toward plans. You might also want to evaluate and predict performance with testing. Lean software testing is a blend of test and operations management techniques developed by Matt Heusser and has been refined over the past decade.

As a result, we can skip the awkward development years and give you the polished lean testing approach. In this chapter, we're going to cover the following main topics:

- What is lean software testing?

- The seven wastes

- Flow and constraints

- Release cadence and strategy refinement

- One-piece flow and **continuous delivery** (**CD**)

- A lean approach to metrics and measurement

Lean software testing defined

To explain Lean as it is understood today, we'll take a giant step back in history, then move very fast, explain the modern meaning, and then inject testing. If you're not a history buff, bear with us; we believe a deep grounding in the concepts will result in a better implementation. So, buckle up.

Here goes!

After the Second World War ended, the American industrial complex went into a massive period of high effort. Fueled by a workforce returning from the war, full of new technology (the washing machine, the mass-produced automobile, and more), and with a hungry customer base outside the US whose manufacturing was depleted by war, the American manufacturing process returned to traditional mass-assembly efforts. That left very little place for those who, during the war, had learned to "do more with less." To a great extent, the outside-of-the-box things, such as W. Edwards Deming and Joseph Juran, found a ready market in Japan, rebuilding from a conflict that drained their resources and was eager to do more with less.

This led to what became known as the Japanese Manufacturing Revolution, including innovators such as Taichi Ohno at Toyota, who defined the **Toyota Production System** (**TPS**). Toyota vehicles were of higher quality in that they had fewer defects and lasted longer (higher resale value) than their competitors, but also because Toyota developed a system to scale manufacturing up with demand. They also moved inventories and build operations to **just-in-time** (**JIT**), instead of having orders that take weeks or months to deliver, while also having stacks of inventory available.

The connection to software is not perfect; software development is a design process, not a manufacturing one. True manufacturing is done by copying files. Yet many of the ideas about how software is delivered apply. We'll discuss why, how, and what to do about it in this chapter.

The idea that new ideas struggle to take root yet can succeed wildly when given fertile soil can happen in every discipline. The next generation of ideas always challenges the current mode of thinking. To follow a line of thinking from Mahatma Gandhi, first, you are ignored, then mocked, then fought, and then your ideas become popular. In our experience, a funny thing happens in those later phases. These ideas are hard to adapt because they challenge thinking. Inevitably, management asks "Can we have that (lean, Agile, context-driven – take your pick) stuff, but not have to change?" This creates a market; someone is willing to pay for some sort of compromise. The nature of free market economics indicates that someone will offer to sell the (compromised) service.

As a result, once a new process innovation becomes computerized, it will almost inevitably be compromised and watered down. One of our mentors, Gerald M. Weinberg, called this *the law of Raspberry Jam* – that is, *the more you spread it, the thinner it gets*. When American manufacturing became aware that these Japanese approaches were resulting in cheaper vehicles developed faster with higher quality, the ideas were bunched together into **total quality management** (**TQM**). The history of TQM, is, well... not very good. The same thing happened with Agile. Scrum is incredibly popular today, yet Scrum, as it is practiced, especially the scaling frameworks as they are practiced, leaves something to be desired compared to the original vision.

When Japanese cars arrived in the US, they could beat US vehicles on price, quality, longevity, and resale value. American companies finally started to notice this and tried to bring the ideas to the US.

From ideas in practice to the term "Lean"

The first attempts to bring the ideas forward resulted in TQM. Three authors, James Womack, Daniel Roose, and Daniel Jones reversed-engineered what the staff at Toyota were doing, calling it the Lean or the TPS. A generation of consultants rose to teach the TPS, often with the same compromises that TQM had. Lean concepts, however, were a little more concrete, with basic steps of identifying the value, mapping the existing flow of work, creating flow, establishing a pull system, and continuous improvement. As you may recall from the previous chapter, there is some intentional overlap: figure out what we are doing, find the flow of the work, and improve it. This chapter will give you the tools to do that measurement and improvement using lean concepts.

Before we jump into lean for software, we'd like to pause for just a second. Building vehicles and building software are fundamentally different. In the first paradigm, we try to do the same thing, over and over again, exactly the same. With software, our goal is to do something different every time. If the work can be replicated and done in the same way, we can write some code and automate it. This means we have to be very careful in taking the ideas from Lean and applying them to software. We've done a fair bit of this work, over the years. This chapter adjusts for those differences, but we'd like to give just one example.

The TPS has a concept called **Takt**, which is the pace of demand. If Toyota can sell 5 million cars per month, then they want to be able to deliver 5 million cars per month. In an ideal system, management measures demand and then pulls the work from the factories, which can scale staff hours up and down, recall retired workers, and so on, to meet the pace of demand. In software, a vice president can walk into an office and say "I think we should develop a plugin architecture like a browser does" and create a dozen person-years of demand in a sentence. Instead of measuring the demand for software (when bounded by imagination, it is infinite), we try to think about how much fully defined work the team has to work on and try to balance that to make sure the backlog doesn't get too big. On the other hand, we can look at the test effort and see if it matches the work that is coming in. If testing is a bottleneck, we can scale back the amount of testing and make it more risk-based. However, we knew we had quality problems and not going very far down our census of risk can lead to bugs that *just aren't found*, we can add testing resources (ick), delay release (worse), or shift our efforts to improve quality earlier. Lean might even have us slow down development since throughput improvements outside of the constraint (bottleneck) are illusions.

Chew on that for a bit.

When we teach lean software testing, we start with a simulation of software development. Instead of having people build something, we have them draw it, with one group acting as the drawers (the technical team), another as the specifiers (writing the requirements), and a third, the process people, moving the paper back and forth. Only the specifiers can see the image to be reproduced, which is a good metaphor for software since classic Waterfall development took ideas, wrote them down, and passed them around. In between the first and second rounds of the exercise, the teams talk about how to improve, but they have to follow the rules as written. In between the second and third rounds, they are allowed to break the rules, so long as the metaphor holds. By round three, we often end up with the drawers and specifiers back to back, using words to talk to each other. Sometimes, they talk in different rooms over the phone. You may recognize this exercise as inspired by something Alistair Cockburn popularized 20 years ago (slide 31: `https://alistair.cockburn.us/wp-content/uploads/2018/02/Crystal2005.07-1dy.ppt`). Here's the text from the PPT:

Draw a drawing (round 1, 10 minutes):

1. Specifiers and artists move to the opposite ends of the room (this corresponds to distributed virtual teams).

2. Specifiers write instructions for their artists regarding what to do (no drawings allowed). One specifier carries messages back and forth and they can watch but not speak to the artist.

3. Artists may write messages back.

4. No SMS or MMS is allowed.

5. No speaking or drawing is allowed between specifiers and artists.

One of the easiest ways to improve performance in the drawing exercise is to get rid of the travel time of the process people. If you think about it, they are doing a job we've already automated away at work with email. One team in one tutorial moved their drawing team into the hallway, "camping out," which the specifiers moved to the edge of the room. Thus, the process people could simply hand papers back and forth. As it turns out, this was one of Taicho Ohno's "seven wastes" – the waste of transport.

The Japanese term Ohno used for waste was "Muda"' waste is a rough translation. By waste, we mean an activity that uses resources that provide no value to the customer – for example, in a physical product warehouse that kept products at unnecessary distances from the team, but every order required one of each item, this would cause transport waste.

Let's talk about the seven wastes.

The seven wastes

Before we dive in too far, there are a couple of arguments we need to cover. First, in software testing, there is the argument that a test that finds no problems is a waste. We're not so sure about that; before we ran the test, there was a risk, and after the test ran, that risk was mitigated. However, we will say that if a test never seems to fail, it might not be worth running. That is especially true if the test doesn't need to run because it would be covered by other tests. For example, you might not need a test to demonstrate the simple "positive" login case if login is a blocking condition for every other end-to-end check. If the login is broken, those other checks will all fail. Likewise, if an automated check doesn't provide much information yet causes a great deal of maintenance effort that could be spent on other things – it "breaks" a lot or is "flaky" due to a changing user interface – then the way that check is constructed could be wasteful.

There's also an argument that nothing is wasted and that these are all tradeoffs. The half-mile walk every day across campus to the team meeting room is not a waste; it is a "constitutional." The team gets to refresh themselves, stretch their legs, and discuss ideas. Those ideas lead to more and better test ideas, and sometimes, they even lead to identifying alternatives; as a whole, they save time and effort. When we talk about waste, we are not talking about that kind of thing, we are talking about *waste*. Silliness. Ridiculousness. Matt once stood up in a meeting and said something close to this: "You're only asking this question because you do not understand the architecture. Changing *that* item will not break *this* one. We do not need to re-test it. If we do re-test it, we'll be a week late and miss our deadline. What do I get when we re-test it and find no additional bugs?" That's what we are talking about here. *Waste.* We'll try to introduce each one in a manufacturing context, and then adapt for software. Here we go.

Waste #1 – transport

We mentioned transport earlier. This is the process of storing mechanical parts in places that require someone to walk distances. If the parts were in bins near the assembly station, the worker could spend their day assembling, not walking. The same can be true in software, except the "parts" are invisible. Essentially, in software, we are the parts. Technical staff can spend multiple hours a day physically walking to meetings, which can be a waste of productivity. One of the large controversies at the time of writing is working remotely versus driving into an office. Between the drive-in, the lunch hour, and the drive home, it is possible for a person to spend 12 hours yet have only 4 hours of productivity. At one point early in its development, Google created townhouses right next to campus, put in sleeping pods in the office, and created buses with wireless internet to pick up employees to get that time back. That's only a partial list; Google also has cafeterias in the office, gyms, and local medical clinics, all to reduce transport waste.

Of course, the easiest way to eliminate transport waste is to let people work anywhere there is internet and power. This creates other concerns about management and productivity. We, the authors, see these as solvable problems, yet we understand the concern. Our approach in this book with the seven wastes is to start where you are and improve what you can. Often, there are plenty of small, quick wins that are easy enough to pick off when working within the existing system; there is no need to blow it up. When we write about the seven wastes, that's where we start.

Note that it is possible to strip all transport, to the point that we sit at our desks all day and just type. Most experts agree that small intentional walks can be good, both physically and intellectually. So, remember, if getting up and stretching every half-hour invigorates you, allowing you to be more productive, then it can't be a waste.

Mary Poppendeick, who wrote software for a factory and then went on to apply lean ideas to software development, also adds handoffs as a kind of transport waste. Carefully reading the rest of this chapter will help you determine that handoffs generally create other kinds of waste and delays. A single person, with a full understanding of the requirements, can simply create the solution – yet that is rarely possible in a business or government organization creating software. Short of an analyst creating spreadsheets, which might arguably be a kind of software, most of this work will have handoffs to one extent or another. That said, just about every assignment we have in our collective memory starts with an opportunity to improve value by *reducing* the number of handoffs.

While we recognize this ideal might not be possible, we also recognize most organizations are so far from the ideal that there is plenty of room for improvement.

Waste #2 – inventory

In manufacturing, it is possible to look at a huge warehouse that is never empty and calculate the value of all the intermediate work products piling up. Some of that inventory could expire or become out of date. Even if it doesn't, the warehouse might represent tens of millions of dollars of investment. At today's rates, every 10 million dollars of equipment placed in treasury bills can yield about $500,000 US dollars per year in interest; that is over a thousand dollars a day. Companies can see a warehouse and understand that the square footage has a cost, that it needs to be rented, heated, cooled, electrified, have insurance, and guards, and could create transport waste compared to a much smaller footprint. Likewise, work in progress, filling up buckets and bins of partially assembled products, has costs that can be calculated.

Unless we work to make it visible, inventory in software is invisible. That's a problem.

One company we worked with had a software process that looked a little bit like Scrum and a little bit like Waterfall. The testers would be working on a 2-week sprint with a number, perhaps sprint 21, on a sprint 21 code branch. The developers would be working on sprint 22 and business analysts on sprint 23. Project managers were looking at sprint 24, and senior managers 25, while operations were trying to get sprint 20 onto production. When the testers found a problem, the developers had to get their heads out of sprint 22, work on sprint 21, do the fix, get it verified, then merge it back. This was a huge inventory problem that no one could see.

Matt suggested visualizing the flow of the work using the main team room. The team room was big; it had room for 60 people to work, plus a side wall as large as a small school gymnasium. The suggestion to put the stories on the wall was rejected, but not because it was too much effort, or to wild, or too hard to maintain. *The idea was rejected because it wouldn't fit; the cards would take up too much space.*

That is a work-in-progress inventory problem.

One common problem in Scrum is getting work to "in testing" immediately before the sprint ends, then complaining testing is slow. These are two problems at once, really: inconsistent demand makes planning impossible (as it isn't possible to test what isn't ready yet earlier), but also the things-to-be-tested inventory is too large.

Excess inventory in the entire software delivery system makes everything slow. When executing a modest idea from inception to production this might take a week; a 3-month backlog means it will take more than 3 months. Excess inventory in tests causes delays in tests in the same sort of way – a feature might take an hour to test, but instead takes a week because there are 4 days of work set out in front of it. These are flow issues that we cover after waste. For now, we start to see the waste in the system.

Waste #3 – motion

Transport waste is walking; motion usually involves your hands. For example, let's say there is some new work to test, sitting on a branch. The tester needs to create a build for that branch (and wait for it), then use a file transfer to push that build to a server, then run a command on that server to create a test environment, then SSH onto that test environment, run setup scripts, and on, and on, and on, to get to the point they can start testing.

If this story doesn't make any sense to you, then congratulations – your situation is more fortunate than most. Perhaps in your office when the programmer checks in the work, if all the automated checks pass, the build system can create a test environment automatically and kick out the location as part of the build report.

The second example is a way to reduce waste motion. It isn't always possible; you might need to create test data. Yet if you have to perform the same activity over and over again, it might make sense to automate it. The cartoonist XKCD came up with a graphical illustration to decide at what point it is worth automating a routine task; we are big fans:

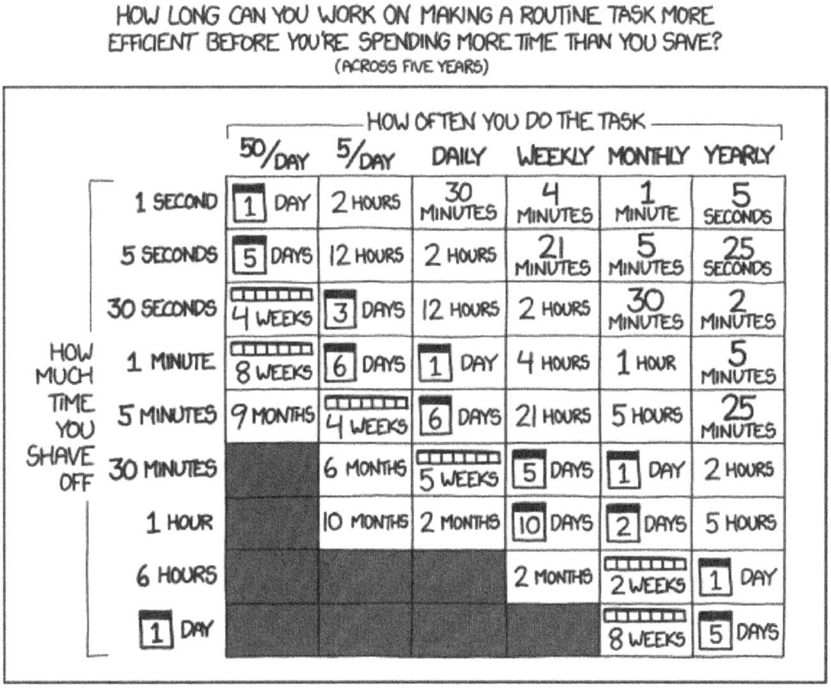

HOW LONG CAN YOU WORK ON MAKING A ROUTINE TASK MORE EFFICIENT BEFORE YOU'RE SPENDING MORE TIME THAN YOU SAVE? (ACROSS FIVE YEARS)

HOW MUCH TIME YOU SHAVE OFF	HOW OFTEN YOU DO THE TASK					
	50/DAY	5/DAY	DAILY	WEEKLY	MONTHLY	YEARLY
1 SECOND	1 DAY	2 HOURS	30 MINUTES	4 MINUTES	1 MINUTE	5 SECONDS
5 SECONDS	5 DAYS	12 HOURS	2 HOURS	21 MINUTES	5 MINUTES	25 SECONDS
30 SECONDS	4 WEEKS	3 DAYS	12 HOURS	2 HOURS	30 MINUTES	2 MINUTES
1 MINUTE	8 WEEKS	6 DAYS	1 DAY	4 HOURS	1 HOUR	5 MINUTES
5 MINUTES	9 MONTHS	4 WEEKS	6 DAYS	21 HOURS	5 HOURS	25 MINUTES
30 MINUTES		6 MONTHS	5 WEEKS	5 DAYS	1 DAY	2 HOURS
1 HOUR		10 MONTHS	2 MONTHS	10 DAYS	2 DAYS	5 HOURS
6 HOURS				2 MONTHS	2 WEEKS	1 DAY
1 DAY					8 WEEKS	5 DAYS

Figure 11.1: Routine task automation chart. Source: https://xkcd.com/1205

The preceding example is an extension of a simple mathematical formula:

- A is the number of times the action is performed per year
- B is the amount of time you save by not repeating the task
- Therefore, savings = A * B * 5

So long as the effort is less than savings, according to the chart, then automation is worth doing.

First, note that the example in *Figure 11.1* plans for 5 years for you to earn your payback. We find it very rare that a software process lasts 5 years. It also assumes you can accurately estimate how long tasks will take. In other words, this chart is incredibly optimistic. If automating a task looks like it won't pay for itself using this chart, perhaps you shouldn't do it.

One final thing to consider under motion is scale. It might not make sense for you to spend 6 months working on a project that will save you 10 minutes a day, but if you can deploy that across a thousand engineers, the project will pay for itself in a couple of weeks. This simple fact could explain why test frameworks are often developed by large companies, then open sourced. Typically, open sourcing the tool will lead other developers to adopt a large company's infrastructure.

Waste #4 – waiting

Waiting has been called the *king of the wastes*, or perhaps the *source* of waste. The examples we've looked at so far involve waiting in some way. The meeting can't start because people are walking to it. Testing can't start because someone is waiting for a test environment; then, the inventory of things to be done is stacked up, waiting for its turn.

Worse, in many business cultures, we view sitting around, idle, as somehow bad. Instead of fixing the waiting problem, we add new tasks. These new tasks are lower value (we'd rather do the thing that is blocked, after all), and they require us to switch as higher-priority tasks come back. One of my colleagues, Sean McMillian, was working in a ticket-tracking system where the tickets that came in were unclear, or confusing, or he didn't have permission to make the needed changes. He would send an email asking for clarification on the first ticket, then grab the second, where he would have the same problem. Eventually, he could get 10 to 20 tickets in-flight, each of which would be working or have a touch time of perhaps 20 minutes to fix but would take a total elapsed time of several business days. If we count the time the task was entered into the system to be resolved, it could be business weeks. Sean did the best he could; he found a way to visualize this inventory (and wait) and presented it to management.

When we make it look like we aren't waiting by picking up another task, we enable at least three kinds of waste. First, we don't solve the waiting problem – we are still waiting. Second, we create inventory waste because our work-in-progress is expanding. In the next major section, *Flow*, we'll explain the deep damage multitasking does mathematically. For now, we can just think of that as waste. Third, we'll create more waste on the second task when the first comes back and we switch – that is, the second task will now take longer as it waits for attention while we finish the first. The solution is not to pick up more work, and very rarely to stand idle. Instead, we need to reduce the waiting. We'll discuss how shortly, and in the *Flow* section.

Interestingly enough, when we work to automate so that we can prevent motion waste, we can create waiting waste. XKCD has a comic for that. The idea that we are doing too much to accomplish today's task is something called the waste of overprocessing:

Figure 11.2: How overprocessing causes waste. Source: https://xkcd.com/974/

Waste #5 – overprocessing

Early proponents of **Extreme Programming** (**XP**) had a slogan: **You Ain't Gonna Need It**, or **YAGNI**. The basic idea behind YAGNI was to not build an all-encompassing extensible framework of frameworks to solve problems. In fact, for most of our early career, when we saw someone try to build an extensible framework that could allow massive change, the changes they would need turned out to be unanticipated ones. Instead, XP taught us to do the *simplest thing that could possibly work*, combined with a discipline that made the code we were writing easy. This ties directly to the concept of overprocessing in lean manufacturing. In manufacturing, overprocessing involves building a product past the minimum specifications. If a customer can't tell the difference between a tolerance to a millimeter and a tenth of a mile-meter, and the product has no particular advantage from perfection, then building a product that is even more perfect doesn't matter.

In software, this might be doing the following:

- Building a website that responds more quickly than a customer can notice – which is less than 250 milliseconds of load time

- Building additional features before we know how the customer will use them

- Not capturing customer use data and adapting our test strategy to the flow of money or flow of users

- Building additional features that don't tie back to value for customers

- Releasing the software in big batches, perhaps quarterly, when we could have a system that enables every-sprint, every-day, or every-change deployments

It doesn't have to be the software; many development processes are full of well-meaning steps that contain waste. For example, let's say a team has a single problem that causes an error, so they inject a "check" step in the process. From now on, for every task, the author has to check something. That problem might only show up every 5 years and only cause a few hours of problems, but now, the entire organization of 100 people has to spend 5 minutes every day or two on a check. We've even seen these lists of checks because some are so exhaustive that we realize no one is doing them at all, having decided that their work does not need performance tests this time, does not need usability tests, and so on. Sometimes, this "think about it for every feature" work becomes a web form where people have to spend time clicking "does not apply" mechanically for 5 minutes for every change. This mechanical clicking can become such a habit that the activity adds no value. What is going on here? What do we call it?

Looking at it through the lens of Lean, the answer is easy: that's overproduction waste.

Waste #6 – overproduction

In Lean manufacturing, overproduction involves producing too much of a product or producing it too early. We might need all the components to assemble a laptop but produce too many hard drives. Not only do the extra hard drives create inventory waste, but the time we spent on them could have been spent on getting every other component ready in time so that we could start assembling the laptops earlier.

In software, projects are often scheduled in odd ways, which causes delays. For testing specifically, there is often a frontend and a backend. There might be a search page, for example, but also a search API. The search API might be done before it is "wired up" to the page. A technical product catalog might be searchable in several rare ways that income code-like text. Instead of waiting for everything to be done, the testers might be able to test the backend while they wait for it to be connected to the frontend. Once the two are connected, the frontend tests can be minimal and focus on the look, feel, output text, output size, and several search results because the API and database have already been tested – that is, frontend testing can focus more on the second half of this sentence: "Assuming the API returns text results as expected, check the page is displayed properly." Once you look for it, you'll see that *splitting* functionality into small pieces, with a little bit of high-level testing on top, can often save time while reducing risk.

Software communication has come to a different understanding of overproduction: relearning. Many software tasks are difficult to learn and master; if we only have to do them every 6 months or less, we are perpetually re-learning. By structuring the work so that we don't forget things, we can reduce waste.

Now, we can finally talk about bugs.

Waste #7 – defects

When manufacturers find a defective part, there is something physical. A malformed yoyo, an automotive part, a broken bit of sheet metal. These go into a bin, either for rework, recycling, or the local dump. A company can measure the waste by measuring the size of the waste bin and counting the number of times it fills up per month.

Again, in manufacturing, an executive can point to a pile of scrap and say "We are losing a hundred thousand dollars a month in scrap, and fifty thousand a month in salary to do the rework to bring malformed parts into compliance!"

In software, unless we make it explicit somehow, the waste of defects is invisible.

Let's talk about how that waste shows up in the world:

- When we find bugs, we have to them because the programmers need to fix the bugs. This also creates a handoff, which is a type of transport waste.

- While the bugs are being fixed, testers have to wait; otherwise, they have to multitask.

- When the bugs are fixed, we have to rework because significant areas of the code need to be retested.

- Any time we spend documenting the bug, conducting analysis on the bug, creating reports, and revising our test strategy to address it in the future is waste. We wouldn't have to do it if we just didn't have the defect in the first place. John Seddon, the British consultant, calls this "failure demand" (https://beyondcommandandcontrol.com/failure-demand/) – that is, additional work that only exists because of some failure earlier in the process. If we had done things correctly, we would not have had to do the documenting/fix/retest steps. Of course, not all defects are preventable, but using the techniques in this book, we have seen order-of-magnitude decreases in defects that are found in end-cycle (regression) testing.

- Defects that escape the customers can cause frustration, customers to go elsewhere, downtime, and even material financial orders. In the worst cases, personal health or financial information can go to the wrong person, **Non-Disclosure Agreements** (**NDAs**) can be violated, stock traders can make the wrong trades, money can be deleted from accounts, insurance checks can be sent to the wrong person or the wrong address for the wrong amount, payroll slips can be incorrect, and payments can go to the wrong person.

Here's just one example: a Fortune 500 payroll company we work with recently made an error when Excelon Development (our company) told it to send over ten thousand US dollars to one of our contractors. The payroll company sent the money but did not deduct it from our bank account, then told the contractor they needed it back! Handling the situation so we had had every legal document signed and agreed to by the parties took a great deal of (lot, expected to be billable) hours, with a total cost dozens of times more than the per-month price on the web-based software we were using to do it with.

Yet at Matt's first annual review as a programmer, when criticized himself for writing too many bugs, his manager shrugged and said "Bugs are going to happen."

To tighten our terms a bit, we'll describe a bug as something that bugs someone that matters. If it bugs a vice president of marketing, what is just "building what you told us to" a week ago could easily become a bug in a second. A defect, in our mind, is something that's clearly wrong. "I don't like that user interface; change it," might be a bug. "When I click submit, I get a 404 error" is a defect.

A warning about prevention

Some people we respect might argue this item is more of a development item, that prevention isn't the role of a tester, and that it is best if we just do the best job we can with the software we are given. We understand the argument. From the 1980s to the 1990s, the literature was full of publications and talks arguing for prevention and zero defect approaches. It wasn't testing, and it didn't work well. Even today, executable specification and shift-left approaches have had mixed success. We are all for jumping in and testing. However, once you've done a little bit of testing, you are likely to get a mental model of the space. You'll realize certain programmers make certain types of errors, while the entire team makes broad general categories of errors. Tracking those errors, bringing them up, and finding ways to prevent the category of error is prevention based on data, and it does reduce the amount of defect waste. There is another argument to be made – that if we get good at working with the team to reduce failure demand, the need for dedicated testers will go away. That may be so; we've seen indications of it on a few high-functioning teams. The sorts of easy errors we listed in *Chapter 1* have become rarer as teams use code libraries that already check for correctly-formed email addresses and calendar dates and so on. To those concerned about it, we say *reduce failure demand anyway*. If you'll forgive the colorful vernacular, we've been doing that explicitly since before we started on the book, *How To Reduce The Cost of Software Testing*, and, at least as of today, we ain't starvin'.

We see simple defects that could have been found and fixed earlier as waste.

(New) waste #8 – ability

While waste of talent isn't one of the seven wastes of the TPS, you can see how it could fit. For example, some time ago, Matt was working as a test coach in a data processing facility. The integrated delivery team had some work come in that was essentially routine – generate SQL statements to update the database under a certain set of rules. The team usually did work in pairs, but they had an odd number that week, so this "easier" SQL work was assigned to a new programmer. The problem was that he did not know the database, he wasn't fantastic with SQL, and he was concerned about asking for help. An assignment that might take a senior programmer 1 hour could take a week for this new hire, and only then after interrupting several people. Matt chose to pair with him; the two knocked the assignment out in 2 hours, and that was only because Matt went slowly to explain what he was doing so that the new hire could do it themselves next time. Training plus getting the work done in a fraction of the time... the alternative sure does seem like a waste, doesn't it?

Another company we worked with genuinely embraced the alternative. One manager walked around, saying with a raised voice, "Know your role! Be your role!" The slogan sounded good. From what we could tell, his goal was to let every department, and every individual, stand on their skills. If a role, department, or person was lacking, overall system performance would decrease, people would notice, and that group would get the attention it needed to improve. Sometimes, the manager would write "Know your role! Be your role!" on a whiteboard. At least once Matt wrote underneath it "What if we tried to figure out what the project needs to be successful, and just do that instead?"

The first idea has some merit. If you routinely "bail out" another team/role, they are likely to never develop the skills to do the work themselves. Our story of pairing to develop skills while increasing speed seems relevant. Another term for this "figure out what needs doing" is managing flow, which we will discuss in a bit. First, let's talk about removing waste in testing.

Removing waste in testing

When we do the drawing exercise, teams immediately find ideas to improve performance. Two, five, 10, 20 ideas. They can write smaller, more concise directions. They explain what keywords mean. They can stagger the people passing messages back, and so on. Cockburn recommends a simple retrospective format, with things to keep, things to stop, and things to start.

The amazing thing is that we don't do this in testing. Instead, we tend to do every project the same as the last one. Every feature is the same as the last one. Most of the companies we work with would spend roughly the same effort testing upvoting on a product review as they would a credit card checkout – at least when we start working with them. Imagine testing is a dial, all features are set to five.

Except they aren't. No one talks about it. Different testers test different amounts. This has some advantages, in that you can turn the dials down to three, two, or one if you are falling behind. Provide no visibility, get the software out, and if there are problems in production, well... whoopsie. Gee willakers. Well, we missed the bug, but the programmers made the same mistake, and the requirements people didn't call it out explicitly in the requirements, so I guess everybody messed up, right?

We can do better.

Consciously adjusting the dials for testing is one way to reduce low-value activity. If we can identify the ways defects are created and work to prevent them (waste #7), we can get away with less testing. Reducing defects also removes a fair bit of waiting, rework, and failure demand. Build, test environment, and testing activities generally contain motion waste, which can be removed. Waiting for requirements and decisions creates a great deal of waiting; it is possible to create a "ready for work" standard on features and tasks that will reduce those delays because the features will be more clearly defined. Careful attention to how the project is structured can reduce overproduction... and the list goes on.

In our experience, once teams are turned on to this, they'll come up with a great many ideas. Many of these ideas can be implemented immediately. Individual workers can usually find improvements that lead to 5-10% more velocity, and teams 10-20%. But the big ideas come from how the work is structured, and communication across teams. These are flow issues. You can find them using the second waste, but understanding flow allows you to make predictions and provide metrics, to make a credible case to improve the pace of delivery.

Now, it's time to talk about flow.

Flow

Imagine you're in an engineering plant. Raw materials come into the plant, where they are painted, assembled, repainted, have a QA inspection, are loaded into trucks, and hauled away. The workers can offload 1,000 widgets per hour into the staging area; initial painting is 750 widgets per hour, assembly is 500, repainting is 750, and the team can inspect 1,000 widgets per hour. What is the net output of the factory?

It doesn't take a wizard to figure out that the factory will produce an output of 500 widgets per hour. Performance improvements regarding the repainting or inspection team are a total waste of time. It would be better if those teams decreased staff, moving them to help with the assembly process. Eli Goldratt's theory of constraints provides some ideas to help us improve performance in such a factory. For example, we want to keep the assembly team working all the time; we might build up a little parts inventory in front of them in case they have a particularly good hour. It also might make economic sense to increase their output in any way possible, such as having extra staff on hand to work during breaks or building an inefficient rig that does appear to make economic sense that only gets 100 widgets per hour – given this setup, that inefficient assembly station nets the factory output by 2,400 widgets per day.

In software, we rarely have any idea what the constraints are or what the bottleneck is. In those rare cases, we know what the bottleneck is, so we are more likely to complain about how inefficient it is than to add resources to improve flow. The following figure is a simplified illustration of our painting story:

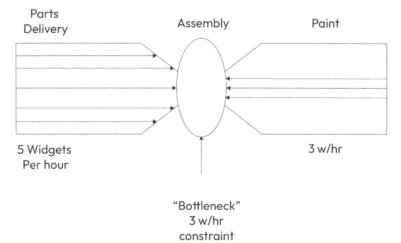

Figure 11.3: Basic constraint theory

Here, we have parts delivery and paint, which are capable of performing five widgets per hour, but we have a bottleneck in the assembly that limits us to three. This is the "constraint." This is simple and intuitive – yet how many teams calculate where the constraints are, structure the work to optimize flow, or adjust testing to improve performance? It's not 0%... but it isn't a very high percentage, either.

From freeways to factories to oil pipelines, engineers understand flow – we just don't think about it enough in knowledge work. For the rest of this section, we'll discuss flow as a system, including some points on measurement.

Visualizing flow – an example

On one project, Matt was working as the lead programmer. The work was mostly maintenance of existing systems, coming through a requirements analyst, and going out to a representative of the business units for testing. Every week, Matt met with his manager for a one-on-one to talk about issues, including career issues. The manager pointed out their hope to move more projects through faster. The problem was that *if Matt moved more projects through, it wouldn't matter*. And he could prove it.

For the past 6 months, Matt had done a weekly tally of his tasks, along with where they were in the process – in requirements, development, developer testing, customer testing, waiting for approval, or deployment. Then, he used Excel to generate a chart. Here's the chart:

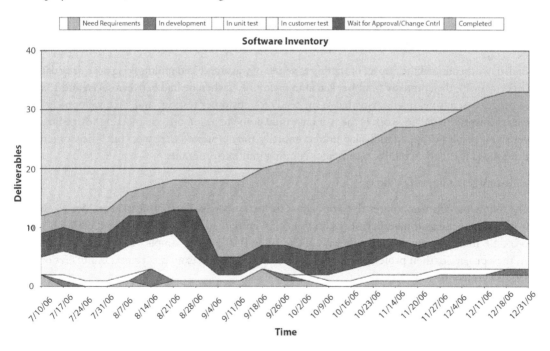

Figure 11.4: A cumulative flow diagram showing emergent
bottlenecks. Source: Matt Heusser, personal work

The line on top is completed; the line below is waiting for testing. Early in the project, the purple line was continually expanding. If Matt shoved more work onto the test, they would have to multitask, which would mean getting work done even more slowly – less value to customers per month! If they did not multitask, then the additional work would simply pile up in front of the test and slowly become outdated, irrelevant, and forgotten. When it was picked up, we'd experience the waste of relearning; overall delivery would slow down!

With the chart in hand, the manager went to senior management, who eventually converted a new web developer position into a subject matter/test analyst. Instead of being in trouble for not getting enough work done (when it didn't matter to the output), Matt provided the information the decision-makers needed about flow so that they could align staffing levels. That is lean software delivery.

The reason the chart is appealing is because *time to market matters*. Another simple measure for value, **cost of delay**, asks us to consider the value we could capture right now if we had the product available to our customers. It may be indirect and more difficult to calculate, but even internal and support projects have some sort of pain for the delay. In addition to not getting the money for the project now, most projects have a limited timespan to add value – so we can't even capture the money later! Yet when we start to do the math on flow and the seven wastes, we see that our work is often not structured to get the most value.

Another way we structure work to inhibit flow is through multitasking.

Multitasking

Earlier, we mentioned the impact of waiting as a kind of waste and said multitasking does deep damage. Let's start with the company Matt worked at in *Figure 11.4*, when he had between seven and 15 items in progress at a time, interleaving between "ready for customer testing" and "in development." The way this would typically work is the worker would come to a one-on-one meeting with a boss and get a new project dropped in his lap until eventually, they protested they were full. The worker then time-sliced the work, a bit like a computer running multiple programs.

Let's look at the impact on flow.

The following figure compares the work effort for two projects. Each project takes 2 weeks. In the first example, the staff member works on project A until it is completed, at the end of day 10, then project B until it is completed, at the end of day 20. In the second example, the work is split, project A, then project B, then project A, then project B. In the second example, project A finishes on day 19, and project B on day 20:

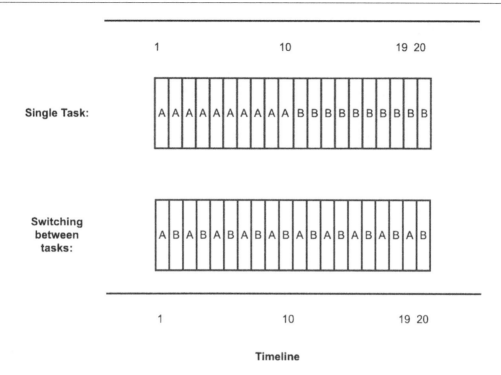

Timeline

Figure 11.5: A multitasking diagram, custom-developed for this book

In this case, all projects are not considered equal. The first set of outcomes are delivered on day (10+20)/2 = average day 15; the second on average day 19.5. With three projects, they are delivered on average day 29. With four, the average day is 39.5. At the time of devising *Figure 11.3*, Matt typically took a notepad with seven to 10 things on it into meetings.

All this assumes that the worker can switch between projects with no effort. It takes a fair bit of brain effort to switch between knowledge work tasks. Jim Benson talks about this in his thin little book *Why Limit WIP: We Are Drowning in Work*. Benson suggests an exercise where you spend 1 minute each writing letters in order, then numbers, then Roman numerals. After that exercise, you spend 3 minutes alternating between numbers, letters, and Roman numerals. You'll find that overall performance goes down dramatically.

When you multitask, you do work of lesser quality, that takes longer to get up to speed, which invariably, mathematically, makes everything take longer in calendar time.

That "time to complete" is something we'll discuss next and is called **cycle time**. It impacts every step of the work effort because the total effort to deliver a project is some of the cycle time of everyone's work.

Measurement – lead time versus cycle time

Executives frequently complain because it takes too long to get anything done. By the time they've completed business case part one, business case part two, and submitted the work to the change control board, they've lost a month. Then, the work takes a month to be prioritized. Then, it sits there and waits for its turn. Finally, it gets worked on.

Cycle time changes the tone of the conversation. Instead of looking at the entire scope of work, we look at two things:

- **Cycle time**: The average amount of time it takes to complete a unit of work as a focused, single task

- **Lead time**: The length of time it takes from work being assigned to it being completed

Figure 11.6 demonstrates the difference between lead and cycle time:

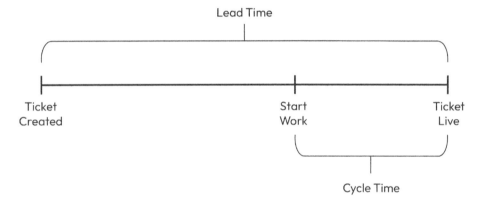

Figure 11.6: Cycle and lead time

Note that most leaders focus on and complain about lead time being too long – but that is not even under the control of the workers! It is instead generally a function of how the work is structured (flow) and the effort of the people working upstream.

Imagine changing the conversation from "Why does it take 6 months to get a project done?" to "From the time you drop a feature onto our team, we can get it on production in 2 weeks." Taking 6 months is a sign the queue for projects is too long; it is a problem outside of the technical team.

Likewise, "Why does a test take so long?" is a tough question. But "From the time you drop a feature on my desk to the time it is tested, it takes on average less than a business day," is answering a different question. As for why testing takes so long, that is likely due to **backwash** on the waterfall. If 90% of features have to be sent back, and they typically need to be sent back 3.5 times, and re-testing still takes a half day, suddenly, the entire process of testing and fixing and re-testing takes more like a week. We believe that some bugs are truly unexpected and won't be found until they're experienced in tests. What we can say is, of the people we've worked with using the techniques in this book, it is not uncommon to see a 90% reduction in problems resolved during the test cycle before the test cycle happens, through ideas such as specification by example. Or, less politely, "figuring out what it'll do, and checking it, before a formal exploration step." Another common option is to interleave exploration and coding, or at least to make the work steps small and fast enough that it looks and feels that way – for example, no QA column on the board, but instead continuous collaboration.

Efficiency and congestion

Imagine that you are on an empty freeway, with nothing as far as the eye can see. How fast can you drive? Likely as fast as you want to – but you'll only get one car to your destination. Planners design freeways to meet demand; they want to get a lot of cars to their destination as quickly as possible. They also understand that a single event, such as a lane closure or a traffic stop, can significantly impact flow.

In a congestion collapse event, the flow goes to zero. A "traffic jam" is an example of this. Congestion collapse is worse; it is when you have a traffic stop and a lane closure and a tire goes out on a bus. Suddenly, no one is going anywhere. These are hard to predict, but one thing we know is that as theoretical capacity approaches 100% (we are getting as many people to our destination as possible), the potential for a collapse approaches 100%. This happened on the old Ethernet networks as well as traditional servers that were overloaded. Failing messages would be re-submitted in a saturated network, then fail again, leading to cascading failures.

The lesson here is that chasing velocity at all costs is not a good strategy for long-term success. Instead, understand the potential of the team, and leave some capacity in reserve. This is especially true for specialized positions, such as database administrators. When you have a single person doing a job, and that person goes out sick or is assigned to something else, the work simply waits. Summing up the amount of waiting in a multitasking environment, we often see that the work itself spends an incredible amount of time waiting around for someone to do something.

As just one example, if we could measure the work precisely (most teams can't) and we know that cycle time is 1 hour (most teams do not even have a standard for a work item, and if they do, they do not have a standard distribution), it is not reasonable to expect a tester to complete 40 items in a week. Meetings, the order the work is dropped, and so on prevent this. It might be better to count the number done and project to predict what is possible.

Metric – touch time

Imagine that you have two stopwatches. The first runs only when an item is being worked on. The second is for the entire feature, from writing it down to operations. Taking the first number divided by the second, you can get a percentage. We can look at the percentage of touch time for a feature while it is in the development team, when it is defined and actionable, or all the way back into the portfolio. One company we worked with had a backlog that was roughly a year and a half of work. This meant that a change that might take a week to implement, but was low in priority, could have an overall touch time of 2% – assuming there were perfect handoffs and single-tasking when the feature was worked on. At the same company, we frequently saw projects that had less than 1 week of engineering work that would take 6 to 9 months to get done, often because the database would be refreshed quarterly and the test data was lost due to multitasking.

Worse, with a 1.5-year backlog, the things at the bottom will simply never be done. By the end of the year, new items of higher priority will appear. If the item somehow miraculously reaches the top, it is likely to be out of date, the analyst who wrote it will have left the company, and so on. Large inboxes lead to waste. Imagine a large inbox at every step of the process and you will see why organizations cannot get things done.

These examples are extreme, but they are worth looking at. Waste and flow theory tells us that when work in progress is too high, touch time falls apart. A touch time of 2% means that if the work is structured differently, it can be done 50 times faster.

Most of the software work we saw at the beginning of our career focused on utilization. Keep people busy. If you've got some free time because of waiting, find something else to do.

We say: No. If you have free time because of waiting, find ways to reduce your waiting.

The logic of flow comes from things that are all roughly equal: cars on the freeway, cubic meters of water, and packets on a telecommunications network. So far, our examples have been skirting around the issue, talking about "work items" or "features." To get from abstract to practice – what the heck are we measuring? One term for this is batch size.

Batch size

If Matt spent a Saturday with his daughter, Julie, making cookies, then batch size would matter. If a tray is 12 cookies, and we have two trays at a time, and cooking takes 2 hours, we might expect 24 cookies every 2 hours. This unit of measurement is known as **batch size**. We typically find that by having a **batch size** that is similar ("about" 2 hours of work, for example), it becomes possible to measure and predict performance. In testing, people do like to measure things, but we get in trouble when we look at things that are fundamentally different and measure them as if they were equal. For example, counting the number of bugs found (or open, or open and closed) on a line graph may look impressive, but if one of the bugs is "no one can log in" and 50 of them are spelling, typographical, and minor visual errors on the screen, the one might be a bigger deal than the other 50 combined. If we measure, for example, the time-to-live of bugs and average them, and fixing typos is easy, our login defect might not get fixed for an extended period.

Likewise, some teams count test cases planned, test cases executed, number failing, number passing, and change over time to calculate when a waterfall project will be done. Those kinds of metrics ignore flow and waiting issues, so they might provide an accurate status of a project that is incredibly ineffectively managed. A second problem is, how big is a test case? Do some test cases take 5 minutes to run, and some 1 hour, some half a day? Having some sort of expected effort behind a test measurable can help both prediction and flow. **Session-based test management**, which splits testing into half-hour sessions, was an attempt to put some measurement and rigor around freestyle exploration.

For software testing, we've generally found a few measures helpful:

- **A feature or story**: This corresponds to the work a programmer does, which is a minimally differentiated piece of work. These are typically half a day to 2 days of effort. Teams earlier in transitioning away from waterfall thinking often start with larger stories that reduce over time. County velocity, or assigning "points" to stories, can be helpful during this transitional period. Some people like it. Our long-term preference is to count stories.

- **A sprint**: How much work can the team do, as a measure of stories? Look at the mean and median. Another way to do that is to take, say, the bottom 90% of work and average it (or find the median) to predict outcomes with more confidence. When it comes to prediction, pick worse-performing periods to predict with a higher confidence interval.

- **Regression testing**: Defining and measuring what needs to be tested for a release, then tightening the cycle time of that process and changing architecture to vastly automate or reduce it, is a mighty lean thing to do. We can even use measurement tools to accelerate that process.

Waiting, work in progress, and multitasking can all be combined to destroy touch time through work queues.

Queues and efficiency

In bottleneck theory, we learned that if something is a bottleneck, we build up work in progress in front of it. That way, the bottleneck is at least always working at 100% capacity. In bureaucracy, we learn to build up work in progress in front of everything. In other words, we have a task that takes 10 minutes but we don't get to it for a week. When the step is done, it goes to the next person, who doesn't get to work on it for a week. Then, the next person takes 10 minutes, but it takes a week, and so on.

Eventually, you have a task that takes 1 hour and takes 3 months to get done. This is all in the name of efficiency. In the workplace, these extreme examples are often things such as reimbursement for taking a college course, which has to go through three layers of management – one for HR and two for finance. However, when you start to look for them in testing, they appear everywhere. At some companies, the project managers are expediters, whose role involves shouting above the clamor to get things done. A shrewd manager of project managers might assign the best project managers to the most important projects… but do we want the success of the company to be beholden to the luck of getting the right project manager?

Arrival time pacing

Before we finish looking at flow, it's worth talking about the arrival time of work. If the testers are working in 2-week sprints and have a cycle time per feature of half a day, with a failure rate of say 10%, it might be reasonable to expect them to get 10 features tested per sprint. However, if the features all drop onto the testers on the afternoon of day 9… forget about it.

Planners understand that when you increase demand, you need to stagger the work. That is why freeways have a quarter-mile of onramp before their lane ends. On freeways with more expected traffic, the on-ramp is larger. The simplest way to "dribble" work onto a group to standardize arrival is to create a pull system.

Limiting work in progress to create a pull system

Finally, we can put our pieces together.

The delivery team has a business analyst, three developers, and three testers. Traditionally, developers "pull" work; when they finish, they shove the work onto the testers and go get more. When that work is done, they shove more work onto the testers.

If you've read this chapter so far, you know this creates all kinds of waste. Another way to look at it is to limit the work in progress to one piece of work per workstation. In this case, the work is a feature (or story) and the workstation is per person. The testers are not ready to receive work from the programmers. The new work cannot be shoved onto the testers. Nor can the developers pull more work, because their workstations are full. Instead, the developers have to help get the software tested.

This can happen with any bottleneck that emerges anywhere in the delivery cycle. One team we were working with simply had to work through a large portfolio of work. The business sponsor's entire role was "web experience director," so they sat around and thought of things for the web team to do. At one point, the team was spending about a fourth of its time either helping define/estimate/refine new ideas or explaining why they were "late." In terms of output, it made more sense for the web experience team to help get the work done, which could be streamlining features or helping to test.

This thinking creates a "pull" system, which can be hard to grasp. Our example is the supermarket milk cooler, where the milk all stands, until someone comes to the end, pulling a gallon of milk, and all the other milk cartons are moved down by gravity. In software, this is the production demand for new work. This shifts our focus, from the concept of a "roadmap" that spirals off into years from now, shoving work onto the team, into the end of the cycle, pulling the newly-finished work out.

In this book, we have focused on two kinds of human exploration in testing – feature testing, where we test a new feature and regression testing, sometimes called **prerelease** testing. There is certainly more to testing than just these elements; there may be usability or accessibility work to do, unit testing that might be done **test-driven development** (**TDD**) style, and there may be A/B split testing for marketing or checks defined early as part of the specification. Our focus is on the human cognitive focus of where to look for risks, and, to a lesser extent, which of those checks to institutionalize in code. The idea of release cadence ties into that regression test piece.

Release cadence

Some companies want a batch size of a "release" so that they can conduct final checking before that release. There are plenty of good reasons for this:

- Making changes is expensive, and the costs of errors are high. For example, let's say the company releases physical hardware on chips that cannot be updated through the internet. The software may ship on DVD ROM with a large amount of data, and customers consider frequent downloads an indicator of a product they cannot trust.

- The company is transitioning from waterfall, and we've always done it this way.

- The software is designed in such a way that changes in one aspect can create unanticipated changes in another area of the software.

- The company likes waterfall and doesn't see a need to change, or the product maps well to waterfall for some reason, perhaps due to the supply change.

We do not see it as our role to judge people who do regression testing, nor to tell them they are "wrong." As context-driven authors, we work with what we are given. One place to start is to standardize the release cadence, or a pace for how long regression testing takes, including how often to run it. Too often, you'll be testing all the time. Too rarely, and all kinds of defects will appear that need to be found and retested, which leads to longer test cycles, which makes regression testing uneconomical, which leads to regression testing happening less often… this is a vicious cycle.

What we can say is that many "regression test" processes are slow, inefficient, and wasteful. Over the years, we've developed a few standard recommendations for companies with a release cadence:

- Document which techniques are finding bugs and eliminate manual steps that offer low value

- Automate the build/test/data setup process to the best extent possible

- Separate the components of the build process so that small chunks can be deployed separately

- Build redundancies and sensors for if a change causes a problem in production

- Automate repetitive manual checking steps for deploys

- The software is released through a "store" that has a long deployment process, or throws out all reviews as irrelevant when the software is updated

We often find that companies can reduce their test/deploy cadence to within 2 hours. From code-complete to in-production in the same half-business day seems like a reasonable goal for most of our customers, but you may be able to do better (or worse).

An extreme example of lean testing may be a continuous flow.

One-piece flow and CD

Imagine a piece of work with a touch time of essentially 100%. Someone is always working on it; software rushes through the pipeline. Of course, people take breaks or have questions that need answers. Getting to a one-piece flow would mean having some way to define what the work does very early on; that isn't always possible. And, in theory, it would mean zero backwash; the tester never finds any defects in exploration. We don't always see that as possible. One way to accomplish this is to collapse the test and programming steps into one, with testers and programmers pairing together – or, in some cases, having the test-focused person be a more capable programmer. Pair programming struggles because companies tend to see it as two people doing one job. Dev/test pairing, on the other hand, has a higher success rate. With dev/test pairing, it is not two people doing one job, but instead two different activities being performed at the same time on the same piece of work – development and testing.

One-piece flow, then, would be a single person (or small group) who takes a single small feature from start to done-done, without significant waiting along the way. When the feature is built (in 1 to 4 hours), they might time a break to coincide with tests running in staging, then they might have a small human final test cycle, and then push to production. This style of work resembles the ideal of CD.

Some of our customers have combined regression automation, multiple deploy points, dev/test pairing (or tri-ing, or mobbing), continuous monitoring of production, and quick rollback to work one piece of software at a time and vastly improve delivery pace. Not everyone wants to go that far, and if that works for them, then it works for them. It's an idea worth looking at and talking about.

> **Flaky tests**
>
> At the time of writing, several experts are debating the value of so-called flaky tests. These are generally customer-facing end-to-end tests that fail often. Solutions exist, such as tracking tests, that fail often and create a report so that they can either be fixed or retired. What we don't see is many people looking at flaky tests through a lean lens, or even really looking closely at all. Most of these tests walk the entire user journey and are long – a typical end-to-end test here might be 1,000 test steps. In our experience with the current state of technology, there is an incrementally increasing chance of infrastructure failure as the number of test steps increases even past a few dozen. Thus, it fails to consider if the probability of failure is low, but the number of repeats (test steps) is high, the probability of failure will be high. Our preference is for many easy-to-debug tests that can be run in parallel or on rotation, separated by a major section of the code, that run with independently deployed features.

Summary

The goal of this chapter was to enable you to look at your software process in an entirely different way, to see every day easy choices as introducing waste. With a little work, you can even start to see not just the waste and bottlenecks but the impact of those bottlenecks on the delivery process. This allows you to suggest concrete changes to help the organization go faster.

To do that, we first explained the history of lean, then tried to explain and adapt it for software with the concepts of the seven wastes, flow-based thinking, CD, and one-piece flow. We ended up with an idealized way to deliver software that few of our customers accomplish. Even the ones writing blog posts about CD fail to achieve that ideal – but most of us can benefit from moving in that direction.

That said, there is a particular reading of one-piece flow, and thought about testing, that we'd like to mention here. Many people have told us that testing is too late, that what we need is prevention, and so on. That's certainly true, as far as it goes – but we don't think it goes all the way. So, yes, many of the organizations we've worked with can see a 90% reduction in defects escaping into tests. This does not mean that testing or test activities "go away." Humans make mistakes; we see some amount of **backwash** in the test process. Likewise, we see extreme risk-management style "What if I do this" testing as a separate and distinct skill from programming, one few programmers have an interest in developing.

Now that we've gotten the theory out of the way, it is about time to get back to dealing with real people, with real motivations and real limitations. In *Chapter 12*, we will dive into some case studies of how these ideas worked out in practice; *Chapter 13* addresses who does the testing and when.

Part 3:
Practicing Politics

The first two parts work well if the software group is aligned, if the goals are shared, if everyone believes that a rising tide lifts all boats, if everyone understands each other's role, and if there is no insecurity. Sadly, most organizations like that have three or fewer employees, one of which is a life partner, and another is a dog. For the rest of us, we need tools to communicate, and set expectations, and boundaries. *Part 3*, is about creating the environment where *Part 1* and *Part 2* can thrive.

This section has the following chapters:

- *Chapter 12, Case Studies and Experience Reports*
- *Chapter 13, Testing Activities or a Testing Role?*
- *Chapter 14, Philosophy and Ethics in Software Testing*
- *Chapter 15, Words and Language About Work*
- *Chapter 16, Testing Strategy Applied*

12
Case Studies and Experience Reports

So far, we've talked about all the pieces of testing, and how to put them together, assuming everyone will know what needs to be done and will do it. If only it were that easy.

Most of the time, people are driven by incentives. Workers (often) want to get the most they possibly can for the least effort; managers and owners want to drive out the most value for the lowest price. All three groups are trying to extract money from customers to pay for their activities. These conflicting expectations lead us to suggest that we should not complain about corporate inefficiency. Rather, we should rejoice that anything ever gets done at all.

We write that not to joke, but instead to emphasize just how difficult change initiatives are. If you're driving a change initiative in testing, it's most likely driven by the middle or lower ranks, without the attention and glitter that comes from a capital-C change initiative. If you are establishing a testing discipline, you'll have the same problem, plus the aforementioned assumptions that the work is trivial, easy, should be done in a specific pre-defined way, and so on.

Most of us are familiar with so-called case studies in business, mostly written as a sales tool. Once the client approves them, they resemble puff pieces: things were okay before (since we all know that no client wants to admit to real problems) and now they are amazing, and so on. These are not designed to help us sell anything but this book, and to do that, we picked stories and examples designed to benefit you. To do that, we didn't go the permission route either. As a result, our loyalty to our customers, our **non-disclosure agreements** (**NDAs**), and basic kindness require us to leave some information out. Some of the details may be changed or lost due to our imperfect memories. One of our bullet points, of the evolution of test strategy, combines information from several projects into a single source. The stories generally come from Matt, but we use the royal *we* for readability. The point here is to convey real lessons from difficult problems through story. To do that, we will cover the following case studies:

- RCRCRC at scale
- A coverage dashboard

- Pair programming and tri-programming

- The expertise paradox

- The evolution of the test strategy

- Professional pushback – dealing with bullies

RCRCRC at scale

Chapter 9 introduced the idea of RCRCRC – of finding test ideas in recent changes, core functionality, risky elements, configuration, recent repairs, and chronic problematic areas. It's easy enough to rattle off the letters RCRCRC and make it sound like a test strategy. With five people, you might get a flip chart, draw a bubble diagram of features, make a list, and spend a day testing. This isn't scientific as much as **heuristic**. Heuristics are fallible methods for solving a problem. A simple real-life heuristic might be to shut the doors when the temperature is warmer outside and open them when it is cooler. This works in the summer for a house without air conditioning, at least so long as it doesn't rain. The informal list the team makes before release might not be backed by a database, but it is quick, easy, valuable, and provides more differentiated coverage than we would get spending a day following some pre-planned process.

Then there was the BigCorp project, with software teams on three continents, in five or six countries. They worked on an IoT app that ran on a mobile phone, integrated with backend services in Europe, and connected to and ran on automobiles in the United States, with data servers on the East Coast, Germany, and in Microsoft's Azure cloud. The total project consisted of a few hundred people – more if you count staff who spent some amount of their day supporting us. More than a project, AutoMe was an entire *program*, with multiple line items on the budget for the application, for after-market (deal support), financing, the next-generation product that was building up as the previous one rolled along, and so on.

At the time, Apple would clear out any reviews for a new push of a mobile application, and the company did not have any of the strategies we discussed earlier for regression testing. As a result, the perception was that the team had one good chance to make a deployment. The general deployment cadence was about every 12 weeks, so if we found a problem on the day after release day, it was much better than 6 weeks in. The last 2 weeks before release, there were supposed to be no new features and testing time. Without dedicated testers, the programmers frequently tooled around a bit and then worked on side projects. With no oversight and no plan, the test strategy came down to how far the leads were willing and able to push their people to do… something. Some of them did. One group had a defined test strategy and embedded testers. It took the full 2 weeks, but they followed the steps and got somewhat repeatable results.

Sadly, the team had two layers of APIs to go through. The program's APIs changed on a similar cadence to the mobile app and there were different versions, but those were mostly patterns that abstracted out the calls to the European data center. Observability was light. So, you might press a button on your mobile device and wait 2 minutes, at which point your doors might unlock, or your car honks. Or, if you were in a garage with no data service, nothing might happen. Or you might think nothing happened, and in another minute, your car's horn would honk. Worse, changes at the API level in the data center were not connected to the mobile app, so the app might "fail" 6 weeks after deployment because an API signature changed.

This isn't particularly unusual for large corporate development, especially a non-software company. It is just unusually honest. In this particular case, our next step was to develop a 1-day test plan.

The 1-day test plan

We cannot take credit for much; we were a catalyst. This included a few components:

- We had to figure out all the features and who was responsible for testing them

- We had to define a test approach, at least at a high level

- We had to find a way to visualize our test status and the results of that 1-day run

- We tried to *optimize* our results with RCRCRC

Most of the ideas we tried have already been discussed in this book. The coverage map contained a list of 10 categories on the wall; each category had eight to 12 features. Some features had micro-capabilities. Once it was defined, teams "signed up" for what they were responsible for, and it was no surprise that there were gaps. The surprising thing was the number of gaps. Due to reorganization, rightsizing, shifting responsibilities, turnover, and contracted teams for projects that had ended, roughly half the board was empty. Building the board took a month, but it took about 4 months to find someone responsible for every feature.

Once we had the list, we started working on a wiki (and editable web page; we used Confluence) for each category that listed the features, then a page for each feature. The pages listed what the feature was and how it worked and included **recipes** for how to test that feature. As the features started to fill in, we created an editable, web-based spreadsheet to act as a red/yellow/green coverage map, to describe how each feature was tested. That gave us our strategy and our coverage map and was enough to get testing.

Recalling the lessons from the dog park from *Chapter 2*, you might agree this approach is not optional. Yes, we defined the features in a high-level way, giving maximum room for whoever was testing to explore. Still, if major test runs were 12 weeks apart, it might be nice to customize them for the actual changes that came down the pike. It was time for RCRCRC!

RCRCRC in the enterprise

A project like AutoMe was not only too big, but the staff were too disconnected from the work to know exactly what changed. Emailing the team leads and asking them to do an RCRCRC analysis by the team would be a fool's errand. No one perceived that they had time for that. But we did have a consultant or two with some discretionary time, so we did our own research. Here's how:

- *Recent*: The release notes for the app provided a list of features that were touched. Another source of code changes was the code itself. git diff makes it possible to get all the changes between two commits.

- *Core*: The API teams were able to provide a list of the most popular APIs. These were the methods people called the most. We also talked to the teams about their user journey and created a few broad, cross-cutting journeys at the bottom of the spreadsheet as macro-features to test.

- *Risky*: The build system provided measures of cyclomatic complexity. According to that measure, code that has more decisions and loops per function is more complex. Our experience is that code that is much more complex is also harder for a human to track. This creates errors because a human might make a change in one place, not realizing that is inside of an if block, and fail to make the change in the else block, and so on. A simple sort allowed us to find the code in the entire application that was the most complex by file type. (There was Java, Kotlin, and Python.) It also allowed us to find the code with the lowest unit test coverage, using **statement coverage** as a measure.

- *Configuration-sensitive*: We did not do much with this, but we did have one spectacular problem when the Apple Watch app crashed on startup. We always **smoke tested** the watch app, where smoke testing was started to see if it smoked. This "C" was a tickler to remind us to ask how much effort to spend on it.

- *Repaired*: The company tracked bugs in Jira; git commits included the Jira ticket number. This enabled two kinds of reports. First, a person could tie the bug to the test strategy that should have found the problem, allowing us to look and see what proportion of test effort to change. Second, we could group bugs by category and feature, to see where the most common changes were. With this, it was possible to use a simple spreadsheet and a little Ruby code to figure out what files changed.

- *Chronic*: Given the repaired spreadsheet, converted into a **comma-separated values** (CSV) file, and a little more scripting code, we could figure out what files changed the most often. The magic didn't stop there, though. By cross-referencing the repaired code with the most complex code, we could find the code modules that had the most bug repairs and were also most likely to introduce new ones. For that matter, the intersection of most changed, most complex, and most bug repairs gave us the truly problematic bits of code.

Once the analysis was done, we drafted a report for each release that recommended how to customize the testing to optimize the results. The report fed into the next cycle of regression testing, with us either adjusting the time invested in the features or creating entirely new rows in the test spreadsheet for one-time things to try.

This approach is designed for multiple teams, in a large system, deployed as a single unit. Teams with independent deployment points, working on contracts with their software interactions designed up front, able to deploy separately, monitor effectively, and roll back easily, might not need such an approach. You could even think of this process as an in-between state to transition toward this. Even for that environment, it is not complete. What we have described so far does not resolve the API changing problem, the performance problem, the problem of unexplored change buildup over time, or the lack of observability. Without these pieces of the puzzle, our test results would be compromised. We did address these, and we will discuss them in more detail in the *The evolution of the test strategy* section.

This section was about putting the basic strategy together. We are proud of it.

> **The least we can do**
>
> While operating norms make it difficult to give proper credit on this project, the least we can do is list a few of the greatest contributors, who include Steve Poling, David Hoppe, Afzal Masra, Matthew Heusser, Vedaswaroop Meduri, Michael Felber, and, yes, Karen N. Johnson.

A coverage dashboard

One of our examples from *Chapter 9* was a coverage dashboard. It's easy enough to pop off a dashboard without explaining how it came to be or was used. So, we'll tell the story of how we developed a real dashboard in more depth, using an example from a company that provides supplies to retail stores. This particular project involved developing a web-based eCommerce frontend so that the customers – the retail stores – could self-service their orders.

Before the dashboard, testing was relatively undocumented. Each person would offer to take a different browser, and we would reconnect at noon to discuss progress. Comments would likely be "Firefox looks pretty good," and so on. There was neither a good discussion of how deeply things were tested, nor on what bugs were found. For that matter, exactly what we were supposed to be testing was changing frequently – there was no source of truth for requirements.

To create a source of truth for documents, one of the testers created a fishbone diagram or mind map of different features. Using a mind mapping tool, they created major components and then had features go off from them. Over time, as the features changed, we added links to the requirements (which were stories in Jira) to the list. Once we had a complete list, we made a web-based spreadsheet (we used Google Drive at the time) with the names of the major components on the left. The environments to be tested were on the right. Then, we agreed on a rubric, or standard, to measure both quality (red/yellow/green) and coverage depth. This discussion of coverage depth was negotiated between the test team and published at the bottom of the spreadsheet. A little bit of scripting code made it possible to enter coverage and get qualities and colors to populate automatically – darker for better coverage, a specific color for quality. Red symbolized some bugs that needed fixing, yellow indicated that there were work issues that someone might want to look into, and green meant that there were no known issues:

Features		Webkit	iOS	Android
	Q:7 C: 9(matt)	Q:6 C: 8 (Sreejit)	Q:7 C. 5 (Paurang)	Q:7 C: 5 (Paurang)
	Q:9 C. 3 (matt)	Q:7 C. 5 (Sreejit)	Q:7 C. 7 Sandhya	Q:6 C: 6 (Paurang)
	Q:6 C: 8 (Sreejit)	Q:6 C: 7 Arun	Q:7 C. 6 (Paurang)	Q:7 C: 6 (Paurang)
	Q:9 C: 6 (matt)	Q:8 C. 7 Arun	Q:7 C. 7 (Paurang)	Q:7 C: 7 (Paurang)
	Q:7 C: 5 (Sreejit)	Q:7 C. 7 Arun	Q:8 C. 7 (Paurang)	Q:8 C: 7 (Paurang)
	Q:6 C: 6 (subid)	Q:6 C. 6 (subid)	Q:8 C. 7 (Subid)	Q:8 C: 6(subid)
	Q:7 C: 5 (Sreejit)	Q:7 C. 5 (Sreejit)	Q:7 C. 5 (Paurang)	Q:5 C: 7 (Paurang)
	Q:6 C: 8 (Sreejit)	Q:6 C: 7 Arun	Q:3 C. 7 (Paurang)	Q:3 C: 7 (Paurang)
	Q:6 C: 6 (subid)	Q:6 C. 6 (subid)	Q:6 C. 6(subid)	Q:6 C: 6(Subid)
	Q:7 C: 8 Beth	Q:7 C. 8 Beth	Q:5 C: 7 (Paurang)	Q:5 C: 7 (Paurang)
	Q:8 C: 7Sandhya	Q:8 C. 7Sandhya	Q:7 C. 7 Sandhya	Q:8 C: 6(subid)
	Q:7 C: 5 (Sreejit)	Q:7 C. 5 Arun	Q:8 C. 8 (Paurang)	Q:8 C: 8 (Paurang)
	Q:7 C: 1 (Subid)	Q:7 C: 1 (Subid)	Q:6 C: 6 (Paurang)	Q:6 C: 6 (Paurang)
			Q:2 C. 10 (Sandhya) Account Preference	Q:2 C. 10 (Paurang) Account Preference
	Q:3 C. 5(Sreejit)	Q:3 C. 5Arun		
	NA	NA	Q:9 C. 4 (Paurang)	Q:9 C. 4 (Paurang)

Figure 12.1: A web spreadsheet testing dashboard

The basic spreadsheet, when it was empty, was a template. We could copy it at any time and begin a new test run. Also, we could "gray out" any areas that we planned to skip testing on, for any reason. If the only thing that changed was the mobile release, we could gray out everything except for iOS. Because the test run was a web-based spreadsheet, if someone wanted to know its status, instead of saying "Firefox looks fine," we could email them a link to the spreadsheet. This allowed the viewer to make their own decisions, restoring their sense of control.

The actual spreadsheet we ended up using was much larger than the one shown in *Figure 12.1* as it had columns for Apple tablets and Android tablets, possibly in different form factors, and also had a column for bugs. When people found bugs, they would put the JIRA code, something like ECOM-1321, and then turn that into a link to a bug. Thus, the viewer seeing that all browsers were lit up red could click on the bug to determine just how bad things were. Interestingly enough, this application did have a high amount of tooling and automation at the GUI level – yet we still found the human exploration process valuable. The tooling was good at telling us when the test environment was down, when the login process was broken, and how to find the largest of the defects, such as add-to-cart failures. The user interface, on the other hand, often had more subtle projects best seen by a human.

Despite significant investment in tooling, the automation fell into disrepair and disuse. Management turned over. When our company, Excelon, was brought back in, half a decade later, to discuss restarting a test tooling initiative, some version of the dashboard was still in place, yet the GUI automation was not just inactive but forgotten. Originally designed to replace the dashboard, the tooling had been replaced by it.

This isn't always the case. Another large project that we did a dashboard for, using the RCRCRC example we looked at previously, eventually did wean itself off heavy quarterly releases and extensive regression bug hunts.

Two things that we see as making a difference are where the test tooling lives and the amount of change in the GUI. Once the user interface becomes relatively stable, GUI test tooling can have more value. Likewise, when the tests are done at the API level, they tend to be less brittle, run more quickly, and reflect real errors when they fail.

There's a strong argument that a test coverage dashboard is a temporary step toward a magical all-singing, all-dancing, deploy-all-the-time approach. We've just seen a lot of naivete and failure in that idealized approach – and a few that can pull it off. *Chapter 3*'s warnings about automation still apply.

That said, there is one more wrinkle of the dashboard to discuss.

Test coverage blinders

From the beginning of this book, we've talked about the problem of planning everything up front instead of following a script. It limits your conceptual plan of action and can even limit your imagination. In the preceding example, we were doing eCommerce work for retailers. The retailer would walk into the back, sometimes in a cooler or freezer, count inventory, and use that to order. Sometimes, they carried a tablet with them that would lose signal. If they had a custom catalog in a list, they might have manually entered a count to order that would not be saved on the backend. This led to a work process where the user updated their order, put the tablet down, went to the laptop, added one more thing, and saw all their changes lost.

There were two problems here:

- Offline mode didn't keep track of changes and retry when you came online
- Updates from a different device would overwrite whatever you had done

Ideally, if you had four items and pressed + and someone else had just changed the number to 10, it would go to 11.

So, there were three problems, as management simply said they did not support multi-device use – arguably four since management also said tablets were not supported.

If you don't want to count management decisions as problems, that's fair, yet they did bug someone who mattered: the customers ended up using tablets anyway; they walked around counting inventory and adding the number needed to "top off." After using the tablet, the user would move to a laptop for final review and order. This made tablet-to-laptop a core use case. The laptop contained spreadsheets with the actual amount they could afford to spend, along with the ability to make cash flow projections.

Instead of stating hard and fast that "tablets are/are not" supported, we suggested a different way: send someone into an empty room for a day or two with several tablets, explore the software, and categorize the defects. With the defects in hand, along with what effort it would take to fix them, we could then choose what to fix and what level of support to offer. We did something similar with simultaneous use and offline mode.

None of these were on the coverage map. Had we focused on the coverage map, a dogmatic definition of what to test, we would have missed important scenarios. Instead, we came up with the problem before a critical mass of customers did, and provided multiple options to management. Instead of being the messengers of bad news, we presented as part of the solution. Another approach we've had some success with is tri-programming.

Pair and tri-programming

Extreme Programming (**XP**) introduced **pair programming**, which has faced significant resistance as the implication is programmers will move half as fast. Honestly, we think that's silly. One dirty little secret of computer programming is that most programmers do not and cannot seem to work a full 8-hour day. Programmers check emails, Slack, message boards, social media, and all other kinds of distractions. There's coffee to get (and re-get), and, for the ones who work from home, laundry to do and sandwiches to make. The little secret of pair programming is that both people need to be on-task. If a typical programmer spends only half the day in deep work, moving to pairs can double the deep work time. That is no significant loss of forward velocity. The second set of eyes and ears can catch problems the first would not have seen.

Ping-pong is a common way to do test-driven development, where one person takes the keyboard and writes a test, and then another person takes the keyboard and writes code to make the test pass. Another common way to do it is with a driver/coder pair, where one person decides what to do and another types it. And yes, plenty of tools exist to enable this for people working remotely.

We find that the language to accommodate pair programming matters. In ping-pong, you have two roles: the tester and the programmer. The person writing the test, who has a critical role, is not redundant – they are doing (a part of) testing work. That's important; it needs to be done. The code that comes out of this work will have fewer defects and a much smaller overall test/fix/repeat cycle than code written by a single person.

One company we worked with took this even further, bringing the tester inside the development loop. They had pair programming, with two programmers, but also a tester, sitting with the programmers, asking questions. Not only could the tester propose the next question in the TDD loop, but they could also talk about what they intended to test for. Thus, the programmers could write the software to comply with these low-level implementation details, often missed in requirements and "stories." Because there were three people actively working on the code, we called it **tri-programming**. The code at this company was built using one of the modern quick-output frameworks, so the testers didn't spend a lot of time twiddling their thumbs. Testers with aptitude who did this tended to be so involved in the work of creation that they turned into programmers. On the other hand, programmers learned to think like testers, internalizing the questions the testers would ask and pro-actively coming up with code and unit tests to satisfy possible problems, using whitelists to screen out input, and so on. That made the code come out at higher quality at every step.

one company we worked with, if you had a question, you'd be redirected to the documentation. For example, one tester had a problem with SoapUI, a testing tool, and was told to look up the answer. Except, of course, the answer wasn't in the documentation. They asked to just pair on it for a few minutes but were told the conversation might interrupt people (they were all working in one large "war room.") So, they scheduled a meeting, which meant they both needed to be present, and they needed to find a free meeting room. 2 weeks later, the meeting finally happened. The peer said, "It's so easy you just do this and... oh." As it turned out, Matt was using a Macintosh, and on Mac, that user interface element didn't exist. The two solved the problem in about 5 minutes – one who knew Macintosh, one who knew the tool.

That kind of knowledge, where one person knows not quite enough, and neither does the other, but together they can solve the problem, happens shockingly often. It is one of the things that makes pair programming so powerful. You might not do pair programming in your work, but in our experience, huge amounts of problems that aimed to be prevented with hours and days of documentation can often be solved in minutes and seconds of pair work.

This brings us to the problem of how people doing testing work are perceived.

Discovering the expertise paradox

A few years ago, we did a training that involved a simulation. One of the testers found an internationalization bug, where they sent a bad input and got a bad output. They pointed out "I found a bug, look!" with great excitement. We were happy. Throughout the rest of the day, we moved on to other ways to test the same application. Aside from reminding us of the bug they had found, the tester didn't participate.

It could have been a communication issue. Perhaps they thought we could "fix" their bug and have everyone test a new release with the fix. That wasn't how we ran it. In any event, the tester didn't seem to find any problems or contribute to the discussion over the next day or two. On the last day of class, in the morning, we found out they had just been promoted to the "senior" pay grade.

What's going on here?

Our sponsor suggested we think about performance differently. This is a person who was easy to get along with, who would do exactly as told, and who never found serious problems that blocked forward progress on the project. They would test around the software a bit and find a bug or two but never really threaten a deadline. When bugs were found in production, well, everyone would shrug, fix them, and move on.

As one leader once said, we can think of testers as having at least three levels of experience.

At the junior level, testers explore the happy path and call it good.

The mid-level tester can make sure the software never ships. They can always find new test ideas and new bugs and make the programmers cry and cackle with glee.

Neither of these are good, are they? They have problems.

It is at the senior level that the person can sit back and think about risk, find the most powerful techniques that find the most information about the software, and figure out if, with our limited understanding, we think we've reached the point that additional testing would not offer value.

Part of the purpose of this book is to accelerate you toward that senior state.

Yet by now you see the problem. The better the tester, the more things they see that might go wrong, the more test ideas they have, and the "more slowly" they test. Thus, to a manager obsessed with metrics, the junior tester looks better – they can do 20 testing tasks in a week! In 2 or 3 weeks, when the customers find the bugs that were missed, everyone can shrug, fix them, and move on. Meanwhile, it is the skilled tester, the one who has the test ideas and finds the bugs, that takes longer and slows everything down. This is the paradox of expertise, a problem we have seen over and over.

Our goal with this book was to go one level deeper – to provide structure to present options to decision-makers. That means a conversation like this: "Sure, we could stop with this level of testing, which would leave us open to the bugs below the cut line – do they matter? Or we could change the priorities, to skip some of the testing I've put at the top and move it down to the bottom."

The same type of logic applies to automation. Typically, whoever writes code to do automated checking writes the cheap and easy tests and ignores the ones that are hard to write, due to limitations of the tool or the structure.

Having test ideas is good; having a lot of test ideas is better. Explaining the risk and making the risk tradeoff publicly available for improvement is better still.

Making expertise transparent

On one project at a small software company, the team decided to skip performance testing. The vice president of engineering position was open, so the CEO was filling it. Matt briefed the CEO on the costs of doing performance testing for their new product launch. Instead of taking the time, the decision was to soft launch, making it available only to a few advanced users. That decision wasn't made by Matt, but instead by the company CEO. And, of course, there were problems with the application, which ran on the same servers as production, with limited resources. This caused all of production to crawl to a halt, with reboots and reinstalls. When it came time for the retrospective on what went wrong, the CEO said "We made a conscious decision. It was a risk tradeoff. What's next?" When the programmers pushed back on this, the CEO clarified "Matt informed me of the risks. It was my call. I'd do it differently next time. What's next?"

There was no more push-back after that.

Later in this chapter, we'll discuss boundaries – that is, how having the right person own the decision can reduce conflict. If the decision is made without management, they end up being the victim. But before we get to that, let's talk about how the test strategy is evolving.

The evolution of the test strategy

Chapter 1 introduced a style of testing: "overwhelm the interface with data." This has advantages as it is quick, cheap, easy, and doesn't even require the tester to have any knowledge of the application. The classic examples of this kind of testing are testing for February 30, or entering a date in the past to purchase plane tickets, perhaps the first day of the 13th month, and so on.

These sorts of test exercises are easy. They are fun. They are low-hanging fruit. And they are representative of the first build delivered to test for many organizations today.

Yet we have come a long way since we started our careers. Date time pickers, phone numbers, and email inputs – these sorts of things are likely to be generated by some open source tool. Instead of hand-creating a whitelist that fails to recognize that is a valid domain, programmers are likely to reuse something else. Thus, on many projects, the classic quick attacks strategy just won't find many bugs. This doesn't mean the bugs don't exist, just that in some companies, the classic and easy test approaches will be of limited value. Instead, we suggest zooming out from the individual feature and looking at more complex workflows, such as path-to-purchase for eCommerce, multi-user scenarios, permissions, and so on. For example, in social media, a simple post and reply might work just fine, but what about a post with a second user replying, and the first user deleting the post before the second user clicks reply? These tests still need to happen; often, the worst security breaches lie behind these more complex attacks.

What we are saying here is that a test strategy depends on context. If the test style in *Chapter 1* doesn't yield bugs, you might be better off performing tests that are more "user journey"-oriented or based on historic bugs. Boris Beizer's *Pesticide Paradox* applies: every method you use to prevent or find bugs leaves a residue of subtler bugs against which those methods are ineffectual. Put differently, once you've used a test technique and internalized the categories of bugs it finds and worked with the team to prevent them, they'll stop showing up. To continue to add value, testing will need to innovate. If testing does not innovate, it will be marginalized in value. Beyond that, the value of testing can be marginalized if the impact can be reduced by resolving production issues quickly. Very few companies are shipping disks in boxes anymore. Annual tax software is one of the holdouts, but it is an update from the internet, or even run on the internet. With the ability to cut/back quickly due to Blue/Green deployments and configuration flags, many companies have chosen to "move fast and break things."

Perhaps due to this marginalized value of tests in some areas, or perhaps in parallel, there is another trend. This one is changing *who* is doing the testing work. This roughly corresponds to the rise of Scrum and the Agile movement. Starting toward the end of the first decade of the 2000s, we saw a change in test organizations, from reporting to executive management to a product group director to testers embedded in teams with a team lead. Then, in some companies, we saw the end of the testing role, changing to **hybrid engineering**, where everyone is a **member of the technical staff**. This can be "soft" hybrid engineering, where everyone has a similar title, but people choose to specialize in "hard" hybrid engineering, where everyone is a programmer first and expected to make real commits to production code. This is especially popular in companies born of the new, cloud-native architectures, that have access to the tools to eliminate some of the larger, more obvious problems. This also occurs in large organizations; Microsoft aggressively pushed plans to eliminate the **Software Development Engineer in Test (SDET)** as early as 2014.

Yet this creates a dilemma. The bugs that remain will be more difficult to spot and require more expertise. At the same time, companies are eliminating the role that has the expertise. This means that the people who remain, on average, need to know *more* about testing than they did when they could rely on testers-as-role.

Another option exists for companies that still have the "business analyst" roles. The business analyst, to some extent, defines and communicates what to build. If they do a poor job, the software that comes out will be inconsistent, and not fit for needs. Having the analysts do the testing allows them to be "bookends" to the development process. To some extent, this allows them to live with the consequences of their actions and provides feedback to help them create better requirements.

Companies pursuing a more *Agile* approach are unlikely to have business analysts, but they may have scrum masters, product owners, product managers, team leads, UI/UX designers, and so on. All of these roles can be seen, on a bad day, to "dump" requirements onto technical staff and walk away. There may be some value in having them stick around to do the testing. Still, even with this model, the expectation remains that programmers do a better job testing their code.

Or perhaps the programmers can do it. There is no right or wrong answer here; test strategy is better or worse in a given context. We think nearly as strategy is transitional; the question is less what is "right" but how we should change for next week, next quarter, and next year.

The biggest change we've seen is radically reducing regression testing (our coverage dashboard) due to continuous integration and test tooling. That environment still begs for feature testing. Occasionally, on the release of a new browser, or a feature that crosses concerns, that will be a need for something more like regression testing. Have a plan for it.

The alternative to evolution – information hiding

A client called once with an unusual situation: regression testing took at least 2 weeks, but the CEO could not figure out exactly what it was the testers were doing during those 2 weeks. The team was distributed, with some people in the USA and some in Eastern Europe, so we brought in Vernon Richards, based in the UK, who was right between both time zones. The testers were using a combination of automated regression test code written in Selenium, along with spreadsheets to run through all the scenarios.

The code was confusing; it seemed to look at every screen and confirm that the user interface elements, buttons, checkboxes, and such still existed. It didn't seem to click anything. Likewise, the test documentation would list a scenario for a screen, a combination of checkboxes and radios, but that was it. Each row in the spreadsheet would just be a different combination. Vernon started with the polite, appreciative inquiry approach, but ran into several red flags where the answers didn't seem to line up with the questions he was asking. We decided to dig deeper and bring Matt in with a less diplomatic, more direct approach to understand how the test strategy was modeled and what they could do differently.

Matt couldn't get answers either.

It's difficult to describe the interactions. Matt would ask what an activity was, to break down the steps, or show him the process, and words would come back, but they wouldn't coincide with anything objective. He couldn't do anything with the information he got. So, he tried to ask the question differently or ask them to run through the process. He'd ask other roles about their experience at testing time. The programmers could describe their unit tests and requirements process, but to them, testing was completely dark. New code came in, bug reports came out. Testing and release management were intermixed, so there was no one else to ask.

Vernon and Matt working together illustrate the **principle of the pair** – that is, *two people doing the same activity are likely to make different errors and catch each other. If they make the same error, then it is likely that was a reasonable error to make given the situation.* More than that, Vernon and Matt intentionally approached the problem from different directions, yet came to the same conclusions.

As it turned out, the lack of information wasn't just happening to Matt or Vernon, but came from the CEO, and was the reason for the assignment. The CEO couldn't figure out if the tester leadership "just didn't get it," or if, possibly, there just wasn't much to get.

The consulting project ended with a brief report that explained the depth of the problem, along with other issues we were investigating.

It's possible the testers simply did not know how to explain what they were doing. Given the distance, there may have been deeper language issues. Still, on some level, we expect there were information-hiding issues. Information hiding for control is designed to make the person appear indispensable. It works... until it doesn't. And when it stops working, the person doing the hiding may find themselves out on the job market, with neither strong skills nor strong references.

A huge part of this book is about how to make your work more transparent, to engage related roles in the work, and to help them understand it. When they don't, bad things can happen.

Speaking of bad things, let's talk about bullies.

Professional pushback – dealing with bullies

Matt was working on a project for a healthcare company. A project manager walked in the room, harried, explaining that they had just come from the steering meeting, and the team now had to add more customizations to the web application before it went live. Not only were there more elements to search through, but the new search filters would be sliders, with new requirements for different types of customers. In particular, while the tool had been designed for self-service, the nursing staff would be able to process groups of customers at a time. The project manager said "And we need it by the same date. You'll need to deal with it." and walked off.

...Time passes...

Matt becomes a project manager in his own right at the same company, determined to fix what might have gone wrong in the past. That meant evidence-based work, with projects compared to other projects for work effort as well as plans for scope creep. Instead of an aggressive deadline, the teams typically had an internal goal, along with an external commitment. The size of this buffer would grow or shrink based on the projected churn, the team's knowledge of the technology, and the reasonably perceived amount of unknowns. While it wasn't a work of art, it did represent a step forward, and Matt was proud of it.

About a year into his project management role, that same programmer from the earlier story came around to Matt's desk. He said "The government insurance plan website is going to be two weeks late [past the commitment date]. You'll need to deal with it."

You'll need to deal with it.

You'll need to deal with it?

How can the same thing happen to the same guy twice, from both sides of the power structure? *What is going on here?*

Back then, that conversation was the beginning of the end. Matt would take criticism from several corners (we'll describe one in the next story) before taking a no-annual raise and going back to technical work. Today, we know exactly what we'd say, we've built the skills and will tell you how. First, though, let's explore how that happened and what it meant.

Power in the workplace

Sean McMillan, a programmer who worked with us at the time, remembers the story, if not fondly. Listening to it, he pointed out something obvious, if slightly painful: "Matt, for whatever reason, you gave off a social signal that you could be bullied."

If someone gives off a signal they can be bullied, it is a bit like throwing raw meat to wolves. That's it. That is all that it takes. But what would that signal be, and how do you drown it out?

In software testing, we frequently hear testers and other members of the technical staff complaining that they are not listened to or respected and that they do not get special perks or appreciation. Yet in our consulting work, that problem is exceedingly rare. Like, maybe it happened, once, to one of us, over a decade ago. What's different?

There are certainly a great many things happening with power dynamics independently. An outside consultant present for 2 weeks will have access to the boss, and the bosses boss, so it would be unwise to try to bully them as you'll lose. We could argue it is unfair to compare the two. Besides, when it comes to bullying, we certainly aren't psychologists. Still, we think we have a little bit to add.

Comparing a consultant to a member of technical staff is a good illustration. Bullies are generally insecure and want to take from someone who has something they can get. This can be time, resources, money, or social status. The primary thing holding them back from taking action is *consequences*. In the case of the consultant, they may lose face by picking a fight. Meanwhile, the consultant is not an employee. Once the assignment is over, they won't have to deal with this person anymore. So, the consequence of "John in marketing might be unhappy with me" is much smaller.

For employees, creating consequences generally leads to risk. The risk is that the person might not like you, or, if the breach was serious enough, they may even attempt to sabotage your career! If they are a game-player, they might spend 20 hours a week getting good at this game-playing stuff – and here you are spending all your time, every week, actually trying to ship software. We kid, of course. We wrote this book for people who are trying to deliver software. The problem is that the game-players will be better at playing games. Our first attempts at enforcing boundaries (more about that shortly) are likely to be inconsistent and sloppy. More than that, people involved with testing, in general, like to be liked. Many of us are agreeable and will do any reasonable thing to help others succeed. Sadly, the definition of reasonable has enough flex that people with that personality type (highly agreeable, likely extroverted) are easily bullied. The challenge is to put the boundaries where they should be and to come up with those consequences.

Let's go back to the example we looked at previously, where our heroes were bullied on both sides of the transaction. What should they have said?

One way to say it

The easiest one to handle is how to respond as a project manager when you're told the project will be late. Here's one way to do it:

> *There seems to be some confusion about roles here. My job is to report the status.*
> *That's an easy thing to do. I'll update the plan, publish it, and let management*
> *know that your team can't meet the original goal and has a new projected date.*
> *That might be fine, I'm not sure. If management has a problem with it, I can*
> *facilitate the conversation between the two of you. You'll be the one to deal with it,*
> *as it is your deliverable, but I'll be happy to help.*

This all has to be delivered with a warm, genuine, friendly smile, but you get the point. The web team isn't performing. My job as a project manager is to summarize and report status. Making this our problem is shifting the responsibility for the performance – it is a *boundary violation*.

The other scenario is a little different because it is more subtle. Being agreeable people, we are likely to find a way to do one more task in the same period. Take that to an extreme, and it makes sense to try to load the team up with all the technical work they can do. Here are three possible answers:

We're currently staffed at a full load to make that October 1 deadline. You can throw it on the stack, and we'll see what we can do, sure.

Or

We haven't broken down the work into chunks yet; we're delivering about 10 chunks a week. That seems pretty big. And breaking it down will take time away from the work we are doing now. Right now, we're on track to be done on October 1; do you want us to take 8 person-hours away to define it long enough to make projections?

Or

That's about 12 new features of work. We've been producing about 10 features a week, consistently; we have 40 to do and the project is due in a month, on October 1. So, unless something changes, I predict we finish all the work around the middle of October. Of course, you're free to make your own projections, or move the priority of the features around, maybe get more staff assigned. We'll certainly try.

Notice that in all these examples, we make it clear there is a problem, we want to help, but we will not accept someone else's problems as our own. Another way some people put this is "Poor planning on your part does not constitute an emergency on my part."

The third example is particularly powerful because it provides data. We've seen examples of this throughout this chapter, and will again when we look at project predictions. For now, even without data, it is possible to leave the ownership where it should be: you committed to one thing, without any slack in the system, and they are asking for more. Say "We'll try," shrug, and do your best professional job. The XP literature suggests that occasional mild overtime to hit a key deliverable might be a reasonable thing and might improve team speed. Relying on it instead of developing a plan is something else entirely.

Bullies can also use our best traits against us. For example, setting an unreasonable project deadline can convince people to internalize that deadline. "The project must go out on July 1," we say, when in fact we had no control over picking the date nor the amount of work to go into the project. Yet we accept the responsibility, and the consequences in terms of burnout and damaged home relationships due. All because of our desire to be liked, our weak boundaries, and, perhaps, a misguided sense of compassion for others.

The solution for this is stronger boundaries and boundary enforcement.

Boundaries in the enterprise

Townsend and Cloud, who wrote the book *Boundaries* and a dozen follow-up works, explain that boundaries are the things that define us – where you end and I begin. Under the law, a physical punch is a boundary violation, but in a Western professional business culture, it is more likely to be two feet of room. That is why people say "excuse me" when they are not touching each other.

In software testing, we propose that for us to be responsible for an outcome, we need to *own* it. The previous two examples are boundary violations because they pushed responsibility to the other people without any control. The solution is to re-assert where they begin and we end.

Now, let's look at two real testing examples.

At one company where we were employed, the vice president of products had a pet project and pulled Matt into a meeting. Matt wasn't a consultant, just an employee, and the vice president wanted to tell him how to do his testing. Their ideas were a document-heavy, repetitive approach, that invested much more time than we had been investing in a few features that were less critical than the smooth operation of the system. Toward the end of the meeting, Matt replied "I appreciate your input into how our team does testing; we'll keep it in mind when we make our decision." The vice president didn't try again, and the two had an ongoing positive relationship.

At another company, Matt came to a meeting a week before Christmas. Employees were about to take off, for the most part, from Christmas to New Year's. Contractors would work. Matt was assigned his first story to test and was shown the process, which was a traditional define-every-click test case. After pausing for a minute, he said "You have to understand, I can't do this. If the community I practice in (context-driven testing) heard about this, I'd be laughed at. I tell you what. How about between now and New Year's, I do some things. I'll test the story my way. I'll produce something to describe what I plan to do, something on what I did, and bug reports. When you come back, we can review and negotiate. And if we can't agree on something, we'll part as friends. Would that work for you?"

Those are two examples of boundaries in testing that worked.

One of our colleagues, Tim Western, reviewed this section, which reminded him of a time he had made a similar offer. The company was locked into a contract to deliver certain documentation, which would slow down delivery without adding any value to his own experience. Perhaps that paperwork had value to *someone*, but it was not Tim. So, he estimated the delay, and the schedule shifted. We have had similar experiences, but instead, by offering to cut elements of the defined process, we could make the deadline. This allows us to short-circuit the classic engineering pyramid, where people talk about things, middle management talks about processes, and senior management talks about money. In our experience, if you can get through to senior management and talk in terms they understand, the technical folks may be able to change the outcome.

Sometimes, the other person simply does not respect your boundaries. When you say you cannot work the weekend, they want to pry into your personal life. When you tell them it is your only son's wedding, they want to know when the events are so that you can work before and after – can't you rent internet on the plane? When they ask why the project is late and you point out it was done 1 hour after a key decision you were waiting 2 weeks for, you get a nasty look, and, within days, you get sudden unexpected reprimands that don't make any sense. It seems that no matter what you do, you can't win.

Well, perhaps you can't. Our shorthand for this style of interaction is **narcissistic communication**.

Narcissistic communication

Again, we have no special mental health training, but we don't think we need it to take notice that some kinds of interaction are just *not quite right*. Where we view communication as about learning, growing, and helping each other, *narcissistic communication is about winning*. Instead of being about the content, the actual project, narcissistic communication is the other person, communicating to you, that you are less than and they are better. They are more powerful, they have control, and you are not as good at whatever it is you are talking about. Agreeable people trapped in these sorts of conversations become incredibly frustrated; they may attempt to jump through hoops to "prove" they are "enough." You have to understand that if the conversation is about power, then admitting you are enough weakens the other person. They don't *want* you to be enough.

For example, Matt needed to be heard, to feel like there was some meeting of the minds. In a heated debate, if the other person says "You made a good point" or "I see what you mean there," Matt at least feels heard. He tried to explain this to someone who communicates in this dominating way once, and the response was that was ridiculous, that "You make a good point" is a way of dismissing the other person and not making any change. If the goal is power and control, you're right. If it is advancing an understanding of each other, however... that's just fine.

In our experience, we've found that what we call narcissistic communication has certain markers, to make it identifiable. Here are six:

1. *Grandiosity*: The other person is always better than you. This is not like a teacher talking to a student, where the desire is to use skills to educate. Instead, the content, such as the rules of chess is just an excuse to show you that you are less than. For double narcissism points, they'll first correct you about something minor, such as the pronunciation of a word, but not tell you how to pronounce it correctly! That is, they don't care about your condition.

2. *Lack of vulnerability*: They won't admit they were wrong, made an error, or apologize. They'll likely say you are a jerk for bringing it up, that "One serious problem with you is you never let things go."

3. *Power and control*: Conversations with them are generally either about who is bigger than who, or, perhaps, teaming up against someone else. This is called **triangulation**. The communication may appear entirely reasonable, even subservient up the chain of command.

4. *Insecurity*: When some external agent appears that says something good about you, they suddenly need to put you in your place. Alternatively, they may be unable to celebrate your successes. Tying that back to item number one, one narcissistic signal is when people are uncomfortable, or incapable, of sitting down and letting anyone else have attention unless that person is a direct superior.

5. *Exploitive/lack of empathy*: Your issues are waived away as immaterial. "Look, I really can't work any later, I'm worried about my spouse leaving me." / "If your spouse will leave you for working late a few nights, you don't have much of a marriage anyway, do you?"

6. *Manipulative*: Specifically, the use of shame, blame, and guilt to control others. You may also notice that their story changes over time, always in a way that is away from vulnerability and personal responsibility.

The term narcissist has entered common language; there are plenty of videos, web pages, and podcasts that explore it in depth. For this book, it is enough to realize that this style of thinking can be momentary, cultural, or become part of the deeper personality. When the thinking becomes so deeply entrenched that it is a fixed part of personality, psychiatrists call it a personality disorder. People with **narcissistic personality disorder**, or **NPD**, leave a trail of destruction behind them.

We've covered the topic here in the context of boundaries. Narcissistic communication styles don't care about your boundaries, because the sender, for some reason, lacks empathy. They might not be a bad person; they might be someone on another continent who has no relationship with you who has a problem and expects you to solve it. They might be having a bad day. The culture could be narcissistic. For whatever reason, the communication style is narcissistic. Remember, these sorts of "conversations" are really about power and forcing you to accept something outside of your boundaries. Understanding your "no" and accepting it means they "lose." The further down the rabbit hole the culture, the less acceptable this will be.

In that case, *what you say doesn't matter*. We can't fix it for you with words. We are sorry. You do, however, have options, and it may be possible to steer. Our broad recommendation is that if you have to deal with the person, becomes, well, boring. Don't spread gossip, don't share stories, don't embellish, just tell them the facts. Then, carefully consider your options:

1. *Grin and bear it*: It's a job. Go home on time, enjoy your social life, live below your means, and save. Develop yourself professionally and look for opportunities to transfer. We've both done a fair bit of this, especially early in our careers.

2. *Create a consequence*: There's an old expression that when you go to prison, you should pick a fight with the meanest, nastiest person there. You probably won't win, but you'll show everyone present that you do not back down from a fight, and if they pick on you, it is going to *hurt*. If you can find a way to just be tough enough that a bully has other targets elsewhere, they may just move on down the line.

3. *Change your organization*: If the culture is sick, but the people are not damaged, you may be able to change some decisions. One way to do that when work is running off the rails is to remind the company of a similar, recent decision that went very poorly. One company we worked with essentially lost the productivity of a team for a year because of a serious overtime project. The second time, we pointed out this was similar, and listed all the people who had quit, along with the results (buggy software and so on). We also used the project prediction story to properly estimate. There was no third time.

4. *Change your organization again*: Go get another job.

Paradoxically, the way to be most effective at your job may be to not care about keeping it. If you can develop yourself professionally to the point where, if you get fired, you have a year's savings and you'll have another job in a month or two, that can position you to say what needs to be said. One term for this is **best alternative to a negotiated agreement** (**BATNA**).

Passive aggressive comments are insults, but when challenged, they can be defended as something innocent. For example, "Must be nice." That is an insult, but if challenged, the other person can shrug and ask "What? I was saying it's nice!"

Boundary enforcement – the power move

At one conference, Matt dealt with someone who spent 3 days with passive-aggressive comments. At the end of day 3, he was explaining a talk he had given that day – about the impossibility of complete testing. The question he asked was "Assume you have a new chief information officer who says this project is too important to have any risk – it must be completely tested. What are they asking for and can you comply?"

The response was "That's not a 1-hour talk! That's a 5-minute talk."

After a pause, Matt looked him in the eye and asked, "…Why you gotta be a ****?"

Yes, Matt used obscenity, in a professional setting. Not after a word or two, but after a weekend of having his boundaries pushed. For someone with an earned reputation for civility, this was, in effect, putting the behavior on notice. The good news is that it stopped.

The two are no longer friends. But as Sean McMillan points out – were they ever friends in the first place?

Declaring a boundary is only the first step. You can say the line is here, and the other person can't cross it. The next step is defending the boundary when it is violated. A narcissistic person may step right over the boundary as if to ask, "What are you going to do about it?" Be prepared to answer – and realize that protecting your boundaries can cost you.

Not protecting your boundaries can cost you too.

If you make your own choice, even if you choose not to defend your boundaries, you can own the outcome. Fail to do that, and you'll always be a victim.

If you choose to stay

We spent a fair bit of time helping with the analysis of the situation, with simple hard truths about what to do about it. Even if you choose to leave, you'll likely need to start for a little while. Here are a few ideas to limit your liability:

- *Recognize the perceptions game*: As speakers of truth, we often think we have no political position; we'll just come in and "tell it like it is." Yet in a political organization, decisions are not made in meetings as much as announced in meetings. When we come in and list the problems with the plan, we make someone look bad. In a narcissistic culture, that means we are messing up someone else's plan. Instead, work behind the scenes.

- *Don't disagree publicly with powerful people*: For the same reasons I wrote earlier. For that matter, assume that any private communications of disagreement will get back to them anyway; you could be labeled a "pot stirrer."

- *Gray rock*: If you notice that someone is creating drama based on what you tell them, stop telling them things! Instead, become straightforward and refuse to speculate. "I really couldn't say" is a fine answer. If they press, ask "Why are you asking?" They'll say they are just curious and ask again, to which you should reply, "I really couldn't say." These two phrases run on repeat until the person goes away. Gray rock enough, and they'll find others to gather information from.

There is another option, which is to try to play the game. Cynthia Shapiro wrote a book on how to play the game, called *Corporate Confidential: 50 Secrets Your Company Doesn't Want You To Know, and What To Do About Them*. From what we can tell, the book downplays the ethical implications of doing what works to get ahead in a certain type of corporate environment, and instead simply explains the game. At the extremes, game-playing leads to deception, falsehoods, and, well… it turns you into the kind of person you might not want to be. *Chapter 14* further explores ethical issues in software testing.

Summary

In this chapter, we told true stories that we thought we be helpful to you in dealing with what humans do in software projects. Large projects have a coordination and synchronization process, which can be done with large charts and abstraction. Each bubble can represent one team's status; click to drill down. Recognizing the expertise paradox, you can explain it and allow management to make more informed choices about the process. Being aware of your boundaries and able to push back can radically change outcomes but also your mental health and your lived experience.

So far, we've tap-danced around who is doing the testing. Is there a tester role? Do the programmers do it? Do we hire people who could program and ask them to write test code? Is it shared by the whole team? Do we have business analysts who also test? Do we bring in specialists for performance?

It's time we talk about who does what testing and when. We'll do this in *Chapter 13*.

13
Testing Activities or a Testing Role?

In the previous chapter, we touched on a few possible models, including business analysts as *bookends*, doing analysis and testing. Yet, for the most part, so far, this book has been intentionally vague about who does the testing work. We've focused on the testing activity instead of testers as people. This expands the role and avoids conversations about generalists versus specialists. If a company has no testers, then everyone is going to do a little testing, which means everyone is going to need knowledge of testing, which increases the need for this book.

It's time for the tough conversation.

In this chapter, we'll cover the following:

- The cultural conflict with the testing role
- Building a risk mitigation team (defects and bugs)
- Faith-based versus empirical test automation
- Shift-left and shift-right
- (Actually) continuous testing

Our goal here isn't to tell you what you should be doing; that's a bit like a doctor prescribing without examining the patient! Instead, we'll give you things to think about as you make decisions in organizational design on where and when testing will happen, along with some ability to conduct experiments and measurements about where testing might be required earlier or later in the development cycle.

Technical requirements

This section will walk you through a technical analysis of your organization to improve it. Having real data will improve your experience. In particular, having access to a real bug tracker and the ability to survey your team on how they spend their time will be helpful. However, we think anyone can benefit from this chapter, even academic reviews that lack an active project. In the section on risk management teams, we'll discuss how to do your own analysis on how to get from wherever you are now to whatever you are doing next.

The cultural conflict with a testing role

In the 1948 movie, *The Treasure of the Sierra Madre*, a group of bandits attempt to trick the hero by claiming to be the Federal Mounted Police ("federales"). When the hero asks to see their badges, the bandit leader responds with the classic phrase, *"We don't need no stinkin' badges."* In the actual movie, the reply comes in three parts: *"Badges? We ain't got no badges. We don't need no badges. I don't have to show you any stinking badges."* The line has gone down in movie history, to be honored (or lampooned) in books, comics, cartoons, and even Al Yankovic's movie *VH1*.

At some point, the idea of having testers as a job emerged. A series of comedic (or perhaps tragic) mistakes had happened since then to marginalize testing as a role, making it a low-, no-, and (in some cases) negative-value activity.

Somehow, companies have started to say, "We don't need no stinkin' testers". Sometimes, sadly, with the same tone as in the original quote. We'd like to explore how we got here, then how the idea of having no testers arose, along with the consequences of that idea.

How we got here – the bad news

We can think of the 1980s and even the 1990s as a simpler age. Software was built on floppy disks that were physically passed around to be installed, then sent to a duplicator to be shipped in boxes. As we discussed before, the impact of a bug so big that it required a physical recall of the packaged software was huge. Likewise, a smaller bug that didn't require a recall could still lead to a bad review in a (paper) magazine, which could effectively kill a product, if not a young, new company. Quarterly (or slower!) releases were common, with a classic waterfall-like hardening phase toward the end. Companies had a desire to make projections on when a project would be finished, so they wanted to know: *"How long will testing take?"*

There are a few "easy" ways to solve this problem. One approach is to look at testing a bit like a naïve person might look at building a bridge. Figure out the work to be done, count the number of bricks, divide the number of bricks you've moved by the total number of bricks to get your percentage done in a week, and then figure out how many weeks are required to get to 100%. To do that one has to break testing into *bricks*, sometimes called test cases. Another approach is the odd benefit of having many people working on a wide variety of projects. At any time, you can ask for the entire company to focus on the number-one priority, and, if you can slice and coordinate the work, that priority-one project can be completed to meet almost any arbitrary deadline. To do that you also need to break the work into small chunks. The drumbeat of "stable, predictable, repeatable" pushed in project management circles, plus cliches such as "if you didn't write it down, it didn't happen" led to a documentation-focused approach to testing. People broke the work down into chunks and documented every small piece. A third approach is to just give up and declare the software to be tested because time ran out. Throughout the book we've discussed strategies to do just that, to adjust the testing to fit any arbitrary timebox. With the documentation focus, the primary idea was to write everything down. Once everything was written down, regression testing turned into re-running all the tests, plus whatever was new, at least until time ran out.

At the time, there were plenty of delays. Builds took a long time and didn't run that often; simply propagating new builds to the team meant an installation process. We're not talking about updating a web server, but instead running an installation program in MS-DOS or Windows. Testers spent a great deal of time simply waiting around. In the first decade of the 2000s, Bernie Berger, a leader in the *Association for Software Testing's* Financial Services Special Interest Group, wrote an article for a testing magazine about a *Day in the Life of a Tester*. A great deal of that article was about waiting for things to be ready to test, poking, prodding, and finding information for more effective testing. The actual act of doing the testing only took a small amount of time, so testers had plenty of time to create documentation. When Matt saw a documented test case for the first time, he was impressed by the professional look – a Word document with columns, steps to follow, and expected results that could be printed and physically signed. It wasn't until later that Matt realized the intellectual content, a typical test case, which would be two pages long, could fit into two or three lines of text. A great deal of the text was repeated, templatized, copied and pasted, or trivially obvious. The important thing is that testers in many organizations actually had time to do this work. The 1980s and 1990s were a time of enormous expansion in software development, with market segments growing at double-digit rates.

By 2001, commercial dollars were starting to move from the desktop operating system to the web, but the web still did not have the rich user experience that the desktop had. It was at that time that Joel Spolsky wrote, *"Daily builds are your friend"* (`https://www.joelonsoftware.com/2001/01/27/daily-builds-are-your-friend/`), which proposed the then-cutting-edge idea of the new delivery of working software every day, from the development to the testing stage – unless the build failed, of course.

That was a time before unit tests and complex merge strategies. Programmers who broke the build, introducing code that failed to compile, might have an insulting trophy placed on their desk until the next person broke the build. Without the defect-impact-reduction strategies we cover in this chapter and elsewhere, and without a good structure, a change in one place could introduce unintended consequences. Organizations didn't measure change impact, so they did feature testing of every feature and regression testing of everything. Pressured by time, some leaders would come up with a shortened test suite. Another blocking condition at the time was that the tooling and automation at the GUI level weren't generally available. Very few commercial products existed to test Windows, typically record/playback with the ability to add logic through a BASIC implementation. Web applications had to be tested through Windows until web automation was available; the Selenium project did not have a public release until 2004. As late as 2008, a topic at Google's Test Automation Conference was how to get "buy-in" to do test tooling – how programmers could get approval to write test code.

In short, the first (and second) build programmers produced were typically buggy, incomplete, and needed repeated rounds of testing. Builds were likely to have basic functionality failing, and the system had major delays. Adding a handoff to test and having test documents seemed like no-brainers. Documentation allowed testing to scale.

This wasn't the case everywhere, especially in Silicon Valley test culture. The 2000s brought a breath of fresh air.

How we got here – developing at internet speed

The late 1990s brought us **Extreme Programming** (**XP**). Teams of programmers, writing unit tests first, striving to interact directly with the customer, and mastering concepts such as patterns led to some incredible improvements in quality. In the beginning, XP recommended a physical build machine, where programmers would merge new builds by hand and create a new version after every story. 2001 saw the release of Anthill Pro, some software that put a loop around the build tool **Ant**, creating a new build for every check-in version control. **Hudson** came out in 2005, which was forked to become the open source Jenkins in 2008. Suddenly anyone who wanted to do **Continuous Integration** (**CI**) could do it in any language while having an amazing web-based dashboard that provided status on any build – for only the cost of the time to support it.

All of a sudden, builds became very fast; so fast that people started to ask what testing was getting them.

Programmers suddenly had tools such as Selenium to do the job they thought testers were doing. To be fair, it was the job some testers were doing – mindlessly following steps written down by someone else a long time ago. At one international test conference in Sweden in 2012, one speaker pointed out that the QA group at his clients simply could not keep up with the release cadence his team was putting out, so the programmers had built an internal (automated) testing process. Eventually, management started releasing software as soon as it passed this internal check. He said, *"You testers are dinosaurs; you're all going to die!"*

Again, to be fair, a lot of testers were solving problems that hadn't existed for a decade. Perhaps they should have gone away. XP had called for an end of the "QA Department." While not universal, it did become common for organizations to move from a "QA department" and a "programming department", to short-term project teams that borrowed from both of these departments, to having long-lived delivery teams with testers embedded.

Some QA organizations resisted these changes. Without the strategies we cover in this book that align time investment to risk, they tended to spend a lot of time and find not too many bugs, while delaying the release of the software. In 2015, Yahoo eliminated its QA department (`https://spectrum.ieee.org/yahoos-engineers-move-to-coding-without-a-net`).

We have to say, that was probably the right call. As early as 2003, Yahoo was saying that it was building individual web pages using PHP. These pages could be tested and deployed separately. As long as the changes were limited to one web page, the errors would also be limited to that web page. Using the strategies we've discussed so far; a tester and developer could knock out several changes a day. Instead, the company appeared to be batching a large group of changes up to be tested and retested toward the end of a long cycle. Where the programmers were able to find technology to enable frequent releases, the testers were unable to find ways to adapt to the new delivery cycle. Like dinosaurs, they had to go away.

There are other factors at play. To technology executives, testers look and feel like an overhead. Meanwhile, computer science is established enough that the typical development manager started out as a programmer – and what programmers do is automate things. If the process-improvement instinct is to make things "stable, predictable, and repeatable" and the programmer instinct is to automate things, it makes sense intuitively to give the testing work back to programmers. Have one person do both tasks and if they hate it, they can automate it.

This makes sense intuitively. The login functionality should work when it leaves a programmer's hands. We don't need a separate role to try to log in, fail, and file a ticket. A programmer should check it by hand. If there is some kind of build problem, a tool could at least try the highest-level features, get an error message, and demote the change back down to the programmer to figure it out.

Finally, we have the lean tools, which show that handoffs and multitasking cause waste. Handoffs can be necessary; few programmer-implementors can design a top-flight user interface. Lean tools tell us that for a handoff to exist, it needs to provide incredible value. Older, documentation-centric approaches that can't respond to frequent changes slow delivery and force it to be batched and released as a group – you get less software in more time.

It's no surprise that companies pursuing modern approaches (as we discussed in the last chapter) driven by these forces often conclude, *"We don't need no stinkin' testers."* We get it. You don't need *that* style of testing, and you might not have been introduced to what we are talking about in this book.

Two things to consider:

First, for those people who want to be in a testing role, you have to add significant value, overcoming the delayed feedback cycles in a handoff process, but also overcoming that cultural assumption of testers being of little value to the process.

Still, risk mitigation and testing need to happen. So, who will do it?

Building a risk mitigation team

You might be familiar with the old question, *"Why didn't testing find that bug?"* It sounds innocent enough. Usually, it is in fact an assertion that testing should have found that bug. The short reason is that someone made a mistake, and people do make mistakes. For the most part, testing exists because people make mistakes. Testing mitigates, or reduces, the risk of a mistake. There are other factors;

testers can think of things no one else thought of or provide other quality-related information such as a feature idea. Still, for the most part, we can think of the defects created, and the tests run as two overlapping circles. Defects that exist outside that circle need to be caught by something else, or else they will escape to the customer.

Here's a simple exercise.

Write down on a piece of paper everything you might do to reduce risk in a project – that is, every type of activity your company runs to catch a problem or find quality-related information. These could be things done by testers, the delivery team, operations, product management, senior management, internal customers, or stakeholders, it doesn't really matter. The point is that someone wonders about something that could go wrong, and then they run some kind of check to figure it out.

We'll encourage you to pause here and make your own list. Later in the chapter, we'll provide a sample list, so please, don't read ahead. Instead, go write some ideas down.

Seriously, go make a list. It'll take five minutes. Then we'll describe the next step, and finally give our commentary. If you really want a good exercise, have everyone on the team write down their ideas. Then have a meeting and pass each person's sheet to the next person – go in a circle until the person has their test list again. Then, with input from others, have them write down their ideas. This gives you an exhaustive list of what people think is done to reduce risks and find problems on software projects. You could go one more round or keep a master list in a cloud-based document, to at least make sure everyone's ideas are exhausted.

There are other columns you can add. For example, you could list every possible type of test you could run, and then have a column that asks if that activity actually happens routinely. Or you could have a column to ask if that activity actually finds any bugs. Or have a column for who (what role) actually performs that type of testing. Imagine running the exercise above, and for one of the activities, everyone thinks it is someone else's responsibility. Yes, that can happen, especially when it comes to what areas of the program are being tested.

Now go make the table. This is the last time we'll tell you. Do it.

Once you've completed the table, someone has to do a little research in the bug tracker. Over the course of a lunch period, go through the last hundred or so bugs and try to find a root category for the defect. That could be "accepts invalid input", "reasonable click leads to error page", "button renamed or missing", "screen render error", and so on. If you're feeling ambitious, go through a few hundred bugs. If you don't track bugs, that's fine, just start tracking problems for two weeks. Realistically, these will be problems found post-commit; it's likely not worth tracking the conversational problem/fixing that happens during pair programming, unit testing, or the prevention that happens with **Test-Driven Development** (TDD). If a debugging session runs for more than two hours, it might be worth writing down, because the programmer's time was wasted reproducing and eliminating a defect. With modern tools, we find these problems are mostly framework and integration issues, which are still worth tracking if they can be prevented. Another possible source of bug fixes is the commit logs in version control. Teams that don't use a bug tracker can put enough detail in the fixes that they can be reviewed and tracked back to the root cause. For teams that track defects with numbers, we've had a fair bit of success putting the issue number on commits, and, in some cases, putting the commit hash in the ticket tracker. If you can, consider tracking where the bugs are found, typically in code review, feature testing, regression testing, or by customers. A *404 error* from using the main functionality that is caught in feature testing would count as one; a second *404 error* found by customers would require a new row.

Once the list of root causes and counts of each exists, make a new spreadsheet that lists the root causes by count (you can just sort the old spreadsheet) and where they should have been found in the existing test process. (You can just add a column and list the activities that should find the defects.)

This approach tells us a few things:

- What test practices are not effective enough, and perhaps need more time

- How they should be strengthened

- What categories are escaping that could be found earlier in the process

- What you are spending time on that doesn't line up with the problems you are actually seeing

Obviously, with the rules we've set up, unit testing and earlier activities can prevent problems before they appear, but that is not the only problem. There is also no guarantee that yesterday's types of bugs will be tomorrow's, so optimizing test approaches to find yesterday's bugs could leave you blind to tomorrow's risks. Numerical counting could be a problem, because "no one can log in" one time is likely more serious than a font size being off a dozen times. Still, this sort of research is better than nothing.

The purpose of the risk exercise

The exercise from the previous section shows you what you are doing now to manage risk, along with what risks are escaping. It also shows, to some extent, how the team is compensating for errors. Compensating for errors is a good thing. When you think about the human body, nearly every critical system is redundant, and in that redundancy, each system reinforces the others. DNA tries to produce humans with two nostrils, two ears, two lungs, two kidneys, and so on. Two human eyes are not redundant; they work together to create depth perception. Hands and opposable thumbs work the same way. The number one cause of death in many countries is heart disease – one of the only systems in the body that is not redundant.

In most cases, testing is cheaper than true redundancy, which might involve coding things twice and then automating the software to take random walks and look for differences. In many ways, this is essentially what model-driven testing is doing, with a cheaper model for testing.

If your organization is doing testing activities, then the people doing it are the risk management team. Formalizing who is doing what and then tracking the results can help you decide which activities to invest your time and resources in. Careful discussion of where bugs are found and who has the aptitude to find them might help you shift the "who" of testing to the right players.

A careful reader might find some similarities here to the discussion in *Chapter 10* about strategy. Where that was based on risk and coverage, this exercise was based on the defects (that we know of) that have escaped in the past.

Before we move on, here's one sample table. It's far from complete, as the list could include beta testing, usability testing, accessibility testing, soak testing, testing on a staging server, and dozens more. As of this publication, a search for 100 types of testing yields plenty of results. The example in the following table is just designed to give a flavor of types of testing frequently run with intention on a software team:

Activity	Who does it	Does it catch bugs
Requirements Review	Delivery Team	Yes
Acceptance Tests	Delivery Team	Yes
Unit Tests	Programmer	Yes
Programmer hand-test	Programmer	Yes
Linting	Tool	No
Code Review	Programmers	No
Continuous Integration	Tool	Yes
Security Scan	Tool	No
Functional Tests	Testers	Yes
Functional Tooling	Tool	Yes
API Tests	Tool	Big ones?
Emergent Testing	Testers	Yes
Regression Test	Tool	Big ones?
Penetration Test	Security/Pen Test	Yes
Performance Test	Tool/Release team	Yes
A/B Split Tests	Marketing	No
Production Monitoring	Ops	?
Synthetic Transaction in Production	Testers	?
Run business on staging	Delivery Org	Yes
Log Review	Testers	Informs test strategy
Emergent Risk Management	Testers	Yes (See section on actual continuous testing below)

Table 13.1 – Sample types of risk management activities

Several items on the list imply test tooling, sometimes called "test automation"; others, such as load simulations, cannot be done without it. Let's talk about that.

Faith-based versus empirical test automation

There's a strange thing that happens when people outside of a field try to direct work they do not understand. The skilled technical writer becomes a typist; the expert on the helpdesk ends up routing requests. Project managers, who can do noble things, become a sort of nag, whose only job is to ask, "Are you done yet?" and update the schedule. The outcomes we get when people who do not understand the work but try to manage it are poor. This leads to either attempts to break down the work into its smallest component (the brick metaphor earlier), or, sometimes, self-service.

For technical writing, self-service is simply having the workers define their own systems. Low-value project managers can be replaced by an Agile tool that shows the board and projects when the work will be done based on velocity. The helpdesk person who is told to only be a phone router will be replaced by having customers make their own helpdesk requests on a web app. The results, sadly, are predictable: the official documents are poor, so each team creates its own, slightly better documents for onboarding and support. The hard-to-explain parts of the project manager's job, like negotiation and alignment, simply do not get done at all. Work feels a little less human and people lose productivity because it takes days to get an answer to a simple question. Sometimes, the helpdesk requests are routed to the wrong team or "bounce around", and answers take weeks to arrive.

If you've been reading along, you know that the automation of testing takes a similar approach. People who don't understand the work have a desire to make it simple, predictable, and repeatable, then get not-very-great results from that documented approach. (It reminds us of the line from Thomas More's Utopia: *First they create criminals, then they punish them.*)

Once the value is low, it's time for self-service – get programmers to do the testing or create the automation. This is another way to restate what we wrote earlier, in *How we got here*.

The odd thing is that often, the people pushing for it have themselves never seen the idealized world they are pushing toward. To be uncharitable, it is as if a bunch of executives around a watercooler spoke in hushed tones and grunts about how "automation is good", deciding "from now on, all testing will be automated!"

Of course, we know this is silly; it is faith-based, not evidence-backed. Indeed, we know a few people who have gone from company to company (to company, to company) preaching this gospel, this thing they themselves have never done. Hired as the expert, they may work on frameworks and foundations for a year or two. Eventually, due to politics or other opportunities, they move on. When we point out the string of failures, we are told "Oh, (Fortune-500 company name)? That wasn't their fault…" There's always a reason.

Faith-based test automation is dangerous.

The math behind faith-based test automation

Imagine you have an existing project. Every two weeks or so, you release software to production; you may have a test/deploy step at the end, while others are working on the fuzzy frontend of the project. We are not excited about this approach; we don't want to argue whether this is "Agile" or "WAgile." It just is a common pattern we see. You want the test automation because the testing results aren't fast enough, and you can't get software released quickly enough.

So, who is going to do the test tooling (by which we mean automating the most obvious parts of test execution and reporting)?

If you ask the programmers to do it, they'll do a poor job and slow down delivery. Ask the testers, and they'll do a poor job long term. That is because companies tend to hire testers who are not the strongest programmers. At the very least, they tend to be multi-skilled, which generally means a little less than a specialist at everything. There are certainly exceptions. Yet, we feel compelled to point out – those are exceptions and that they slow down delivery. The testers can't do it as a "spare-time activity", as by definition the test process is already too slow. The next option is to hire automators, either on a contract or in a new role. If hired on contract, the tests are likely to go away when the contracts do. If the work is done by new employees, it is possible to keep up and integrate the work into the delivery cycle. In a year or so, there will be enough test tooling built up to reduce the regression-test cycle time.

Analysis: By increasing delivery costs by 5-10% and creating an entirely new discipline with the **Software Development Engineer in Test** (**SDET**), it is possible to radically reduce the regression-test step. This means programmers see large errors more quickly, perhaps right after they are introduced. Overall velocity might increase by perhaps as much as … five to ten percent.

Wait a minute. What is happening here?

Possible outcomes

The most common outcome we've seen is that complex, long-term test tool projects get scrapped. Another is that we create an entire role to handle the creation of tools. We have seen some success with starting new projects expecting programmers to produce tests for new features that are more like demonstrations. These include the acceptance tests; running them shows that nothing (big and obvious) broke. We've seen less success trying to introduce this for new stories in flight. The idea here is not to develop an automated proof of concept for a high-level smoke test of the entire system. Instead, create the demos for the changes. Those systems are likely to break, and the programmers can design the user interface changes for testability. Eventually, entire subsystems will be covered. If the interfaces are designed well enough to be deployed independently, we can turn off regression testing in subsystems one at a time.

For legacy systems not designed for testability, it may just be that the juice isn't worth the squeeze. Also, try to keep the promises that the tooling offers in mind. Looking at a tool to predict outcomes simply will not have the same value as a full-time project manager, but a project manager is more expensive. Tools created by non-testers to do testing will be faster and look cheaper… and they can be brittle and cause painful debugging. Low- and no-code tools have some promise; they enable the tester to create a high-level demonstration. Still, it's important to note the difference between this automation and what a careful inspector can do.

Another place we've seen tooling succeed is at the API level, where there is no slow GUI, and the setup and debugging are easier. In addition, API tests are generally useful for both web and mobile applications; they will continue to be useful if some new form factor is invented. The combination of a large number of API tests, a few GUI tests, and careful human testing around a specific feature change can drastically speed up delivery cycles. To see how to enable that, we'll next discuss shifting left and right, and actual continuous testing.

Shift left and shift right

One way to think of the waterfall model is that we build the wrong thing, then check it against the value for the customer, and then build the right thing. That is, it is not until the testing step that we actually check whether the ideas are going to work. The "Shift Left" paradigm is a plea to show quality earlier in the process. That might mean inviting programmers to participate in the requirement creation process or coming up with specific, clear acceptance criteria. Those acceptance criteria can be expressed as tests, either in plain English or BDD-style. For example, the requirements for valid and invalid passwords could include examples of valid and invalid passwords; not just "Must be at least 8 letters, of which one is a number and one a special character and one uppercase", but actual examples of valid and invalid passwords. One bank we worked with, for example, would accept "&", "<" and ">" as special characters. Yet, because they had meaning in HTML, they would be stripped out during a login attempt. As a result, users could create a password, but never log in! A discussion of examples of special characters with the team could have prevented this problem. That is what shift-left is all about, catching problems sooner by coming up with ways to check earlier.

Shift-right isn't quite the opposite. Instead, the idea is to shift testing activities into production. With effective production monitoring, teams can notice 400 (bad request), 401 (unauthorized), 402 (forbidden), 404 (requested URL was not found), and other error messages, including where they came from. Division by zero and interpreted code crashes tend to show up as 400 errors, so paying close attention to technical operations could help to find a problem just minutes after it shows up. The ability to roll back code through blue/green deploys or config switches might mean bad code lives on in production for minutes. Synthetic monitoring or running through a series of read options on repeat is another way we can catch large errors as soon as they are introduced. We can also catch performance problems. An excellent team could connect a performance problem to a change, roll the change back, and work on the fix at their leisure.

The classic approach to change management is, "If there are problems, slow things down and do more checks." Shift-right is more of a weightlifting approach to change management: If it hurts, do more of it.

For the final part of our discussion on *"When does testing occur?"*, we'd like to mention the idea of actually testing continuously.

(Actually) continuous testing

The term **continuous testing** typically means building the code and creating a test environment for every version-control change, then running all the types of tests against it – unit, integration, API, and GUI. In pseudo-code, which looks like this:

```
while (<CT server is on> {
Wait for a change
Check out the code
Perform a build, report errors
        - Create build artifacts
- Run unit tests, report errors
Create a test environment
Run API tests, report errors
Run end to end tests, report errors
}
```

One of our reviewers, Stephen Spady, pointed out that continuous testing could include post-release, and running synthetic transactions against the live system. We don't always see this in practice (notice the word *typically* in the previous paragraph) – but it would be a better world if we did. That would force end-to-end checks to be structured so they could run in production, making for more modular systems disconnected from data and test environments.

In practice, there's a little more to continuous testing, as you need to set up test databases and fake users, you might need to fake API endpoints, and so on. The real server probably just waits for changes, then creates a child process to actually perform the build. If you have multiple endpoints or many branches, there may be many server processes running, plus you need to define reporting, who gets the error messages, and so on. Still, that's the basics of it.

The continuous testing practice we have described here can be very helpful. It creates a feedback loop that happens early. Waiting until the end of a sprint to run automation is likely to reveal a ton of problems that need to be checked to see where they were introduced. Tying it to a specific change means we know exactly where to look to fix problems. Yet this approach is also shallow. All that is happening is that the same test ideas you had yesterday are run over and over. The one thing we know about the code in each build is that it is different than yesterday. If it was the exact same, the automated checks would have no value.

One way to avoid this shallow approach is to set aside some amount of time for testing new ideas that go beyond today's features. This is most likely new potential uses of the software, or combinations of uses that could happen due to a series of recent features used in the concept. Feature testing is unlikely to find these because they are cross-cutting concerns. Another possibility is the release of a new browser, operating system, or device.

Teams can set aside anything from a half-hour per week per person for up to four or eight hours per week (or more) to deal with these additional concerns. They can appear in the workflow as stories. That is, the Product Owner would explicitly know that instead of future progress, the team is investing blocks of time in risk management. The team can track them as blocks of time, or, more likely, just store them in a spreadsheet or tracker to be removed or rotated when they are complete. This is another way to get rid of an expensive regression testing process – just test everything over the course of the week you are delivering. If something big breaks at deploy-time, use shift-right tools to find the problem and eliminate it quickly. Of course, it is possible the team is not yet mature enough to eliminate the regression step at the end. Or that they are so mature they don't need continuous regression tests.

The idea here is to invest time in emergent test ideas, tracked in a backlog, just like development effort. Think of it as a list of risks worth exploring once, reminiscent of our census of risk in *Chapters 9* and *10*.

Continuously check with tools; explore with humans frequently enough we might call it continuous. The computer does the things we want to do over and over, and the human answers the one-time "what if?" questions. Both of these are strategies to invest in mitigating risk. Re-run the exercise at the top of this chapter, then adjust the test strategy to invest in areas that can find real bugs. To do that, you'll need to spend less energy testing something else, so take a look at the techniques that don't find bugs, exploring the risk and what would happen if a bug did emerge. In many cases, the low-yield approaches would yield low-value bugs, or the bugs would be caught by some other technique.

Summary

This chapter tried to widen the idea of testing, asking about all the activities done to reduce risk, who does them, and when. To that end, we explored the idea that testers are out of fashion, then gave you the tools to look at the wider picture in your current organization and steer toward improvement as you defined it. We took one more crack at discussing test tooling and whether your approach is based on data or faith. The chapter then went on to expand the view of quality, to the left and the right, and covered the concept of adding the exploration of risks as a broad topic with a tracked list of risks ordered by a decision maker.

Make no mistake, we're strong advocates of an actual person who thinks of their role primarily as a tester of software. We realize this is against the spirit of the age, to which we shrug. Organizations that eliminate the tester role and try to push it down to everyone else will then need everyone to have a higher knowledge of testing – someone has to champion, drive, and teach. You might call that person … a tester.

If you are at least a tiny bit suspicious that two testers would be advocating for testing as a role, well, there is a term for that: *conflict of interest*. In the next chapter, we explore ethics in software testing.

14
Philosophy and Ethics in Software Testing

In math, we can say that if an expression is true for any given number *N*, it will be true for *N*+1. Then, we prove it's true for 1 and find we've proven the claim true for all integers. That is a *proof by induction*. Testing has sort of the opposite problem. If we don't observe problems running the software in a specific way, that doesn't prove that there will not be problems the second time around. If we test twice in a row, that doesn't prove that there will be no error the third time. Thus, we cannot prove the software correct; we can merely indicate the conditions we ran it in and the problems we found.

If all testing can say is, "We don't know if the software works, we can just show that it appeared to not show errors at some point in time under some conditions", well, that isn't very valuable, is it? Beyond that, people will ask us to do it anyway. Specifically, they'll ask if the software is "good enough." Then, if there are problems, someone will say, "Well, my goodness, those technical people (who we put under immense pressure to say things are okay) said it was okay; what's their problem?"

To resolve that, we need to leave the land of **science, technology, engineering, and math (STEM)** and enter the land of philosophy. Specifically, this chapter will cover the following topics:

- Philosophy and why it matters in testing
- Branches of ethics and ethical reasoning
- Practical ethical issues in testing
- Scientific thinking and logical fallacies
- How we wind up in hell and how to escape

Don't worry; we'll be gentle.

Philosophy and why it matters in testing

"Is the software good enough to go to customers?"

"Have we tested well enough?"

"Is this new feature worth building?"

These sorts of questions arise in testing all the time. To answer them, we need to define "good" and we need to define "enough." Philosophy, which stems from the root words *philo* (love) and *sophy* (of learning wisdom), seeks to answer that. Our quick shorthand for philosophy is the study of the good, the right, the true, and the beautiful.

How can we possibly even talk about "good enough" without philosophy?

This topic comes up from time to time. People want techniques, tools, tips, and actionable ideas, not philosophy. Yet, given what we just wrote, how is that possible? One of the writers, Matt, asked this question to someone he trusted with a philosophy degree. She replied, *"Some people are stupid."*

We wouldn't go that far. Instead, we'd look at the problem: why do people think philosophy is a waste of time?

The short answer is that there is no easy answer.

Consider the simplest of questions:

1. What is the ideal ratio of testers to developers?
2. How do we know we are done testing?
3. When should we create an automated test for a bug?
4. How long should a sprint be?

Now let's look at some easy answers:

1. Two developers per tester
2. When the acceptance tests pass
3. Always create an automated test for every bug
4. Two weeks

And now some more philosophical answers:

1. It depends
2. It depends
3. It depends
4. It depends

Imagine being a leader trying to set policy for an organization. You don't have one question; you have a thousand questions. Can't you just ask an expert, get an answer, and do it?

Well, yes, you can. You can go out and find a solution that solves someone else's problem (maybe) at some point. Will it solve your problem? Will it introduce more problems? We don't really know.

"It depends", of course, isn't the end of the conversation. It is a start. The expert should talk about the issue.

Let's look at sprint length in scrum.

Sprint Length: it depends

Beyond three weeks, teams lose a sense of urgency about the work. This also creates disincentives to creating small stories. However, if the team has a traditional regression-test phase that it wants to bring into the sprint, three weeks can be a reasonable limit. One-week sprints that have all the formal ceremonies can feel a bit rushed, as you have kickoff on Monday and then a retrospective and demo, plus a production push, on Friday. That leads to 4.25 hours of meetings in one week, which is more than 10% of the time (3 + 0.25*5 days a week). Of course, there is no law that says there needs to be a demo and retrospective every single sprint. Meanwhile, teams that have eliminated regression-testing as a phase can eliminate the concept of the sprint, moving to frequent deploys with just-in-time demos and retros. For example, team members can put sticky notes somewhere, perhaps on a web page, and when the page has five stickies, they do a retrospective.

What we wrote is slightly philosophical. It depends on where the team is (the context) as well as the value system—the team could find the time pressure of one-week sprints to be a good thing and the meeting costs worth paying. That is a question of value.

"Just start with two weeks" can sound compelling in comparison, but it has a problem we'll discuss in a bit. Generally, when people give broad instructions, they are implying a model such as Shu Ha Ri.

Shu Ha Ri: learning by osmosis

Many martial arts start with form and repetition. In a martial arts *Kata*, you do the same thing repeatedly without an opponent. Real combat is nothing like Kata, yet Kata can be the first step. World-class athletes such as Wayne Gretzky and Tiger Woods tell comparable stories of practicing the same move over and over until it becomes muscle memory, even though what will happen on the field will be different every time. **Shu Ha Ri** (守破離) is a Japanese martial arts term that codifies this idea. They correspond roughly to the guild concept of apprentice, journeyman, and virtuoso.

During *Shu*, you are given precise instructions or rules to follow.

In *Ha*, you recognize the rules are more like guidelines or heuristics.

In *Ri*, you reject the idea of rules and simply do the needful. The virtuoso has transcended the concept of rules and limits due to their expertise. They know what needs to be done, and they do it.

When it comes to coordinating and organizing humans to move in a particular direction, we typically need a rhythm and order; sprints need to have some length. Context-driven testing and test philosophy tend to start people out on the *Ha* level. This can be very disconcerting for people who just want to be told how to do something. Heuristics can help, but they do not always apply and have exceptions.

A few years ago, in the speakers' room at the **Agile Roots** Conference, one speaker was talking about Shu Ha Ri and how you have to tell people what to do. Matt disagreed. The speaker provided the example of teaching someone to cook eggs—you have to start with a recipe card.

Really? Matt asked if the speaker had ever actually taught anyone to cook eggs. What he does is get out two wooden spoons, two frying pans, and two eggs and have the student mirror his movements, making comments about what is happening as it happens. There might be a few comments that are more like hard rules (undercooked eggs can make you ill), but for the most part, the goal is to let the learners experience and think for themselves and put themselves in the driver's seat.

The point here is that *Shu Ha Ri* is not the only way to approach creating rules around workflow. *Shu* can force them to do the work in a way that does not make sense to them. You see this when people say things such as, "I was only following the process." If you do not own the process and instead just do what the process tells you, you cannot take responsibility for the outcome. That might be fine at a fast-food company where the rules are to cook the fried potatoes at a certain temperature for a certain period of time, so they always come out exactly the same. The company is taking responsibility for the outcome. In software, Scrum was designed to give the team time to finish the work without interruptions, buying time against a too-fast company decision loop. XP was designed to get the software to production quickly, moving faster than the multi-year company decision loop. Adopting a process that solves a different problem than you have seems like a bad idea. In those cases, following someone else's *Shu* guidance might be a mistake. Is that the case for you? Well, it depends.

Joking aside, the goal of this book is to give you enough information to act at the Ha level—to own your own process while having some guidelines and good advice. We wanted to cook along with you—while warning you about undercooked eggs—to the extent possible through the written word.

That's what we've tried to do with this book—show you how we would test, explain some of the choices, and then leave it up to you to analyze. To do that, we need to discuss what we value and talk about our own values. One way to do that is with a points exercise; we've done a few in this book. We are about to do one more to determine what executives actually want.

A tough question: what do you want?

When we come into a project as consultants, we are frequently asked to improve things. Testing takes too long, quality is poor, the projects lack predictability, delivery teams seem slow to answer questions that come from customers, management doesn't get the information they need about quality to make key decisions, time to market is too slow, projects delivered lack key features, and the amount of work delivered in a given period (velocity) just feels low. "Can you fix that for us?", they ask.

Well, it depends.

The question is, what do you want?

- Do you want more speed or better testing and more information?
- Do you want decreased time to market or more features for major releases?
- Do you want high quality or more velocity?
- Do you want technical staff to respond to questions quickly or more velocity?

There are a few ways for teams to structure the work to get a nice handful of these, but it is unlikely that we will find a solution that gives us everything. So, management, what do you want? Pick one and we will get it for you. You cannot have your cake and eat it too.

As consultants, we are likely to face an unblinking stare and an answer such as, "Look, if I wanted to get just one thing, I could do that myself. I want all of it. All of it. That is why we spent all this money to bring in a world-class expert. I want it all."

The next steps are difficult.

A typical consulting assignment involves starting with a *vision* for the way the world could be. From there, we conduct an *assessment* to determine the state of the software world. The next step is conducting a *gap analysis* to see the differences between the two, which leads to recommendations on how to fix the gap. Yet before we start, we hit a snag; the vision is for an impossible all-singing, all-dancing future.

One possible interim step is a survey. Give the stakeholders 100 points and ask them for a complete list of what they want to invest in. Then do a little math with the answers, looking at the mean (average), median (numbers in the middle), and standard deviation (distance between answers) for each set of answers.

This could allow for some synergies. **Synergy** is the idea of combining two or more things to create something greater, making one plus one equal three. For example, if the two most popular ideas are reduced time to market and predictability, then small stories and sprints become appealing. In the case studies where we dropped formally documented test cases and created a coverage map and a visualization of coverage/quality, a one-day release process would allow us to both reduce the test process while improving transparency, allowing for a single unified view of what to do.

Before we can start improving things, we need to understand what the goal is. If the goal is unclear, surveys and points can help create consensus. Another approach is to simply declare things and gauge the reaction. Frequently, we find people who are used to define steps will react to our made-up and wrong definitions. This can break the logjam and get things flowing. The challenge, then, is for us to let go of our egos and be "wrong", even though what we did was an intentional process to deal with someone who refused to take a stand. Okay. Fine. We are "wrong." By virtue of this, we now know, or have a better idea, of what "right" is. That gives us what we need to move forward.

Pointing out how much we value things can create a democratic process and lead to consensus. Another thing it can do is *point out differences*. If one team manager wants 100% more velocity and another wants 100% higher quality, that is the start of a conversation about values. To have that conversation, we need to understand a little philosophy. We hope you can understand why we felt we needed to include this chapter in the book. Maybe it's a little shorter than other chapters, perhaps a little later, but it's necessary and important.

Speaking of "maybe later but necessary" brings us to the idea of ethics in testing.

Ethics and ethical reasoning in testing

If you've been in testing long enough, you'll probably face a moment where someone asks you a simple and obvious question in a group setting and the boss gives you *the look*. The look says, "You better think real carefully about how you answer that."

Wait a minute.

The person who is asking is a director. Vice president. CIO. CEO, maybe. Are you telling me I'm supposed to lie to our internal executives? That can't be right. We mean, it should not be right. If we are not supposed to lie to them, then what are we supposed to do?

In our experience, there are five broad approaches here:

- **Tell the truth**: "The software currently has 75 show-stopper bugs. On average, we introduce one new show-stopper for every five we fix. Given our current rate of fixing twenty per week, we do not see how we could put this responsibly into customers' hands until January."

- **Lie**: "Everything looks on track for November." This is deceptive. We do not say exactly what "on-track" means or what will happen in November. The customer thinks that means a release of the full completed functionality while we mean that work will continue in November. When you use a vague term to mislead someone knowing they will take one interpretation when we mean another, that is *equivocation*. When you say true things that paint an untrue picture, that's more like *dissembling*. In this case, no reasonable person would interpret "on track for November" as "going to keep developing in November" given the context. That's just a lie.

- **Avoidance**: Look at your shoes. Do not make eye contact. Try to be invisible. If you are called on, demure and defer—"I think Bob is better positioned to answer that." Another term for avoidance is, "Unless they ask a direct question, we don't really have to answer."

- **The way of the weasel**: "We have some issues. On a red/yellow/green scale, I would say the project is orange." It's worth noting that we produced this example by putting peers in a simulation where all the data pointed to goals being impossible. We then pressured them to say things were going fine.

- **The way of the super weasel**: This is for predicting and avoiding situations where the truth is uncomfortable. In one case, Matt literally told a boss, "Look, the CIO is going to be in that meeting, and if I am asked questions, I will tell the truth. I don't think you want me in that meeting. Should I just not go? Would you rather I plan to take that particular day as time off?" The super weasel prevents the direct question.

We dare say that as authors, we've never lied to customers, nor have we taken the weasel way. While under pressure and trying to navigate something difficult, Matt has taken the way of the super weasel at least once, whereas Michael has done avoidance. Going to bed that night, we've never felt good about it, never slept well, never been happy. Our goal with this book is to help you navigate ethics in a way that does make you feel good.

So, there is one practical example of a conflict between what we think is "right" and the incentives in the system. A **conflict of interest** happens when we are conflicted between two matters. The classic example is a member of a board of directors who owns a vendor that an organization is voting on using, but testers have conflicts of interest all the time between what is "right" for the company and what is "best" for their careers. This is where ethics comes into play.

Sadly, the dictionary is not that helpful when it comes to ethics, which we'll generally define as the study of moral principles that govern our choices. To understand that, we'll look up morals, which are standards of belief and behavior concerning what is acceptable or right. If "right" is "morally good or acceptable", we seem to find circular reasoning. Ethical frameworks can help us move from definition to practice

Ethical frameworks

A few years ago at a conference, one of our peers complained that an action was unethical. We asked according to what ethical standard or framework. The answer that came back was, "Well, that's the thing about ethics, right? There is no standard, each person has their own."

This tells us that this person had never bothered to do any serious inquiry into ethics. Do not be this person.

Ethical frameworks don't need to trap us. Instead, they give us ways to make tradeoffs. We'll explain the three most popular—utilitarianism, deontological ethics, and virtue ethics:

- **Utilitarianism**: Summed up by the phrase "the most good for the most people", utilitarianism seeks solutions that provide broad benefits to all. The US government needs to consider such things (public good) when it confiscates land to build a road, collects a higher tax from people who have the means to pay or distributes income to the needy. One common utilitarian tactic is to ask, "If you had no idea who you would be when you were born, would you want this policy to exist?" Another is to ask, "What happens if everyone does this?" If it makes the world a better place, creating a virtuous cycle, that's good. If it creates a corrosive effect, a vicious cycle, maybe create policies to prevent it.

- **Deontology**: This is the philosophy of moral obligations. Ideas such as "parents are obligated to support a child" can be based on utilitarianism (roving gangs are bad) but also on deontology. To be duty-bound to report, or obligated to care, even the "citizens' duty" to vote, can be arguments from deontology. In the TV Show *The Wire*, Lieutenant Daniels is constantly mistreated by his management, yet consistently returns to his beliefs in the chain of command.

- **Virtue Ethics**: This focuses on what a good person does and pursues that. If a good person would not lie, we pursue an ideal where we tell no lies. Stoicism, an ancient Western philosophy we practice, provides us with four cardinal virtues of **justice**, **prudence**, **temperance**, and **fortitude**.

The four cardinal virtues

Justice is the idea of giving people what they deserve. This includes both criminal justice (punishment) but also rewards to those who are deserving. That includes the idea of merit.

Prudence, or practical wisdom, involves the wise use of resources, such as money and time.

Temperance covers self-discipline. The classic issue of temperance, moderation in drinking alcohol, has become so popular that the term is totally associated with alcohol in many circles. Still, it includes not overeating, exercising, not spending excessively even if you can afford it (prudence), and so on.

Fortitude is moral courage, especially in the face of negative consequences. Speaking truth to power can require fortitude. Picking fights you can't win out of spite is not so much fortitude as it is a lack of prudence.

The virtues are often depicted as ladies with items. Justice may be the most well-known, holding scales to weigh items (or a sword). Prudence is often depicted with a mirror or snake. Fortitude might have a club, broken column, helmet, armor, or a tamed lion. Temperance pours water into a wine glass.

The cardinal virtues appear in ancient literature, from Plato's *Republic* to *Wisdom of Solomon*. The Christian tradition adds three theological virtues: faith, hope, and charity (or love), along with *The Corporal Works of Mercy*. *The Corporal Works of Mercy* are actions to do more than ideals, and they include feeding the hungry, giving drink to the thirsty, clothing the naked, visiting the imprisoned, sheltering the homeless, visiting the sick, and burying the dead.

There are plenty of virtues: patience, perseverance, determination, self-dignity, humility, modesty, sincerity, tact, integrity, gratitude, and so on. Sometimes they play off each other; to practice one would make another impossible. In fact, in his book *That Hideous Strength*, C.S. Lewis states that, "If evil cannot convince you that a good thing is bad, the next trick is to try to convince you that something good is more important than something better". An example is elevating patriotism over the humanity of someone else.

Before we dive into more testing case studies, we'll leave you with an example of an honor code that combines deontology with virtue ethics; the honor code of the US Air Force Academy at Colorado Springs, Colorado: "I shall not lie, cheat, nor steal, nor tolerate those among us who do. Furthermore, I resolve to do my duty and live honorably."

Classic ethical challenges

The road to Abilene. A family in Texas discusses what to do on a Sunday afternoon. Someone mentions taking a drive to Abilene, the next town up the road. Eventually, everyone loads up into the car with broken air conditioning and takes the road, ending up at a store, looking around, and driving back. Once they return, everyone slowly realizes that no one wanted to go to Abilene; they just thought everyone else wanted to.

The Asch Conformity experiments. Put a person in a room with ten others and four lines on the screen. When a proctor comes in and asks, all ten agree that the third line is the longest (it isn't). Will the actual real subject agree to get along or will they stand firm? The overwhelming majority of the people go along with the crowd, either assuming they are understanding something incorrectly or just not wanting a fight.

The Stanford prison experiment. A professor simulated the environment of a prison in the school, complete with prison guards with khaki clothing, mirrored shades, and billy clubs. The prisoners were forced to wear prisoners' outfits. Over the course of a few days, the group devolved into evil behavior, with the warden (professor) finding he enjoyed it too much.

These examples tell us that we all have the capability for evil, and even the desire for the most good for the most people (utilitarianism) can lead to a bad outcome. The goal is to prepare us to think and reason in terms of ethics.

Now let's get real.

Practical ethical issues in testing

Your boss drops by your office, bragging. "I was just in a meeting with Linda; she was bugging me about the technical requirements and the answers she needed to move forward on the project. She said she told me she needed them a week ago. I said, 'I don't know what you are talking about.' She looked so foolish. She said she had emailed me today, as well as several times this week. I told her she was wrong. It was so embarrassing for her." He sits down, logs in, and checks emails. "Yup. There it is, four requests over the past week. DELETE. Forget about it, Linda. You're not getting that information from me."

This actually happened to Matt, almost word for word. Within six months, Matt transferred bosses. Within eighteen, he had left the company.

What is going on here?

The problem here is multi-layered. On one level, it was transparent that one department was attempting to make another look foolish while making inroads into their territory. On another, the boss is testing your courage and loyalty. The move is also a bit of a *double-bind*; if you say something, you are not loyal enough to be trusted. If you say nothing, you've demonstrated a lack of *fortitude*, showing that you are not brave.

One option is to become a yes-person. Laugh along. Poor Linda, such a sucker. We suspect that isn't you because you kept reading this chapter to get here. Another option, which Matt did, was to turn back to his desk, keep his head down, and start looking into a transfer. Why? Because to do otherwise is to risk genuine retaliation.

Another option is, if the boss is new, to look the boss in the eye and say, "You need to understand that we don't behave that way here. Now you have some tough decisions to make. The easiest one is to find the document and email it to Linda with an apology. If you don't do that, you could explain to me why I shouldn't take some further action."

The problem with this, of course, is retaliation. If you announce that, you've announced you are an enemy to someone who has the authority to fire you. More importantly, you've created a *power imbalance* by asserting yourself. If this boss cares about appearances and power (and their language indicates that they absolutely do), then making some sort of assertive statement is declaring yourself a risk. At the very least, the boss is likely to keep you at arm's length, away from the best assignments and promotion possibilities. They might even block a transfer.

Another option is to try to speak to Linda, Linda's boss, or someone else about what you heard.

Given how remarkably difficult it is to win in this situation, the next few sections are going to cover how to prevent putting yourself in it.

Skipping test steps and the good news

One story we routinely heard is the boss who orders people to either skip testing, comment out/ignore failing test information, or fake test results. We put those in ascending order, as they fall into different levels of ethical problems. The first two sections of this book were designed to give you, the reader, tools to make the test process transparent. Done well; management can understand the risks. If they want to skip one level of testing in order to test integration to save a week, they can. If, of course, the lower-level testing has all kinds of problems, then the integration and debug stages will be more painful. Still, if you've informed management of the risks and they still tell you to skip, here is a magic phrase: "If you'll take responsibility for it, sure, we can do that. Just send me an email."

That phrase works wonders. First, it will cause the leader to pause. Wait. Can they take responsibility for this decision? If the answer is yes, fine, they'll send you an email, and the problem is solved. If they won't, well then, carry on with what you were doing before.

Ignoring test results and faking test results are more problematic. In utilitarian terms, if everyone did that, we'd have a bunch of bad software. In deontological terms, it is sort of ignoring the purpose of the testing role. In terms of virtue ethics, it is delaying the inevitable (fixing) to feel better for a short time. "Going along to get along" is an integrity violation that lacks temperance. It's a non-starter.

Usually, these things are done subtly by pushing the decision to someone else. In 2021, BMW and VW were fined nearly a billion euros for faking emission results. You can see how that could happen. An executive repeats, "We must pass the emission standards" and, "I don't care how you do it; just get it done" enough times, and some poor technician just goes and changes the rows in the spreadsheet. When it all comes out, the executives can shake their heads and say, "We certainly didn't mean *that!*"

Avoiding this sort of scandal is easy. When you're asked to do something wrong, have the boss put it in writing that they'll take responsibility for it. If they won't do it or if it is a "secret", don't do it.

We realize that to some extent integrity is a luxury. If you are Jean Valjean, stealing a piece of bread to help his starving family, we won't judge you. But pause for a minute … are you Jean Valjean? Is your integrity worth a small raise, a bonus, not taking the risk of a demotion? Remember, as Christopher Nolan has the main character say in *Batman Begins*, "It is not who we are underneath but what we do that defines us."

While we've heard these stories over and over again, there's a funny thing about them: neither Matt nor Michael have ever been asked to do them. Bear in mind, for the first half of his career, Matt gave off the vibe of someone who could be bullied. Yet, despite that, he also gave off a vibe of personal integrity.

This leads to the integrity axiom: if people know you are not willing to lie, they won't ask you to.

Most of our section on ethics is about doing the right thing and helping others see it. We want to make it easy for them, not hard. By taking our principled stand, we often run the risk of making people look bad and creating enemies. Before we leave this section, let's talk about helping people save face.

Decisions are not made in meetings

Sometimes, we, the testers, want to swoop in and save the day. We want to go to the meeting to discuss a project, hear something wrong, and jump in talking about how wrong it is: "We cannot take this step; we must take another step."

Meanwhile, the decision had already been made. We just made some people look really bad. The political people are asking what our agenda is and whose side we are on. And here we are, on the side of truth, not being liked by anyone.

You see, decisions aren't made in meetings. At least, they often are not made in meetings. Instead, they are made before the meeting by a collection of "inner ring"-ers, distributed over time and space. The purpose of the meeting isn't to gather input; it is to announce the decision.

If you find yourself with strong opinions trying to change policies, start building your coalition behind closed doors. Figure out what the decision will be. If you can, get in on the decision loop. Help other people accomplish their goals. Be concerned, at least a little, with helping people save face. When the time comes for you to get decisions made in your favor, you are much more likely to get the outcome you hoped for. If not, you can know in advance to not waste time and hurt feelings in person.

Scientific thinking and logical fallacies

When we think of science, we think of repeatable experiments. That is, if you submerge a bar of Ivory soap in the water a hundred times and see that it always rises to the top, you can conclude that Ivory soap floats. Francis Bacon's idea of the scientific method was to identify a hypothesis, conduct an experiment, and come to conclusions. Karl Popper adds a bit to that, suggesting that science is much better at disproving things than proving them. According to Popper, we can't really prove things, as much as say that a point (water freezes at 32 degrees Fahrenheit) is demonstrated reliably enough that we can assume it is true and build on it. These approaches have analogs to testing.

Science gets a little more difficult when we get to things that are not reproducible, such as historical artifacts and economics. Still, we can apply something such as scientific thinking. To verify a historical document, we can look at where it claims to come from, how old the oldest copies are, and how different they are, as well as compare the writing to writings from the claimed era, and so on. In economics, we can look for similar situations and apply logical thinking.

There is another way to approach large datasets: starting with an agenda and then looking for data that correlates with our answer, ignoring data and explanations that can lead us in a different direction. Without an agenda, this process can be a valuable part of, say, an RCRCRC analysis that looks at log data for interesting collieries. For instance, at one company, the average page load was lower than expected. We dug into the data and found that the bottom one percent of page loads were so slow as to actually throw off the number. Eventually, we realized someone from a remote outpost using satellite internet was consistently downloading large files that were updated every day. For another example, you might have two sets of data in spreadsheets and flip between them, looking for patterns. **Michael Bolton** named this kind of analysis **blink testing**. Done as a simple pattern match, it can be a kind of blind experiment. Done as a search for numbers to support a pre-drawn conclusion, we get into the land of non-scientific thinking. If you come to a conclusion that explains the data when many conclusions are possible, you get into real trouble.

Another thinking (or perhaps not-thinking) trap can be found in logical fallacies.

Logical fallacies

Junior developer Johnny is accused of not working at all, all afternoon, for several days in a row. He denies it. The programmers who accuse him say, "Of course, he would say that."

This statement doesn't actually add any evidence; it doesn't help us prove anything. Yet it can be persuasive. That is what logical fallacies are. They sound good and can convince people, but they don't actually provide weight or evidence. Formal logic that can be picked up by math or computer science is a bit beyond our scope (we'll talk about it in the additional readings toward the end of the chapter), but we hope to at least help you figure out what is not true.

Here are a few of the most common fallacies:

- **Ad hominem**: This is where we attack the person, not the idea. "Joe doesn't have any training in computer science, so what could he possibly know about performance testing" is an ad hominem argument. It can be persuasive; we don't expect strangers on the street to have answers about advanced particle physics. But it doesn't actually address any concrete ideas Joe has put forward.

- **False dilemma**: This is where many options are intentionally limited to two. For example, test this module (all day today) or not, when we could invest 15 minutes into testing, 30, an hour, a half-day – or we could test it next week, or 15 minutes per day over the next week, and so on.

- **Equivocation**: The logical fallacy of equivocation is where a person uses a vague term in two different ways in a conversation in order to make an invalid point seem valid. Anyone can equivocate when they use a vague term and let the audience interpret it in different ways. "We're going to do whatever we need to do here" could be an equivocation if the project manager thinks "whatever" can include slipping the schedule while an executive thinks that means sleeping at the office.

- **Straw man**: This is a simplified, weaker version of what the person is arguing against set up so it can be torn down. For example, "The all-manual test brigade is just afraid because they are not technical and can't code."

- **Hasty generalization**: Two data points don't always make a trend. When people complain the software is "slow", ask questions and seek data.

- **Bandwagon**: An example of this is, "300,000 software testers can't be wrong; join the ranks of the certified at `CertifiedTesting.com`". Matt actually got a flyer in the mail much like this several years ago.

- **Elitism**: "Only a few of the best have risen to become Miagi-Do testers. Will you be one of the elite?"

If you listen to enough complaints about the work, you are likely to hear a lot of logical fallacies. You may be able to start listing and labeling them. This brings us to Heusser's theory of fallacies: *When people start throwing around fancy Latin words and labeling each other's arguments as fallacies, the hope of actual learning from each other slips fast.* Instead of saying, "That's a false dilemma!", try to gently explain the other choices. When you stop assuming good intent, the hope for collaboration dies.

One thing we've noticed about those logical fallacies is that they are often used to deflect responsibility. Change the subject, change the subtext, change who needs to change. In the face of that, we dare propose another way: Of personal responsibility.

How we wind up in hell and how to escape

Doctor Jordan Peterson, the Canadian clinical psychologist, once said that sitting at your mother's deathbed is a tragedy. However, there can still be some redemption in it; it could bring your family together. Now, consider a scenario where you are sitting at your mother's deathbed, and "you and all your idiot siblings are arguing." This is what he describes as hell: "You walk away from a situation like that, sick of yourself and sick of everyone else as well" (`https://www.youtube.com/watch?v=iDcOuTdjq8E`). According to Peterson, that kind of hell includes suffering from self-imposed misery, and if you work to make it the best possible outcome it could possibly be, it could still be a tragedy but maybe not hell.

Let's say you are in hell. Start with the described situations involving the lying, the deception, and the politics. Add in some double binds. Perhaps the insecure leaders see you as a threat, so if you succeed, they must find a way to attack you, and if you fail, you've failed.

So, you're in hell. Now what?

Two science fiction authors, Larry Niven and Jerry Pournelle, wrote a book about escaping hell. Titled *Inferno*, it is a modern retelling of Dante Alighieri's epic poem of the same name. In the story, the hero trudges through the nine layers of hell and brings people along with him. Norman Spinrad summarizes it this way: you escape hell "by accepting moral responsibility not merely for your past actions but even for the fate of your fellows in a manifestly unjust universe."

If you serve ten years doing software testing, someone probably owes you an apology for five of them.

You could complain and be a victim. Of course, you are a victim! The list of unjust and unfair things that have happened to us is too long to count. Yet being a victim robs you of the chance to improve. After all, if it is not your fault, it is not your obligation to fix it. And why try when some malevolent force has it out for you will just get you anyway? You could look for a guru to tell you what to do, someone to give you easy, *Shu*-level answers to your problems. That's an easy choice, and if things go wrong, you can blame the guru—you only did what you were told! But that isn't a position of personal responsibility. It won't get you out of hell. You could cut corners and lie. In the dark cultures, as we imply in this chapter, it seems reasonable—everyone else is doing it and it seems to be working. There are a few problems with this. First, in our experience, the truth tends to come out eventually. What comes up must come down. Deception in testing tends to delay the inevitable, but it is inevitable. Second, you will be a scoundrel, and if no one else knows it, you will know it. The best case then is a sort of self-misery. If you can manage to kill your conscience and not feel bad about your choices, well, we feel even more sorry for you.

Finally, there is another way: taking responsibility for yourself and others. Your responsibility means we cannot tell you, in advance, exactly what to do. Heads-down and transfer-soon is right for you. Certainly, we advise working within the system instead of fighting it. You can send an email clarifying what the boss asks and say that you are willing to comment out tests with their approval. You can try to resolve the issues before the meeting. There's no need to go out of your way to make someone look bad unless you recognize fraud, and even then, tread carefully, but get out of hell on earth. Don't stay there.

An astute reader will probably realize our recommendations may lead to loss: financial loss, reputation loss, and pain in the marketplace. That is certainly true. Responsibility for self and others probably involves self-sacrifice, and self-sacrifice usually involves giving something up.

This book is about testing. We aren't going to spend time lecturing you about finding meaning in your life by helping others, although we will say that those who remain free and unencumbered by life tend to be a little less fulfilled as they age. The responsibility of getting fed, having clothes, going to school, and growing up… these things have provided us with some of our own deepest meaning.

Just don't take responsibility beyond what you should.

Put the responsibility in the right place

A typical software career might involve dozens (hundreds? thousands?) of attempts to push the onus (duty or responsibility) for decisions onto someone else. A simple example would be a schedule foisted on a team without their knowledge, followed by pressure, evaluations, and failure if the team doesn't meet the schedule.

Early in his career, Matt worked on a large project worth millions of dollars. And, of course, it was late and buggy. It was a large systems integration/upgrade project. There were a few things we could push out a little (reports that needed to run quarterly or annually), but for the most part, there needed to be a real cutover. At the end of the project, every single technical employee was called individually into a room to discuss the root cause of why the project was late. Matt's reply was, "I'm sorry, remind me again why we ever thought it would be on time?", followed by a genuine discussion of how it was originally estimated. When it became clear the original estimators lacked the subject matter expertise and data to make accurate predictions, Matt's manager said, "Get out of here", and that was the last he ever heard of it.

In this story, the responsibility of the technical team was to estimate, but it was not their responsibility to come up with the original plan, which was not backed by data.

Likewise, while we don't agree to mark tests as run if they have not, it is possible that someone in authority takes a look at the risks and suggests skipping tests or ignoring failing automated checks. Generally, we would suggest forcing that into writing by email. This *forces* the authority to either give you more time, compromise, or take responsibility for your choices.

If an authority puts in writing to skip some testing, they are saying it is their responsibility, not yours. One perfectly reasonable response to that situation is to say, "Okay", shrug your shoulders, and leave work on time to spend time with friends and family.

Take responsibility, but don't let someone else violate your boundaries to push their responsibility onto you.

Summary

Testing is where we really find out what is going on with the software. Before that, it's easy enough to fake or cover-up. During testing, we get objective results: the software demonstrates errors or it doesn't. Unless, of course, we do an intentionally poor job, skip testing, or fake results. If you are never faced with a situation where you have an incentive to do the wrong thing, well... you're more fortunate than most.

In this chapter, we talked about philosophy, which allows us to compare things and come up with our own standards for good, better, and best. From there, we dove into ethics, including how to make difficult decisions under pressure with mismatched incentives. Finally, we talked about hell on earth and how to escape it.

The reality is that most testing involves sitting down in air-conditioned offices where food is plentiful and physical danger is nearly unheard of. We don't want to discount verbal and emotional abuse, but we do want to offer the perspective that most of the time, on some level, if we experience pain in testing, we are volunteering for it. Our goal here was to give you tools to guide you toward decision-making that would help you sleep at night in a warm comfortable bed without starving.

Part of the problem with communication is that we misunderstand each other. When John said he was "done" yesterday, he wasn't lying, he just meant that the "code was complete" but not "ready for production." Words matter, which is why we'll be talking about them more in *Chapter 15*.

We tried to hit the highlights of philosophy with this chapter to mine for the gold. If you'd like to keep digging, we have a few more books for you.

Additional readings for the serious philosopher

- *Logic and Rational Thought* by Frank Harrison covers symbolic logic and logical fallacies. It has direct application in testing complex logical statements, building logical arguments, and detecting fallacies. As an advanced undergraduate textbook, it is not an easy read, though the logical fallacy section is worth it on its own and is easy/fun.

- *Who's To Say? A Dialogue on Relativism* by Norman Melchert is an easy read; you can cover it in an afternoon.

- *Thoughts of a philosophical fighter pilot* by Rear Admiral James Stockdale explores how to be a modern stoic and not let externals get you down. He tried to live it in a prisoner-of-war camp, spending multiple years in solitary confinement and over a year in leg irons.

15
Words and Language About Work

Of the logical fallacies and tries in *Chapter 14*, the one that worries us the most is probably equivocation. Vague words can do more than defer pain – they can actively deceive. Then, when you are caught, the perpetrator can use a different definition of the word, which is more defensible. Of the problems that we discussed in *Chapter 13*, narcissism probably scares us the most. Narcissistic conversations appear to be about some objective reality (the "content") but are more likely to be about power. Even if you don't fall into either of those traps, having only genuine conversations with genuine people, you can still get messed up by having different assumptions about what the words mean.

In this chapter, we will cover the following topics:

- How context-driven testing looks at testing compared to the other schools
- Precise language and how to spot imprecise alternatives
- Wordsmatter (versus "words matter") – examples
- Process versus skill

Context-driven testing and the other schools

In *Chapter 8*, we introduced the idea of Agile software development, which is typically contrasted with Waterfall development. We also introduced context-driven testing, without providing much contrast, except as it was understood in the Waterfall and V-Model.

There are, however, various ways of thinking about the purpose and role of testing. One we'll dive into in some depth later is the idea of process-oriented testing, which can be summarized as "plan your work; work your plan." That sounds sensible, on the surface. Yet testing exists because people made a mistake; something unplanned happened. In our experience, many of the best test ideas are unplanned and emergent. Context-driven thinking allows for the possibility of learning from the process and coming up with new ideas at the moment. That allows for planning, but much less of a prescriptive, pre-defined process.

Brett Pettichord, a co-creator of the context-driven school, characterized four different ways of thinking about testing that he called the "four schools"(http://web.archive.org/web/20070311211805/http://www.io.com/~wazmo/papers/four_schools.pdf). That was before the rise of Agile software, so we'll credit and reference his work but update it a bit. You'll notice areas we have discussed in this book. What the schools tend to do is focus on some elements and ignore others.

Communication between members of the schools can be frustrating as most people don't declare an allegiance, and can use the same word to mean different things, or different words to mean the same things.

The Agile school

Everyone on the team is responsible for quality, perhaps by creating workable examples. Agile software teams are frequently blurring the lines between roles, focusing on the outcome instead of your work versus my work. Projections tend to be data-backed. Instead of studying the theory of where errors come from, or coming up with risk management scenarios, Agilists are more likely to believe that they can come up with enough meaningful scenarios by just having the customer and technical team talk to each other. This group is likely to have an interest in test automation and test-driven development. As an example of values, Agile testers are likely to consider a bug tracker a problem; bugs should be fixed as soon as they are found, or at least in the same sprint.

The DevOps or CD school

Each role is responsible for testing their work in some way. Product managers conduct external customer-facing testing about what to build, designers perform usability testing, programmers write unit tests, and before code is released, it runs through a battery of automated tests, including API and end-to-end. Generally, regression testing is only considered as a special form of one-time event, such as when trying to change payment systems. DevOps proponents (more specialized as **platform engineering**) start with an automated deployment pipeline, then add one fast test to the end that runs as part of the pipeline. These groups rarely discuss test design and are especially prone to missing test scenarios. However, they focus on mitigating problems in production with identification and rollback strategies. Platform engineering puts a focus on creating an automated test environment (server, mobile device) in the cloud based on any given commit, as well as automated checks as part of that build. As an example, a platform engineering team would look at security, accessibility, API, end-to-end, load, and performance tests as repeatable processes best automated, and then placed inside the Continuous Integration Loop.

The analytical school

Instead of talking to customers about how they would use the software, this group came from a time in history when there was a specification, applying rigorous techniques to identify test ideas, including combinatorics and pairwise approaches. The analytical school generally has a mathematical bent and is more interested in coverage, state machines, tables, and decision trees. These ideas are critical for telecommunication switching equipment, network routers, some databases, file systems, and other input/transformation/output-based software, especially without a GUI and the poor user and their ability to click anyway. Analytical school thinking seems almost scientific as it breaks software down into test exercises using techniques; who runs the tests, how and when is not the focus of the work.

The factory school

The emphasis here is on turning testing into an assembly line with fewer mistakes. It is from the factory school that we get test cases, test plans, and the idea of "turning the crank" to have humans execute testing. Factory school students are likely to do things such as count the number of bugs found per day or week to find indications about quality or measure success by the number of test cases executed in any given period. Factory school proponents want a clear, repeatable process that anyone can follow.

The quality school

When these people say QA, they mean **quality assurance**, following the life of a project to make sure good work is done at every step. To a quality school proponent, testing is "too late;" if the process were just done right, testing would be minimal, or, perhaps, not need to exist. Exactly how we assure quality by following the process typically means a set of reviews after every step. The steps tend to follow the WaterfallWaterfall, but not always. We'll talk more about QA versus testing toward the end of this chapter.

The context-driven school

This emphasizes people (and skill) as the success or failure element of a project. Factory school thinking would define the testing to be done and then, since anyone can do it, outsource it to the cheapest locale. Context-driven testing tends to merge thinking, planning, testing, learning, and informing the next test into one activity, thus the exemplar for context-driven is probably exploratory testing. At the same time, context-driven thinking considers the whole process, recognizes ideas from outside, and asks "What would work here?" This book was designed to be context-driven, as frustrating as that might be for our publishers, who were hoping we would plan our work and work our plan! Given that the context of this book is different, we ended up doing a little of both.

Some time ago, Matt was talking to an Agile tester, complaining the software he had been brought in to work on was untestable. It was a report, pulled out of a database, generated by **SQL**. "*What are you talking about?*", Matt asked, as he explained how to pull the live data from the database into cells, calculate totals, and set up fake data. Alternatively, someone else could take the requirements and create their own SQL, and the two could run and compare results. After about 15 seconds came the realization: by "untestable," the programmer meant they could not press a button and have things happen and get test results. Furthermore, they saw no way to write such a program. By "testable" they meant "test-automatable."

Even that view, of test automation, which is prevalent in the Agile, DevOps, and factory schools, only automates a small portion of the entire test process, as we discussed in *Chapter 4*. Those *automated checks* don't add any value until the first time they run without an error. At that time, they don't add any value – until there is a regression bug. And regression bugs are only a small percentage of defects in the entire system.

The premise and value system Matt was talking about were different enough that they used the same word yet meant something entirely different.

One thing you can do to overcome this is explicitly state where you are coming from. That doesn't mean you have to wear an "*I'm context-driven!*" T-shirt to meetings, nor obnoxiously fight over words. We certainly don't advocate correcting other people's language. However, you can define your own words clearly.

Several professional groups have clear definitions of words. Bugs, defects, faults, errors, tests, test cases – they have definitions to use. We can see two benefits from this type of effort. First, there is less chance you'll use the same word to mean different things. Second, there is less effort spent arguing about definitions; people start on the same page.

Having said that, arguing has some merit. By declaring what you mean when you use a term, you create the potential for groups to learn, grow, and change. Rigorous definition may be good, but the medical term for stiff definitions that never change is **rigor mortis**: the stiffening of death.

One of the benefits of context-driven thinking is that it can embrace, adapt, and extend to match others. A context-driven thinker can operate in an Agile or DevOps environment, but then it becomes even more important to use precise language.

Damian Synadinos, who we will introduce later, puts it this way: "*The words we use to label the problem might all affect our perception of the problem.*" We will go further: the paradigm we use to make sense of the situation will impact our perception of the situation, and what to do about it. Understanding where other people come from will help us find the language to use to express where we are coming from – and what we propose to do.

Precise language

You ask the boss what to do: should you test more, fix bugs, or release the software? They say you need to think outside the box.

Wait, what?

The government agency who ordered your custom software complains it doesn't work on their tablet. The boss says this should all be clear in the contract, so you check the specification, where it says very clearly "Users shall use the input device to enter values, search, and update. All elements shall be Create, Read, Update, Delete complete."

The input device? Is that a keyboard? Mouse? Tablet? We don't know.

Most spoken languages, but especially English, are ambiguous. You can play a game, play guitar – you can play a role in a play. You can even play the fool. Each of those uses is different. Usually, we can figure out what the meaning is, but often, words are open to different interpretations. If you want a great example, consider the requirement that the software "handles errors." This could be as simple as a pop-up message stating that something went wrong, to as complex as a schema to back out transactions and try again, several times, over a period of days. Matt even once consulted for companies doing federal funds transfers, and, ironically, his role included handling errors and describing the complex back-out retry process.

In our experience, imprecise words sneak in a few different ways:

- **To defer decisions**: In the input device example, the people writing the specification couldn't agree, so they just wrote something down to call the contract done. The real decision would need to be made later.

- **To delegate decisions**: In the earlier example, when the boss refused to decide, they pushed it on the team. If the team made a mistake, the boss could then credibly say, "I never made that decision; this is the first I've heard of it." If things go well, they can take credit.

- **On accident**: The words are either open to interpretation or regional dialect or life experiences are different enough to cause problems. The first time Matt was asked if he wanted a pop someone from the Midwest, he looked at her awkwardly and said, "No, but I'd like a Coke if you don't mind." Now, Matt lives in the Midwest, and he still calls it soda.

- **To equivocate**: With equivocation, the speaker intentionally uses words the audience will take away. If they are called on their misleading words, the speaker can say they meant the more defensible term. When executives at automakers said something like, "You don't understand, the vehicle needs to pass emissions tests, and it needs to do so by the end of the quarter. Are we clear?" they can credibly claim they never meant the test results should be faked. They can even be outraged!

Except, of course, it's bull. All of it. Even the accident. While some of it may be unavoidable, we believe the majority is due to a lack of care, and a failure to learn the background of the other person.

The alternative to ambiguity is precision.

Precision in a non-scientific language can be difficult. Try to define one word, and you'll see the definition consists of six more. Of those, two will need to be defined:

- **Avoid circular definitions**: Use a word or term itself in the definition – for example, calling a test plan a "document that plans testing."

- **Build decision tables**: Long prose descriptions tend to have combinatorics in them. Break out the spreadsheets and list the possibilities. Go through the list, and eventually, you may find conditions that are not covered – or covered twice.

- **Ask questions**: One requirement document said, "*The software will respond within fifteen seconds*", yet reports took 2 to 3 minutes. The decision to fix it was to put up a pop-up where reports were being generated. So long as the pop-up came up within 15 seconds, that was good enough. There was no easy fix here, but this wasn't exactly a transparent choice – it was more of an equivocation.

- **Read everything and play the worst case**: Most of the time, we talk about fair play, good intent, and good faith. When looking for ambiguity, assume bad faith. Get cynical. Assume the author of the document, the leader of the conversation, and the person explaining is trying to trick you.

Assuming bad faith is exhausting. We also don't find it to be fun. The goal here is not to make anyone look bad or end any friendships. Instead, it is to train the people we are talking with to think through their ideas and express them clearly. So, be up-front. If the team has been burned by unclear terms lately, explain the problem, and that you are going to play critic's advocate for a bit. Help people work through their thinking; don't attack them.

Over time, try to get the team to have aligned intent and outcomes. Shared understanding, agreement, and alignment will go a lot further than having the same silly arguments again and again. One way to get there is to understand the intent of the feature – what the customer is trying to accomplish. When the intent is not accomplished, all the different ways to interpret things in the world don't matter.

This kind of thinking about how we communicate is a sort of self-test we can perform. Get the people in the organization to think this way, and they can test their work, including their running code.

Beyond precision (the text itself) we still have other factors to consider, including subtext, context, and imprecision. A catch-all term for this is "wordsmatter," which no, is not a typo.

Wordsmatter

Our friend, Damian Synadinos, does a series of talks titled "wordsmatter," with no space between words and matter. We can see the different meanings. Jerry Weinberg, our mentor, was fond of the example of the term "*Mary had a little lamb*;" by changing the key focus word, we could change the meaning.

"*MARY* had a little lamb" – as opposed to someone else, who does not.

"Mary *HAD* a little lamb" – this is past tense. What happened to it, is it missing or dead?

"Mary had a *LITTLE* lamb" – did she eat it? Why was it small? Was it smaller than the ones the other children had?

"Marry had a little *LAMB*" – do the other children have different animals?

Here, we have a five-word sentence that is one of the most common and well-known in the English language, and we have found a half-dozen different possible *subtexts*, or underlying themes, for the words. Our writing has the initial text, the *subtext*, and the *context*. The circumstances that form the setting for whatever we are discussing, so it can be understood, are the *context*, from which **context-driven testing** takes its name. We pay careful attention to *context* and *subtext*. For example, when a customer is defining work, they may often say something like "...And don't forget to do (seemingly unrelated thing)," such as creating an automated smoke test for the next major release of a project. We advise digging into that and understanding the importance of it. It will probably be something you do not want to do. That is why they have to keep bringing it up, as you keep giving signals you aren't going to do it. These can be subtle; you might not even realize you are saying it. That is how *subtext* works. It might not be related to your expertise. Unless you can explicitly get it waived as not your responsibility, we recommend doing it first. In our experience, when a customer says, "*Don't forget to do (x),*" if you do everything else but do not get X done, the customer is likely to feel you did not listen to them.

Do not say, "*We didn't get around to it*" or "*We didn't have time to do it.*" If the customer calls it out explicitly, then the subtext indicates that the work must be done. Either do it (first!) or find a way to get it waived. In writing.

The benefits of being imprecise

Anyone who has worked with us, or who has read a great deal of our work, is likely to wonder at this point, "*Wait, Matt and Michael, what are you talking about? You're incredibly imprecise. That is practically your brand!*"

And in a way, that is true.

Communication theory teaches us that messages have three components: the sender, the receiver, and the message itself. If you say "Mary had a little lamb" to someone in the city who eats lamb routinely, they might take your message differently than a shepherd. There are a few ways to get around this. One is to be more precise with your words: "Mary had a small lamb she is raising as a pet." Another is to understand where the other person is coming from, using words they will understand. At conferences, we frequently say something like, "Don't forget, the thing with the stuff is at 7:00 P.M. at the place." This is at least partially a joke. Generally, when we say it, it might be something like a board meeting for a non-profit, which all members are welcome to attend, yet in practice tend to be board members and those with key initiatives to represent. This style of conversation only works when the sender and receiver are well-aligned. Indeed, it is a social sign of alignment. Being aligned allows groups to skip the awkward fights over definitions, and instead, we use short-hand language. "*The project needs to be exactly like OSU, only we are changing the width of the fields to match their database*" is the sort of thing we might have heard at one project. In a sentence, the two understand how to get started: fork the code from OSU, check the database definitions for the new client, adjust the record sizes to match, and source the data from the new database. An outsider would have a dozen questions, or worse, not ask questions and get frequently stuck.

As a result, online, we both tend to use a sort of folksy charm in our language. It helps people connect, but we do run the risk of our audience misunderstanding us. Given that the various communities don't even agree at all about the meaning of the word "test," there is a fair bit of room for misunderstanding. One alternative is to spend half of our writing defining our terms, as you see in academic journals. Another is to have a sort of cheat sheet for the organization that explains how we see the world. Here's a quick cheat sheet for this book:

Most People Say	...But We Say	Because
Test automation	Tool-assisted testing/checking	What humans do while testing is so wildly different than what computers do.
High-quality software	Something specific about what the software does	Show what you mean, don't tell. Avoid labels.
Developer	Programmer	Anyone working in the process of software is a developer.
Tester	Person doing testing	We want to meet teams where they are in a variety of contexts.
QA	Oh my gosh, anything else	
Black-box	Testing as a customer	Effective testers use every bit of information they can, including the internals.
Clear-box	Testing as a programmer	Focus on the style instead of an abstract concept.
Test plan	Here's what we're going to do	Conflate the idea of the document with what we will do, and when we'll do it. This may cause an artificial separation between programming and testing.
Test case	Test idea or thing to test	Differentiates away from a poisoned word.
Best practices	**Heuristics, patterns, practices, my favorite practices, ideas that have worked for me**	`https://context-driven-testing.com/`

Table 15.1 – Common terms versus those in this book

By now, you can see that the words we choose influence how people think about things. If we say, "best practice" people look to someone else, some authority, to tell them what to do, believing there is "one right way." On the other hand, terms such as "heuristics" and "ideas that have worked for me" push the worker to examine the context, see if the practice will work, and take personal responsibility for their decision. The term "patterns" in a software context is particularly illustrative of this. A pattern resolves a system of competing elements – it is a "solution." However, it also introduces new problems! Patterns should only be used when you have the problem the pattern solves, when the solution is worth the cost of the investment, and when the value system of the team indicates the new problems are not as big as the problem they solve. The **Agile Manifesto**, for example, told us to focus on working software *over* comprehensive documentation, that "While we find value in the items on the left, we value the items on the right more." It's certainly conceivable that a government project might value comprehensive documentation – perhaps a mission to Mars or a nuclear test simulation. The authors of the manifesto were expressing a preference for their style of work on their preferred projects – competitive, market-driven projects with customers who paid with their wallets.

Note how the choice of words influences how we think about the work, and even the work itself – that is, how the work is framed. One common way to look at testing is simply a thing that has to be done to get the work out. If that's the case, then all someone has to do is (something mumble), then check the box that the software was tested. If that is the case, then it makes sense to reduce costs by eliminating testing.

Choose your words wisely.

The list in *Table 15.1* is designed to get you thinking about terms that can create a mindset that leads to poor outcomes. We suggest you make your own; we'd love to share them as comments. We've created a post on the Excelon Blog (`https://xndev.com/blog/`) called *Chapter 15, Word Lists* where you can add your own.

Two of the bigger ways words can frame conversations are with a process mindset, and with tooling and automation. We'll examine those words next.

Process versus skill

An accounting class might discuss teams as either a cost center, a profit center, or an investment center. A cost center is simply the cost of doing business and should be kept to a minimum. A profit center has expenses but also generates revenue. Cutting a salesperson back from a profit center will decrease expenses, but if it decreases revenue more, it is a mistake. Investment centers have costs and profits, but also save some of the money to invest in a positive cash return.

The most simplistic view is that the sales staff are a profit center while the people building the software are all cost. Thanks to **Software-as-a-Service (SaaS)**, companies are increasingly able to see development as an investment. After all, development creates the software, which is itself valued as a projection of future cash flows. Still, testing as a discrete activity is likely seen as a cost.

For decades, we've seen the idea of testing as too late touted loudly in the literature. This idea here is that with a stable, predictable, defined process, we could *prevent* errors. After all, "Defects become more expensive to fix the later phase they are discovered." We'd push back quite a bit against that. From what we can tell, that idea came from a paper by Boehm and Pappacio, *Understanding and Controlling Software Costs*, and was popularized by Steve McConnell. The numbers in the examples tend to be more illustrations and thought experiments than hard data. Even if they were hard data, they were written at a time in history when calendar time and phase were interchangeable – the days of the Waterfall. Consider a Waterfall process running on a mainframe in 1988 when that paper was written. That process might have 2 months each of requirements, design, programming, integration tests, and system tests, and 2 weeks to deploy and work through issues. Now, think about an Agile team doing that cycle in 2 days. A problem introduced in requirements and caught in programming by the Waterfall team might take more meetings and signoffs to fix than one caught in production by the Agile team, especially if they are using the mitigation techniques to enable DevOps as discussed in this book.

Now, think about how "quality"-oriented processes evolve.

Most "quality" processes are built on past mistakes. If the requirements are bad, the organization asks for a requirements review. In a Scrum context, if the stories are bad, the whole team needs to review and agree the stories are good enough to go forward, in the sprint planning meeting. If the stories aren't actionable, a Scrum team might have a "kickoff" meeting to get product, test, and programming together to come to a shared agreement before things start. If the acceptance criteria are unclear, leading to arguments about edge cases and what the software *should* do, the team can require defined acceptance criteria at the beginning. All of these are a little investment in quality up front to defer pain later. Sounds good so far, doesn't it?

The problem comes when we have an error that occurs once and might never occur again, and we add a required check. Every story needs X style of testing now. If the team does all the required activities, delivery can take two, three, or four times as long. This is where we get the "DevOps" and "CD" organizations, which can take 2 or 3 weeks from code-finished to code-in-production. Another approach is to make a wish list of things the teams should do, which is widely ignored.

The alternative is skill development.

From the outside, a skilled chess player's moves look like chaos, like winging it. In reality, the chess player is tracking several independent variables in their mind, in real time, thinking perhaps two, three, four, up to seven moves ahead. Given the number of pieces on the board, seven moves will contain tens of millions of possibilities. Chess players get better by playing chess, over and over, while software testers get better by testing software. In *Chapter 12*, we introduced the idea that juniors simply do not see that the possible combinations are errors and finish earlier because they have fewer test ideas. Skill in testing matters.

Unless we are careful with what our words imply, we can be trapped by the dominant paradigm in the business today: process. The process wants us to document everything, to have a checklist for all the possible test ideas, and plan the testing so we can pass it off to more junior people and have less risk.

Let's speak clearly. Without skill, the process is an exercise in futility. A manager can create a template for stories, listing the project, who the author is, who the reviewer is, the story name, the story description, and so on. A manager can create a process that requires these things to be filled out, and reviewed, including acceptance criteria. A manager can create a checklist for the review. But filling the forms out well and having the work come together to be good software? That takes skill. **Context-driven testing** puts the tester in the seat of the decision maker on what to test with limited time and with ambiguity and conditions of uncertainty. This book provides you with the tools to identify risks, make the approach transparent, and provide management with tools to steer and feedback on performance. Still, the process takes skill.

Meanwhile, organizational tenure is going down. We also have the senior tester problems from *Chapter 12* – the system tends to look at them as problems because they cause delays. What is the solution?

If you've read this far, you can probably guess our answer: be very clear about your words, be transparent about your work, learn to predict the outcome of different approaches… and be right.

Predicting outcomes, knowing what will happen before it happens, and figuring things out a few moves before they do happen, will take a lot of skill. It will be more than a little bit like playing chess. It will also resemble something else we described in this book – modeling a finite state machine. When other people with a different perspective start asking questions, model the possible approaches, predict the outcome, and explain why you think the context-driven approach leads to a better outcome. Note that the context-driven approach is fundamentally humanistic and based on the good judgment of the people doing the work. The organization may not value that, but if that's the case, you likely don't want to work there anyway. Organizations that take this more humanistic approach tend to win in the marketplace in the long run.

One extreme example of this process versus skill problem is thinking about test tooling.

Testing and checking

We tried to be careful with our words in the first few chapters, avoiding the term **test automation** in favor of **test tooling**, or **automated test execution and evaluation**. As we see it, actual testing is a process that gathers information about the system, makes inferences about proper behavior, conducts experiments on software under test, and then uses the results of those experiments to inform the next test. The process then needs evaluation and reporting. The entire process, from input to result, is testing. At the time of writing writing, computers cannot do that.

One test training program, **Rapid Software Testing** (**RST**), takes the extreme approach of using a separate word for what computers do, referring to it as **checking**. In the world of RST, checking is, *"The process of making evaluations by applying algorithmic decision rules to specific observations of a product"* (see `https://www.satisfice.com/blog/archives/856`). This is what computers do: anticipate what a problem might be, set up the software, run it to a point, and check for that potential error. This lacks design, learning, and adaptation, along with any elements of evaluation and reporting that are not planned up-front. By emphasizing those activities, RST's chosen language reinforces skill and gives skill prominence.

While this book has tried to make a distinction between the parts of testing that computers are good at, and the human parts, we still use common vernacular, such as unit tests. It seems a bit much to try to change an existing term of art. We do find unit tests developed in the TDD style the most interesting because they evolve with the work as part of a discovery process. This process can involve learning and adjusting. To TDD proponents, the regression test suite that pops out of the end is an interesting side-benefit, not the main goal.

Before we leave wordsmatter, we would like to cover one more bugbear: quality assurance, or QA. To do that, we need to talk about Ken Pier.

Yes, we can assure quality

Both authors of this book, Matthew and Michael, had the opportunity to learn about software testing by working directly with Ken Pier at Socialtext (`https://xndev.com/2015/04/goodbye-to-a-giant/`). Ken wrote the Microcode for the Xerox Dorado, the second commercial personal computer, and went on to spend 20 more years working at Xerox's **Palo Alto Research Center** (**PARC**). You may recognize PARC from such inventions as the computer mouse, windowed operating system, object-oriented programming, and the Ethernet protocols that came to drive the internet.

Ken also had one other valuable point of reference in that he was in Silicon Valley when the personal computer revolution happened. While today when we think of Silicon Valley we likely think of major websites and applications, in the 1970s, Silicon was literal, with Hewlett Packard leading the conversation about physical chips on Silicon. Ken once explained that the term "tester," at the time, was a manual role to physically solder chips onto a board and see if a configuration worked. Indeed, "smoke testing" was putting everything together, flipping a switch, and looking to see if the pieces created smoke. This would be an overload, which was bad.

Around that time, a new role appeared, with someone to work more abstractly in software to check if the code was fit for use. The person worked in an air-conditioned office, wore professional attire, had a college degree, and did not want to get their hands dirty. We don't mean that metaphorically, but literally – hardware testers got dirty assembling parts. To differentiate this new role companies chose to call the role "quality assurance."

Testers find bugs and often expect someone else to decide if those bugs are to be fixed. Thus, they cannot assure quality. The term QA has ties to manufacturing, where it usually involves designing and monitoring software processes to prevent errors (thus the perspective of the quality school). Over the years, there has been a concerted effort to reject the term QA and use the term tester – or, at least, to reframe QA as "quality assistance", "quality analyst," or, as Pete Walen has called it "question asker."

We have mixed feelings.

First, there is little risk that, today, any decision-maker believes quality is the responsibility of QA. If the question is "Why didn't QA find that bug?" and the answer is "We did, and it was low priority, and product management chose to add features instead," that is usually the end of the conversation. Beyond that, in our work, we focus on understanding what we call **commander's intent**, to understand what management would decide if they had time to be fully briefed. QAs who understand the commander's intent can skip heavy documentation, waiting, and conversations for priority. If they do it right, there is no problem.

Second, and more importantly, QA is something we can do.

The whole tempest in a teapot seems to come about from a misunderstanding of the word's meaning. Here's the definition as of 2023 according to the Oxford English Dictionary:

Assurance (noun)

/ə'ʃʊərəns/

[countable] a statement that something will certainly be true or will certainly happen, particularly when there has been doubt about it. Synonym guarantee, promise

> *They called for assurances that the government is committed to its education policy.*

Unemployment seems to be rising, despite repeated assurances to the contrary.

Notice that assurance is simply a statement that something is true or will happen.

Let's consider a scenario.

Mike Pettee lives one town over from Matt, about 15 minutes away in Otsego, Michigan. Matt has made the trip to Otsego hundreds, thousands of times in the 20 years he has lived in Allegan, Michigan. He knows the road and timing by heart. Mike's wife Amber is trying to plan dinner and wants to know for certain what time he will arrive. Matt says he'll plan to arrive by 5:30 P.M. and certainly will be there by 6 P.M.

Did Matt offer his assurance? Why yes, he did.

Does Matt control every aspect? Why, no, of course not. His car could break down; he could get a flat. In the space between Allegan and Otsego, right about the Moose Lodge, there is a cell phone dead zone, which could cause more delay.

When testers say they can't assure quality because they don't control everything, well, goodness, nobody controls everything. Of course, something could go wrong. When Matt gets his flat tire, in the dead zone, and has to hail someone to take him to the Moose Lodge where he calls a tow truck, and then calls the Pettees, what is going to happen? Are the Pettees going to be upset about Matt's lack of assurance? Why of course not. That would be silly. Most people realize there is a difference between assurance and insurance. Likewise, while the dictionary lists a guarantee as a promise, assurance is missing a key part of a guarantee – which is the remedy for failure to comply.

Software testers who are called QA could be put in awkward positions. For example, if the code is not fixed, because the bug is not worth fixing, how could they *assure quality*?

But that is an easy one. Just declare you cannot. "*My role is quality assurance; I don't think that's a quality decision, but it's not mine to make.*" This happens on occasion in manufacturing, where the QA believes something is non-compliant and is overruled; companies have a policy for it. In the regulated industries there may be signatures, documents, and processes, but someone can decide to move forward. Being able to say "*My role is quality assurance; I don't think that's a quality decision, but it's not mine to make*" or writing it in an email could provide career coverage, but more importantly, it could cause someone else to reconsider the decision. Done well, it could materially impact the outcome for the better. So, what is the problem, exactly?

There might not be a problem either way, tester or QA. The problem would come without really understanding the words and their impact, thinking through them, and consistently sending a message aligned with those words.

"Words...", as Damian Synadinos might say, "*words smatter.*"

They really do, because, in review, Damian pointed out that he meant the term another way – as a smattering of words (`https://www.youtube.com/watch?v=A92ACXV2TGc`).

This ambiguity thing might be a problem.

Summary

We ended our dance around test and quality by talking about how communication can go wrong. One of the simplest ways is when we argue past each other, using the same words but meaning different things. In this chapter, we started with some of the assumptions about meaning in the different schools of testing, then talked about the benefits of precise language, and then provided some examples of how to influence word choice.

Our dance around test and quality is coming to an end. In the next chapter, we'll use what we've put together to discuss the mobile test strategy, take a look at the uses of AI for testing, and review a few of our core ideas.

Further reading

For a deep dive into ambiguity, consider Zwicky and Sadock's *Ambiguity Tests and How to Fail Them* (`http://www.web.stanford.edu/~zwicky/ambiguity-tests-and-how-to-fail-them.pdf`). This is not for the faint of heart; Arnold Zwicky is an emeritus professor of linguistics who has been working in the field for nearly 60 years. His classic paper was published in the journal Syntax and Semantics in 1965, was president of the Linguistic Society of America, and is a fellow of the American Academy of Arts and Sciences.

16
Testing Strategy Applied

Our original outline ended with our discussion of words and language in *Chapter 15*. At one point, we discussed what the last chapters should be. The broader ideas for this chapter evolved as we wrote the book and asked, *"What's changed in the past year, and what is missing?"* One of the prominent changes was the release of public **large language models** (**LMMs**), such as **OpenAI**. While knowledge of their practical application is limited, we felt remiss not to include them somehow.

Slowly, the structure of the chapter took form. We could apply the ideas in the book to two domains—a reference implementation of a test strategy for a mobile application or a critical examination of the use of **artificial intelligence** (**AI**) in testing. By the end of the chapter, you should have a greater understanding of how we think about testing so that if someone asks you to develop a test strategy, you can walk through the process.

In this chapter, we're going to cover the following main topics:

- A sample mobile test strategy
- AI in software testing
- A few thoughts to leave with

A mobile test strategy example

A few years ago, we were surprised when mass-developed applications did not have web pages; they were developed mobile-first. Today, we would say that mobile applications are the dominant style for new software development. Yet our book doesn't spend a great deal of time and effort on them. So, before we close, we decided to design a hypothetical test program for a large mobile app. We'll start with what makes mobile application testing different, describe a system of forces, and then describe a test strategy that addresses those forces.

Let's start with some bullet points on why mobile application testing is different and challenging:

- Mobile apps have a wider variety of form factors, operating systems, and screen resolutions.

- In the laptop web application market, access to the internet is stable. People do not experience much downtime. When they do, it might be during a thunderstorm when the power is out and everything is down. Mobile applications move from Wi-Fi hotspots with high bandwidth to cell towers between cell towers. They hit bandwidth limits for their carriers or sometimes turn bandwidth off for apps. Roving bandwidth can be slim to none; dead spots still exist not very far from populated areas or with certain carriers.

- While some tools can create both Android and mobile versions, some companies still maintain separate Android and iOS teams.

- While it is possible to make mobile apps that don't really connect to the internet, such as a video game, most mobile applications use APIs to send and retrieve data from back-end databases or to interact with the broader world. Even a simple stand-alone video game might publish the scores of players, download advertisements, or allow in-game purchasing. That means the application uses APIs. At the same time, the iOS mobile application uses APIs and a website or the Android mobile app might use the same APIs. That creates a timing problem when someone wants to roll out changes to one but that change is not yet ready for the other consumers of the API.

- Common solutions to the outlined problem are **semantic API versioning** and coordinated rollouts. Semantic versioning allows a tool to specify a major version of the API and for the API to publish breaking changes as a new major version. This radically reduces the risk of breaking changes. Yet it is still a common practice to do coordinated rollouts to break API changes, trying to "time" the website, iOS, and Android versions. For that matter, the company could have Mobile Watch, Oculus, Meta-Wayfarer, Automobiles, and other **Internet of Things (IoT)** objects that use the API as well.

- Mobile devices have new failure modes, such as heat warnings, battery exhaustion, loss of Wi-Fi signal, and slowness due to a lack of memory or too many processes running at one time. Some of these may be difficult to impossible to run on a simulator. As a result, some amount of human exploration of real physical devices tends to find defects that automation and simulators do not.

- As of this publication, mobile applications generally are published in a store. These stores can take two days to two weeks to review. Deploying a new version involves writing release notes of what changed, creating a new version number, and possibly (if the functionality has significantly changed) eliminating the reviews. Groups with fantastic reviews may want to keep reviews, running the risk that they are out of date, while app developers with poor reviews may want a periodic clearing of old reviews. Apps can also be "sideloaded" directly into the device.

- The basic modalities for a mobile app are native, web-based (through a browser), and hybrid, where parts of a browser window run inside a native application.

For this list of issues, the easy thing for testing to do is to have versions of APIs and a hybrid app that can be tested in a browser window sized to match the display of a common phone (or tablet). Sadly, life is rarely easy.

We'll describe a sample mobile application that is essentially a combination of things we have tested before in a complex ecosystem and then propose a strategy for it.

Our sample mobile app

The Maximo Toothbrush is a Bluetooth-enabled, electrically charged toothbrush that can interact with a phone to send signals about the length of the brushing and the area of the teeth brushed. The mobile phone app, in iOS and Android as separate builds, requires users to log in with a popular mobile authenticator tied to an email or a social media account. Users can use the app to see an image of teeth, with coverage increasing in brightness until an area of the mouth is *covered*. This is done through a camera in the phone combined with AI image recognition and brush/mouth recognition. Users can track their brushing progress by week and month, purchase games to gamify the brushing process, post their success on social media, and even report their brushing quality to insurance companies to reduce premiums. There is a children's version of the app that allows parents to monitor progress; the children can earn points to collect virtual objects to decorate their avatars.

The preceding list isn't all that different from tools that exist today, though there are a few from different domains. Here's our breakdown of the things to test:

- The major subsystems are the web app, mobile app(s), API, toothbrush mechanicals, and toothbrush software (camera and Bluetooth interactions). We'll consider the mechanicals (duration of battery, number of charges, and so on) outside of our scope here. Just for grins (pun intended), we'll have a kids' app and a version of the kids' app that works for a console system such as the Nintendo Switch.

- For our purposes, the company does not have versioned APIs and the app is native with two different builds, one for the iPhone and one for iOS.

- Programmer testing, unit testing, as well as database testing, will occur at a low level. There will be operational risk management, data center testing, planning for cutover in case of a data center disruption, and so on. We'll focus our testing on the first bullet point.

Once you understand the dynamics of the software project, it is time to design a test process to match. On real systems, these evolve in sync with the software effort, but we have a chance to step back and design one to match without having to worry about the "as-is" or evolved state.

Designing a test program

Beyond testing each individual component, it becomes hard to detangle software engineering from coordination. We will try.

For the toothbrush, the main element of testing is the interaction between the device and the phone. By creating a virtual phone and virtual device, it is possible to simulate the device, drive it, and observe the interactions between the two. Once unit testing is done, the testing activity exercises the new functionality as it is used, as well as considers *abuse cases*. From a testing perspective, the most interesting cases will be those that cause the software to fail, seize up, time out, and so on. Testing these extreme cases, sometimes called **soap opera testing**, also tends to provide broad general coverage of the intended use. This book focuses on software, so we will not get into testing how the brush head works, but there is work to be done with just the software interactions. If the simulator (running in software on a computer) remains an accurate rendition of what the mobile app does, new toothbrushes can be released on a schedule set by the hardware team. This does require coordination for major hardware and mobile updates, along with planning for backward compatibility. The team will develop automated **smoke** checks to walk through the most common use cases, then test the entire system by hand before major releases, using either the web app or an instrument that simulates it and shows signals. The web app might have a debug to provide both.

The *web app* will include a frontend that is designed to run independently, which can be checked by humans. That frontend will call APIs, which can be created using service virtualization, a test environment that runs in the cloud, or in the staging environment. For each micro-feature, a human will explore the work, either before or after the commit. Once the code is in version control, it will be picked up and checked by continuous integration. To do this sort of automated checking, the company needs the ability to set up a staging server in the cloud with a known URL and a way to point the web app to that test environment to make API calls. The web app also needs to be tested against a variety of browsers (at the time of writing, Edge, Chrome, Firefox, and Safari for Mac). The team described an expected level of support, and testing, by browser, determining how much time they will invest in each.

The *APIs* can be tested by contract tests. The APIs themselves may call other APIs, so the team wrote a dependency mapper back to the databases. This makes it possible to create a **constellation** of dependencies in the cloud for any API at any time. Developers can then load up a database with the **Canonical Test dataset** to run exploration, add new API-level tests for the change, and push the change into version control, where continuous integration will run the API through a check of the expected behaviors. This can happen again when the code is merged into the trunk. Non-breaking changes can roll out at any time; more complex changes require coordination. The three major teams (iOS, Android, and Nintendo) are each responsible for testing their changes. Major API changes will be rolled out using a blue-green deployment, so they can be cut over and rolled back quickly. Without version control, the largest API changes may need to use named APIs, where the version of the mobile app is embedded into the API name. Over time, this becomes untenable, and the team will need to move toward API versioning.

The *mobile apps* will have to check the code that runs during the Continuous Integration loop, just as the API tests. These can include two levels of tooling: frontend checks that use mocked API endpoints and end-to-end checks of the entire system as a system deployed in the cloud. Continuous integration will create an artifact that is a mobile build, which can be picked up by a human and slide-loaded onto a physical device for exploration. In all these cases, authentication and payment will be mocked out. A final check can run against a more robust staging server during the releases that require integrated coordination.

The *kids' app* will have a separate development organization with its own test function. The structure of the teams will determine how they perform testing, with app functionality, avatars, gamification/games, push to social media, and the rewards center all separate. These functions are highly interdependent, as the games can show the avatars so can the core app functionality. As a result, the team has a traditional scrum/scaled agile framework case with tooling running under continuous integration all the time, but there's a two-week coordination phase at the end of the six weeks of development. The mobile apps work on a similar cadence.

The preceding examples cover the basic functions. Accessibility, load, internationalization, and security are also serious considerations that are done via human exploration for new changes, as well as runs as part of the continuous integration process. In practice, running all the tests all the time tends to delay the builds without adding much value. One fix for that is to run them less often or rotate them. In our example, we'll run everything on new pushes to a branch, but we'll only run these tests twice a week in master, as they have already been checked on a branch and are unlikely to regress. After all, if testing is about risk management, then the cost of cloud computing resources for all those CI runs should be a consideration!

This chapter doesn't provide us with the space to cover each system in depth, but we'll likely identify the features, the depth of coverage provided by the checks, the gap, and the cadence of deployment. Then, we can develop systems to mitigate that gap. That might involve making lists of risks and deployment cadence. In some cases, teams just won't write automated checks. It might be too hard, the technology might be too new to be driven, or the old checks might go out of date when we have a major user interface change and they are simply abandoned. Sometimes too many defects slip through the checks—they are a decent smoke test but just not comprehensive enough. In those cases, it's time to go back to listing the functionality, documenting coverage, and creating maps to testing dashboards to plan the work before every major deployment, then coordinate test environments, versions, and deployments.

Mobile system coordination and deployment

The example sounds easy. Just make a list of all the things, make sure people do their jobs, and everything will be just fine. It is not. The CI system, running on simulators, is likely to lure the users into a false sense of security. Meanwhile, it is likely to throw false errors. These are real errors in the sense that the software is not doing what we expected it to do last week, but they are false because having it do something else was the fundamental nature of our change.

To be successful, someone needs to track the changes that matter and coordinate the teams. When we have more than half a dozen teams in more than one continent and mobile apps that, if mis-launched, will take a week to re-launch (waiting for the store), there's typically a pre-release testing stage. We are not excited about this and see it as a temporary step. However, when the impact of a problem is high, when we cannot simply push a fix in an hour or two when non-versioned APIs are part of the solution, sometimes we still need to deliver on a cadence. The release train metaphor can be slightly helpful here, as every eight weeks or so, the train leaves the station. That allows for six weeks of independent development by teams and two weeks of coordination and testing. If a feature isn't ready, it isn't merged into the trunk. If that means that at that exact time, the train leaves the station, the change will need to go on the next train. From a lean perspective, one goal would be to get testing down to a day and the number of cycles down to (ideally) one, perhaps two. Once that's done, the difficult work is coordinating breaking API changes, which can be fixed through technical solutions. Versioned APIs allow the teams to essentially deploy separately, with only coordination needed to roll out unique and major features that crosscut through the entire application.

Our goal with this section was to show how we have combined the strategies in this book to address testing across systems and sub-systems, as well as where the tools in this book (mind-maps, test dashboards, risk lists, and lean metrics) can be plugged in for improvement.

Now that we've taken you this far, what's missing?

You can pause for a moment or two before we go on. We'll even put an image here to take up a little space so you don't accidentally jump to the next section.

Figure 16.1: A placeholder so you don't read ahead. Image credit: Julie Heusser

The human element

The strategy we outlined in the preceding section, for the most part, could be used by any of a dozen software groups we know of. Remove the IoT component and that number jumps to hundreds. Yet many of those groups struggle with software quality. They have **continuous integration and continuous deployment** (**CI/CD**) runs that take too long and test too many builds, which break too often when the problems are not actually bugs. The exceptions are the holes in coverage that no one knows about or wants to talk about.

The preceding description isn't terribly wrong. However, it is missing some key details about where our testing strategy comes from and how it evolves. Let's look at the example strategy (the toothbrush mobile app tool) from a different angle.

As we see it, there are five major parts to the testing:

- **Each sub-system team comes up with a way to test their features independently**: By subsystem, we mean the web app, the mobile apps (there are several), the API, and the brush software components. It's also possible to structure the work with pure, multi-stack feature teams, but that isn't the case here. To test their components independently, each team will use the techniques in the book, both for new features and regression.

- **Each sub-system team has a way of releasing candidate testing**: Each product group will develop its own feature map, its own way of measuring coverage, and ways to visualize and publish it. In a work-from-the-office environment, the real-time coverage map is on display in the team room. For remote workers, it is a web page. The groups develop documents with the recipes for how to test. Most importantly, these need to be done with skill, consistently used, and explained to new hires. "If you don't write it down, it doesn't exist" has three extensions: "If you write it down and no one reads it, that's worse", "Even if they do read it, everything that you write down creates a maintenance obligation", and "If you write too much down, people will not be able to figure out what matters." Comprehensive is the enemy of comprehensible. As a result, people need skills to identify what needs to be tested, model it, and describe it in ways that can be heard. Then they need the skills to figure out when and how to document that.

- **Continuous integration, artifacts, and test environments**: The test process can be accelerated by pushing regression testing into the build. This process can also deal with test environments and sample test data.

- **Ancillary testing**: Accessibility, load, security, and internationalization can be their own programs or pushed into the build. In this case, the company will use automated tools on each build and special programs as needs evolve.

- **Coordination and final deployment**: This also will take some visuals, perhaps a key issues list. Tools exist to help; you can create a top-defects list that is pulled out of the bug tracker, a daily standup, and a project management threads list. A person, or a small group of people, needs to coordinate the timing of the release. This often turns them into a hero; when that person leaves, the organization will feel pain. Management's role is to create capacity so people can go on vacation but testing can have a significant role in organizing, describing, and tracking the work to be done.

Putting that together, one could argue the techniques in the book in the first description we gave, and that is true. A five-paragraph strategy will not go on to elaborate all the details we spent a few hundred pages building up. Yet when you dig into the details, the test strategy was built out of our puzzle pieces, lean testing, and development models chapters. Below that, at the implementation level, the strategy comes from the first five chapters about test approach, tooling, test data, and specialized testing.

Does yours?

AI in software testing

In the early 19th century, a group of workers, mostly weavers making clothing, organized a rebellion against a new technology that threatened their jobs. Over the course of months, they raided empty shops at night, destroying the new tools and forcing employers to employ the traditional professions. The new technology was the steam-powered loom. The group leading the rebellion was called the Luddites.

Today, the term Luddite is applied to anyone who resists technological change. Change we have had, and it is welcome! Just a few decades ago, people were employed to press buttons on elevators, answer phones for catalog orders, connect every telephone phone call, type letters, and help every person check out their groceries. By and large, those jobs have gone away to be replaced with self-service. The common argument with AI is that testing is next.

Let's be clear—we think it's nonsense.

Time will tell. Conceptually, it is possible that this section will not have aged well in a year or two because some wiz-bang tool comes out that you can send a web link or mobile app to to get test results.

The thing is, that's nonsense. If it isn't nonsense, humanity will face far more existential challenges than where the demand for testing work went.

But it is nonsense. Total nonsense. Silly. Wrong.

A curious reader might read this and infer that we are saying we have ethical and competence concerns about some of the people currently touting magical AI pixie dust. Our only response is to shrug. As the saying goes, "If the shoe fits..."

If we are to take such a stance, duty requires us to discuss the state of AI tools, what is possible, and what modest evolutionary improvements could be made using them.

The state of AI tools

Most of us understand the concept of **linear regression**—taking a thousand data points and a tool can generate a line and make predictions. In November of 2022, the OpenAI foundation released **ChatGPT**, a linear regression tool for words. That is, ChatGPT absorbed a large part of the internet and looked at every word. Given a few words, it was capable of predicting the next word. Many of us have seen that in the autocomplete feature in Google's search bar and for our texts. ChatGPT went further with a conversational interface that mimics human interaction. Thus, you can ask a question to ChatGPT and get an answer. You can take four or five bullet points and ask it to create a paragraph or give it a paragraph for copy-editing. Except for the examples in this chapter, we did not do that with this book. The name for this kind of AI is an LLM. LLMs require a fair amount of computing power, but that amount is getting smaller. In April of 2023, it was 36 cents per query to run (`https://www.digitaltrends.com/computing/chatgpt-cost-to-operate/`). The interface for ChatGPT is a text ask-and-answer format; it is unclear how long the tool will remain free. Our examples used ChatGPT 3.5. ChatGPT 4.0, at the time of authoring this book, has a small monthly fee.

In addition to LLMs, another recent AI innovation is tools that create images. These tools can recognize faces and put faces on images, make replacements, do 3D modeling, and change the angles of characters. Typically, they use a base image, though the presence of base images for image models and text for LLMs may create copyright issues.

Given that the tools can create images, that LLMs can create dialogue, that movies are just a series of pictures with small changes, and that we already have tools to create audio from text, it seems logical that we should be able to create movies with these tools.

Let's be clear. As of today, that is a ridiculous and silly idea. Not only does it not work, but if it could work, the cost of the computing power would be prohibitive. We need a series of innovations to make those pie-in-the-sky dreams possible.

As dreamers have come up with ways to use AI to create movies, dreamers are also coming up with ways for AI to automate testing away. In this chapter, we'd like to present a more balanced view of what you can do today. The upcoming list is not exhaustive—this is part of one chapter, not the entire book. Our goal is to give you a feel for what you can do now.

Possible ways to use AI for testing

A disciplined test-driven development proponent can use something such as ChatGPT to create unit tests. Describe the transformation and allow the tool to create the tests.

For example, imagine creating a method in C called `powerof` with this signature:

```
int powerOf(int base, int power);
```

We used the following prompts to set up the request:

I have a function in C called powerOf() that takes two integers and returns the first raised to the power of the second. Can you give me ten test examples as a CSV file that have the first number, the second, and the expected result, using numbers between zero and ten?

Assume the method PowerOf, discussed above, has this function signature: int PowerOf(int base, int power) can you please create some unit tests in cppUnit that exercise this method?

We got this result:

```
void testPowerOfPositive() {
    CPPUNIT_ASSERT_EQUAL(8, PowerOf(2, 3));
    CPPUNIT_ASSERT_EQUAL(9, PowerOf(3, 2));
    CPPUNIT_ASSERT_EQUAL(1024, PowerOf(2, 10));
}
void testPowerOfZeroExponent() {
    CPPUNIT_ASSERT_EQUAL(1, PowerOf(5, 0));
    CPPUNIT_ASSERT_EQUAL(1, PowerOf(10, 0));
}
void testPowerOfNegativeExponent() {
    CPPUNIT_ASSERT_EQUAL(0, PowerOf(4, -2));
    CPPUNIT_ASSERT_EQUAL(0, PowerOf(7, -3));
}
```

Notice these examples are what we might call weak or confirmatory checks. They are fine, as far as they go. The last set, the power of negative, is particularly interesting; 4 to the -2 power is actually 1/16th. Integers in C are whole numbers; there is no 0.025, so the code tells us the right answer is 0. These sorts of things can force conversations.

We asked ChatGPT to test limits, bad data, and overflow, and it generated these examples:

```
void testPowerOfOverflow() {
    // Test for potential overflow with large exponents
    CPPUNIT_ASSERT_EQUAL(0, PowerOf(10000, 10000));
}
void testPowerOfBadData() {
    // Test with bad data (e.g., negative base and exponent)
    CPPUNIT_ASSERT_EQUAL(0, PowerOf(-2, 3));
    CPPUNIT_ASSERT_EQUAL(0, PowerOf(2, -3));
}
```

Again, these snippets of code create more questions than answers. PowerOf to the ten thousandth power will certainly go beyond the limits of the int type, but should the result be 0? We might want to throw an exception to be caught within a try/catch block. -2 to the 3rd power is not zero—it is -8. So, you can use an AI tool to generate code, but you'd better check it out yourself.

When it comes to testing ten thousand to the ten thousandth power, one thing we would look for is performance—how long does it take? It might be interesting to wrap the call in a timer and set some arbitrary limit. No call should take more the 1/4th of a second, about the time it takes a human to notice a delay. The AI tools might be able to help you write such a test, but they won't come up with an idea for such a test... yet.

Besides that, in our experience, real code is messy. It has a surprising number of dependencies. Even with dependency injection, the generator may need to know how the base object works. GitHub Copilot is the first tool to integrate code completion with an integrated development environment; it can do some simple tasks. For example, in Visual Studio Code, we asked GitHub Copilot to generate a regular expression to determine if a number was a phone number. It gave us not one suggestion but ten, suggesting phone numbers with nine different date formats:

```
phone_number_regex = /(\d{3})-(\d{3})-(\d{4})/
#regular expression to determine if a number is a zip code
zip_code_regex = /(\d{5})/
#regular expression to determine if a number is a date
date_regex = /(\d{2})\/(\d{2})\/(\d{2})/
#regular expression to determine if a number is a date
date_regex = /(\d{2})\/(\d{2})\/(\d{2})/
#regular expression to determine if a number is a date
date_regex = /(\d{2})\/(\d{2})\/(\d{2})/
#regular expression to determine if a number is a date
date_regex = /(\d{2})\/(\d{2})\/(\d{2})/
#regular expression to determine if a number is a date
date_regex = /(\d{2})\/(\d{2})\/(\d{2})/
#regular expression to determine if a number is a date
date_regex = /(\d{2})\/(\d{2})\/(\d{2})/
#regular expression to determine if a number is a date
date_regex = /(\d{2})\/(\d{2})\/(\d{2})/
#regular expression to determine if a number is a date
date_regex = /(\d{2})\/(\d{2})\/(\d{2})/
#regular expression to determine if a number is a date
date_regex = /(\d{2})\/(\d{2})\/(\d{2})/
```

Again, as of writing, we see large language models enabling the user to generate template or boilerplate code, along with saving us time from performing a Google search. This is not automating testing, but it might be automating parts of testing.

Another potential use of AI in testing is test data generation. There are plenty of tools that can come up with a list of first and last names and birthdays across a distribution, perhaps with start and end dates for effective coverage that do and do not overlap with the system date. Ironically, ChatGPT will not do that, as it is concerned that you'll be using it for fraud. What we can do with ChatGPT is the famous triangle example.

The triangle problem asks for three sides expressed as numbers from zero to ten. Then, it states whether those three sides make a shape that is scalene (all sides different), equilateral (all the same), or not a triangle at all (two sides combined are less than the third or one side is zero). We asked ChatGPT to come up with ten examples of test data. This is what it found:

3	4	5	Scalene
5	5	5	Equilateral
7	7	10	Isosceles
2	4	7	Not a Triangle
9	3	9	Isosceles
8	8	8	Equilateral
6	8	10	Scalene
4	4	5	Isosceles
3	5	3	Isosceles
11	6	6	Not a Triangle

Table 16.1 - ChatGPT test data for triangles

This allows us to use ChatGPT as the oracle. Isolate the code that calculates the triangle type, make a call to the ChatGPT API to ask for ten random examples, and run the code over and over again, getting different examples each time. While that would add a **model-based testing** feel to the code (without much effort to code the model), it could be a problem, as ChatGPT changes over time. One Stanford study (`https://finance.yahoo.com/news/over-just-few-months-chatgpt-232905189.html`) found that ChatGPT's ability to perform math functions had decreased over time, as the constant use by humans trained it in different unexpected ways, just like a human brain.

For now, it's perfectly fine to have AI tools generate test data, but you'll need to check the data. We'd suggest creating a great deal of test data (currently, the tools tend to generate up to 50 to 100 examples at a time), running it through, and storing it instead of API calls for new data on every run.

Another approach that has been touted lately is asking the tool to generate test cases. For example, given an eCommerce site and a particular scope (such as the product page), AI tools can tell you how to test it. Yes, a tool such as ChatGPT can generate a list of ideas. We find these ideas to be incredibly superficial. Yes, they can save you from typing, but these are the sorts of things that a professional tester following the advice in this book would not bother to do. You could ask the tools to write boilerplate code to load a web page and click it using a fashionable open source automation library; sometimes they can do so, or they can at least save you some time crafting it. The thorniest problems in test automation are often finding a locator on a screen; we have had much success asking the tools to help with that. ChatGPT runs on old data collected from the internet, so it cannot click on your web page; pasting the source will only work on the most rudimentary of websites. Google's Bard claims to be able to read current web pages. As of today, it generates code that looks right but typically generates locator strings much more like a human would when guessing the locator as opposed to actually locating the object to click on it.

Other forms of AI in testing

Machine learning is a more primitive form of AI than LLMs. With machine learning, the software looks at large amounts of data and makes predictions. A supervised machine learning algorithm might look at trends in order over years (and seasons and days within those years) to make predictions about future orders or to help us understand how many units to produce to keep shelves stocked. Those sorts of predictions fail in the face of "black swan" events that are unseen by the data.

Machine learning can also be used in an unsupervised mode to infer meaning about groups. One classic unsupervised task is to look at a million poker hands ranked and infer the rules of the game.

There are practical applications of machine learning for testing, such as guessing locators when an object moves, capturing the image, and, should the now-passing test be marked as acceptable, changing the locator in the code itself. On a more complex scale, machine learning can also be used in fraud detection, complex logistics, and so on.

The bottom line for AI testing

For our purposes, we think of AI as having the computer solve problems in a non-linear way, creating answers we could not have considered ourselves. That is, the computer creates or improves the algorithm to solve the problem. Today, the algorithms are smart enough to take something very close to the spoken word and return an answer. It's important to note that the computer isn't really thinking; it is mimicking human thought. In one of our experiments, the built-in Skype AI claimed to find accessibility problems in web pages that did not exist. When asked for references, they came from web pages that were similar from a different domain.

For now, look to the tools to accelerate your boilerplate code and solutions. If you want test ideas, first do the test work, then push for different kinds of test ideas, special conditions, special characters, and so on. Then, add anything you haven't already thought of. For now, the data simply is not reliable. Think of it as a first-year college student on a deadline, stringing words together into something that looks like a correct answer. This might accelerate your work, but be careful. When people make claims about their magic AI that does everything for you, ask them for examples.

A few thoughts to leave with

Gerald M. Weinberg used to come up with quick, easy, pithy sayings to remember the key points of his work. We may not be Jerry Weinberg, but we do recognize that a few of our ideas compress well into his format. We have collected a few of our favorites here:

- **The consultant's gambit**: There are probably obvious problems insiders can't see because of company culture that outsiders will see.

- **The maxim of documented testing**: At the end of every human-run, pre-designed, documented test is a hidden expected result: … and nothing else odd happens.

- **The first corollary**: This assumption is particularly difficult to automate.

- **The second corollary**: If you try to automate the search for the hidden expected result, you'll get a whole lot of false errors.

- **The maxim of test automation**: Even if a test could be automated, the second time it runs, it fails to be test automation and becomes change detection.

- **The exception**: High-volume, empirical, data-based tests or simulate them by injecting randomization. You'll need some automated oracle to know what the right answer is. One version is the previous version of the software.

- **The magic formula**: Developer unit tests, acceptance checks that can be automated, and human exploration.

- **The Dijkstra conjecture**: Program testing can be used to show the presence of bugs, but never to show their absence!

- **The Heusser proposition**: Testers who can take responsibility for what is not technically possible and somehow do it anyway can write their own ticket. Or, we, the willing, led by the knowing, have been doing the impossible …

- **The automation cost fallacy**: Automation isn't cheap, free, or instantaneous. While code might not rot, as the source code changes around the test code, this will create additional maintenance efforts. Mature user interfaces and clean separation of components can keep these costs to a minimum.

- **The rule of (traditional, pre-defined) test automation**: The majority of defects found by "100% test automation" organizations are not found by tooling running regression but instead by humans doing other activities.

- **The other source of all kinds of evil**: A naive misunderstanding of how humans uncover problems versus what computers can do is the source of many troubles in software delivery.

- **The automation decision dilemma**: When it comes to a computer running unattended and producing results, the tool can likely check everything for errors (and it becomes change detection) or it can check specific things (in which case it ignores everything else). Finding a middle path requires future knowledge of what might change that would be wrong, divined as different from what might change that would be right. As it turns out, it is very difficult to get a computer to have this pre-calculated or *a priori* knowledge.

- **Automation delay**: This is the delay caused by test automation that fails, which needs to be checked, corrected, and re-run.

- **The complexity conundrum**: The harder it is to set up and run conditions for a test, the more tempting it is to skip. This also means the more likely it is to have bugs hiding in it.

- **The four cardinal virtues**: These are justice (giving people what they deserve), prudence (practical wisdom), temperance (avoiding extremes of pleasure and self-discipline and seeking appropriate pleasures at the right time and place), and fortitude (courage).

In addition to our thoughts on testing, we have thoughts that are purely on documentation. Not the documentation of testing, but the documentation of anything on an intellectual project.

Thoughts on documentation

The documentation dilemma: You may have heard that if you don't write it, it doesn't exist.

The first corollary: If you write it down and no one reads it, that's worse. In that case, you have simply produced waste.

The second corollary: Even if they do read it, everything that you write down creates a maintenance burden. It will either need to be updated as things change or you'll have out-of-date documents.

The third corollary: If you write too much down, people will not be able to figure out what matters (comprehensive is the enemy of comprehensible).

Summary

This book represents the very best of our ideas on how to conduct testing. They were honed over honest work that equates to over five decades of experience, two hundred interviews formalized as podcasts and many untold informal conversations at conferences and over the web. Through this work, we attempted to provide a fully integrated view of testing and quality that offered something really unique, as well as the tools to analyze your work situation, come up with your own strategy, and measure and improve it.

"Go forth and test" might be a little cliche, but that is our goal—to put things in your hands that you can use when doing testing.

That said, we feel obligated to say just one more thing about doing testing.

A few times at Excelon, we've tried to hire a consultant, someone respected who speaks at conferences, to actually do test work with us. The look they often give is one of distaste. They make a face, step back or somehow indicate that they are better than sitting in a chair doing testing. Certainly, it is fair that training, consulting, and teaching are all ways to accelerate value over one person doing the work. But that work itself? We see it as worthy and noble in its own way.

We don't see testing as something we are above or beyond. We enjoy it and want to do more of it.

And, we must admit, writing this book was hard. This may even be the most difficult professional activity we've done yet. It symbolizes a major work, at least to us. Still, a few decades in each, it feels like we are only getting started.

At the end of *Star Trek VI, The Undiscovered Country*, Captain Kirk is ordered to retire, but he instead takes his ship out for one more ride, ordering his navigator to go to the "second star to the right and straight on 'till morning." That line is borrowed from Peter Pan, the boy who would not grow up. It signals that Kirk is not ready to retire and also that his mission of exploring was *fun*.

Let's test some software together.

Soon.

Index

Symbols

A

B

Packtpub.com

Subscribe to our online digital library for full access to over 7,000 books and videos, as well as industry leading tools to help you plan your personal development and advance your career. For more information, please visit our website.

Why subscribe?

- Spend less time learning and more time coding with practical eBooks and Videos from over 4,000 industry professionals

- Improve your learning with Skill Plans built especially for you

- Get a free eBook or video every month

- Fully searchable for easy access to vital information

- Copy and paste, print, and bookmark content

Did you know that Packt offers eBook versions of every book published, with PDF and ePub files available? You can upgrade to the eBook version at packtpub.com and as a print book customer, you are entitled to a discount on the eBook copy. Get in touch with us at customercare@packtpub.com for more details.

At www.packtpub.com, you can also read a collection of free technical articles, sign up for a range of free newsletters, and receive exclusive discounts and offers on Packt books and eBooks.

Other Books You May Enjoy

If you enjoyed this book, you may be interested in these other books by Packt:

Software Test Design

Simon Amey

ISBN: 9781804612569

- Understand how to investigate new features using exploratory testing
- Discover how to write clear, detailed feature specifications
- Explore systematic test techniques such as equivalence partitioning
- Understand the strengths and weaknesses of black- and white-box testing
- Recognize the importance of security, usability, and maintainability testing
- Verify application resilience by running destructive tests
- Run load and stress tests to measure system performance

Test Automation Engineering Handbook

Manikandan Sambamurthy

ISBN: 9781804615492

- Gain a solid understanding of test automation
- Understand how automation fits into a test strategy
- Explore essential design patterns for test automation
- Design and implement highly reliable automated tests
- Understand issues and pitfalls when executing test automation
- Discover the commonly used test automation tools/frameworks

Packt is searching for authors like you

If you're interested in becoming an author for Packt, please visit `authors.packtpub.com` and apply today. We have worked with thousands of developers and tech professionals, just like you, to help them share their insight with the global tech community. You can make a general application, apply for a specific hot topic that we are recruiting an author for, or submit your own idea.

Share your thoughts

Now you've finished *Software Testing Strategies*, we'd love to hear your thoughts! Scan the QR code below to go straight to the Amazon review page for this book and share your feedback or leave a review on the site that you purchased it from.

https://packt.link/r/1837638020

Your review is important to us and the tech community and will help us make sure we're delivering excellent quality content.

Download a free PDF copy of this book

Thanks for purchasing this book!

Do you like to read on the go but are unable to carry your print books everywhere?

Is your eBook purchase not compatible with the device of your choice?

Don't worry, now with every Packt book you get a DRM-free PDF version of that book at no cost.

Read anywhere, any place, on any device. Search, copy, and paste code from your favorite technical books directly into your application.

The perks don't stop there, you can get exclusive access to discounts, newsletters, and great free content in your inbox daily

Follow these simple steps to get the benefits:

1. Scan the QR code or visit the link below

https://packt.link/free-ebook/9781837638024

2. Submit your proof of purchase
3. That's it! We'll send your free PDF and other benefits to your email directly

Made in the USA
Monee, IL
17 December 2024

74292603R00208